# BATMAN WAR GAMES
## ACT ONE OUTBREAK

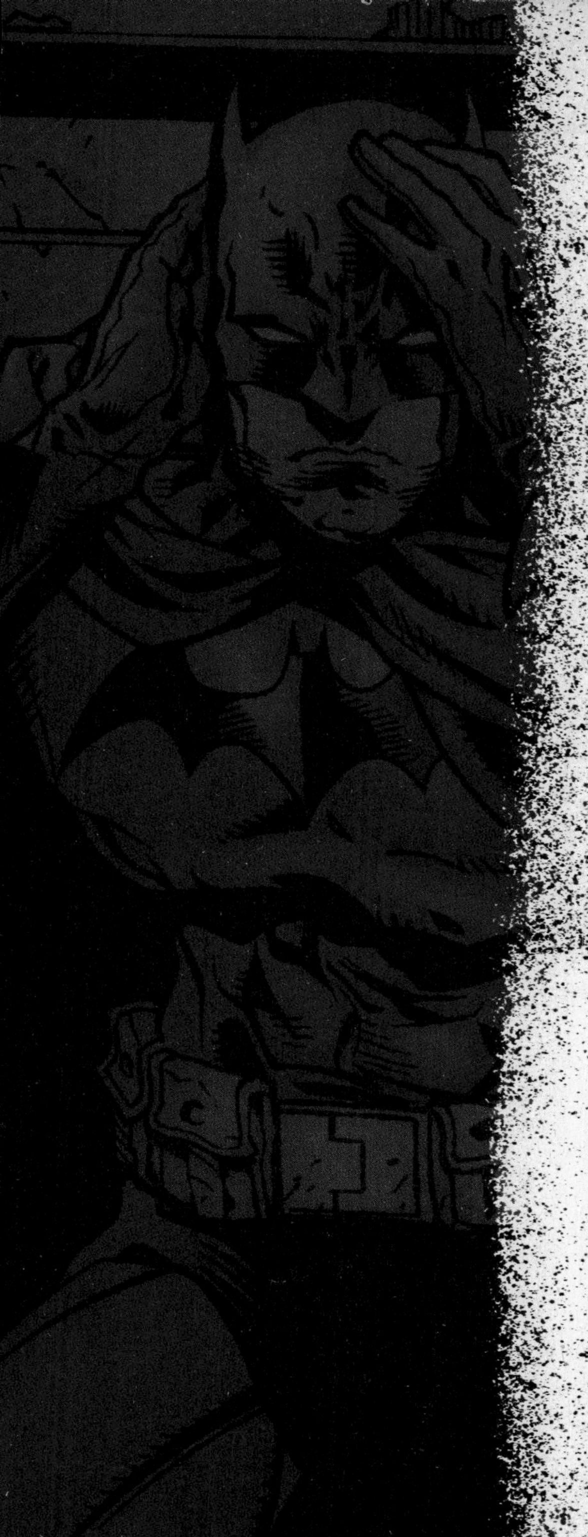

**BATMAN: WAR GAMES ACT 1**



DC Comics, 1700 Broadway, New York, NY 10019 --
a Warner Bros. Entertainment Company
Printed in Canada. First Printing.
ISBN: 1-4012-0429-5
Cover illustration by James Jean

ED BRUBAKER
ANDERSEN GABRYC
DEVIN GRAYSON
DYLAN HORROCKS
A.J. LIEBERMAN
BILL WILLINGHAM
WRITERS

RAMON BACHS
AL BARRIONUEVO
GIUSEPPE CAMUNC
PAUL GULACY
KINSUN
MIKE LILLY
SEAN PHILLIPS
BRAD WALKER
PETE WOODS
PENCILLERS

RAUL FERNANDEZ
NATHAN MASSENG
TROY NIXEY
ANDY OWENS
JIMMY PALMIOTTI
SEAN PHILLIPS
FRANCIS PORTELLA
RODNEY RAMOS
LORENZO RUGGIER
AARON SOWD
INKERS

PHIL BALSMAN
PAT BROSSEAU
JARED K. FLETCHER
ROB LEIGH
NICK J. NAPOLITANO
CLEM ROBINS
LETTERERS

BRAD ANDERSON
TONY AVINA
STEVE BUCCELLATO
LAURIE KRONENBERG
GUY MAJOR
JAVIER RODRIGUEZ
GREGORY WRIGHT
JASON WRIGHT
COLORISTS

BATMAN CREATED BY
BOB KANE

# BATMAN
## WAR GAMES
### ACT ONE

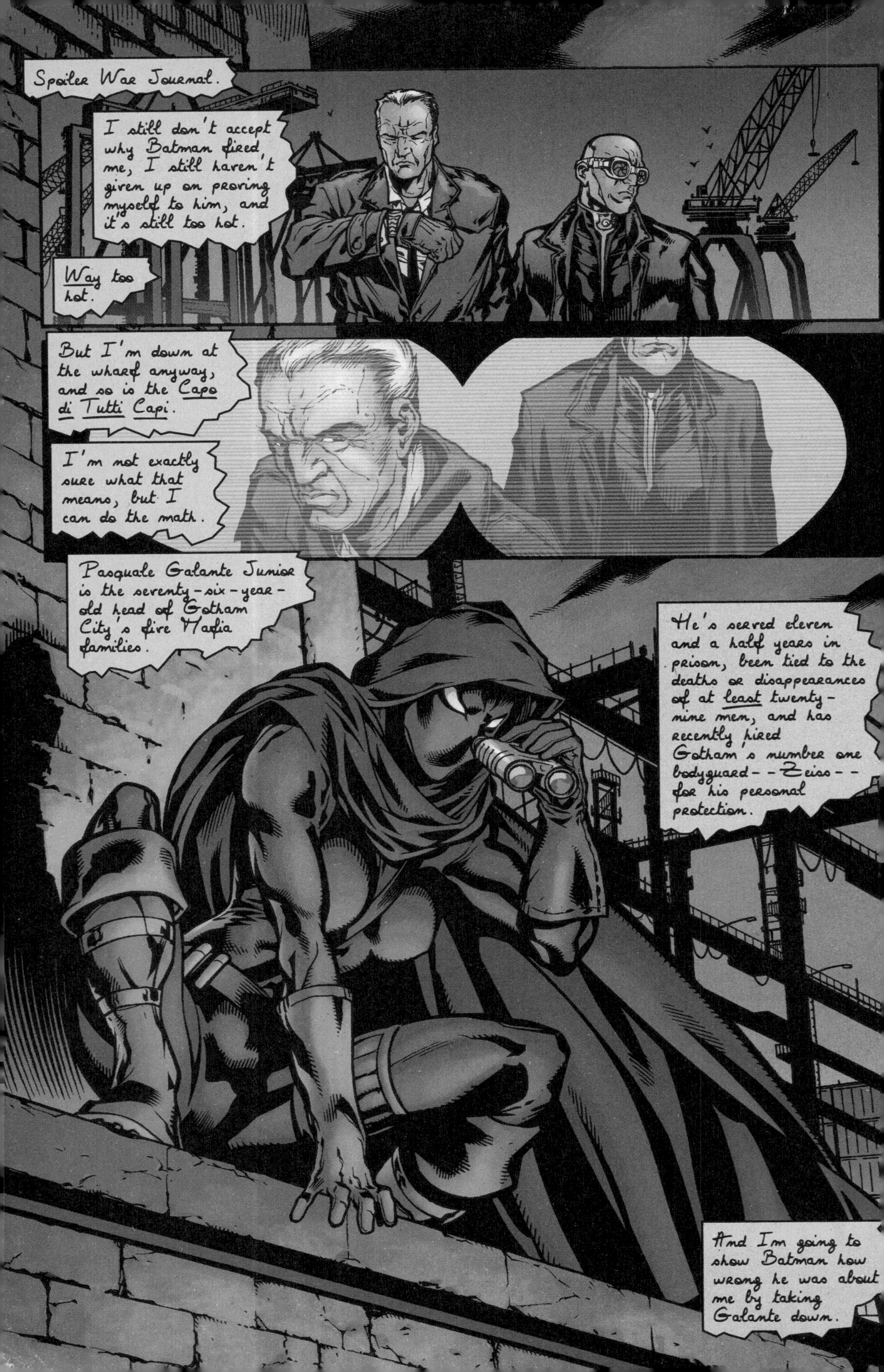
Spoiler War Journal.
I still don't accept why Batman fired me, I still haven't given up on proving myself to him, and it's still too hot.
Way too hot.
But I'm down at the wharf anyway, and so is the Capo di Tutti Capi.
I'm not exactly sure what that means, but I can do the math.
Pasquale Galante Junior is the seventy-six-year-old head of Gotham City's five Mafia families.
He's served eleven and a half years in prison, been tied to the deaths or disappearances of at least twenty-nine men, and has recently hired Gotham's number one bodyguard--Zeiss--for his personal protection.
And I'm going to show Batman how wrong he was about me by taking Galante down.

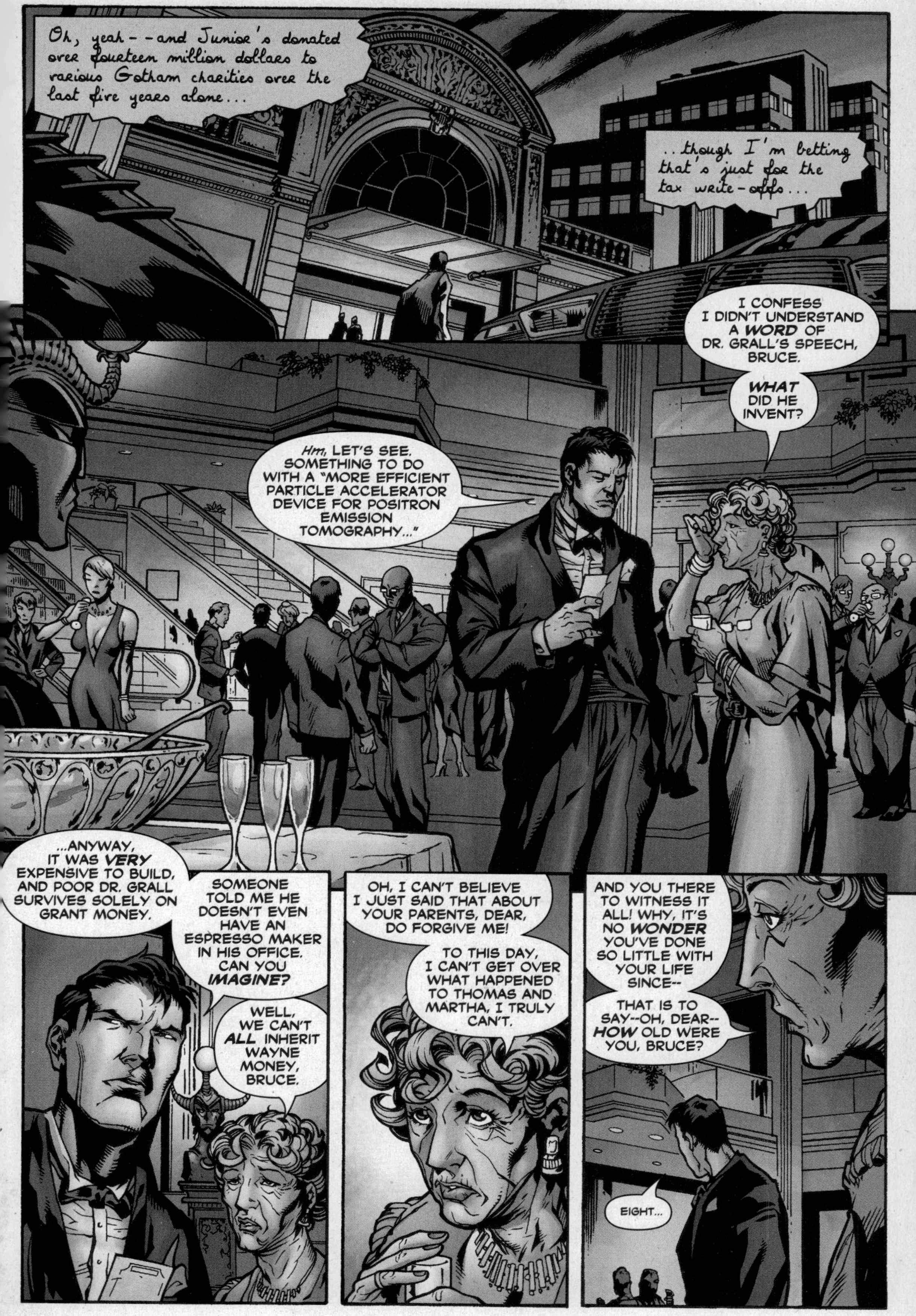

Oh, yeah--and Junior's donated over fourteen million dollars to various Gotham charities over the last five years alone...
..though I'm betting that's just for the tax write-offs...
I CONFESS I DIDN'T UNDERSTAND A WORD OF DR. GRALL'S SPEECH, BRUCE.
WHAT DID HE INVENT?
Hm, LET'S SEE. SOMETHING TO DO WITH A "MORE EFFICIENT PARTICLE ACCELERATOR DEVICE FOR POSITRON EMISSION TOMOGRAPHY..."
...ANYWAY, IT WAS VERY EXPENSIVE TO BUILD, AND POOR DR. GRALL SURVIVES SOLELY ON GRANT MONEY.
SOMEONE TOLD ME HE DOESN'T EVEN HAVE AN ESPRESSO MAKER IN HIS OFFICE. CAN YOU IMAGINE?
WELL, WE CAN'T ALL INHERIT WAYNE MONEY, BRUCE.
OH, I CAN'T BELIEVE I JUST SAID THAT ABOUT YOUR PARENTS, DEAR, DO FORGIVE ME!
TO THIS DAY, I CAN'T GET OVER WHAT HAPPENED TO THOMAS AND MARTHA, I TRULY CAN'T.
AND YOU THERE TO WITNESS IT ALL! WHY, IT'S NO WONDER YOU'VE DONE SO LITTLE WITH YOUR LIFE SINCE--
THAT IS TO SAY--OH, DEAR--HOW OLD WERE YOU, BRUCE?
EIGHT...

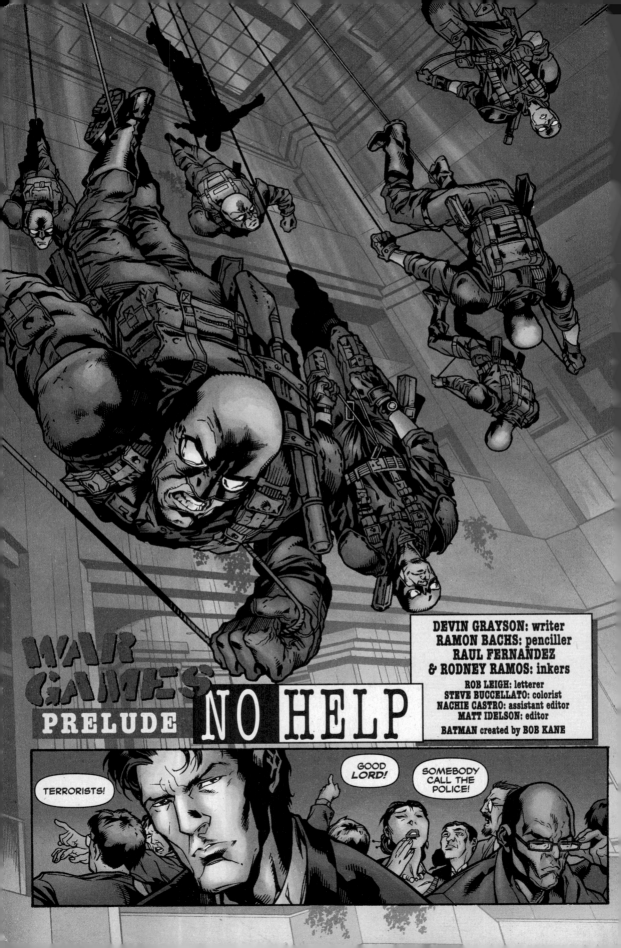

WAR GAMES PRELUDE NO HELP

DEVIN GRAYSON: writer
RAMON BACHS: penciller
RAUL FERNANDEZ
& RODNEY RAMOS: inkers

ROB LEIGH: letterer
STEVE BUCCELLATO: colorist
NACHIE CASTRO: assistant editor
MATT IDELSON: editor

BATMAN created by BOB KANE

TERRORISTS!

GOOD LORD!

SOMEBODY CALL THE POLICE!

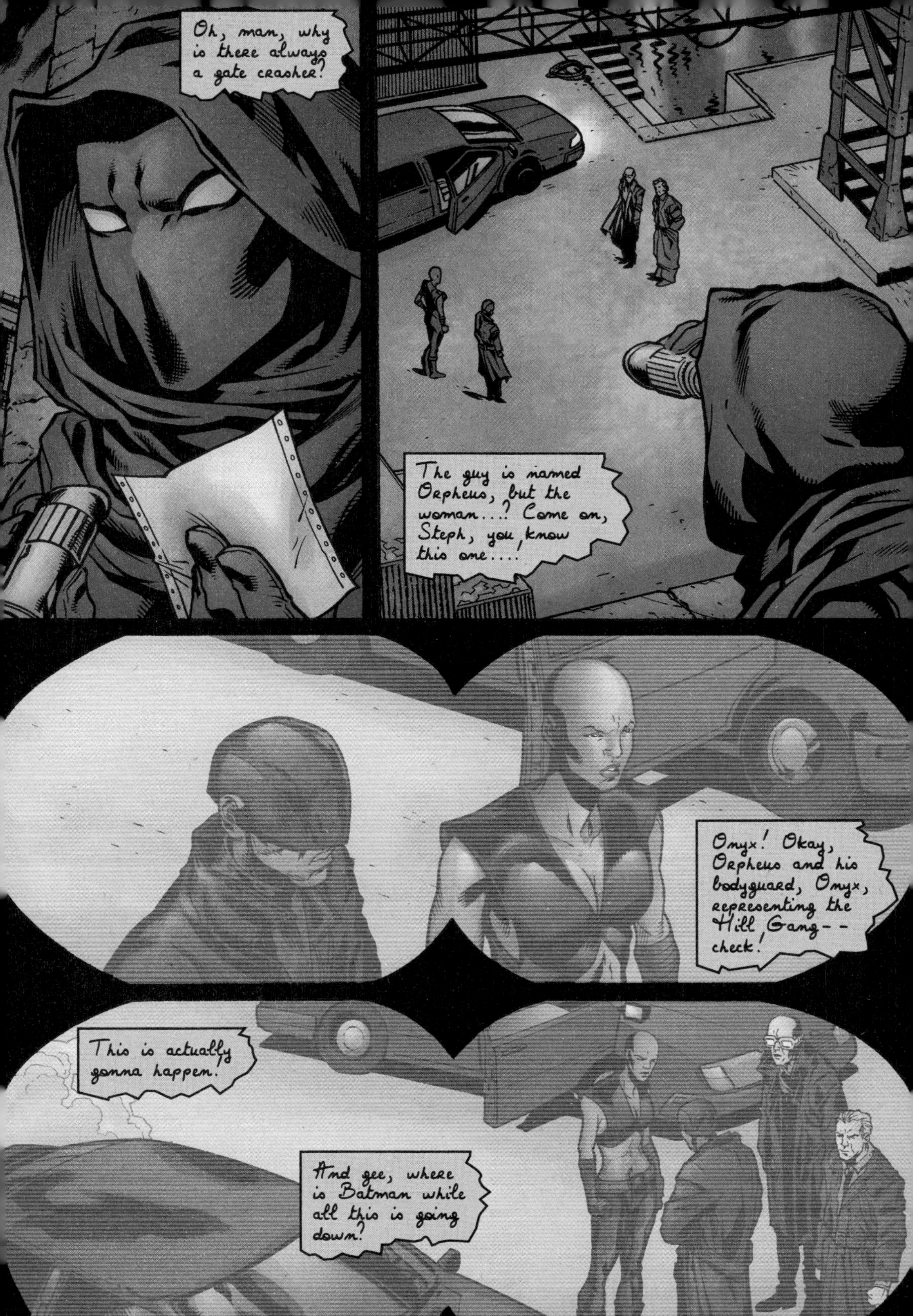
Oh, man, why is there always a gate crasher?
The guy is named Orpheus, but the woman...? Come on, Steph, you know this one...!
Onyx! Okay, Orpheus and his bodyguard, Onyx, representing the Hill Gang--check!
This is actually gonna happen.
And gee, where is Batman while all this is going down?

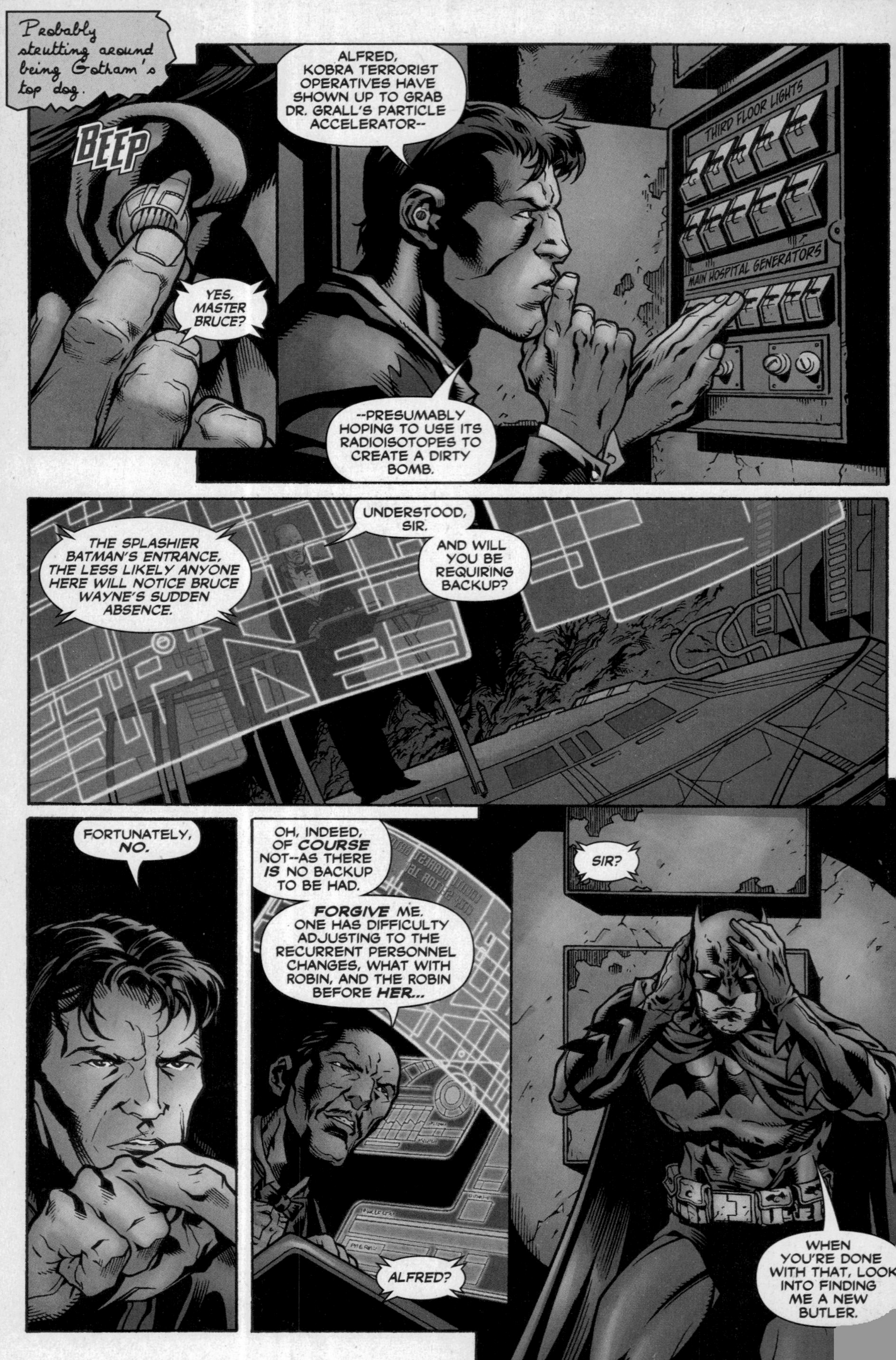
Probably strutting around being Gotham's top dog.
BEEP
ALFRED, KOBRA TERRORIST OPERATIVES HAVE SHOWN UP TO GRAB DR. GRALL'S PARTICLE ACCELERATOR--
THIRD FLOOR LIGHTS
MAIN HOSPITAL GENERATORS
YES, MASTER BRUCE?
--PRESUMABLY HOPING TO USE ITS RADIOISOTOPES TO CREATE A DIRTY BOMB.
THE SPLASHIER BATMAN'S ENTRANCE, THE LESS LIKELY ANYONE HERE WILL NOTICE BRUCE WAYNE'S SUDDEN ABSENCE.
UNDERSTOOD, SIR.
AND WILL YOU BE REQUIRING BACKUP?
FORTUNATELY, NO.
OH, INDEED, OF COURSE NOT--AS THERE IS NO BACKUP TO BE HAD.
FORGIVE ME. ONE HAS DIFFICULTY ADJUSTING TO THE RECURRENT PERSONNEL CHANGES, WHAT WITH ROBIN, AND THE ROBIN BEFORE HER...
ALFRED?
SIR?
WHEN YOU'RE DONE WITH THAT, LOOK INTO FINDING ME A NEW BUTLER.

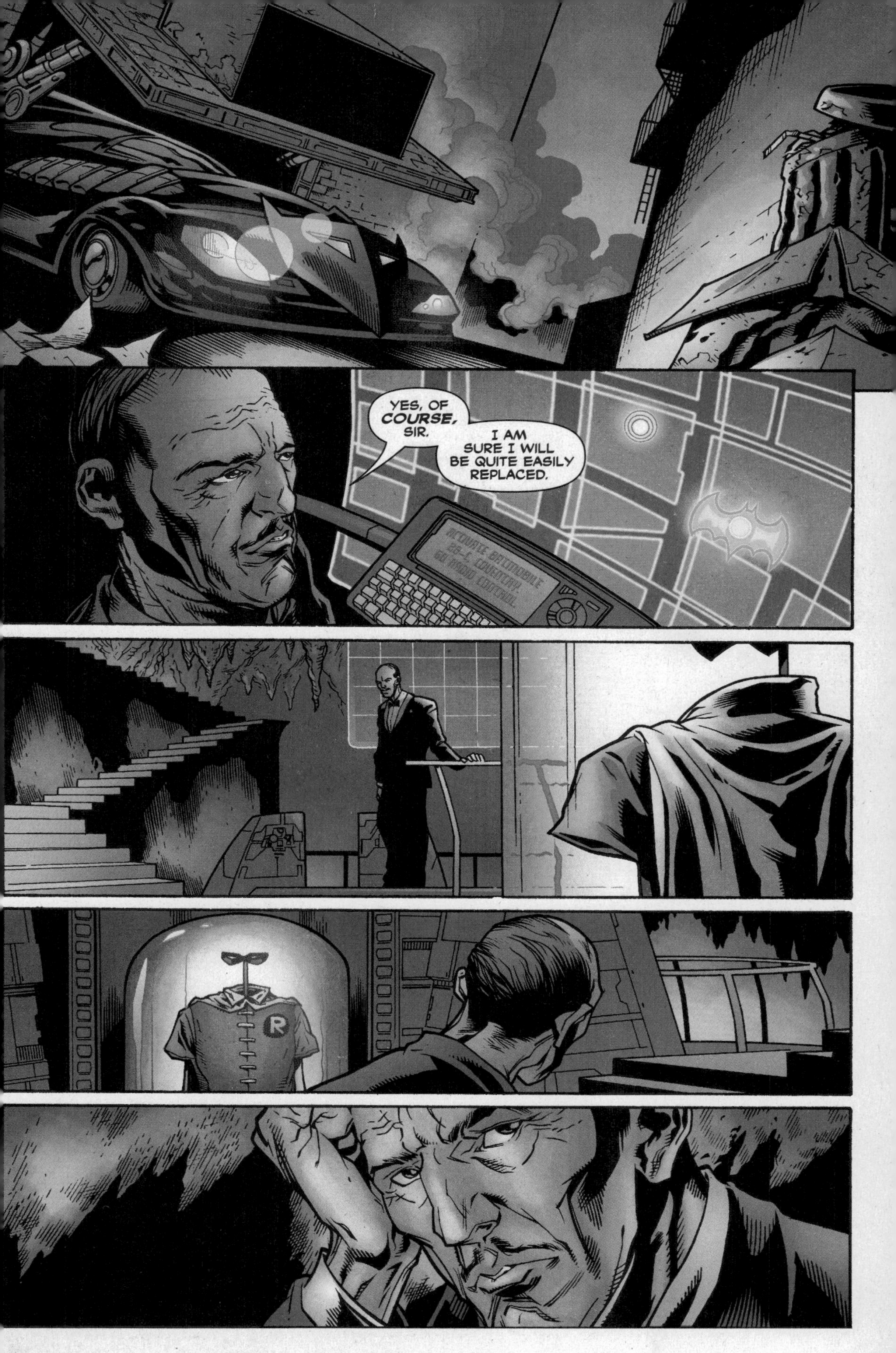
YES, OF COURSE, SIR.
I AM SURE I WILL BE QUITE EASILY REPLACED.

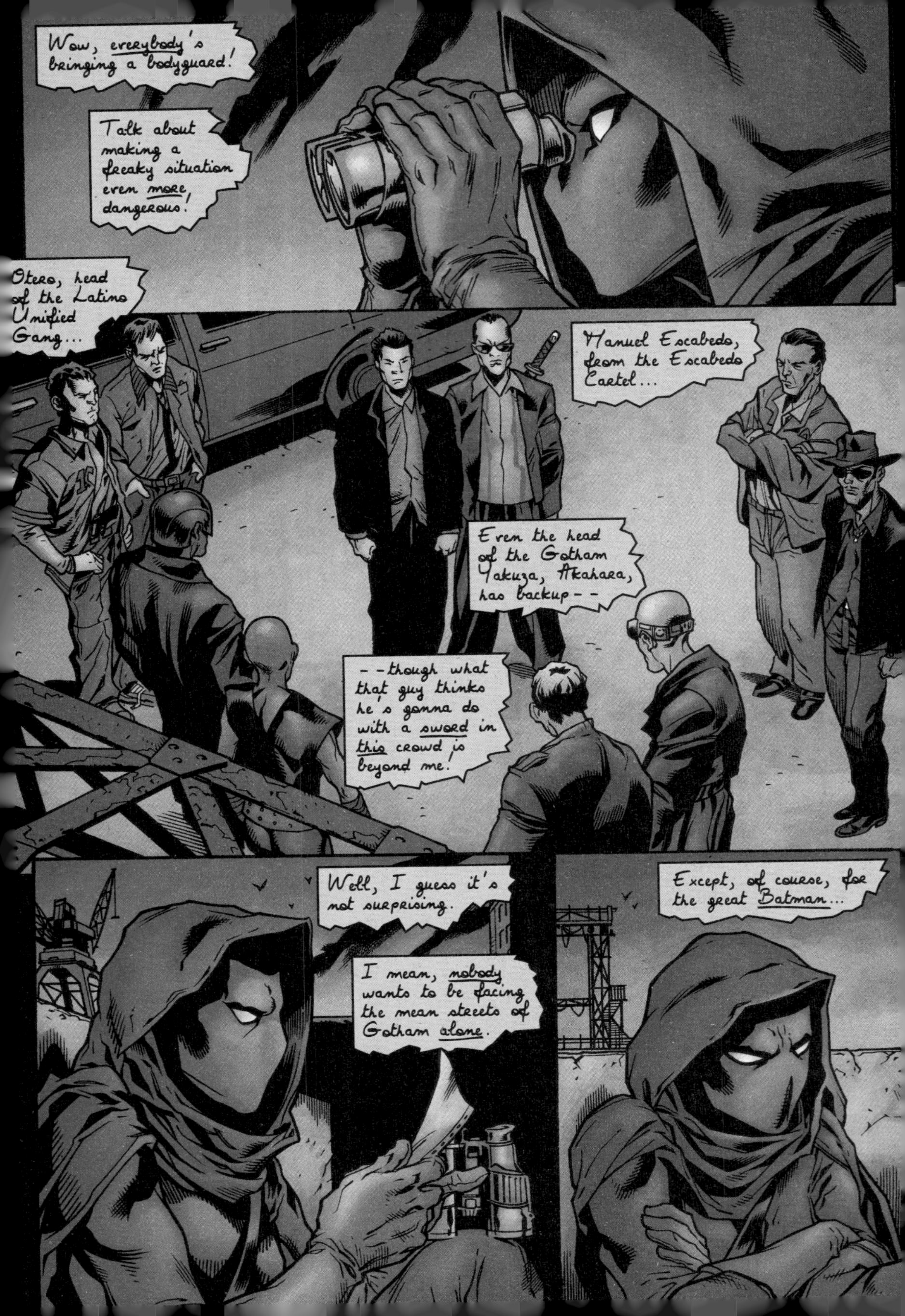
Wow, everybody's bringing a bodyguard!
Talk about making a freaky situation even more dangerous!
Otero, head of the Latino Unified Gang...
Manuel Escabedo, from the Escabedo Cartel...
Even the head of the Gotham Yakuza, Akahara, has backup--
--though what that guy thinks he's gonna do with a sword in this crowd is beyond me!
Well, I guess it's not surprising.
I mean, nobody wants to be facing the mean streets of Gotham alone.
Except, of course, for the great Batman...

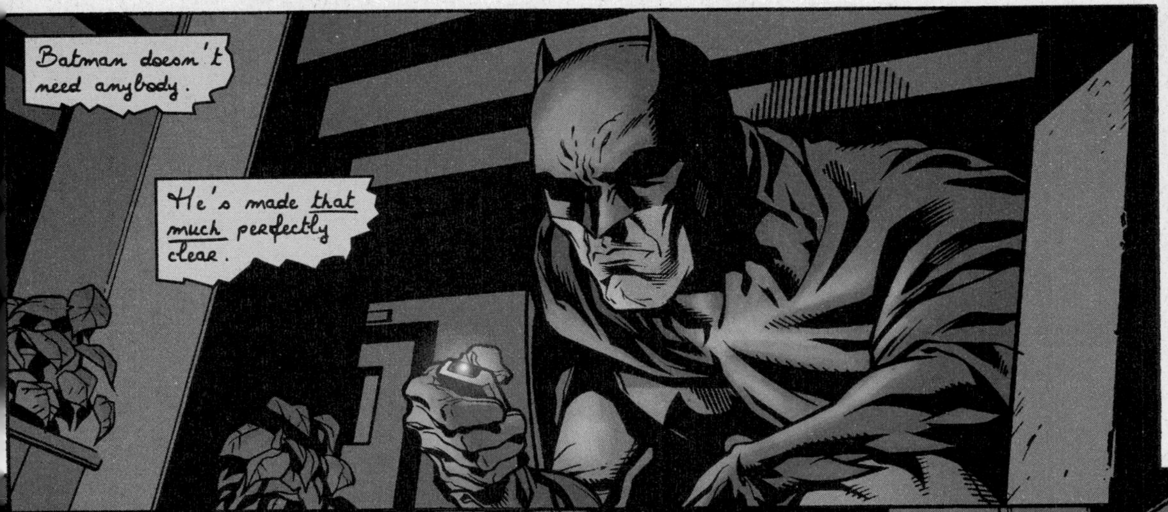
Batman doesn't need anybody.
He's made that much perfectly clear.
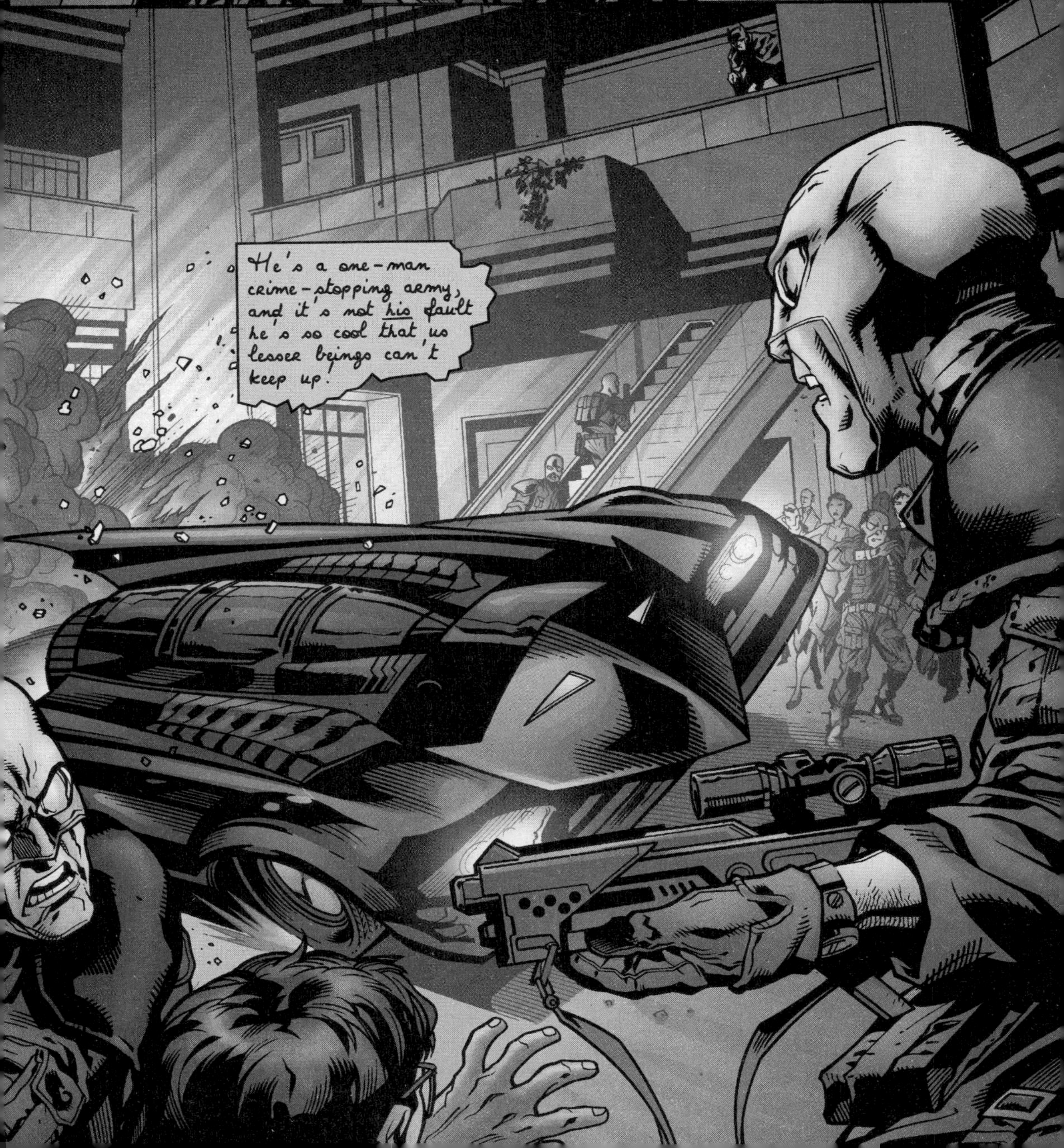
He's a one-man crime-stopping army, and it's not his fault he's so cool that us lesser beings can't keep up!

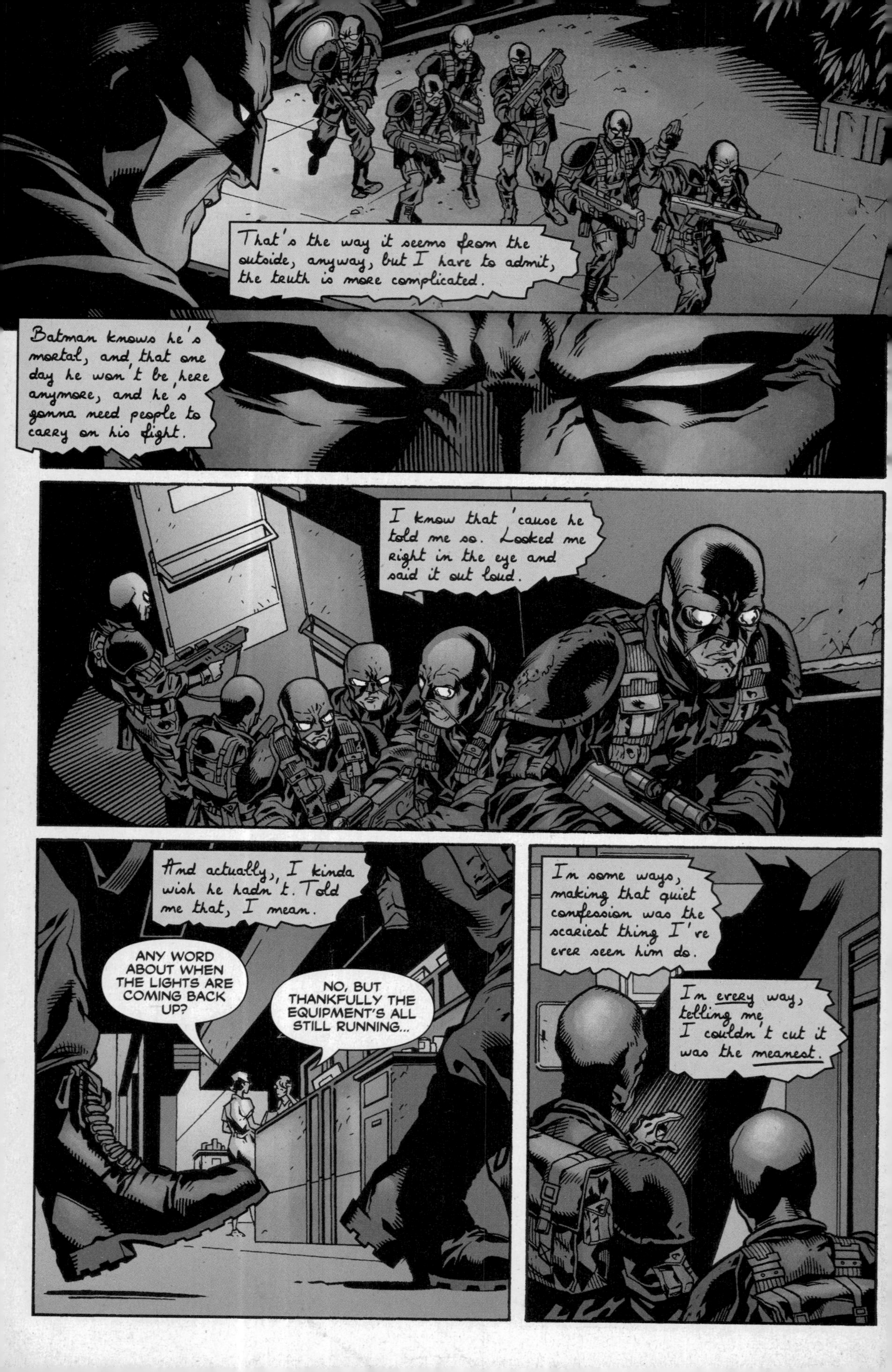

That's the way it seems from the outside, anyway, but I have to admit, the truth is more complicated.
Batman knows he's mortal, and that one day he won't be here anymore, and he's gonna need people to carry on his fight.
I know that 'cause he told me so. Looked me right in the eye and said it out loud.
And actually, I kinda wish he hadn't. Told me that, I mean.
ANY WORD ABOUT WHEN THE LIGHTS ARE COMING BACK UP?
NO, BUT THANKFULLY THE EQUIPMENT'S ALL STILL RUNNING...
In some ways, making that quiet confession was the scariest thing I've ever seen him do.
In every way, telling me I couldn't cut it was the meanest.

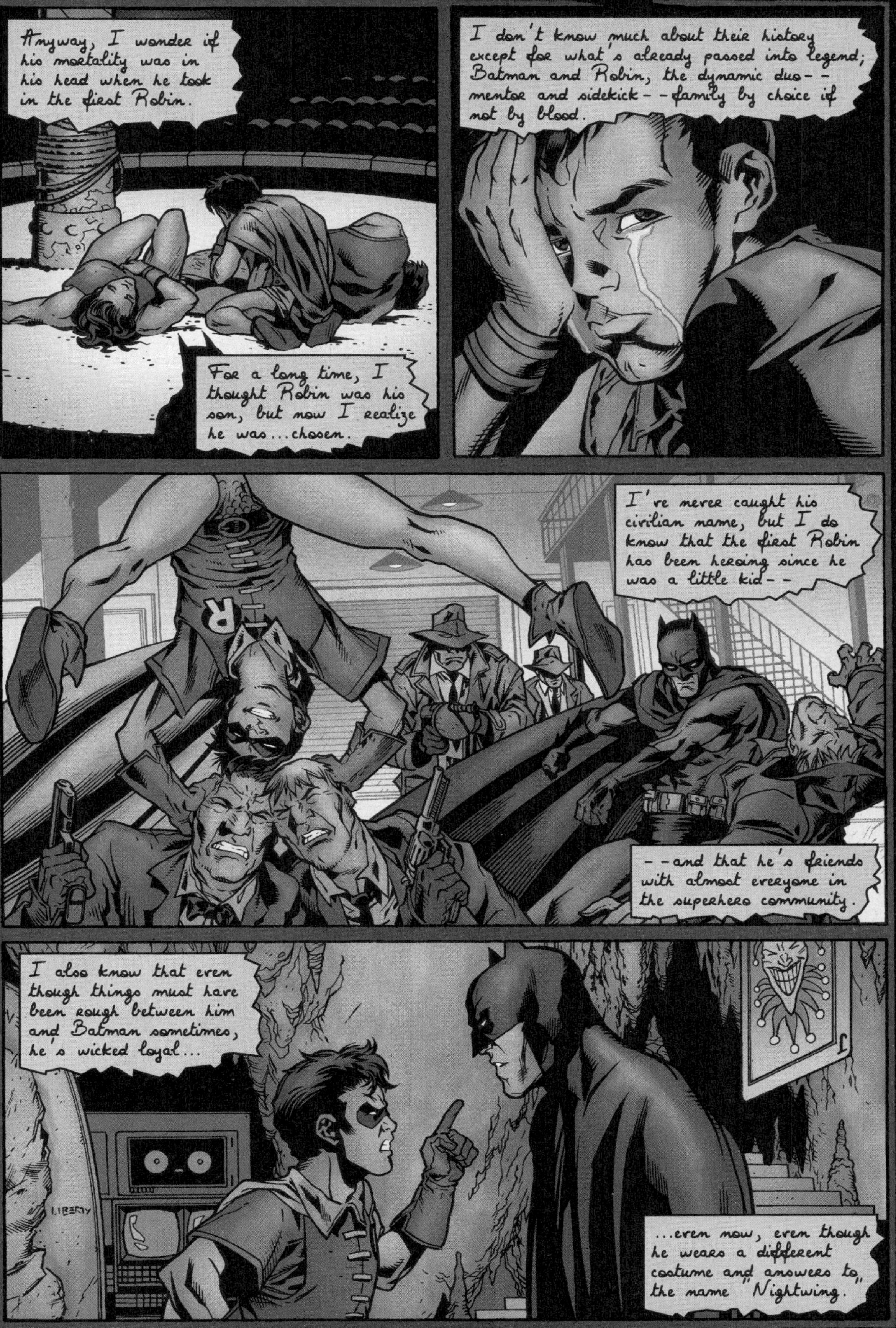
Anyway, I wonder if his mortality was in his head when he took in the first Robin.
For a long time, I thought Robin was his son, but now I realize he was...chosen.
I don't know much about their history except for what's already passed into legend; Batman and Robin, the dynamic duo--mentor and sidekick--family by choice if not by blood.
I've never caught his civilian name, but I do know that the first Robin has been heroing since he was a little kid--
--and that he's friends with almost everyone in the superhero community.
I also know that even though things must have been rough between him and Batman sometimes, he's wicked loyal...
...even now, even though he wears a different costume and answers to the name "Nightwing."

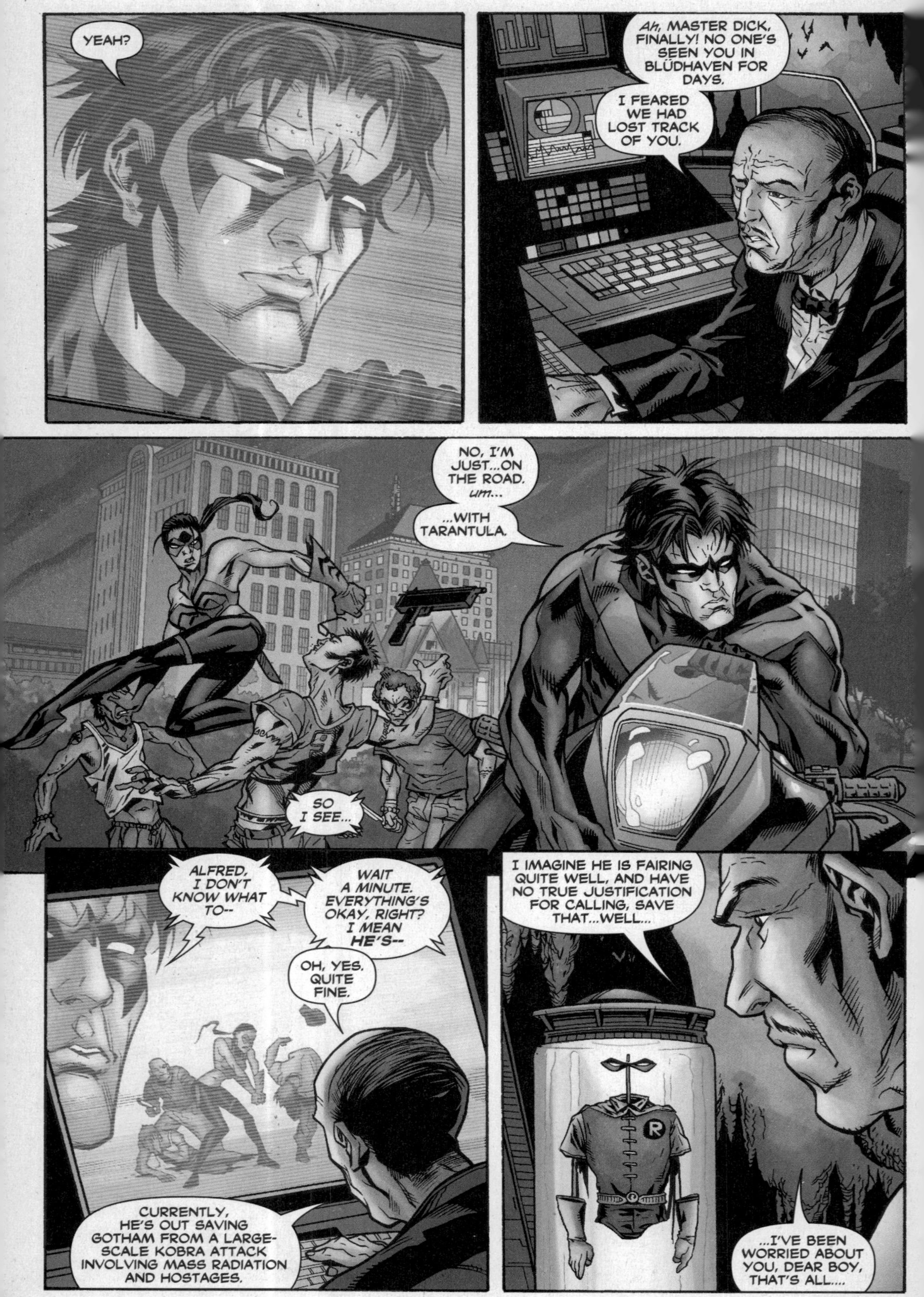
YEAH?
Ah, MASTER DICK, FINALLY! NO ONE'S SEEN YOU IN BLÜDHAVEN FOR DAYS.
I FEARED WE HAD LOST TRACK OF YOU.
NO, I'M JUST...ON THE ROAD. um...
...WITH TARANTULA.
SO I SEE...
ALFRED, I DON'T KNOW WHAT TO--
WAIT A MINUTE. EVERYTHING'S OKAY, RIGHT? I MEAN HE'S--
OH, YES. QUITE FINE.
CURRENTLY, HE'S OUT SAVING GOTHAM FROM A LARGE-SCALE KOBRA ATTACK INVOLVING MASS RADIATION AND HOSTAGES.
I IMAGINE HE IS FAIRING QUITE WELL, AND HAVE NO TRUE JUSTIFICATION FOR CALLING, SAVE THAT...WELL...
...I'VE BEEN WORRIED ABOUT YOU, DEAR BOY, THAT'S ALL....

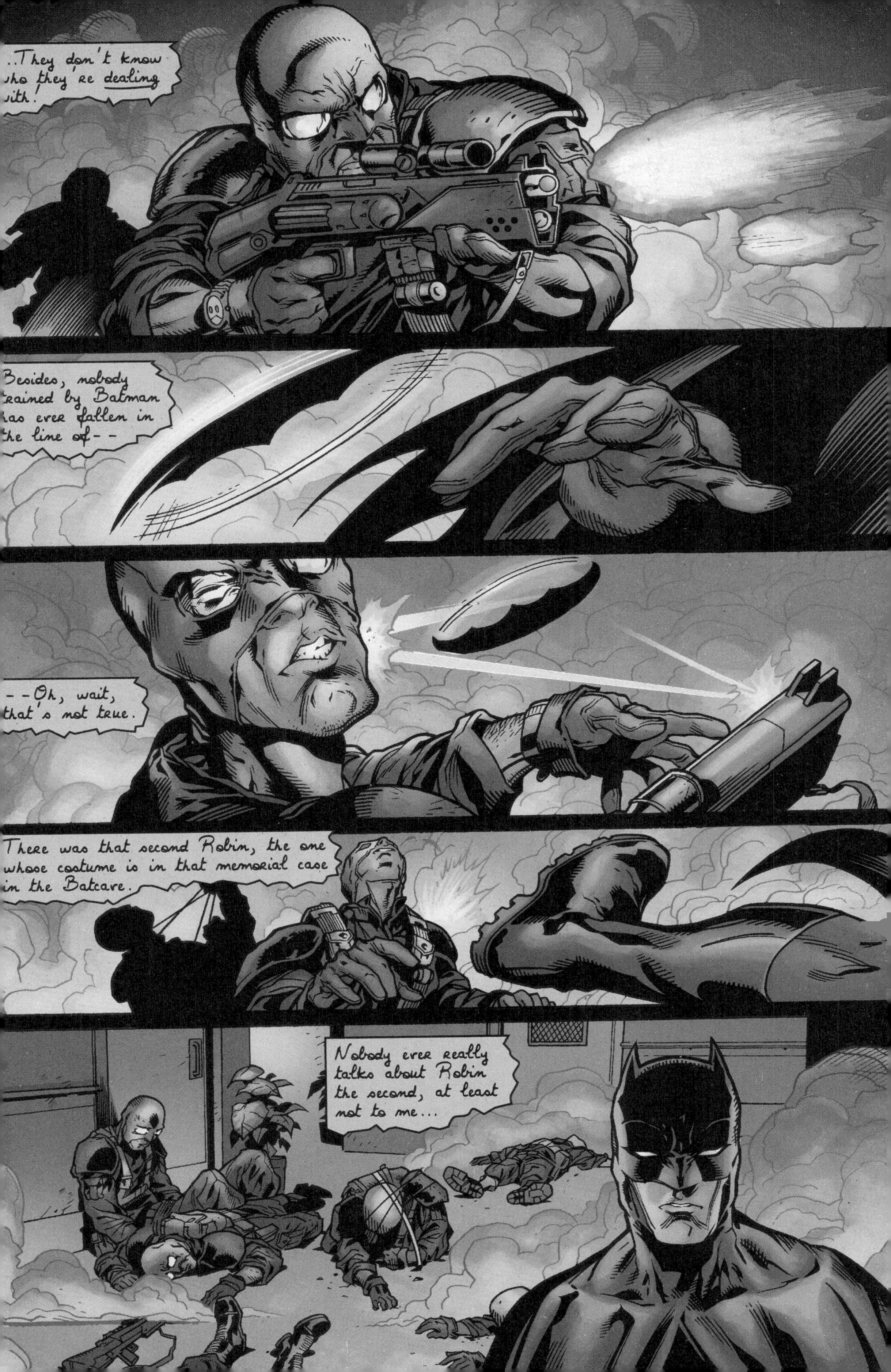
..They don't know who they're dealing with!
Besides, nobody trained by Batman has ever fallen in the line of--
--Oh, wait, that's not true.
There was that second Robin, the one whose costume is in that memorial case in the Batcave.
Nobody ever really talks about Robin the second, at least not to me...

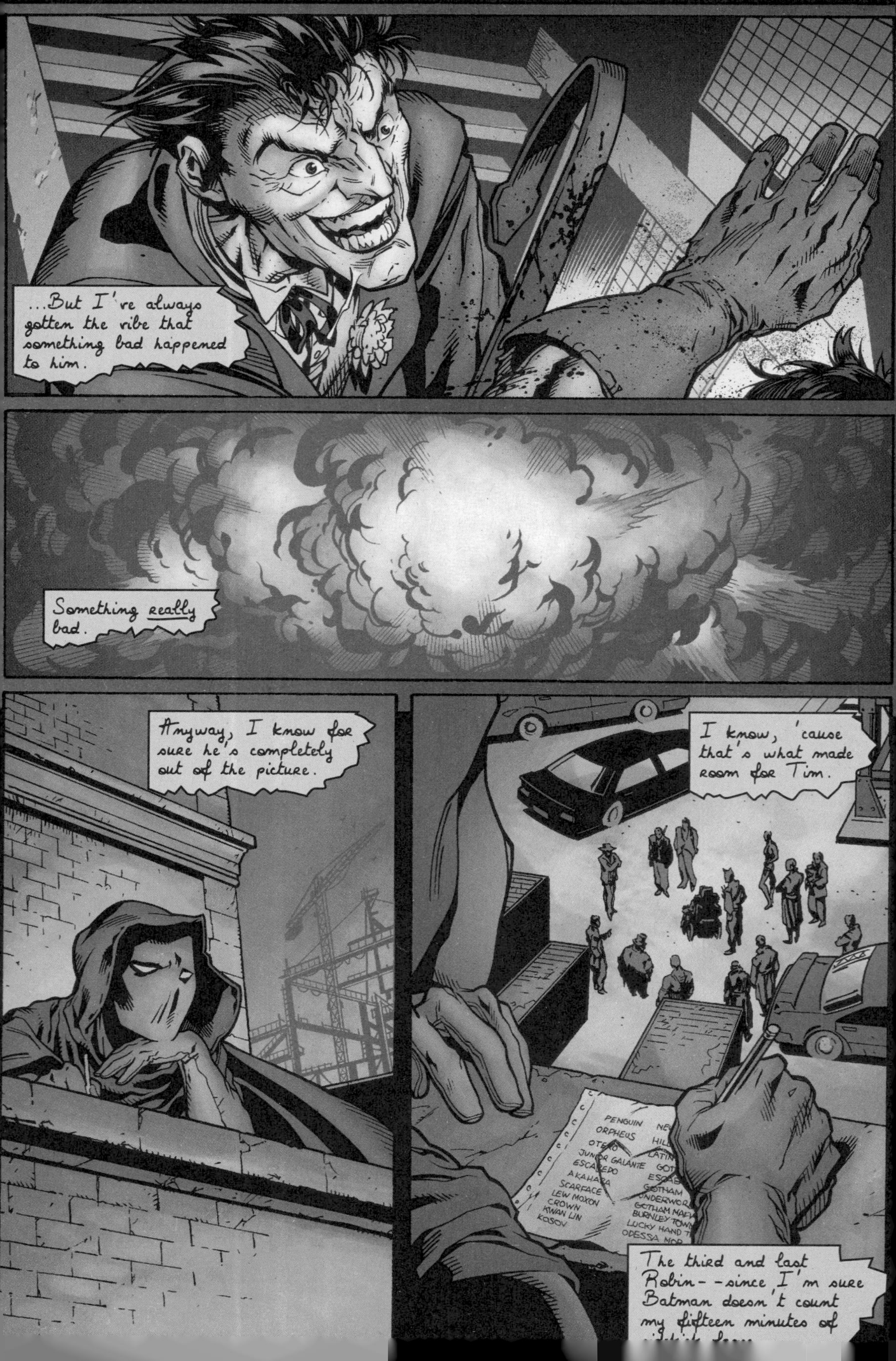

...But I've always gotten the vibe that something bad happened to him.
Something really bad.
Anyway, I know for sure he's completely out of the picture.
I know, 'cause that's what made room for Tim.
PENGUIN
ORPHEUS
OTERO
JUNIOR GALANTE
ESCAREPO
AKAHARA
SCARFACE
LEW MOXON
CROWN
KWAN LIN
KOSOV
The third and last Robin--since I'm sure Batman doesn't count my fifteen minutes of

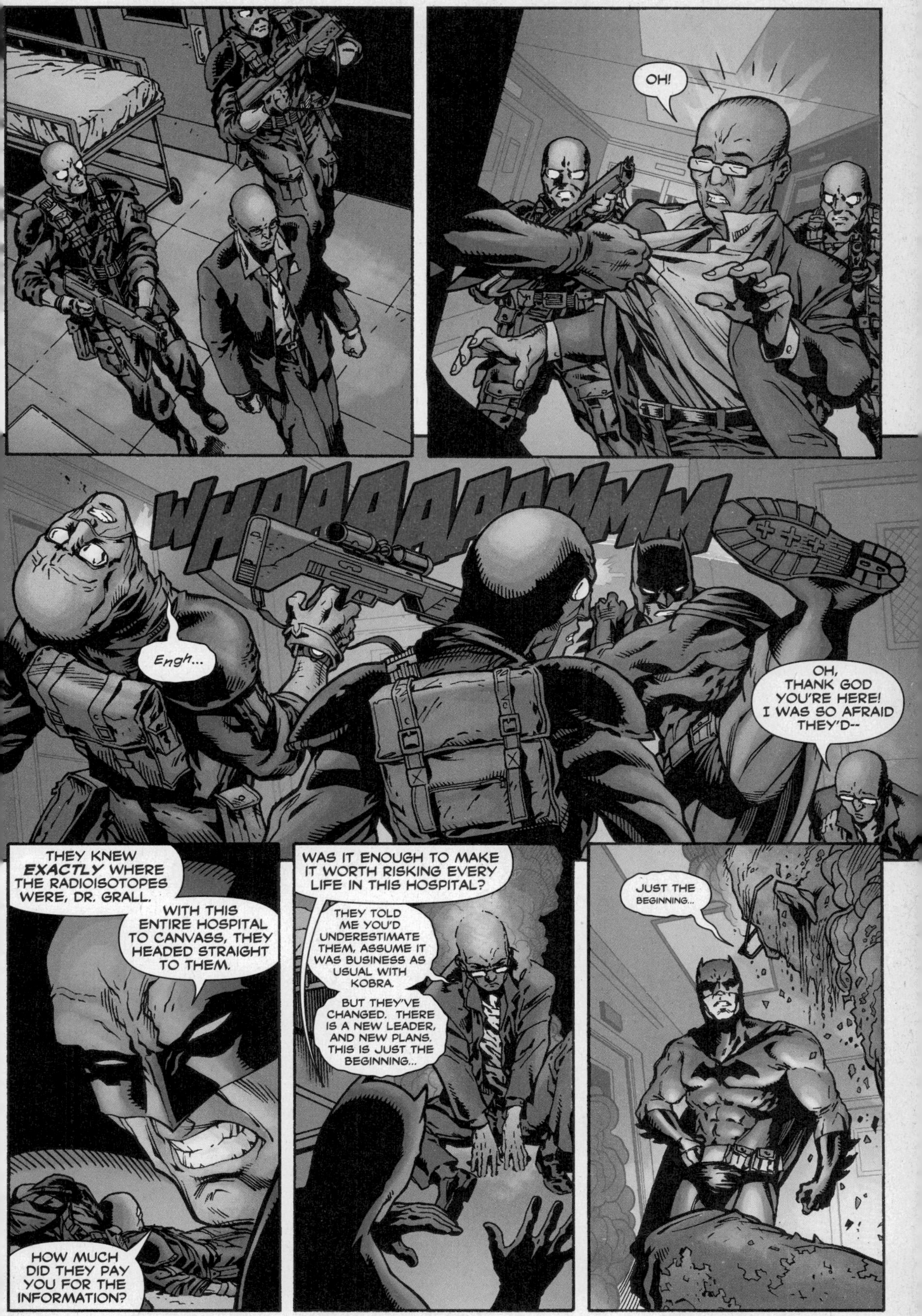
OH!
WHAAAAAAMMM
Engh...
OH, THANK GOD YOU'RE HERE! I WAS SO AFRAID THEY'D--
THEY KNEW **EXACTLY** WHERE THE RADIOISOTOPES WERE, DR. GRALL.
WITH THIS ENTIRE HOSPITAL TO CANVASS, THEY HEADED STRAIGHT TO THEM.
HOW MUCH DID THEY PAY YOU FOR THE INFORMATION?
WAS IT ENOUGH TO MAKE IT WORTH RISKING EVERY LIFE IN THIS HOSPITAL?
THEY TOLD ME YOU'D UNDERESTIMATE THEM, ASSUME IT WAS BUSINESS AS USUAL WITH KOBRA.
BUT THEY'VE CHANGED. THERE IS A NEW LEADER, AND NEW PLANS. THIS IS JUST THE BEGINNING...
JUST THE BEGINNING...

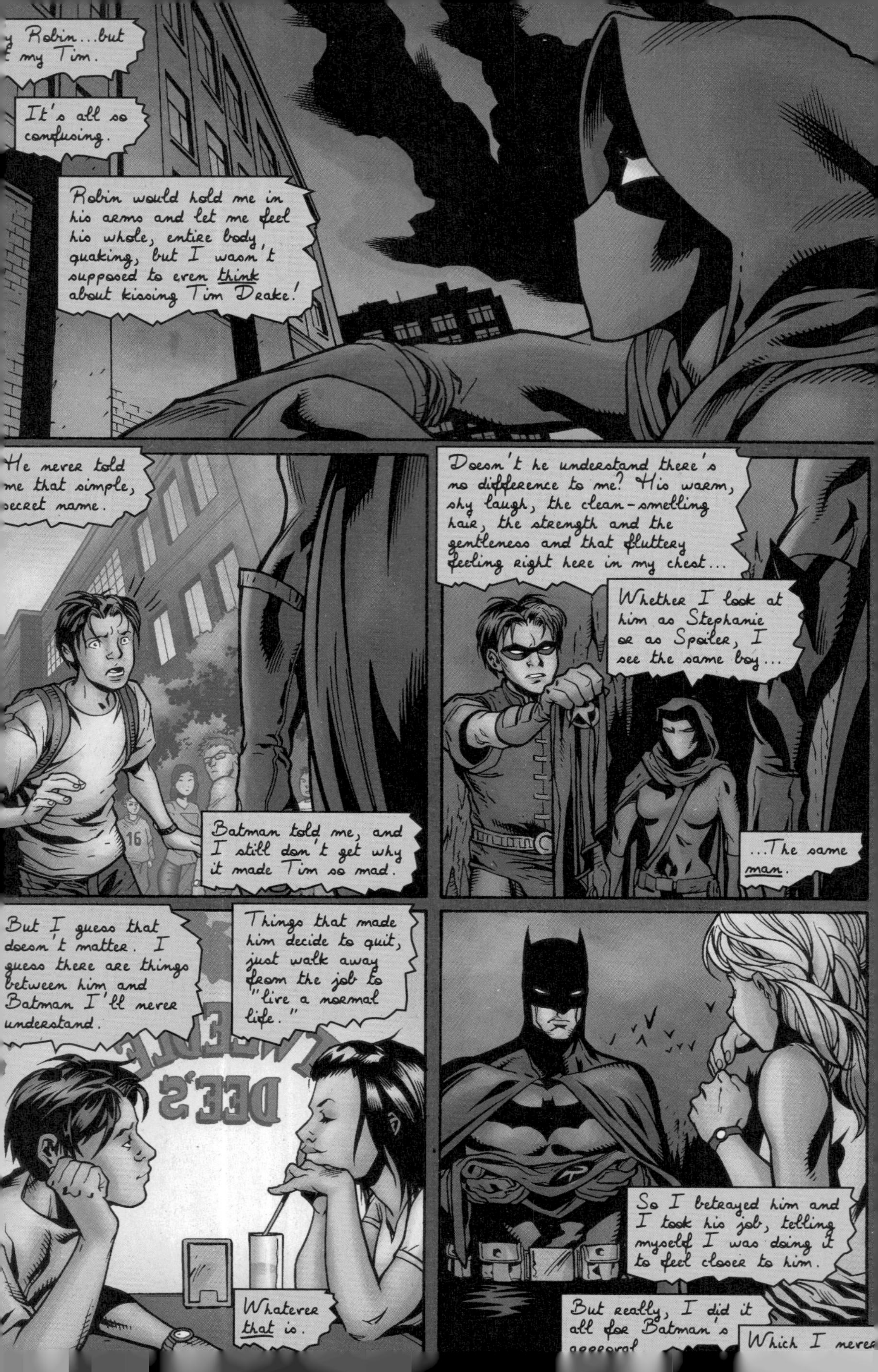
Robin...but my Tim.
It's all so confusing.
Robin would hold me in his arms and let me feel his whole, entire body, quaking, but I wasn't supposed to even think about kissing Tim Drake!
He never told me that simple, secret name.
Batman told me, and I still don't get why it made Tim so mad.
Doesn't he understand there's no difference to me? His warm, shy laugh, the clean-smelling hair, the strength and the gentleness and that fluttery feeling right here in my chest...
Whether I look at him as Stephanie or as Spoiler, I see the same boy...
...The same man.
But I guess that doesn't matter. I guess there are things between him and Batman I'll never understand.
Things that made him decide to quit, just walk away from the job to "live a normal life."
DEE'S
Whatever that is.
So I betrayed him and I took his job, telling myself I was doing it to feel closer to him.
But really, I did it all for Batman's
Which I never

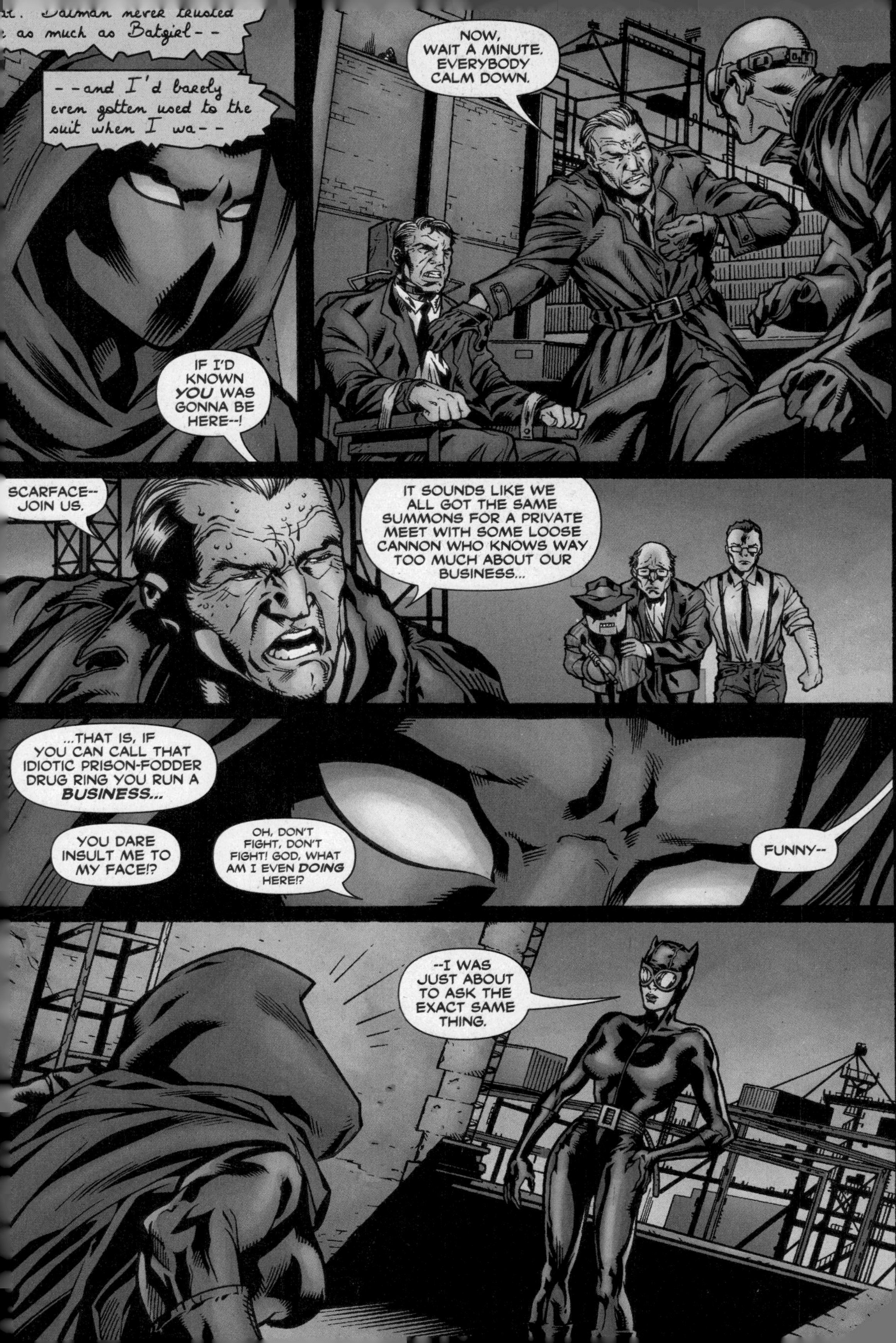
Batman never trusted as much as Batgirl--
--and I'd barely even gotten used to the suit when I wa--
NOW, WAIT A MINUTE. EVERYBODY CALM DOWN.
IF I'D KNOWN YOU WAS GONNA BE HERE--!
SCARFACE--JOIN US.
IT SOUNDS LIKE WE ALL GOT THE SAME SUMMONS FOR A PRIVATE MEET WITH SOME LOOSE CANNON WHO KNOWS WAY TOO MUCH ABOUT OUR BUSINESS...
...THAT IS, IF YOU CAN CALL THAT IDIOTIC PRISON-FODDER DRUG RING YOU RUN A BUSINESS...
YOU DARE INSULT ME TO MY FACE!?
OH, DON'T FIGHT, DON'T FIGHT! GOD, WHAT AM I EVEN DOING HERE!?
FUNNY--
--I WAS JUST ABOUT TO ASK THE EXACT SAME THING.

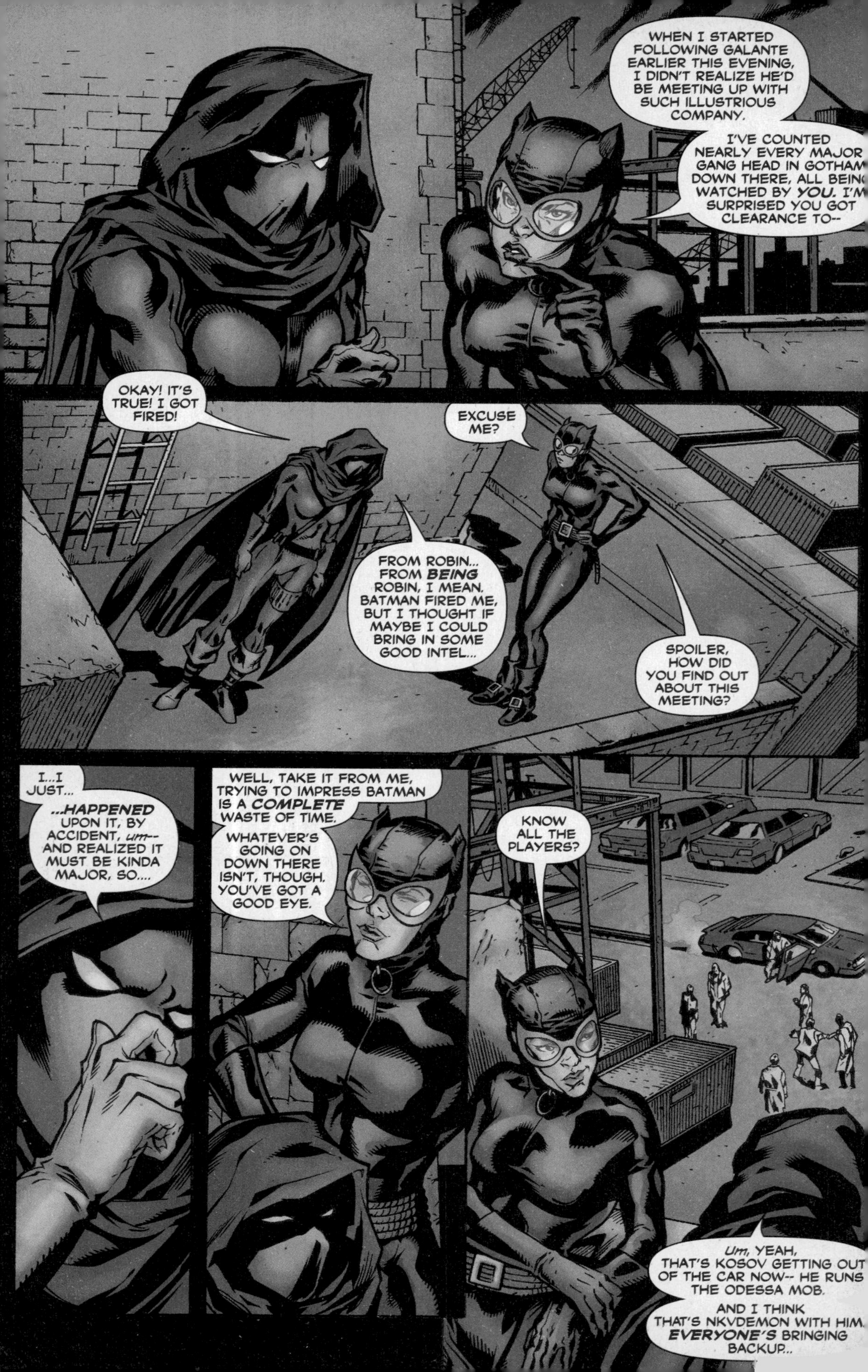
WHEN I STARTED FOLLOWING GALANTE EARLIER THIS EVENING, I DIDN'T REALIZE HE'D BE MEETING UP WITH SUCH ILLUSTRIOUS COMPANY.
I'VE COUNTED NEARLY EVERY MAJOR GANG HEAD IN GOTHAM DOWN THERE, ALL BEING WATCHED BY *YOU.* I'M SURPRISED YOU GOT CLEARANCE TO--
OKAY! IT'S TRUE! I GOT FIRED!
EXCUSE ME?
FROM ROBIN... FROM *BEING* ROBIN, I MEAN. BATMAN FIRED ME, BUT I THOUGHT IF MAYBE I COULD BRING IN SOME GOOD INTEL...
SPOILER, HOW DID YOU FIND OUT ABOUT THIS MEETING?
I...I JUST...
*...HAPPENED* UPON IT, BY ACCIDENT, *um*-- AND REALIZED IT MUST BE KINDA MAJOR, SO....
WELL, TAKE IT FROM ME, TRYING TO IMPRESS BATMAN IS A *COMPLETE* WASTE OF TIME.
WHATEVER'S GOING ON DOWN THERE ISN'T, THOUGH. YOU'VE GOT A GOOD EYE.
KNOW ALL THE PLAYERS?
*Um*, YEAH, THAT'S KOSOV GETTING OUT OF THE CAR NOW-- HE RUNS THE ODESSA MOB.
AND I THINK THAT'S NKVDEMON WITH HIM. *EVERYONE'S* BRINGING BACKUP...

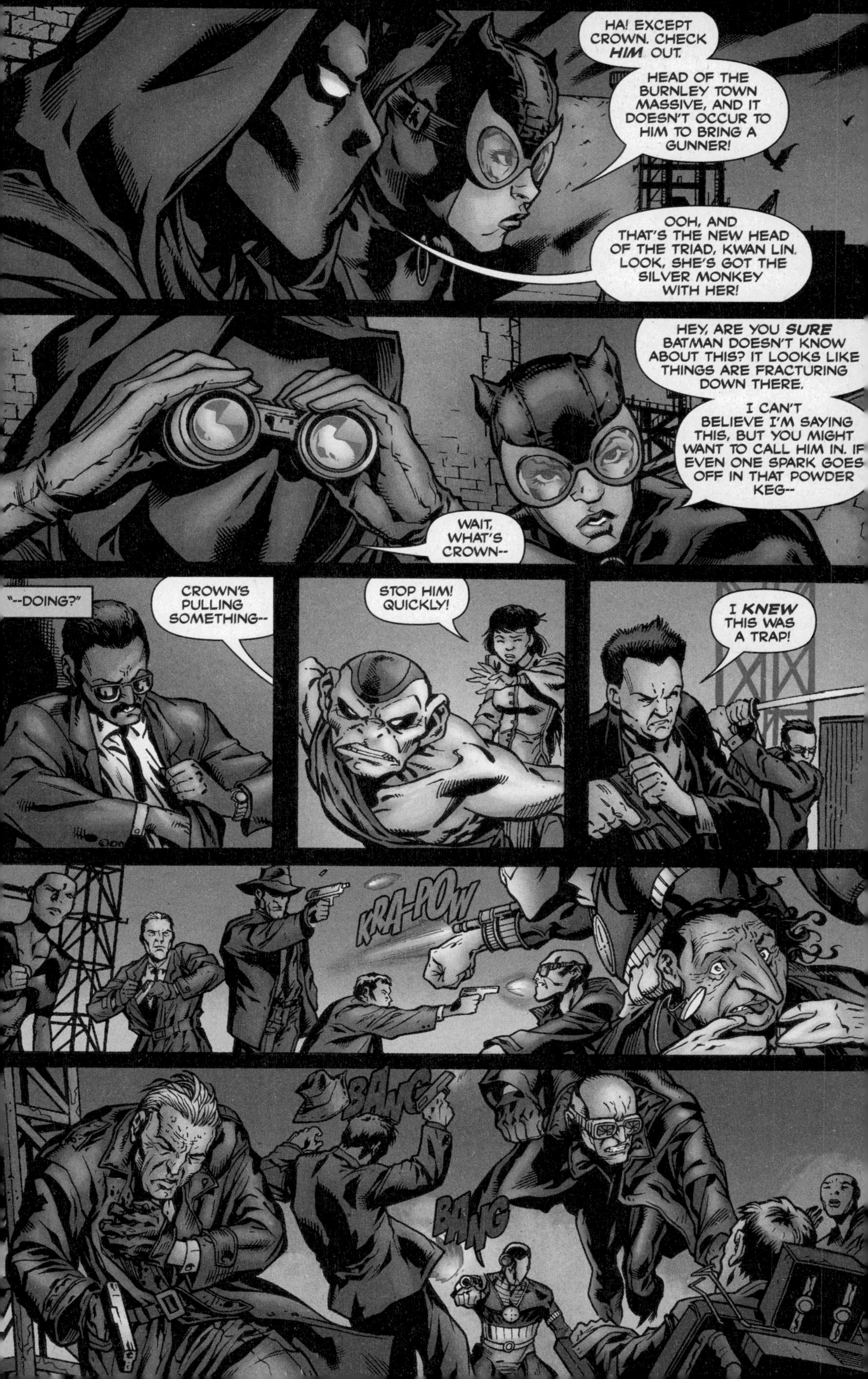
HA! EXCEPT CROWN. CHECK HIM OUT.
HEAD OF THE BURNLEY TOWN MASSIVE, AND IT DOESN'T OCCUR TO HIM TO BRING A GUNNER!
OOH, AND THAT'S THE NEW HEAD OF THE TRIAD, KWAN LIN. LOOK, SHE'S GOT THE SILVER MONKEY WITH HER!
HEY, ARE YOU SURE BATMAN DOESN'T KNOW ABOUT THIS? IT LOOKS LIKE THINGS ARE FRACTURING DOWN THERE.
I CAN'T BELIEVE I'M SAYING THIS, BUT YOU MIGHT WANT TO CALL HIM IN. IF EVEN ONE SPARK GOES OFF IN THAT POWDER KEG--
WAIT, WHAT'S CROWN--
"--DOING?"
CROWN'S PULLING SOMETHING--
STOP HIM! QUICKLY!
I KNEW THIS WAS A TRAP!
KRA-POW
BANG
BANG

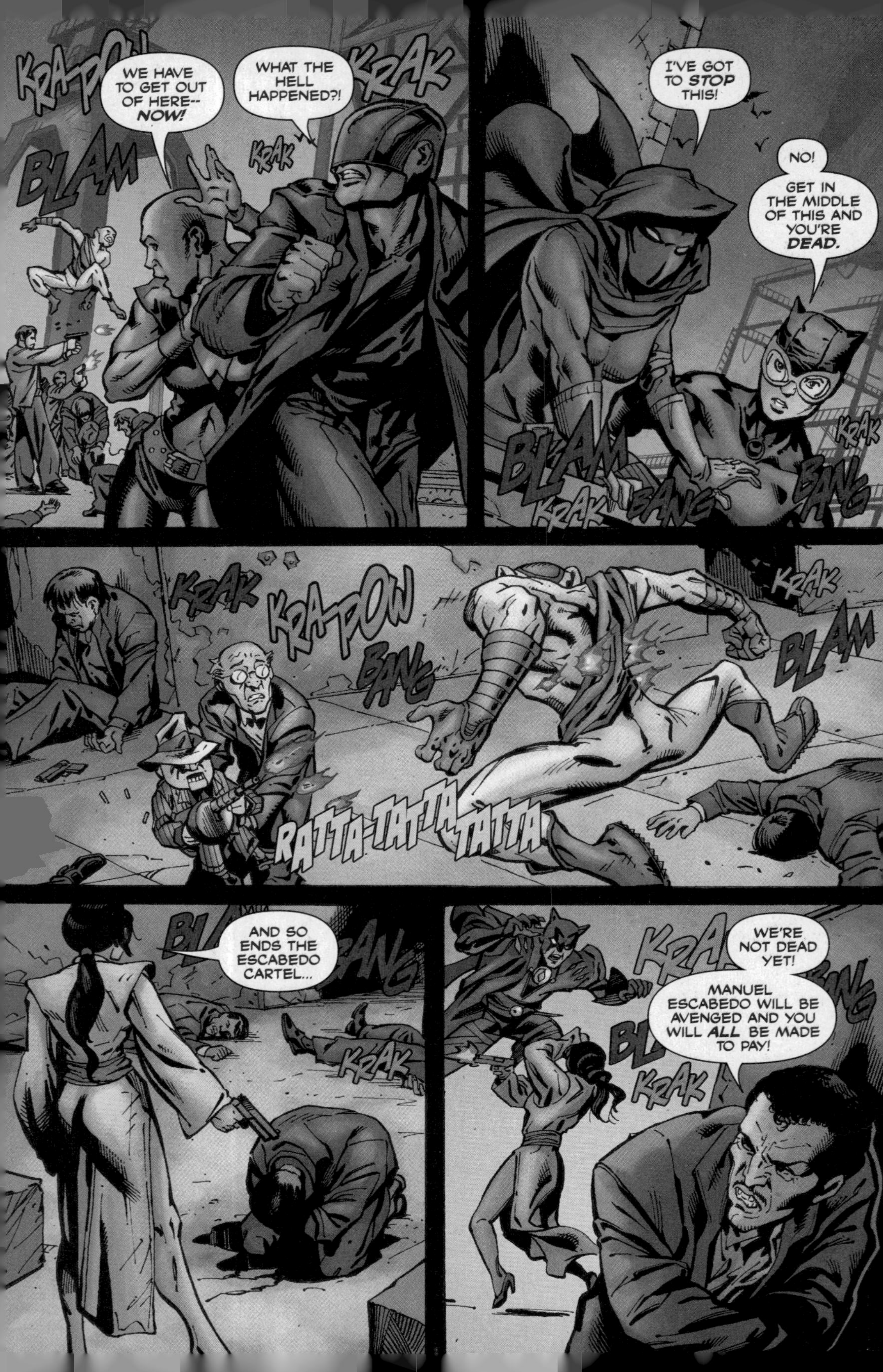

KRA-POW
WE HAVE TO GET OUT OF HERE-- NOW!
WHAT THE HELL HAPPENED?!
KRAK
BLAM
KRAK
I'VE GOT TO STOP THIS!
NO!
GET IN THE MIDDLE OF THIS AND YOU'RE DEAD.
BLAM
KRAK
BANG
KRAK
BANG
KRAK
KRA-POW
BANG
KRAK
BLAM
RATTA-TATTA-TATTA
AND SO ENDS THE ESCABEDO CARTEL...
KRAK
WE'RE NOT DEAD YET!
MANUEL ESCABEDO WILL BE AVENGED AND YOU WILL ALL BE MADE TO PAY!
KRAK

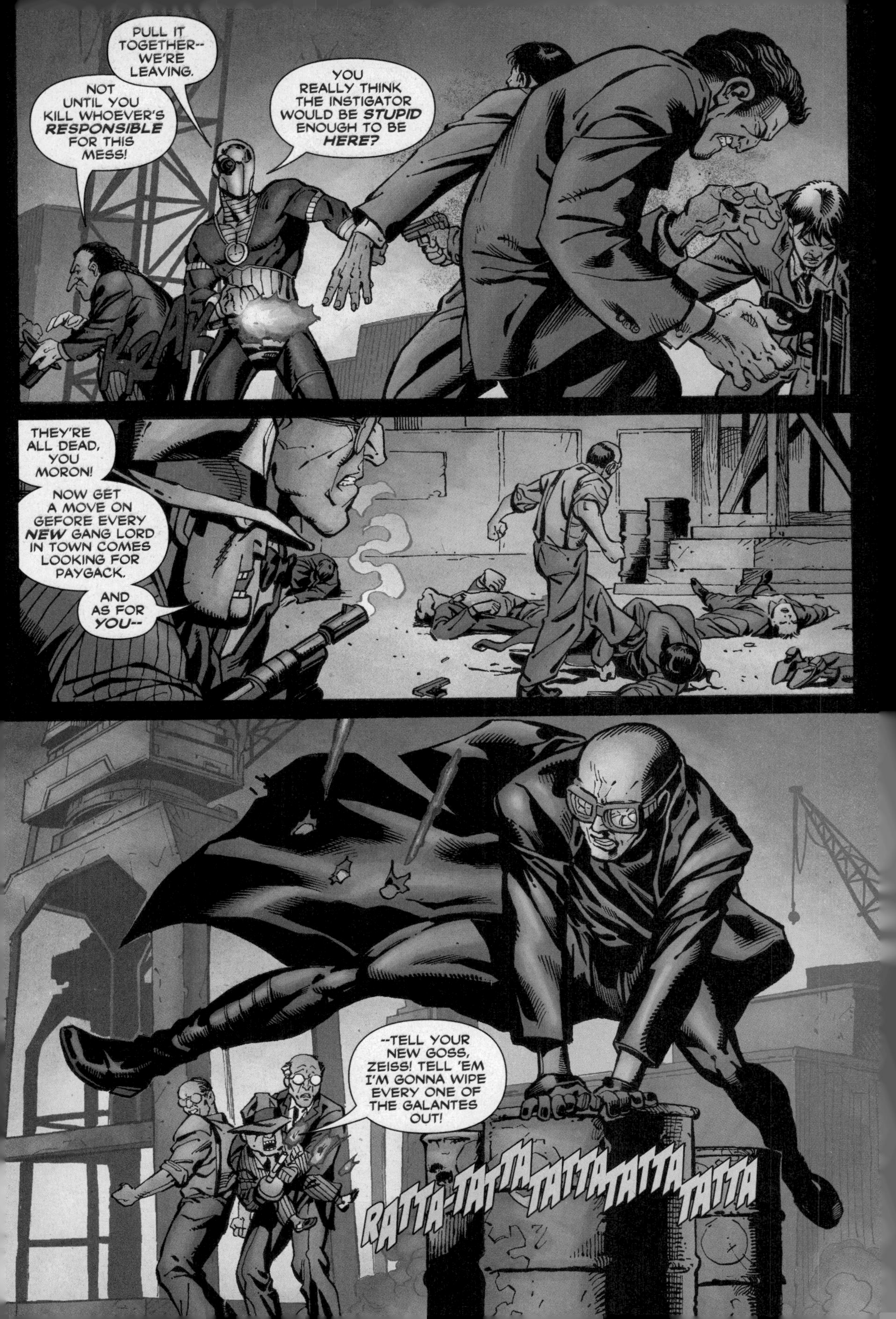
PULL IT TOGETHER-- WE'RE LEAVING.
NOT UNTIL YOU KILL WHOEVER'S ***RESPONSIBLE*** FOR THIS MESS!
YOU REALLY THINK THE INSTIGATOR WOULD BE ***STUPID*** ENOUGH TO BE ***HERE?***
THEY'RE ALL DEAD, YOU MORON!
NOW GET A MOVE ON GEFORE EVERY ***NEW*** GANG LORD IN TOWN COMES LOOKING FOR PAYGACK.
AND AS FOR ***YOU***--
--TELL YOUR NEW GOSS, ZEISS! TELL 'EM I'M GONNA WIPE EVERY ONE OF THE GALANTES OUT!
RATTA-TATTA TATTA TATTA TATTA

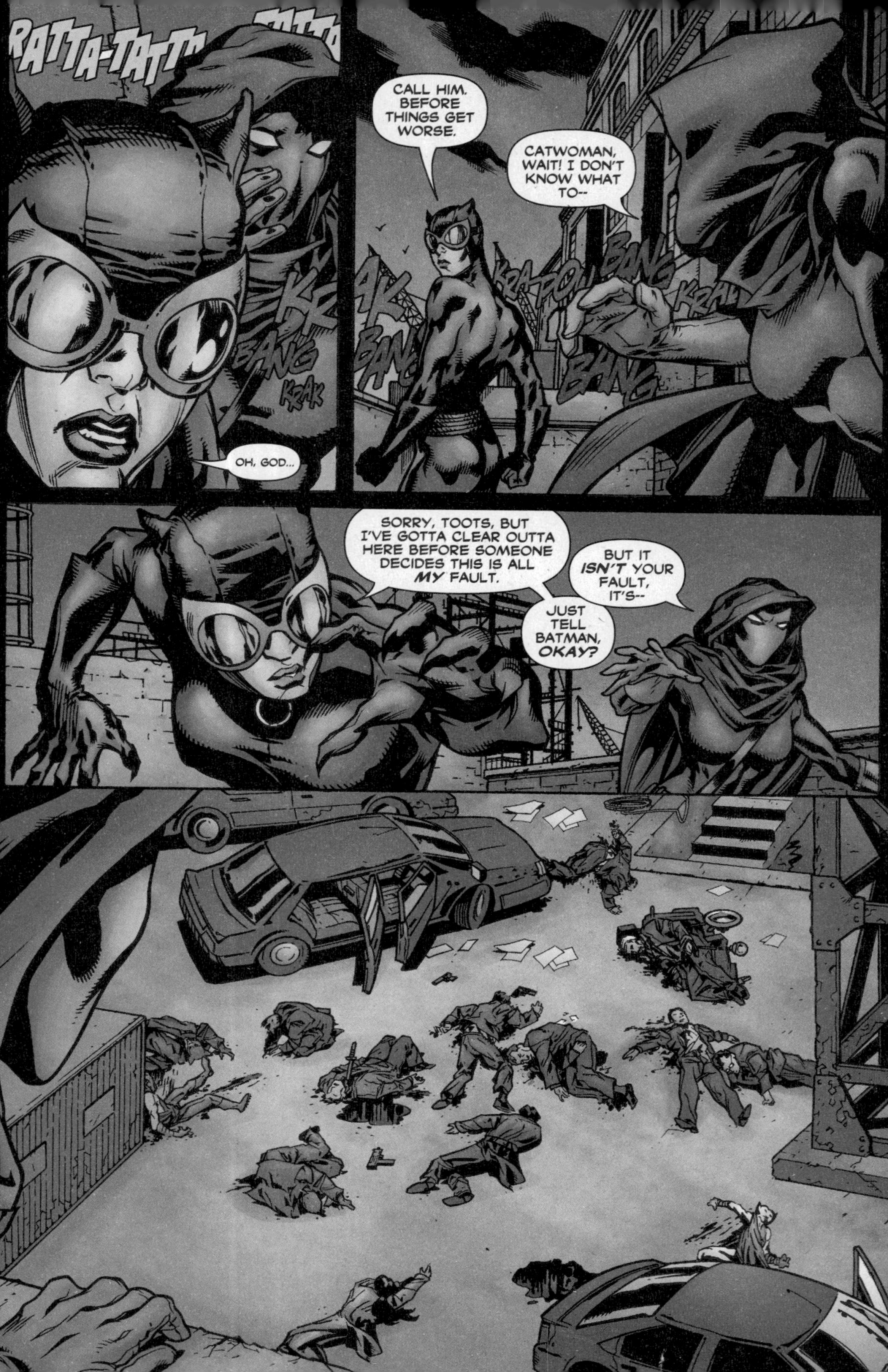
RATTA-TATT
OH, GOD...
CALL HIM. BEFORE THINGS GET WORSE.
CATWOMAN, WAIT! I DON'T KNOW WHAT TO--
BANG
KRAK
SORRY, TOOTS, BUT I'VE GOTTA CLEAR OUTTA HERE BEFORE SOMEONE DECIDES THIS IS ALL MY FAULT.
BUT IT ISN'T YOUR FAULT, IT'S--
JUST TELL BATMAN, OKAY?

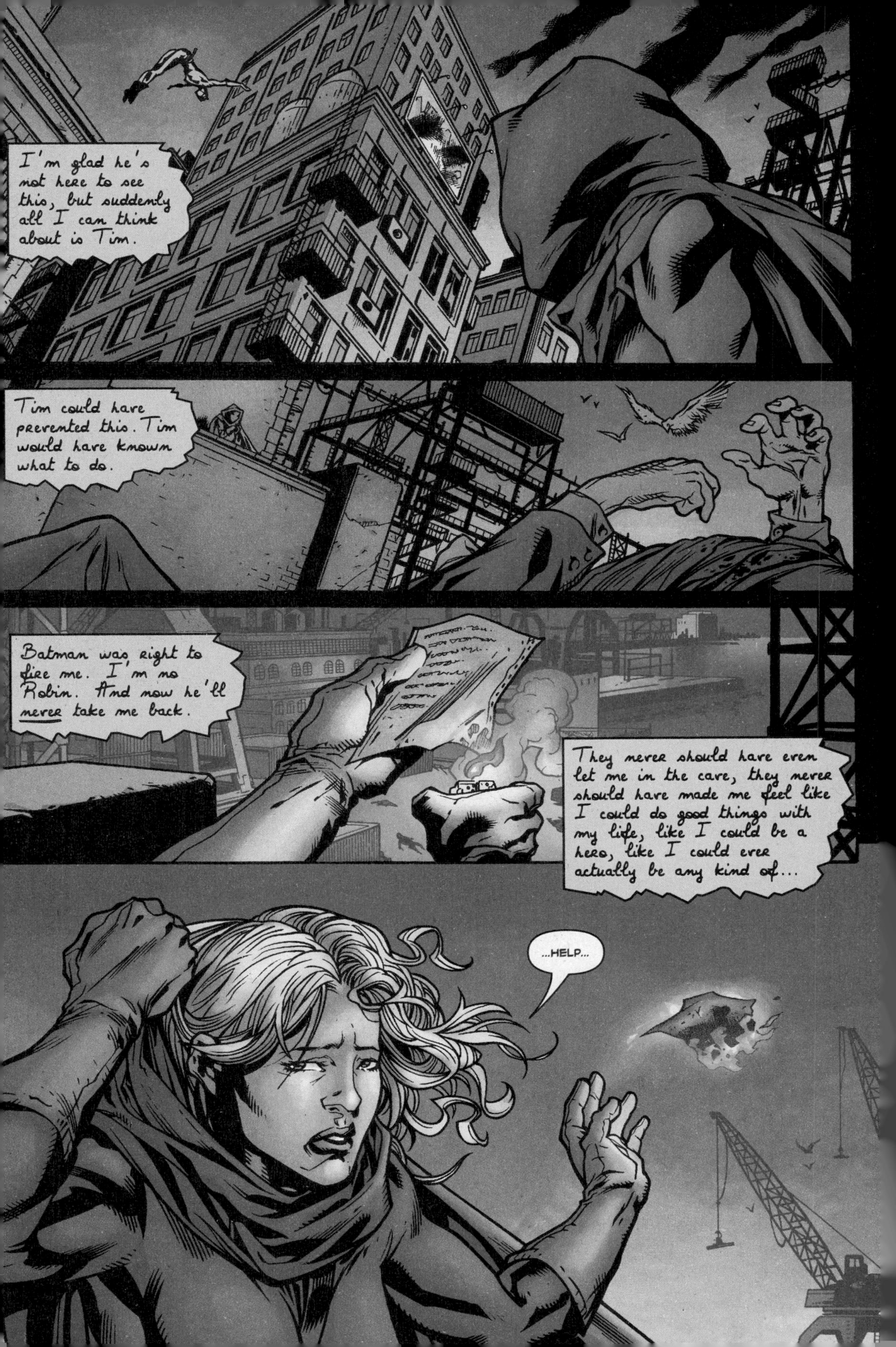
I'm glad he's not here to see this, but suddenly all I can think about is Tim.
Tim could have prevented this. Tim would have known what to do.
Batman was right to fire me. I'm no Robin. And now he'll never take me back.
They never should have even let me in the cave, they never should have made me feel like I could do good things with my life, like I could be a hero, like I could ever actually be any kind of...
...HELP...

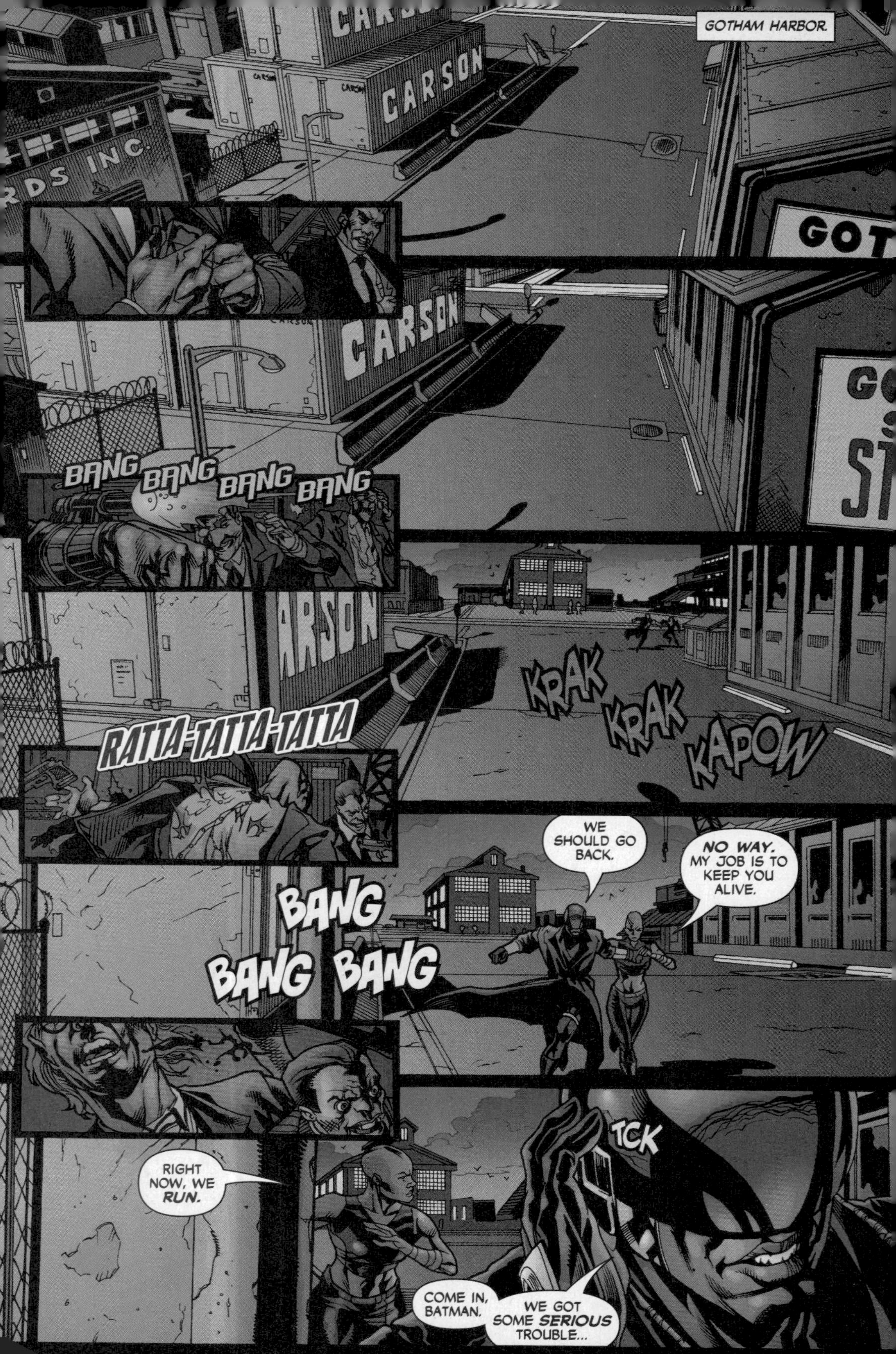
GOTHAM HARBOR.
BANG BANG BANG BANG
RATTA-TATTA-TATTA
KRAK KRAK KAPOW
WE SHOULD GO BACK.
NO WAY. MY JOB IS TO KEEP YOU ALIVE.
BANG BANG BANG
RIGHT NOW, WE RUN.
TCK
COME IN, BATMAN.
WE GOT SOME SERIOUS TROUBLE...

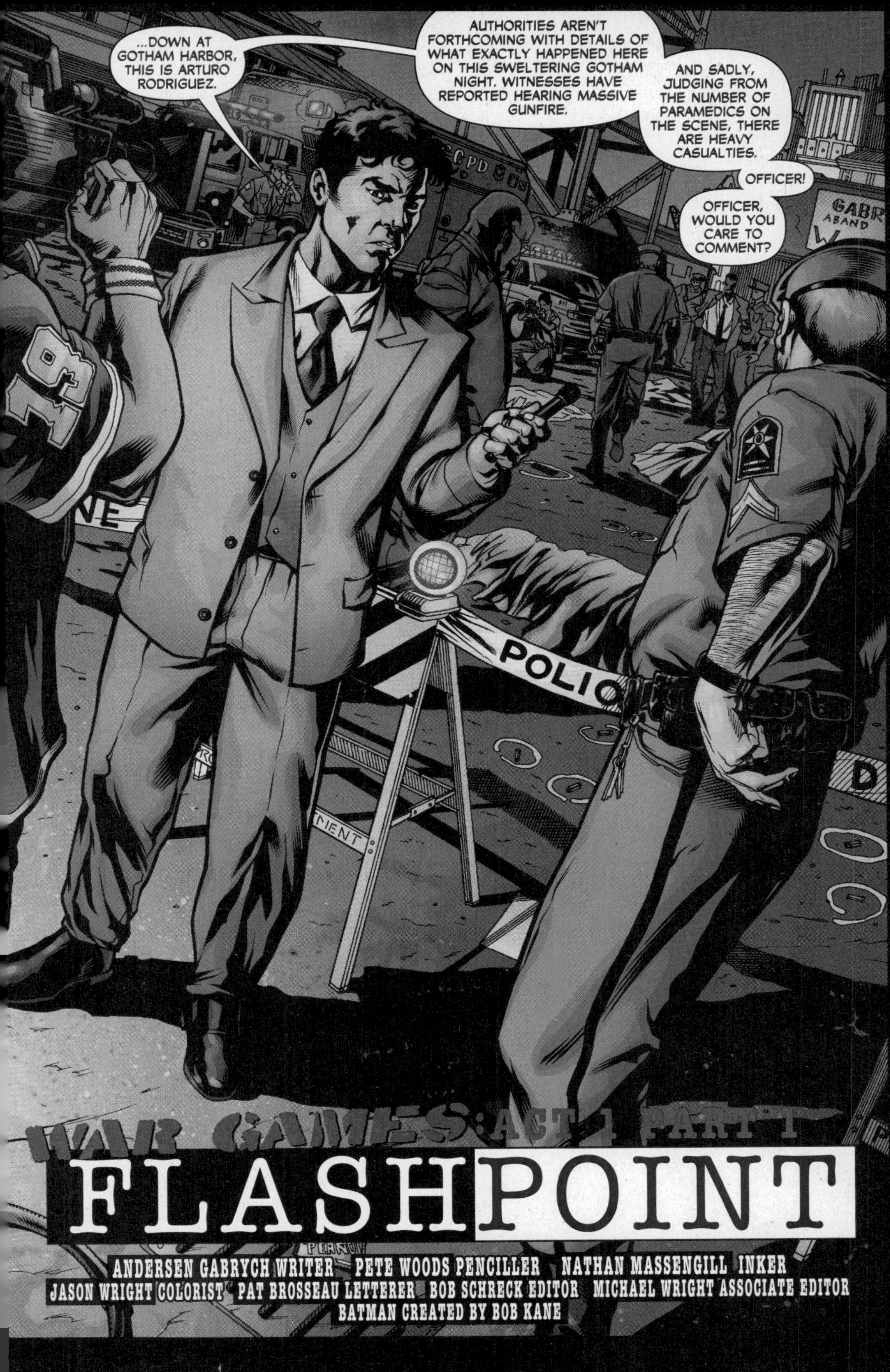
...DOWN AT GOTHAM HARBOR, THIS IS ARTURO RODRIGUEZ.
AUTHORITIES AREN'T FORTHCOMING WITH DETAILS OF WHAT EXACTLY HAPPENED HERE ON THIS SWELTERING GOTHAM NIGHT. WITNESSES HAVE REPORTED HEARING MASSIVE GUNFIRE.
AND SADLY, JUDGING FROM THE NUMBER OF PARAMEDICS ON THE SCENE, THERE ARE HEAVY CASUALTIES.
OFFICER!
OFFICER, WOULD YOU CARE TO COMMENT?
WAR GAMES: ACT 1 PART 1
FLASHPOINT
ANDERSEN GABRYCH WRITER PETE WOODS PENCILLER NATHAN MASSENGILL INKER
JASON WRIGHT COLORIST PAT BROSSEAU LETTERER BOB SCHRECK EDITOR MICHAEL WRIGHT ASSOCIATE EDITOR
BATMAN CREATED BY BOB KANE

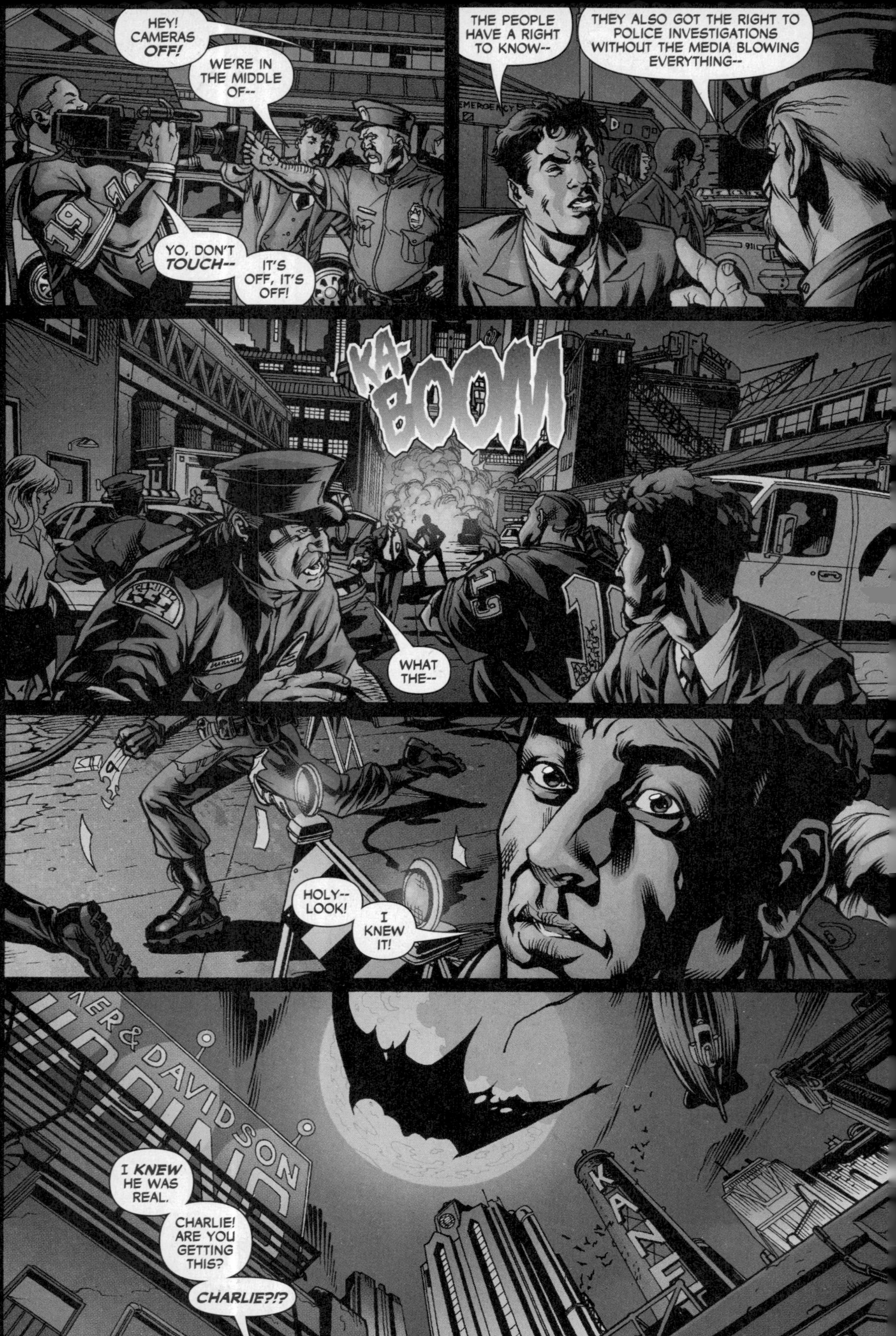
HEY! CAMERAS OFF!
WE'RE IN THE MIDDLE OF--
YO, DON'T TOUCH--
IT'S OFF, IT'S OFF!
THE PEOPLE HAVE A RIGHT TO KNOW--
THEY ALSO GOT THE RIGHT TO POLICE INVESTIGATIONS WITHOUT THE MEDIA BLOWING EVERYTHING--
KA-BOOM
WHAT THE--
HOLY-- LOOK!
I KNEW IT!
I KNEW HE WAS REAL.
CHARLIE! ARE YOU GETTING THIS?
CHARLIE?!?
DAVIDSON
KANE

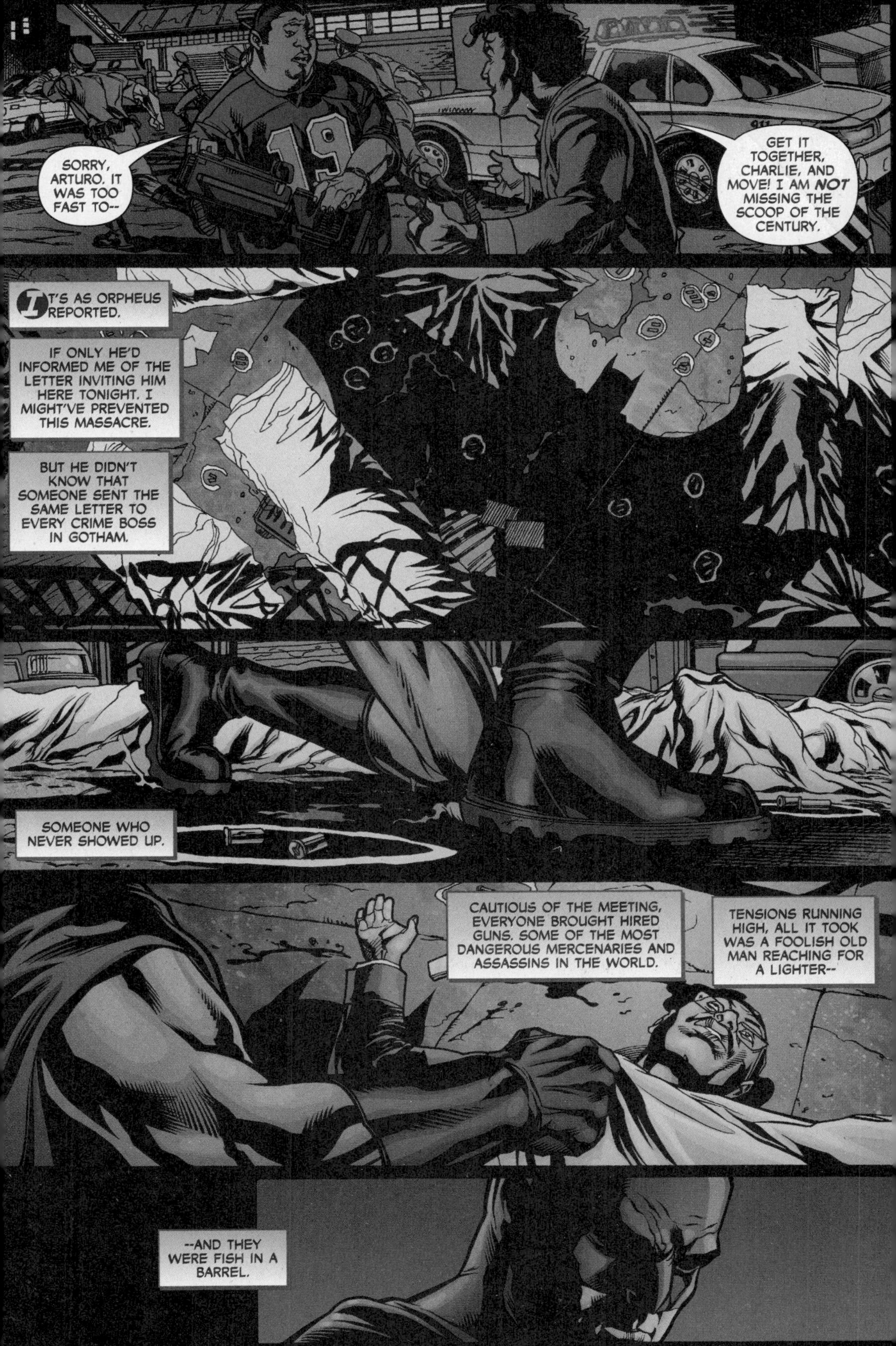

SORRY, ARTURO. IT WAS TOO FAST TO--
GET IT TOGETHER, CHARLIE, AND MOVE! I AM **NOT** MISSING THE SCOOP OF THE CENTURY.
IT'S AS ORPHEUS REPORTED.
IF ONLY HE'D INFORMED ME OF THE LETTER INVITING HIM HERE TONIGHT, I MIGHT'VE PREVENTED THIS MASSACRE.
BUT HE DIDN'T KNOW THAT SOMEONE SENT THE SAME LETTER TO EVERY CRIME BOSS IN GOTHAM.
SOMEONE WHO NEVER SHOWED UP.
CAUTIOUS OF THE MEETING, EVERYONE BROUGHT HIRED GUNS. SOME OF THE MOST DANGEROUS MERCENARIES AND ASSASSINS IN THE WORLD.
TENSIONS RUNNING HIGH, ALL IT TOOK WAS A FOOLISH OLD MAN REACHING FOR A LIGHTER--
--AND THEY WERE FISH IN A BARREL.

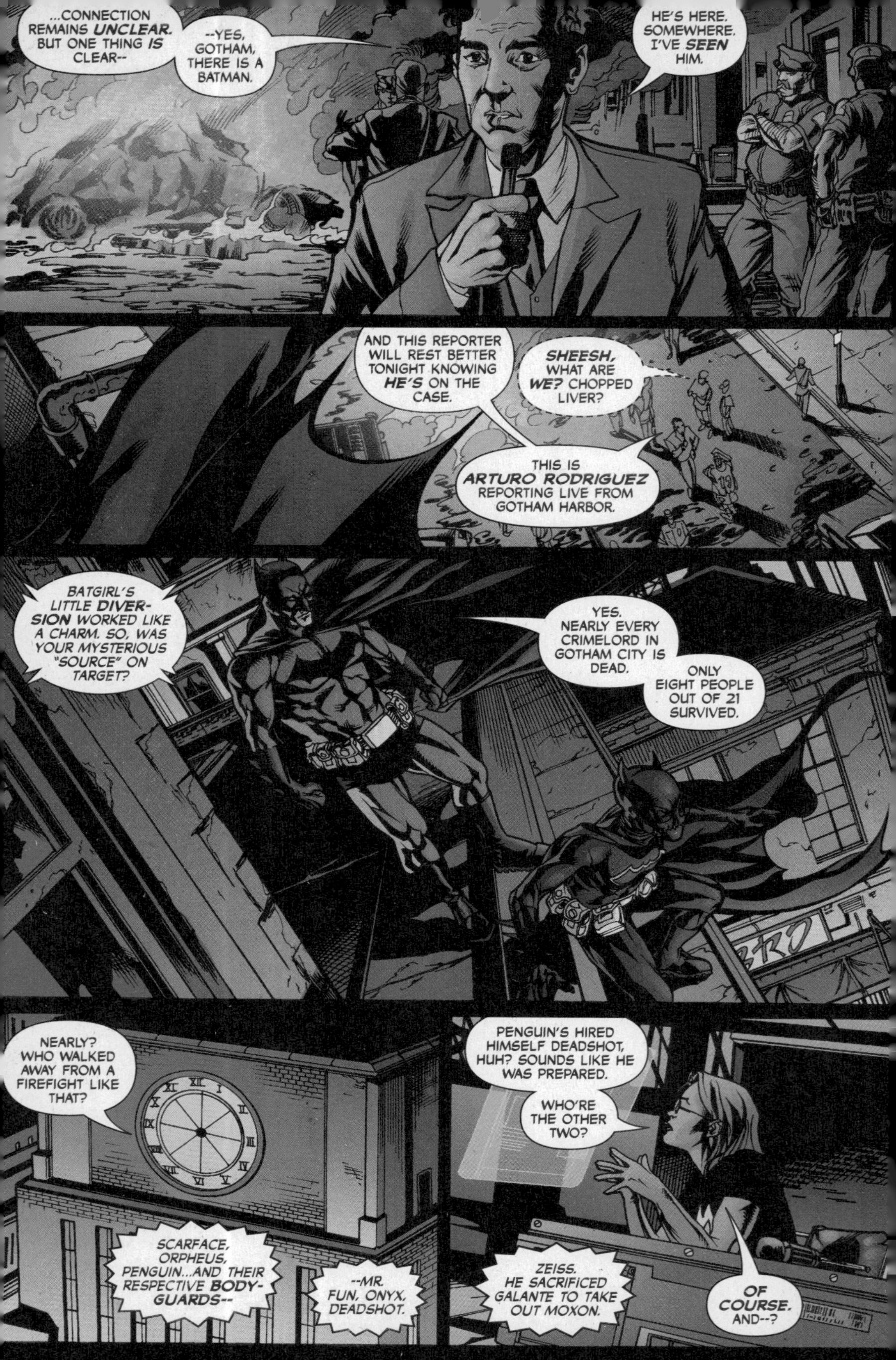
...CONNECTION REMAINS UNCLEAR. BUT ONE THING IS CLEAR--
--YES, GOTHAM, THERE IS A BATMAN.
HE'S HERE. SOMEWHERE. I'VE SEEN HIM.
AND THIS REPORTER WILL REST BETTER TONIGHT KNOWING HE'S ON THE CASE.
SHEESH, WHAT ARE WE? CHOPPED LIVER?
THIS IS ARTURO RODRIGUEZ REPORTING LIVE FROM GOTHAM HARBOR.
BATGIRL'S LITTLE DIVER-SION WORKED LIKE A CHARM. SO, WAS YOUR MYSTERIOUS "SOURCE" ON TARGET?
YES. NEARLY EVERY CRIMELORD IN GOTHAM CITY IS DEAD.
ONLY EIGHT PEOPLE OUT OF 21 SURVIVED.
NEARLY? WHO WALKED AWAY FROM A FIREFIGHT LIKE THAT?
SCARFACE, ORPHEUS, PENGUIN...AND THEIR RESPECTIVE BODY-GUARDS--
--MR. FUN, ONYX, DEADSHOT.
PENGUIN'S HIRED HIMSELF DEADSHOT, HUH? SOUNDS LIKE HE WAS PREPARED.
WHO'RE THE OTHER TWO?
ZEISS. HE SACRIFICED GALANTE TO TAKE OUT MOXON.
OF COURSE. AND--?

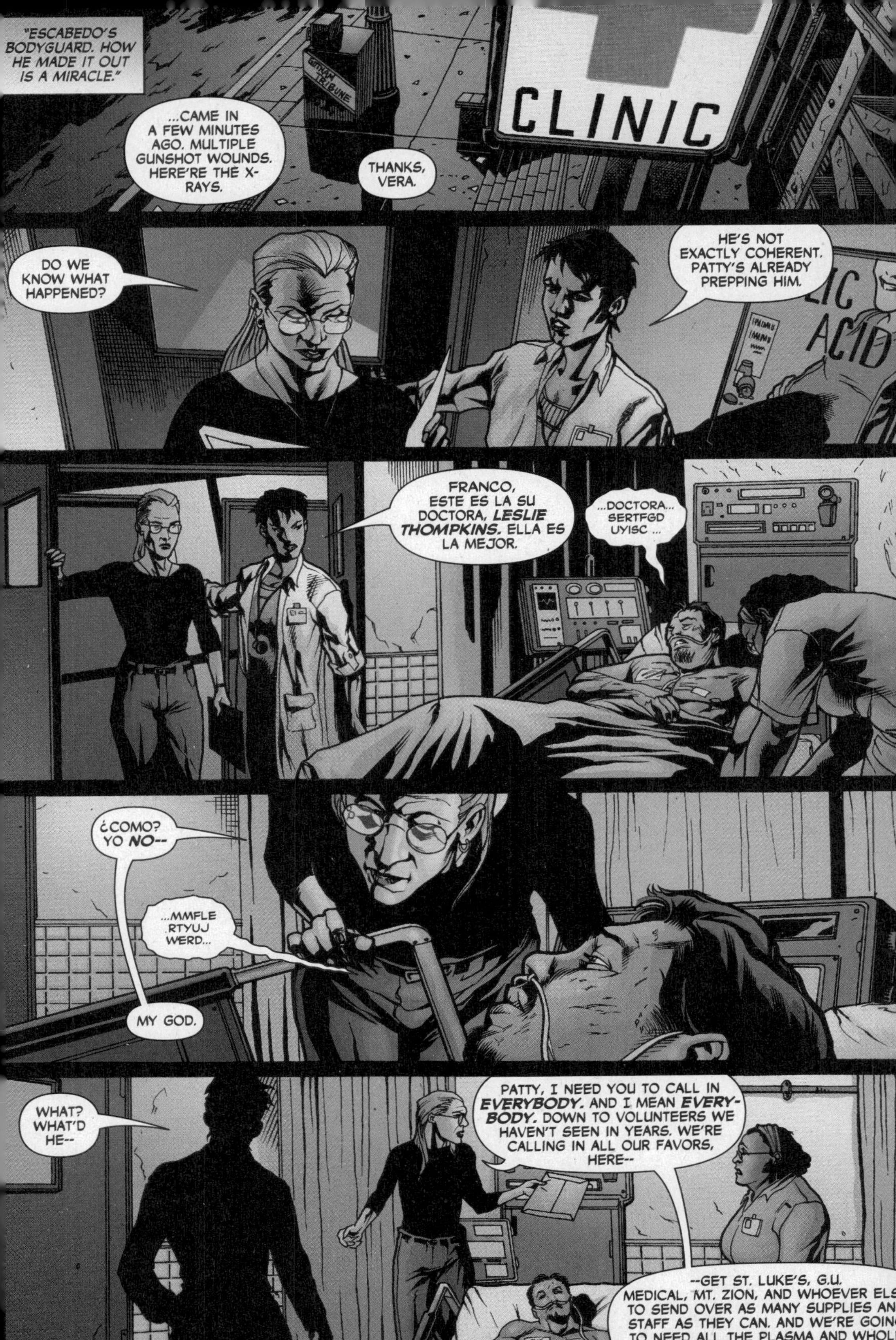
"ESCABEDO'S BODYGUARD. HOW HE MADE IT OUT IS A MIRACLE."
CLINIC
GOTHAM TRIBUNE
...CAME IN A FEW MINUTES AGO. MULTIPLE GUNSHOT WOUNDS. HERE'RE THE X-RAYS.
THANKS, VERA.
DO WE KNOW WHAT HAPPENED?
HE'S NOT EXACTLY COHERENT. PATTY'S ALREADY PREPPING HIM.
FRANCO, ESTE ES LA SU DOCTORA, LESLIE THOMPKINS. ELLA ES LA MEJOR.
...DOCTORA... SERTFGD UYISC ...
¿COMO? YO NO--
...MMFLE .RTYUJ WERD...
MY GOD.
WHAT? WHAT'D HE--
PATTY, I NEED YOU TO CALL IN EVERYBODY. AND I MEAN EVERY-BODY. DOWN TO VOLUNTEERS WE HAVEN'T SEEN IN YEARS. WE'RE CALLING IN ALL OUR FAVORS, HERE--
--GET ST. LUKE'S, G.U. MEDICAL, MT. ZION, AND WHOEVER ELSE TO SEND OVER AS MANY SUPPLIES AND STAFF AS THEY CAN. AND WE'RE GOING TO NEED ALL THE PLASMA AND WHOLE BLOOD ANYONE CAN SPARE...

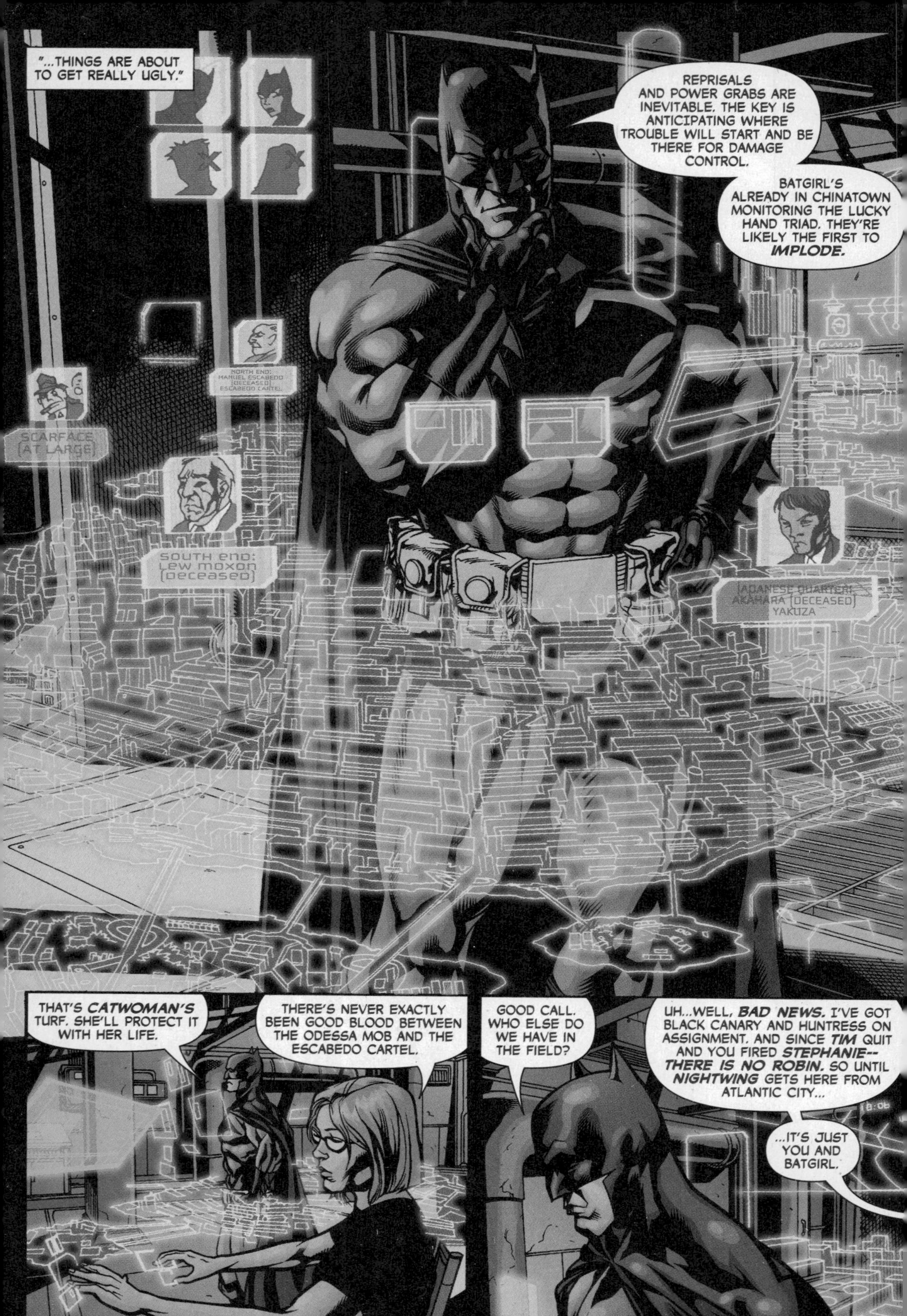
"...THINGS ARE ABOUT TO GET REALLY UGLY."
REPRISALS AND POWER GRABS ARE INEVITABLE. THE KEY IS ANTICIPATING WHERE TROUBLE WILL START AND BE THERE FOR DAMAGE CONTROL.
BATGIRL'S ALREADY IN CHINATOWN MONITORING THE LUCKY HAND TRIAD. THEY'RE LIKELY THE FIRST TO *IMPLODE.*
NORTH END: MANUEL ESCABEDO (DECEASED) ESCABEDO CARTEL
SCARFACE (AT LARGE)
SOUTH END: LEW MOXON (DECEASED)
JAPANESE QUARTER: AKAHARA (DECEASED) YAKUZA
THAT'S *CATWOMAN'S* TURF. SHE'LL PROTECT IT WITH HER LIFE.
THERE'S NEVER EXACTLY BEEN GOOD BLOOD BETWEEN THE ODESSA MOB AND THE ESCABEDO CARTEL.
GOOD CALL. WHO ELSE DO WE HAVE IN THE FIELD?
UH...WELL, *BAD NEWS.* I'VE GOT BLACK CANARY AND HUNTRESS ON ASSIGNMENT. AND SINCE *TIM* QUIT AND YOU FIRED *STEPHANIE-- THERE IS NO ROBIN.* SO UNTIL *NIGHTWING* GETS HERE FROM ATLANTIC CITY...
...IT'S JUST YOU AND BATGIRL.

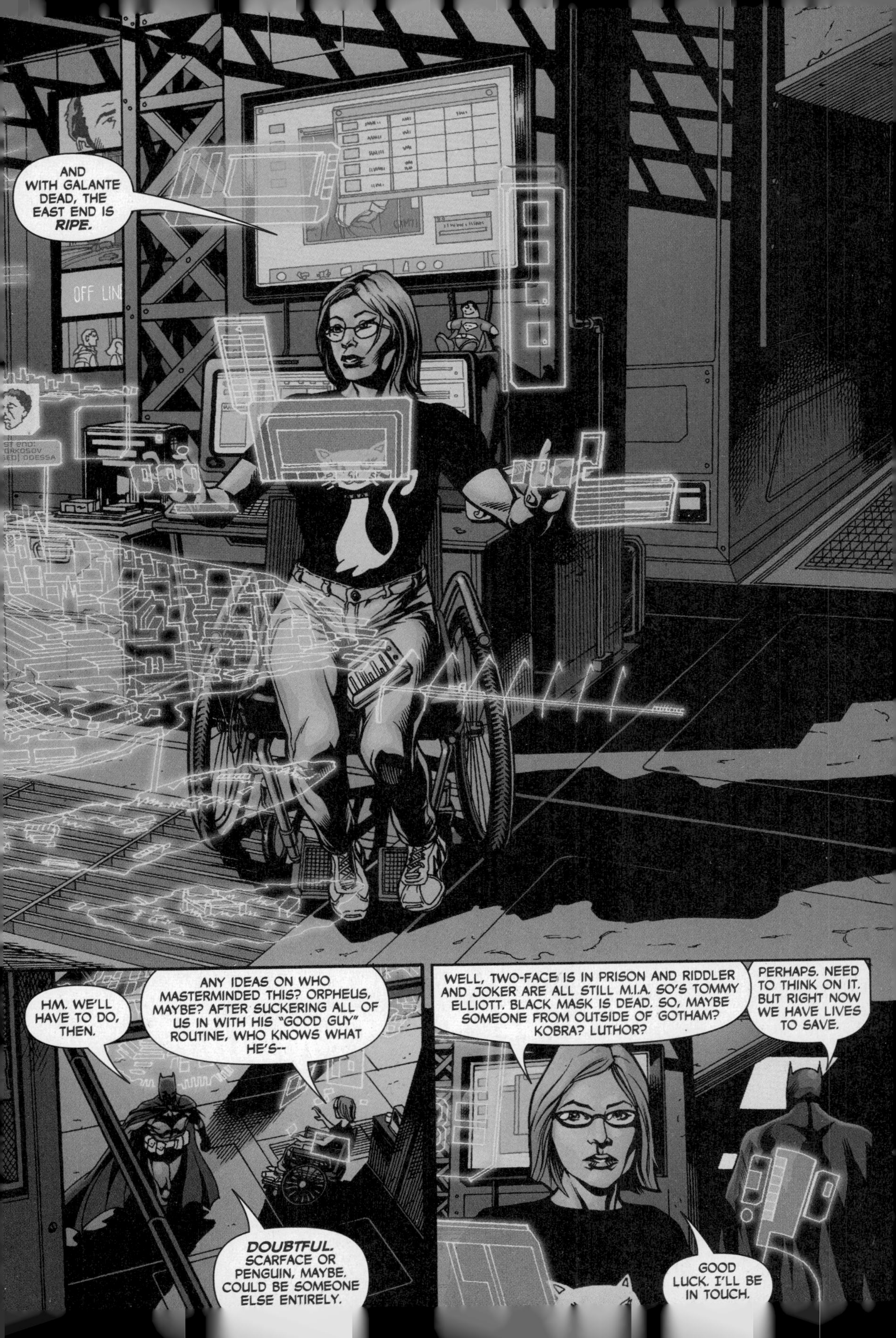

AND WITH GALANTE DEAD, THE EAST END IS RIPE.
OFF LINE
HM. WE'LL HAVE TO DO, THEN.
ANY IDEAS ON WHO MASTERMINDED THIS? ORPHEUS, MAYBE? AFTER SUCKERING ALL OF US IN WITH HIS "GOOD GUY" ROUTINE, WHO KNOWS WHAT HE'S--
DOUBTFUL. SCARFACE OR PENGUIN, MAYBE. COULD BE SOMEONE ELSE ENTIRELY.
WELL, TWO-FACE IS IN PRISON AND RIDDLER AND JOKER ARE ALL STILL M.I.A. SO'S TOMMY ELLIOTT. BLACK MASK IS DEAD. SO, MAYBE SOMEONE FROM OUTSIDE OF GOTHAM? KOBRA? LUTHOR?
PERHAPS. NEED TO THINK ON IT. BUT RIGHT NOW WE HAVE LIVES TO SAVE.
GOOD LUCK. I'LL BE IN TOUCH.

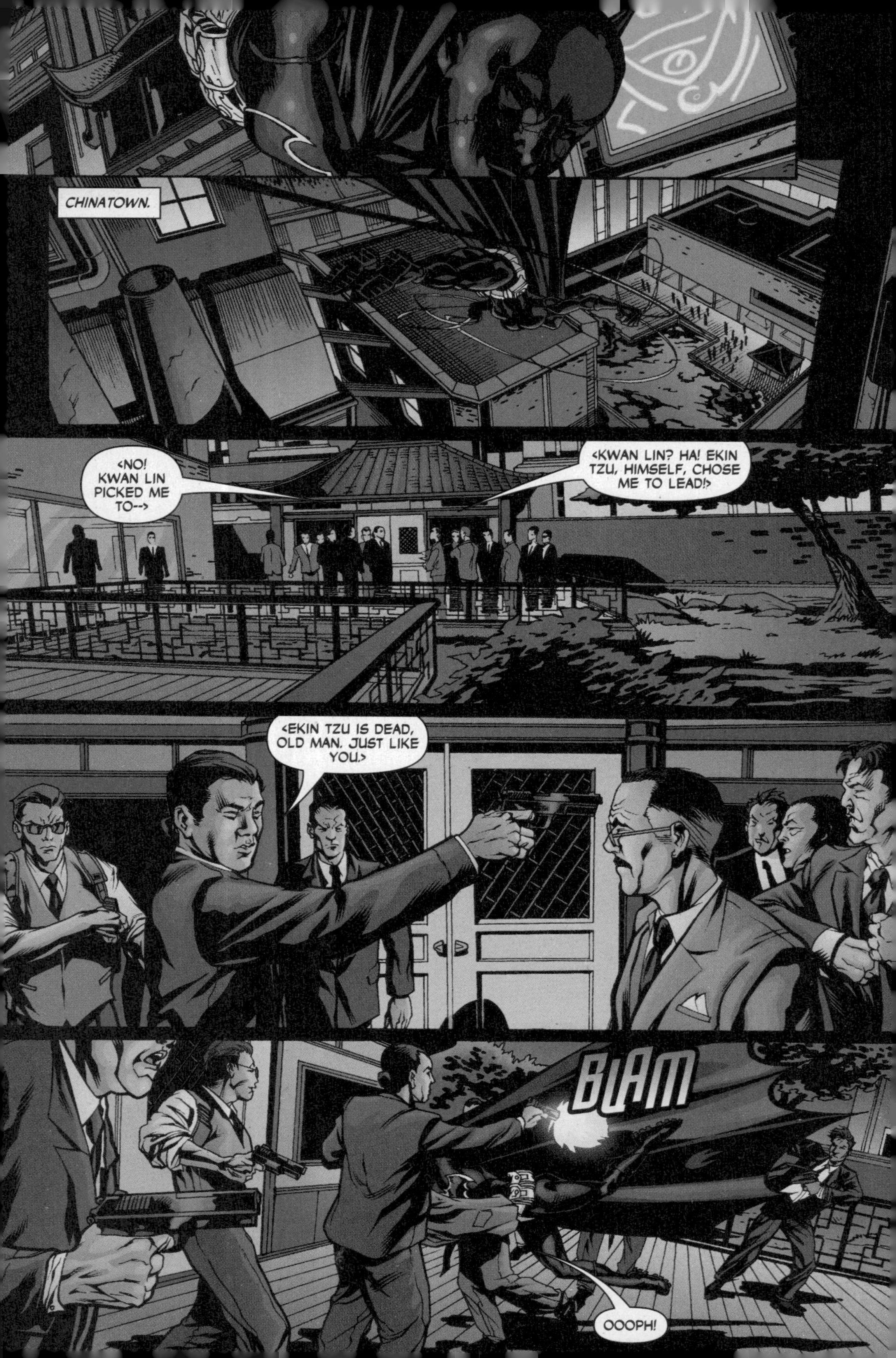
CHINATOWN.
<NO! KWAN LIN PICKED ME TO-->
<KWAN LIN? HA! EKIN TZU, HIMSELF, CHOSE ME TO LEAD!>
<EKIN TZU IS DEAD, OLD MAN. JUST LIKE YOU.>
BLAM
OOOPH!

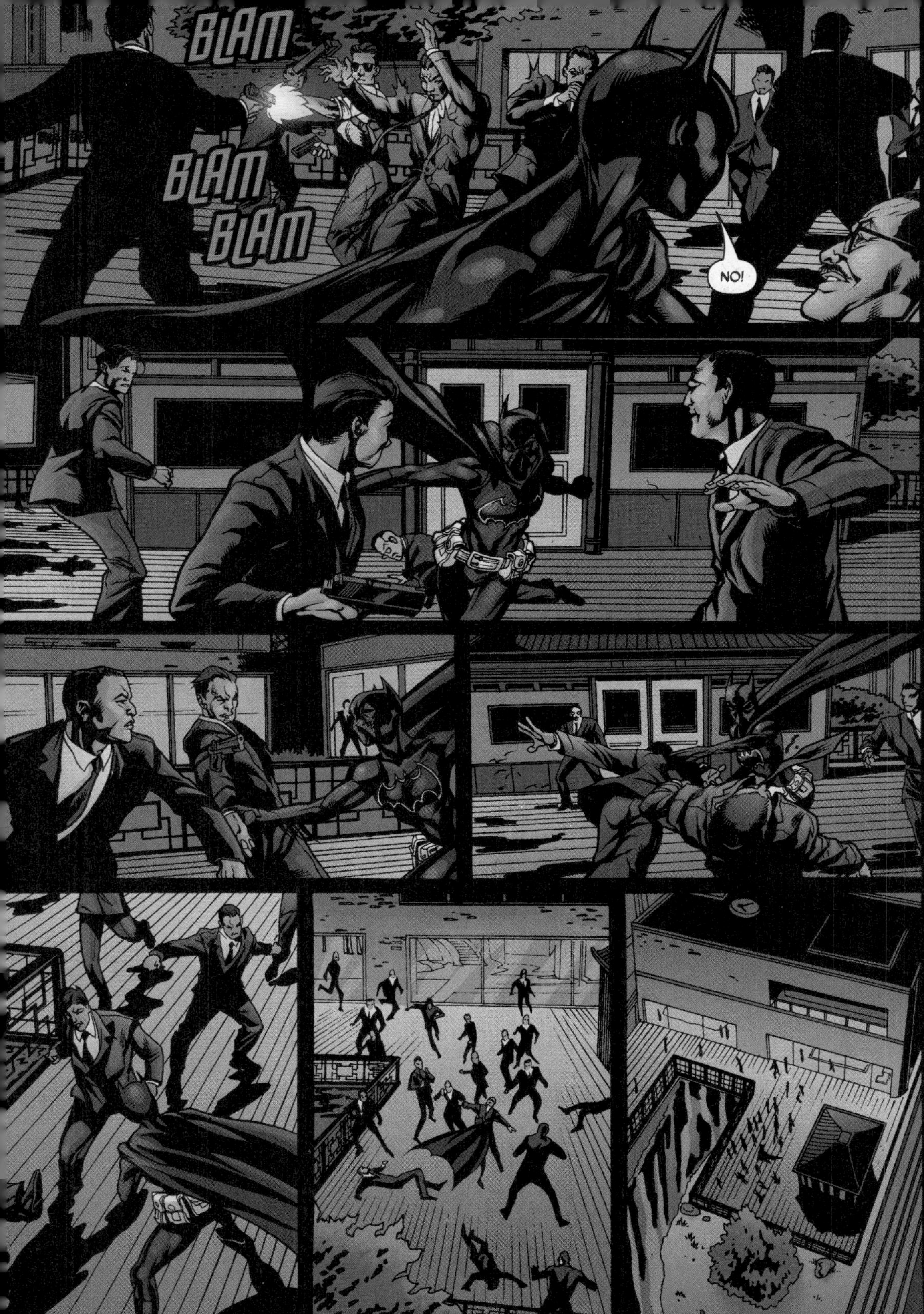
BLAM
BLAM
BLAM
NO!

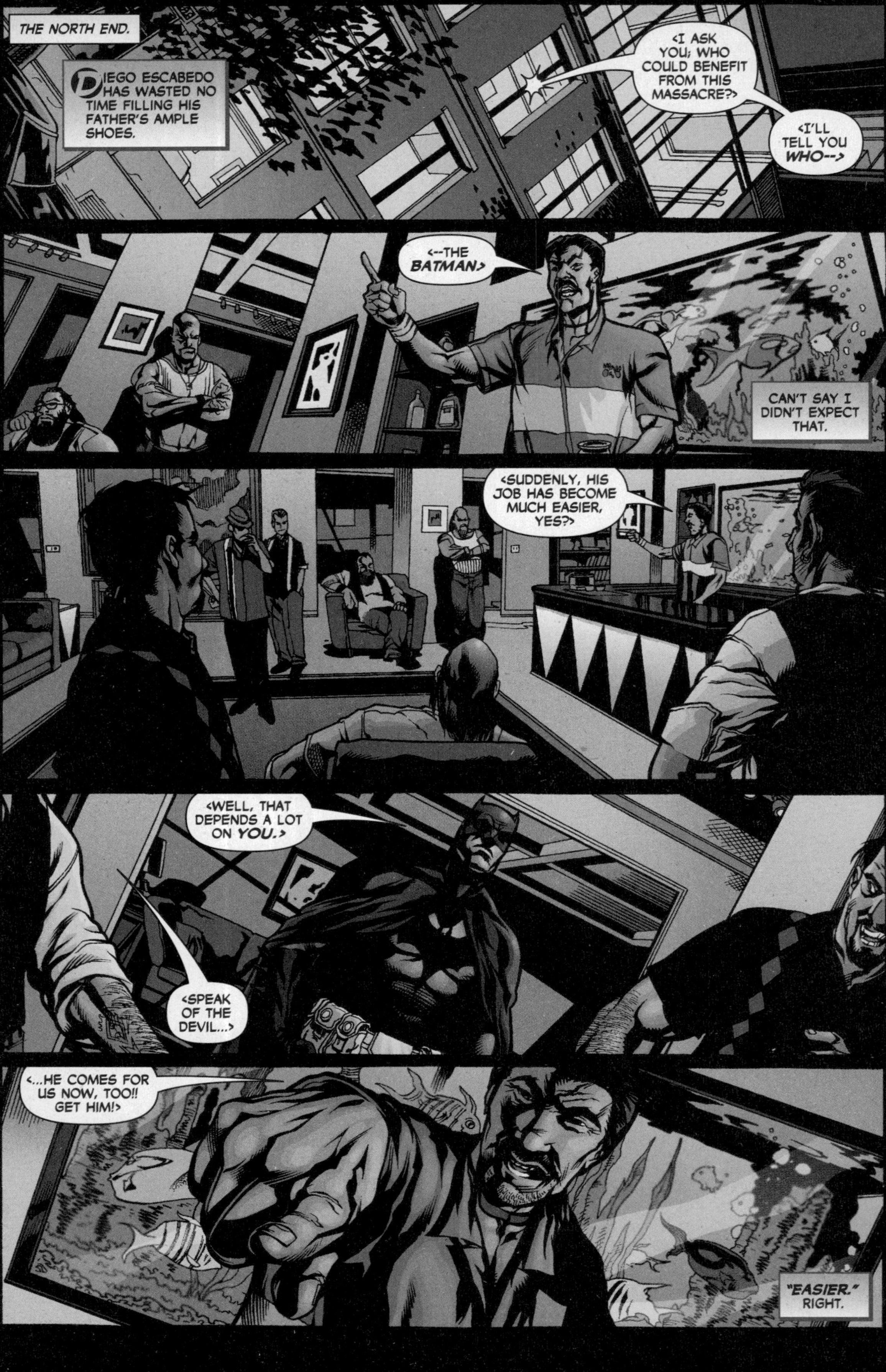
THE NORTH END.
DIEGO ESCABEDO HAS WASTED NO TIME FILLING HIS FATHER'S AMPLE SHOES.
<I ASK YOU; WHO COULD BENEFIT FROM THIS MASSACRE?>
<I'LL TELL YOU WHO-->
<--THE BATMAN>
CAN'T SAY I DIDN'T EXPECT THAT.
<SUDDENLY, HIS JOB HAS BECOME MUCH EASIER, YES?>
<WELL, THAT DEPENDS A LOT ON YOU.>
<SPEAK OF THE DEVIL...>
<...HE COMES FOR US NOW, TOO!! GET HIM!>
"EASIER." RIGHT.

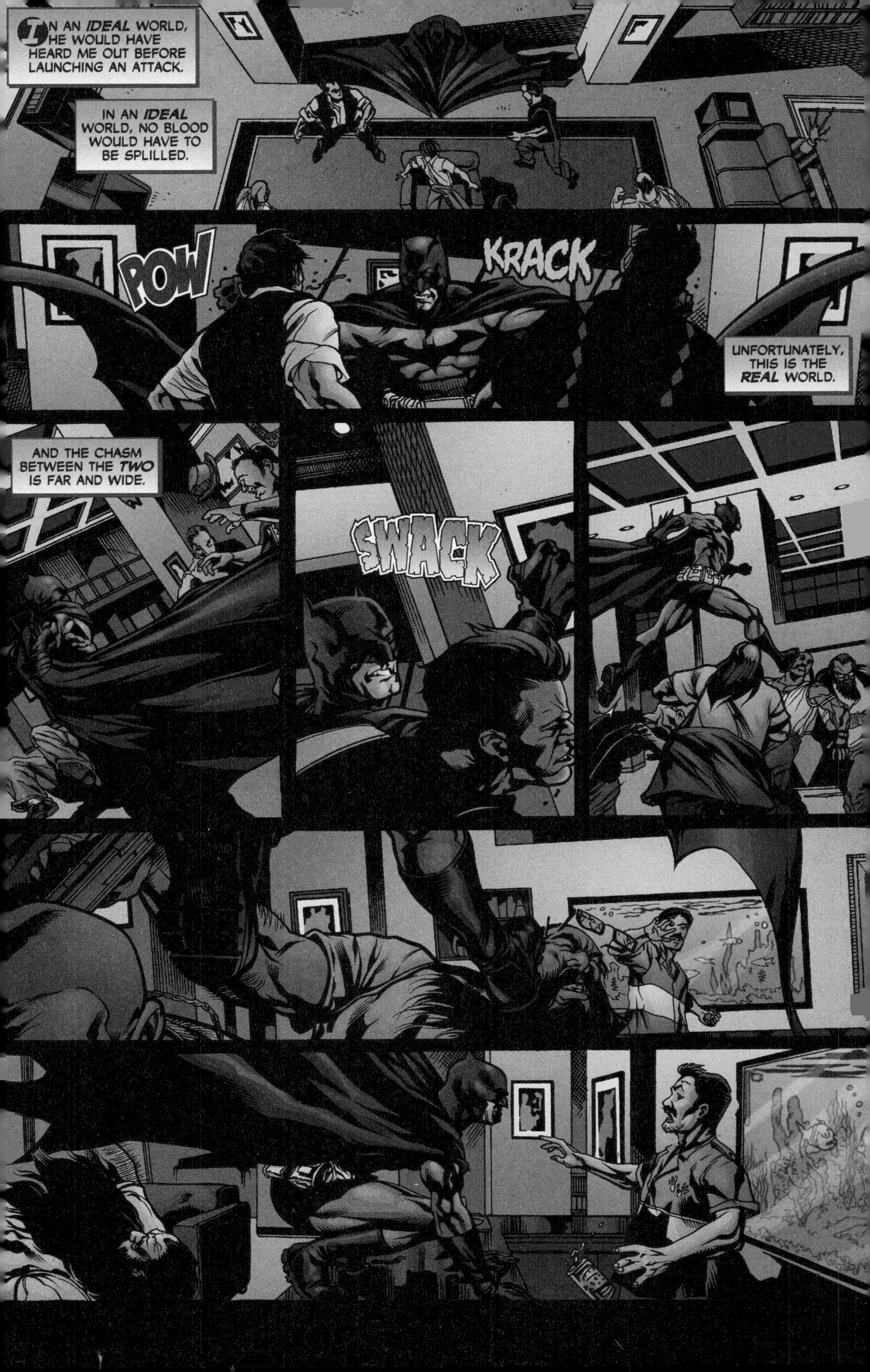
IN AN *IDEAL* WORLD, HE WOULD HAVE HEARD ME OUT BEFORE LAUNCHING AN ATTACK.
IN AN *IDEAL* WORLD, NO BLOOD WOULD HAVE TO BE SPLILLED.
POW
KRACK
UNFORTUNATELY, THIS IS THE *REAL* WORLD.
AND THE CHASM BETWEEN THE *TWO* IS FAR AND WIDE.
SWACK

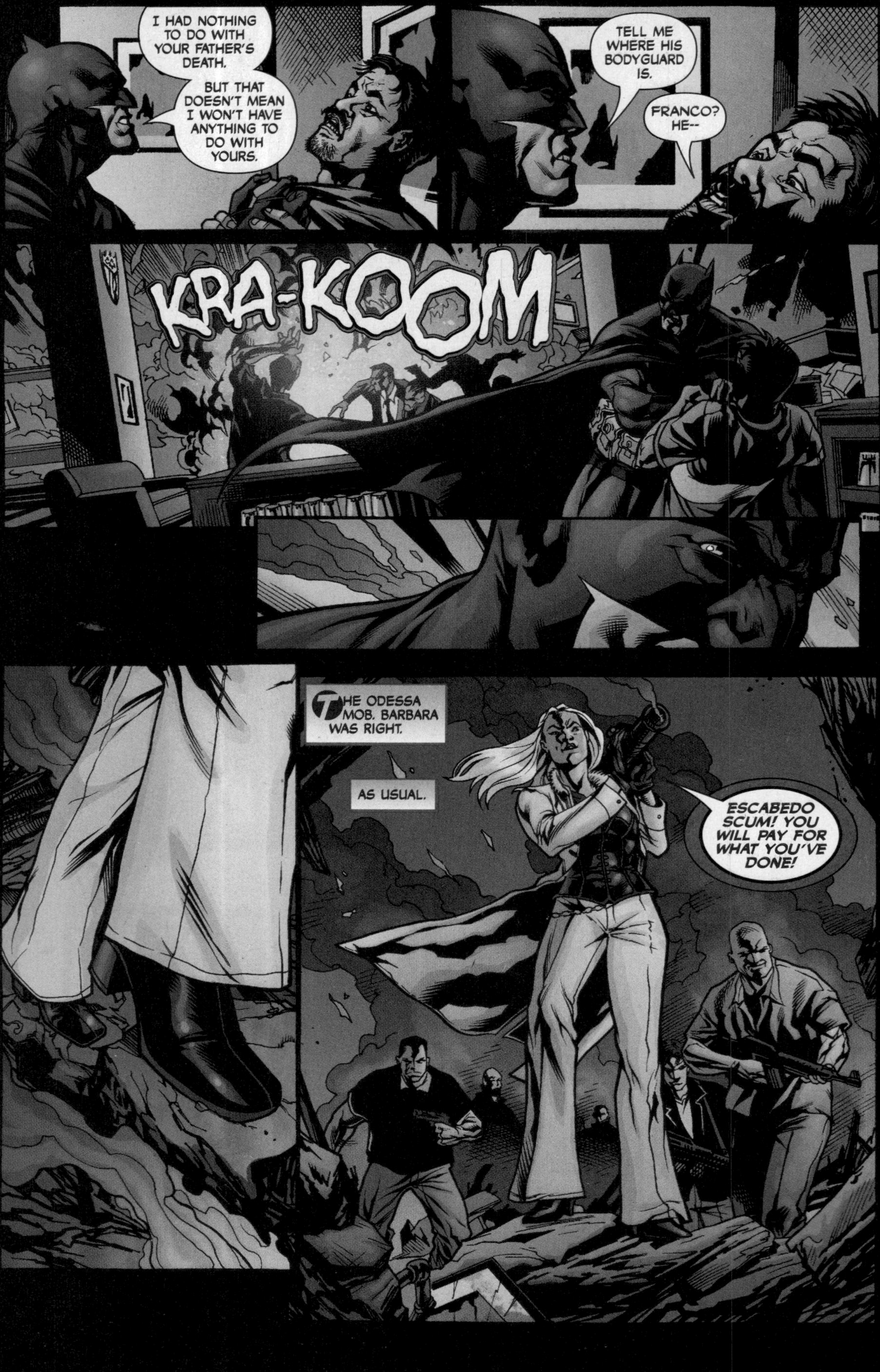
I HAD NOTHING TO DO WITH YOUR FATHER'S DEATH.
BUT THAT DOESN'T MEAN I WON'T HAVE ANYTHING TO DO WITH YOURS.
TELL ME WHERE HIS BODYGUARD IS.
FRANCO? HE--
KRA-KOOM
THE ODESSA MOB. BARBARA WAS RIGHT.
AS USUAL.
ESCABEDO SCUM! YOU WILL PAY FOR WHAT YOU'VE DONE!

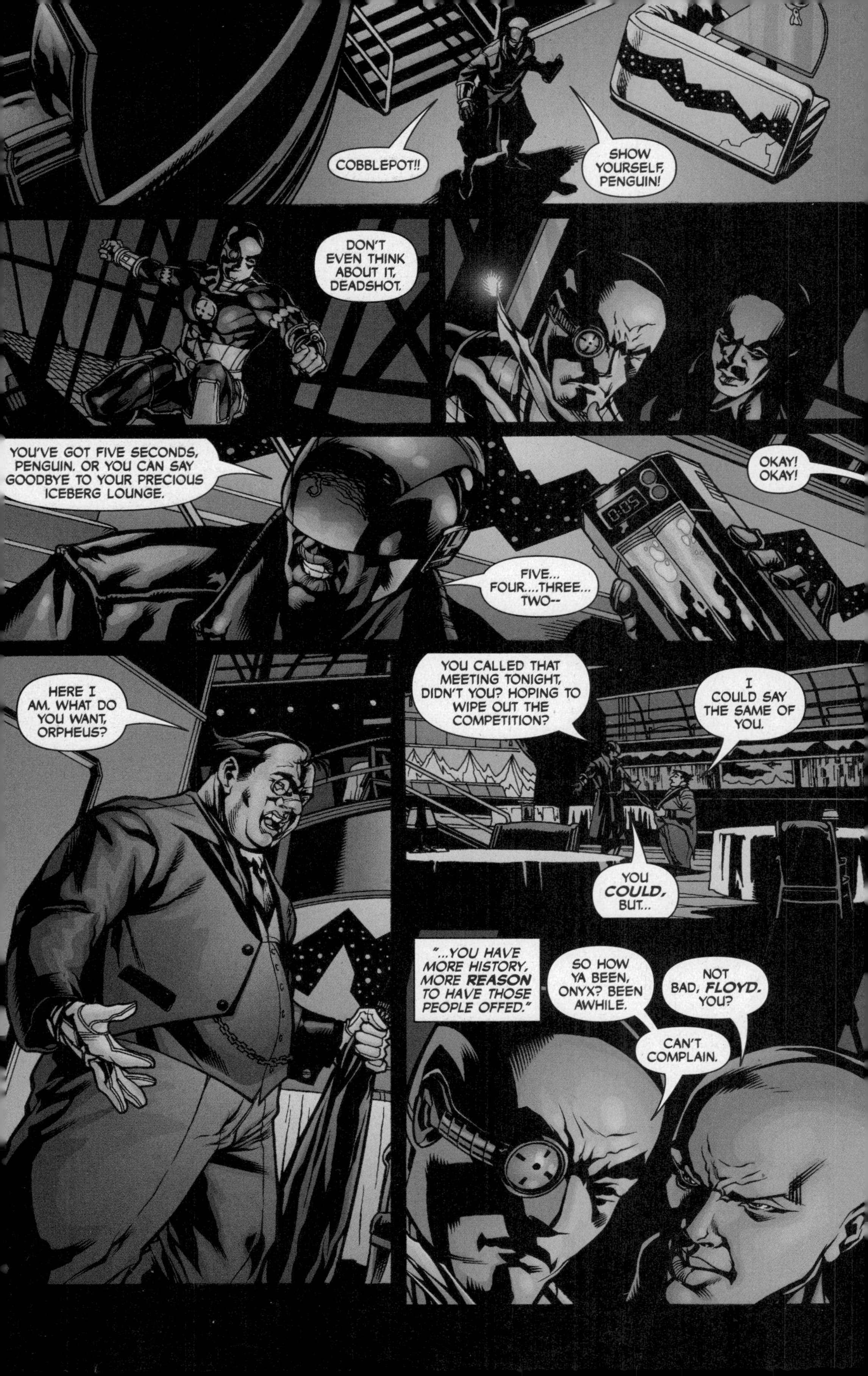
COBBLEPOT!!
SHOW YOURSELF, PENGUIN!
DON'T EVEN THINK ABOUT IT, DEADSHOT.
YOU'VE GOT FIVE SECONDS, PENGUIN. OR YOU CAN SAY GOODBYE TO YOUR PRECIOUS ICEBERG LOUNGE.
FIVE... FOUR....THREE... TWO--
OKAY! OKAY!
HERE I AM. WHAT DO YOU WANT, ORPHEUS?
YOU CALLED THAT MEETING TONIGHT, DIDN'T YOU? HOPING TO WIPE OUT THE COMPETITION?
I COULD SAY THE SAME OF YOU.
YOU COULD, BUT...
"...YOU HAVE MORE HISTORY, MORE REASON TO HAVE THOSE PEOPLE OFFED."
SO HOW YA BEEN, ONYX? BEEN AWHILE.
NOT BAD, FLOYD. YOU?
CAN'T COMPLAIN.

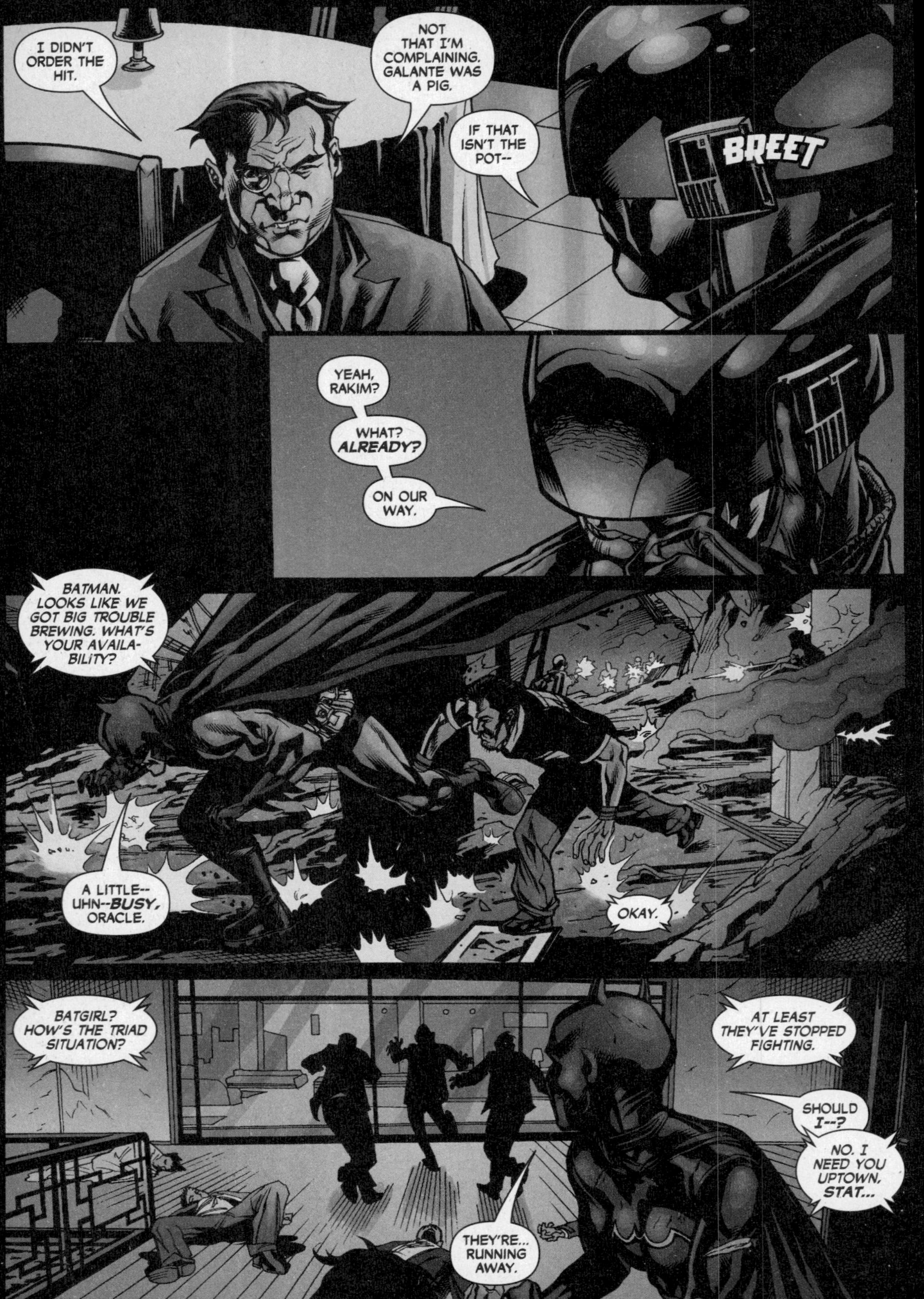
I DIDN'T ORDER THE HIT.
NOT THAT I'M COMPLAINING. GALANTE WAS A PIG.
IF THAT ISN'T THE POT--
BREET
YEAH, RAKIM?
WHAT? ALREADY?
ON OUR WAY.
BATMAN. LOOKS LIKE WE GOT BIG TROUBLE BREWING. WHAT'S YOUR AVAILA-BILITY?
A LITTLE-- UHN--BUSY, ORACLE.
OKAY.
BATGIRL? HOW'S THE TRIAD SITUATION?
AT LEAST THEY'VE STOPPED FIGHTING.
THEY'RE... RUNNING AWAY.
SHOULD I--?
NO. I NEED YOU UPTOWN, STAT...

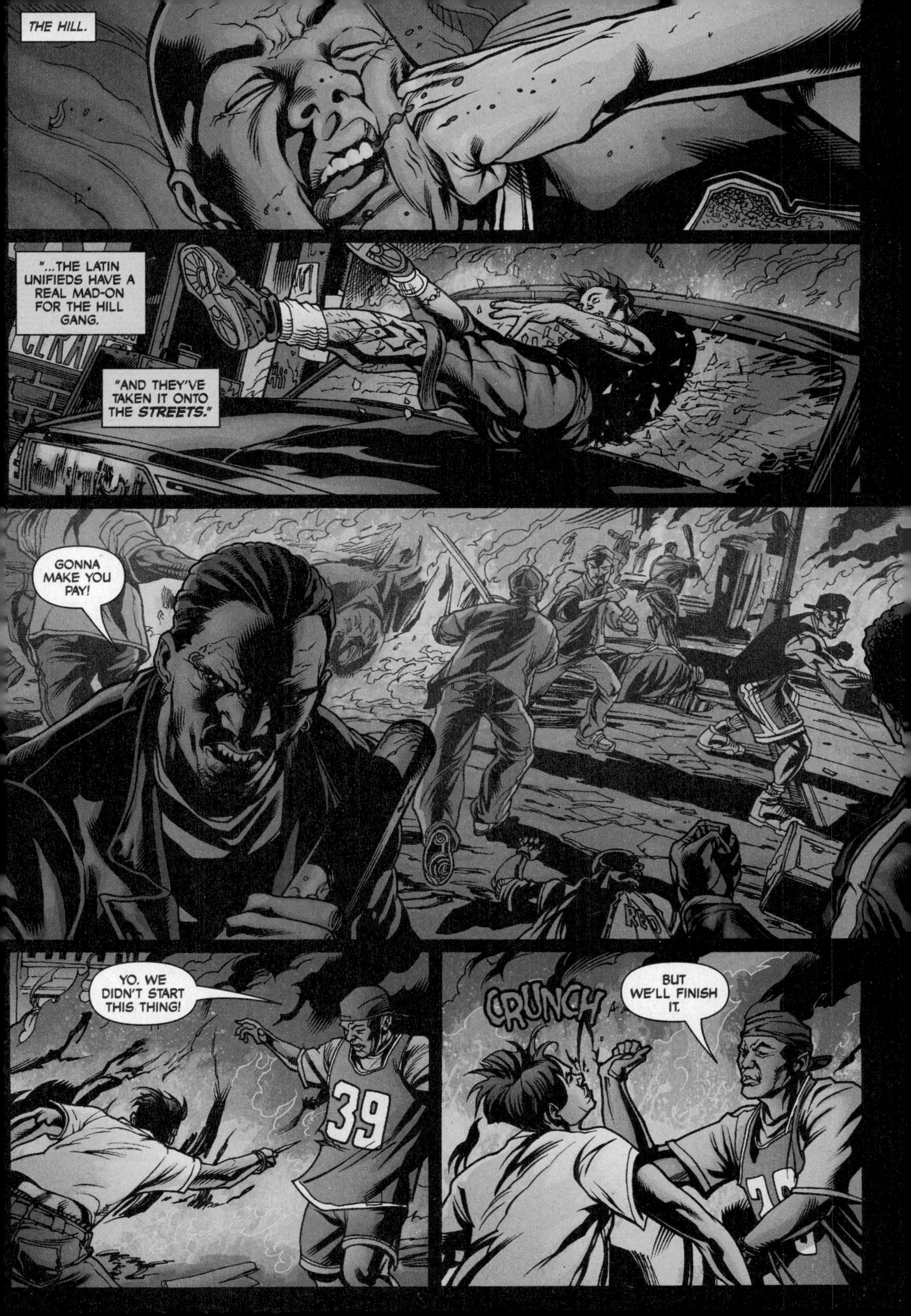
THE HILL.
"...THE LATIN UNIFIEDS HAVE A REAL MAD-ON FOR THE HILL GANG.
"AND THEY'VE TAKEN IT ONTO THE *STREETS*."
GONNA MAKE YOU PAY!
YO. WE DIDN'T START THIS THING!
CRUNCH
BUT WE'LL FINISH IT.

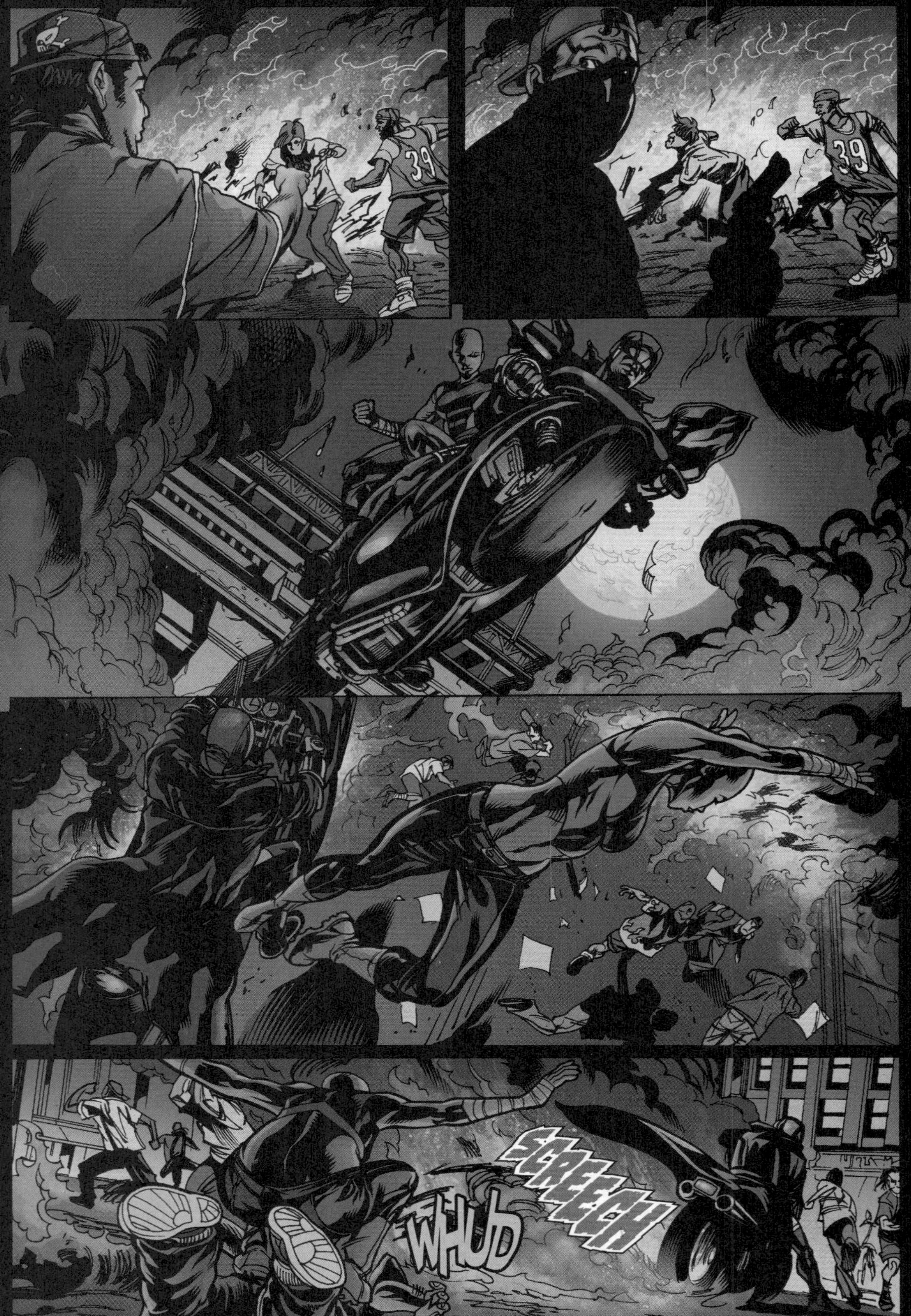

SCREECH
WHUD

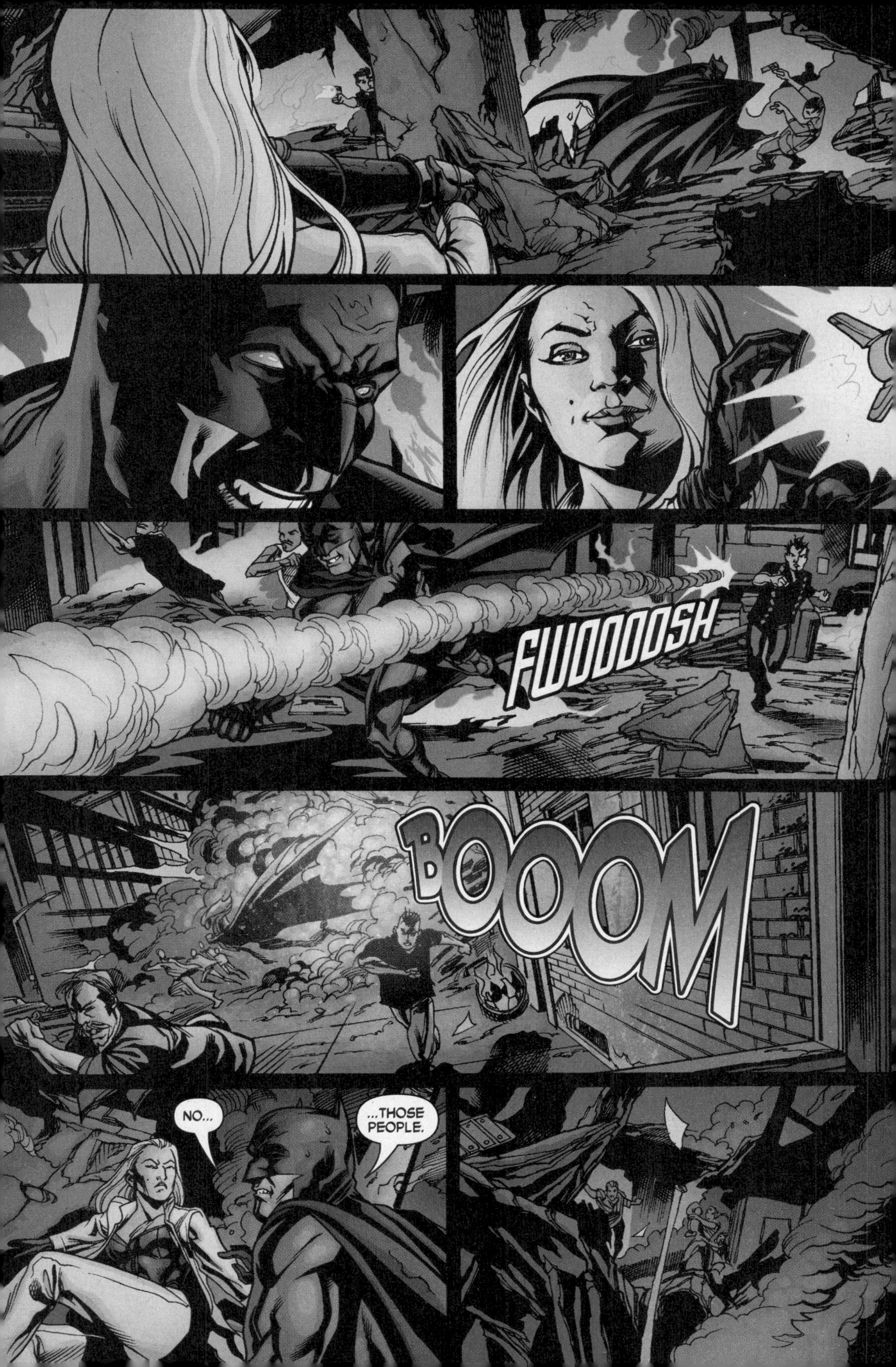
FWOOOOSH
BOOOM
NO...
...THOSE PEOPLE.

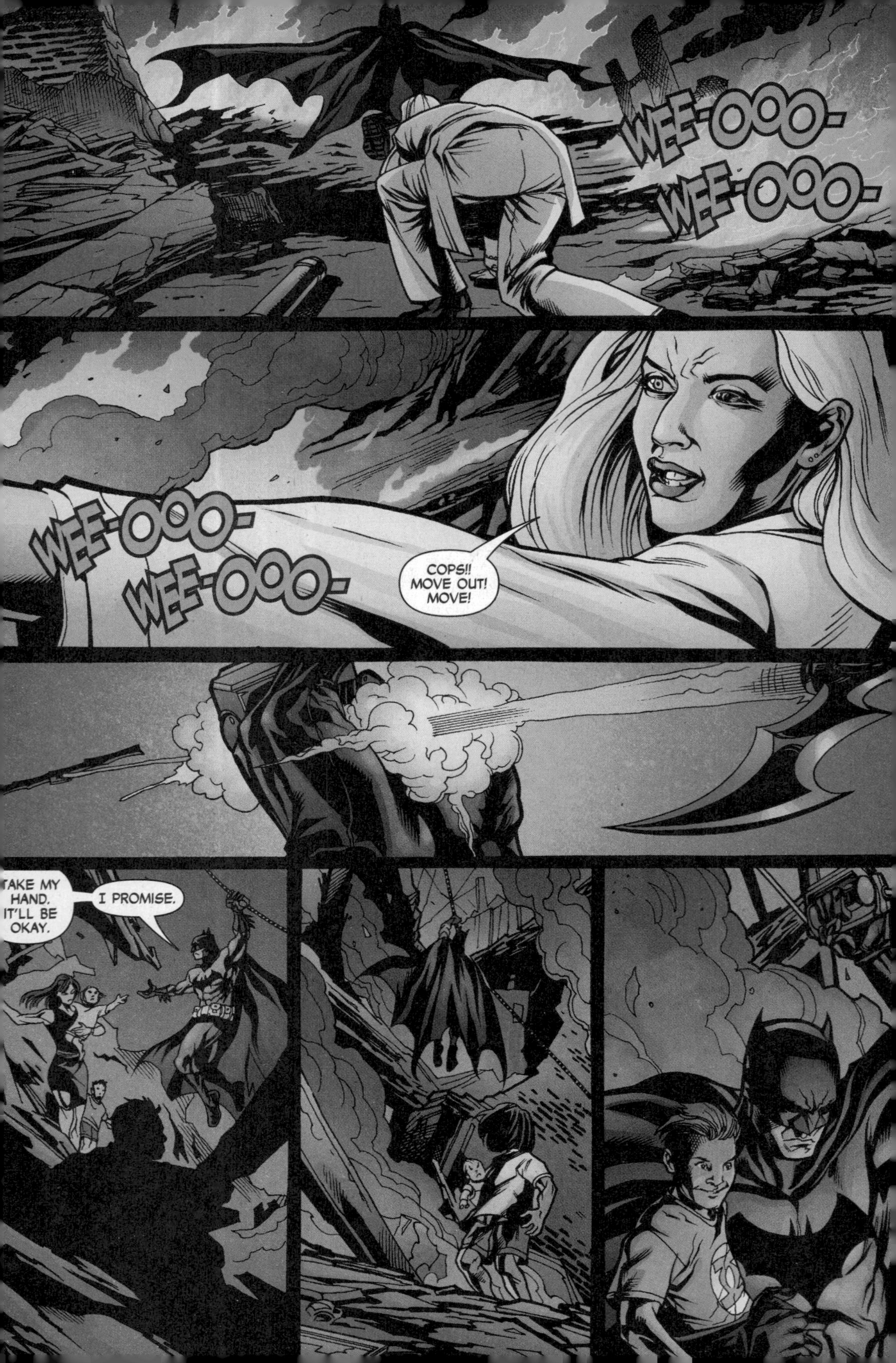
WEE-OOO-
WEE-OOO-
WEE-OOO-
WEE-OOO-
COPS!! MOVE OUT! MOVE!
TAKE MY HAND. IT'LL BE OKAY.
I PROMISE.

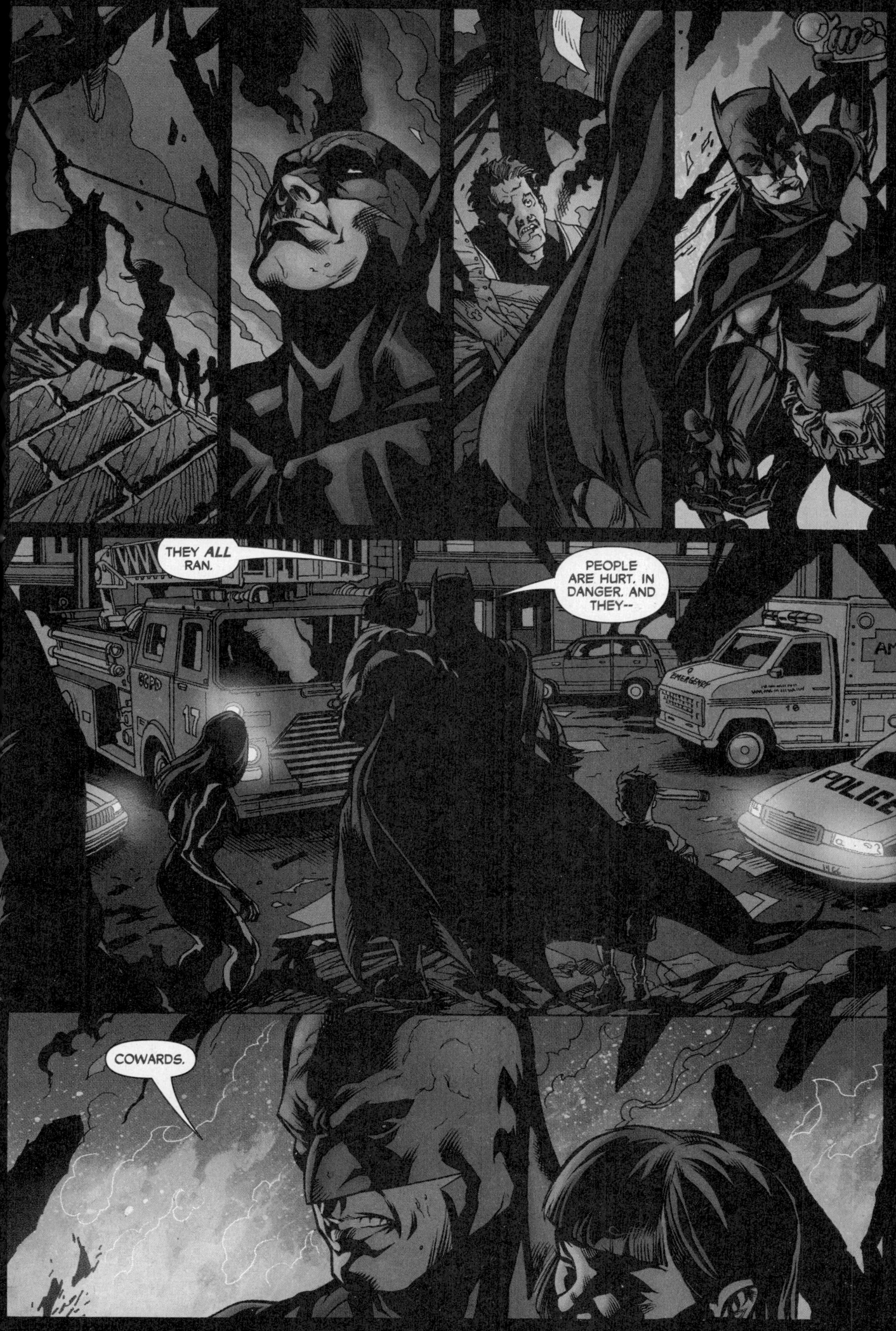

THEY ALL RAN.
PEOPLE ARE HURT. IN DANGER. AND THEY--
COWARDS.

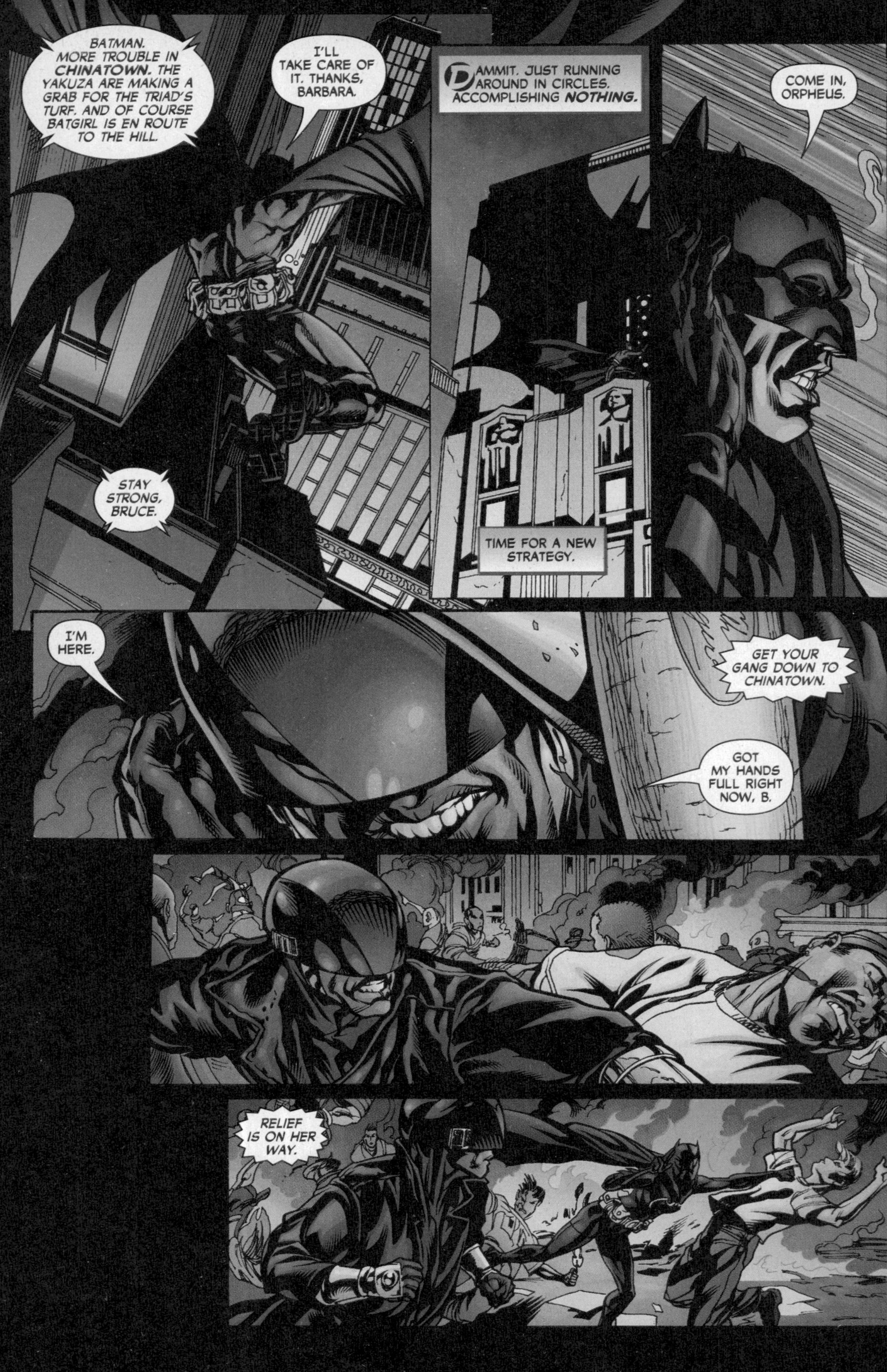

BATMAN. MORE TROUBLE IN CHINATOWN. THE YAKUZA ARE MAKING A GRAB FOR THE TRIAD'S TURF. AND OF COURSE BATGIRL IS EN ROUTE TO THE HILL.
I'LL TAKE CARE OF IT. THANKS, BARBARA.
STAY STRONG, BRUCE.
DAMMIT. JUST RUNNING AROUND IN CIRCLES. ACCOMPLISHING NOTHING.
TIME FOR A NEW STRATEGY.
COME IN, ORPHEUS.
I'M HERE.
GET YOUR GANG DOWN TO CHINATOWN.
GOT MY HANDS FULL RIGHT NOW, B.
RELIEF IS ON HER WAY.

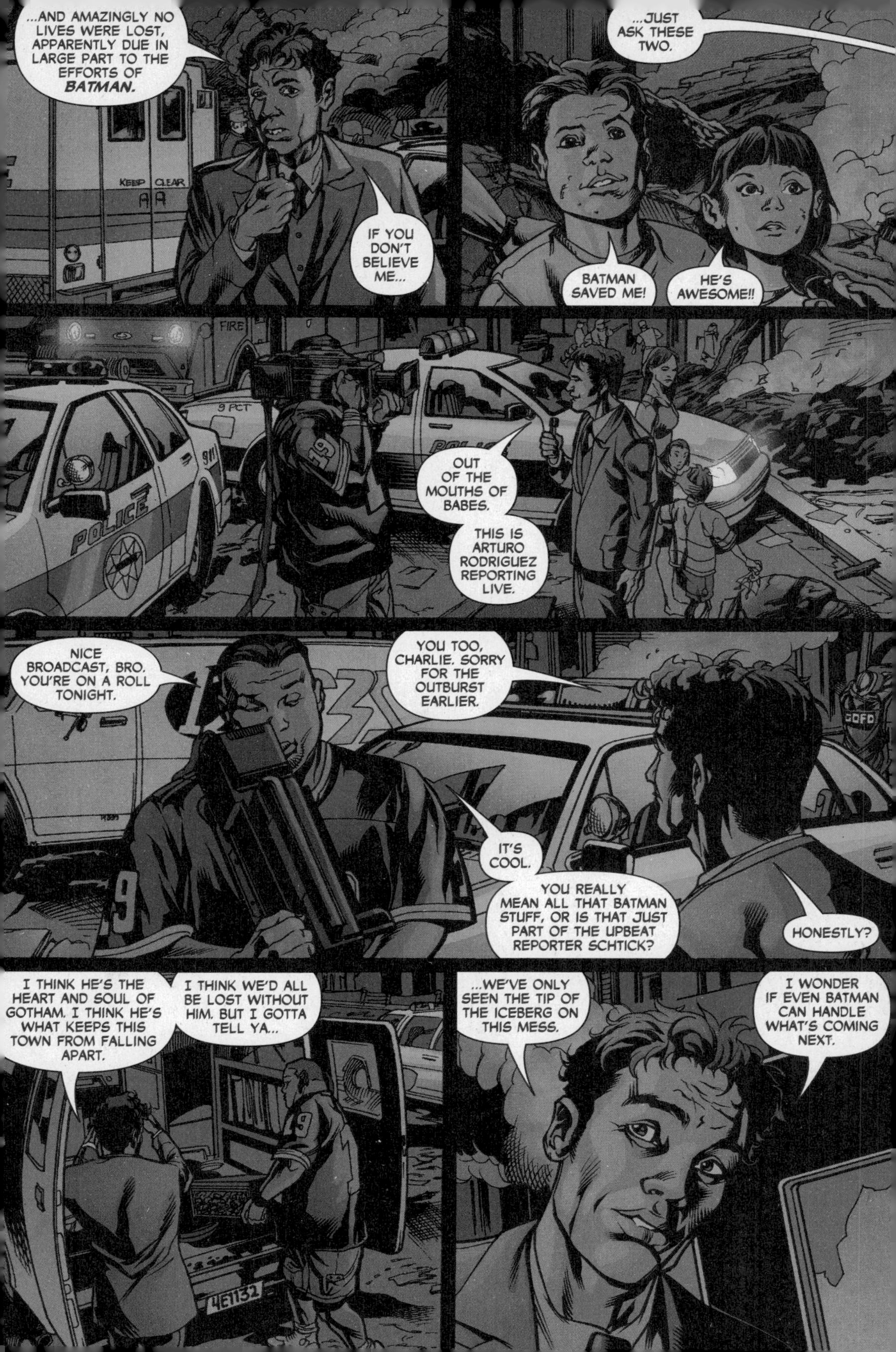
...AND AMAZINGLY NO LIVES WERE LOST, APPARENTLY DUE IN LARGE PART TO THE EFFORTS OF *BATMAN.*
IF YOU DON'T BELIEVE ME...
...JUST ASK THESE TWO.
BATMAN SAVED ME!
HE'S AWESOME!!
OUT OF THE MOUTHS OF BABES.
THIS IS ARTURO RODRIGUEZ REPORTING LIVE.
NICE BROADCAST, BRO. YOU'RE ON A ROLL TONIGHT.
YOU TOO, CHARLIE. SORRY FOR THE OUTBURST EARLIER.
IT'S COOL.
YOU REALLY MEAN ALL THAT BATMAN STUFF, OR IS THAT JUST PART OF THE UPBEAT REPORTER SCHTICK?
HONESTLY?
I THINK HE'S THE HEART AND SOUL OF GOTHAM. I THINK HE'S WHAT KEEPS THIS TOWN FROM FALLING APART.
I THINK WE'D ALL BE LOST WITHOUT HIM. BUT I GOTTA TELL YA...
...WE'VE ONLY SEEN THE TIP OF THE ICEBERG ON THIS MESS.
I WONDER IF EVEN BATMAN CAN HANDLE WHAT'S COMING NEXT.

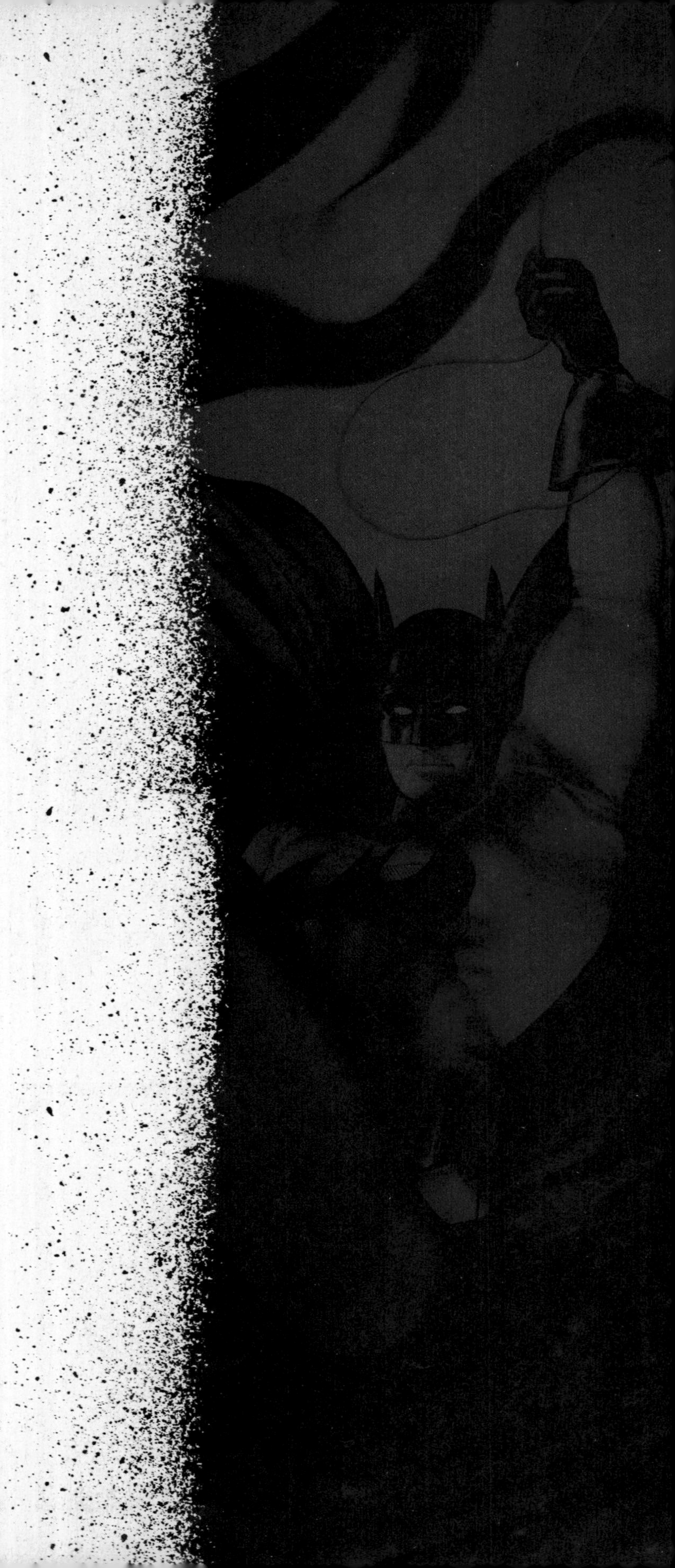

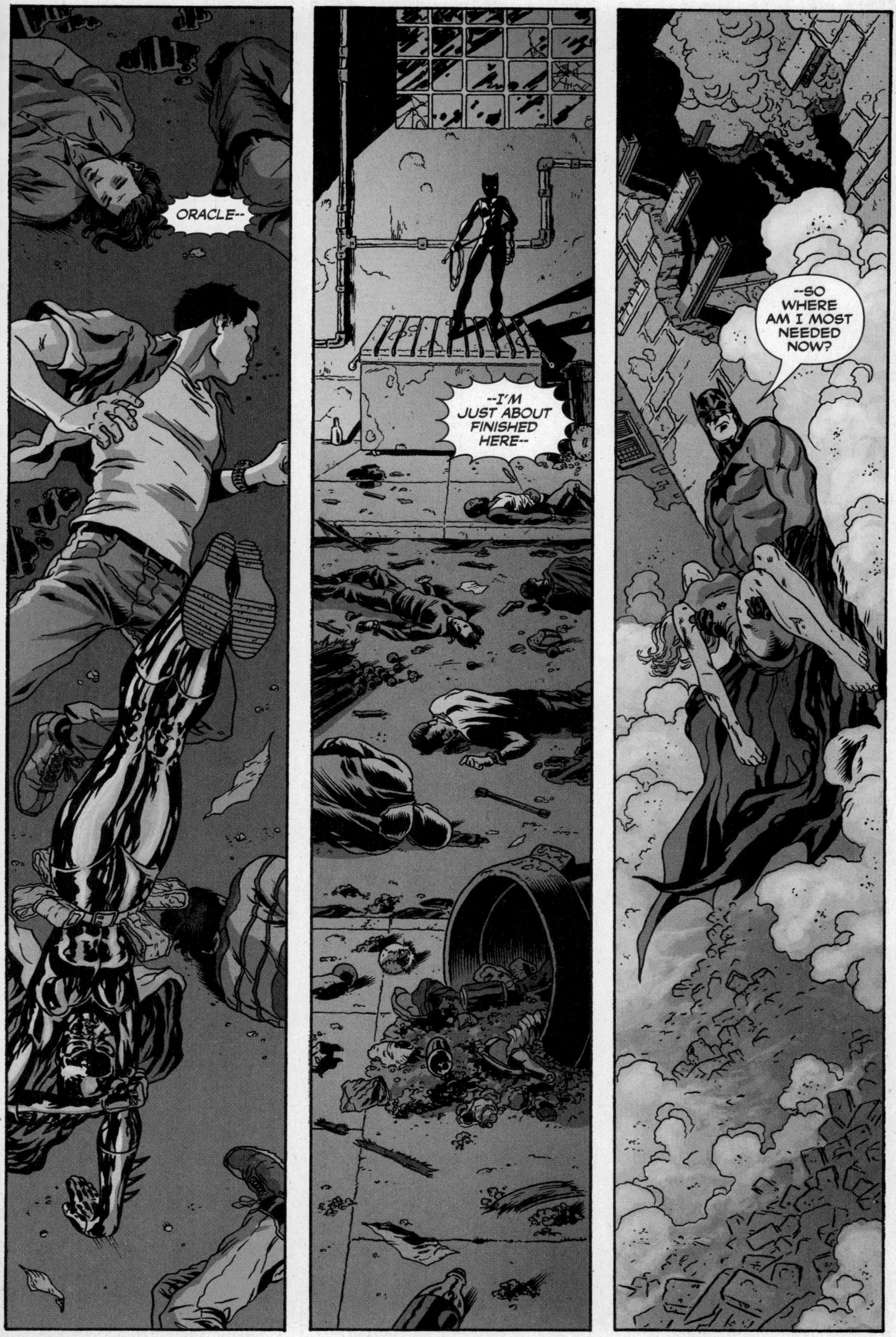
ORACLE--
--I'M JUST ABOUT FINISHED HERE--
--SO WHERE AM I MOST NEEDED NOW?

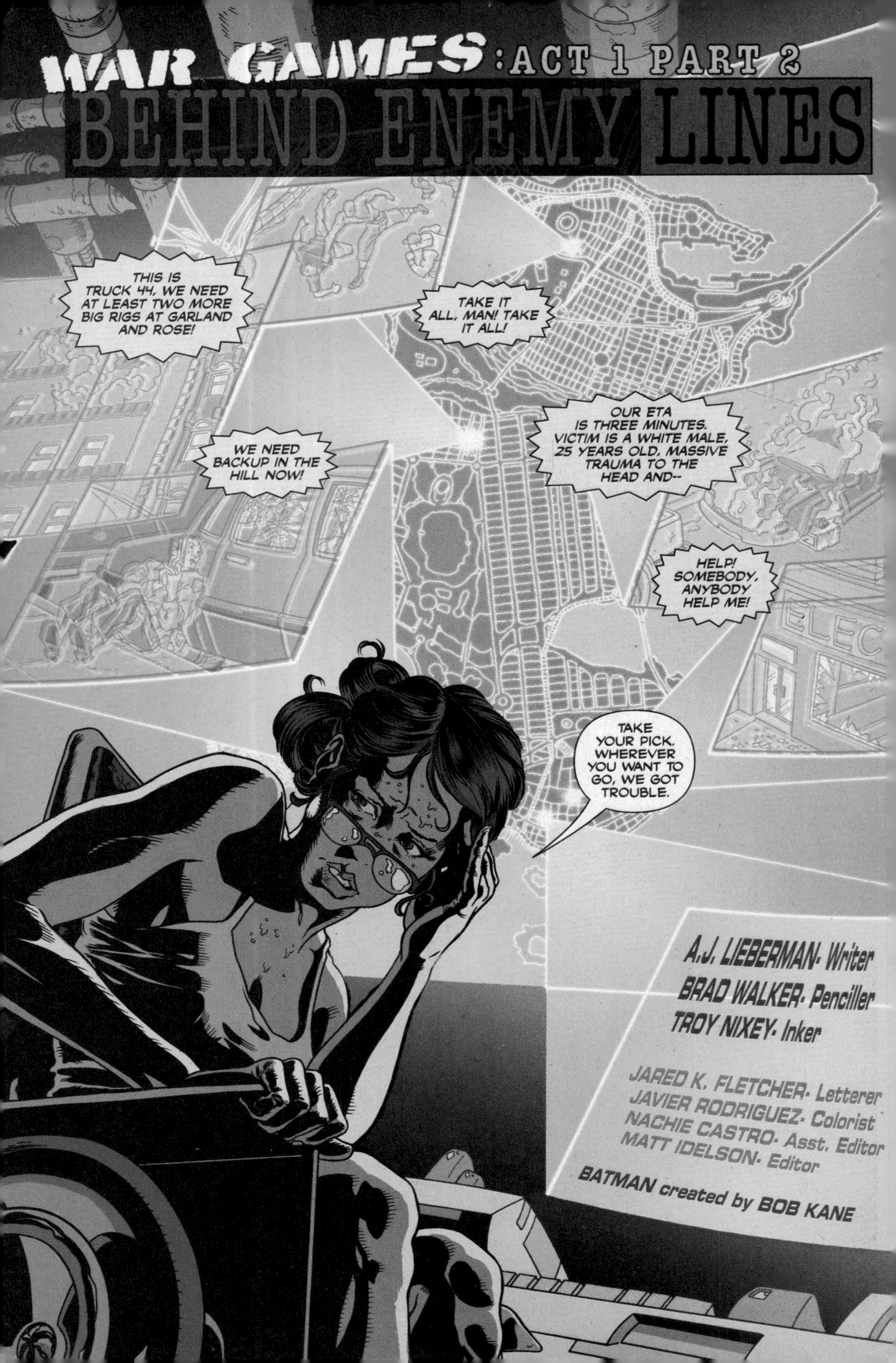
WAR GAMES: ACT 1 PART 2
BEHIND ENEMY LINES
THIS IS TRUCK 44, WE NEED AT LEAST TWO MORE BIG RIGS AT GARLAND AND ROSE!
TAKE IT ALL, MAN! TAKE IT ALL!
WE NEED BACKUP IN THE HILL NOW!
OUR ETA IS THREE MINUTES. VICTIM IS A WHITE MALE, 25 YEARS OLD, MASSIVE TRAUMA TO THE HEAD AND--
HELP! SOMEBODY, ANYBODY HELP ME!
ELEC
TAKE YOUR PICK. WHEREVER YOU WANT TO GO, WE GOT TROUBLE.
A.J. LIEBERMAN- Writer
BRAD WALKER- Penciller
TROY NIXEY- Inker
JARED K. FLETCHER- Letterer
JAVIER RODRIGUEZ- Colorist
NACHIE CASTRO- Asst. Editor
MATT IDELSON- Editor
BATMAN created by BOB KANE

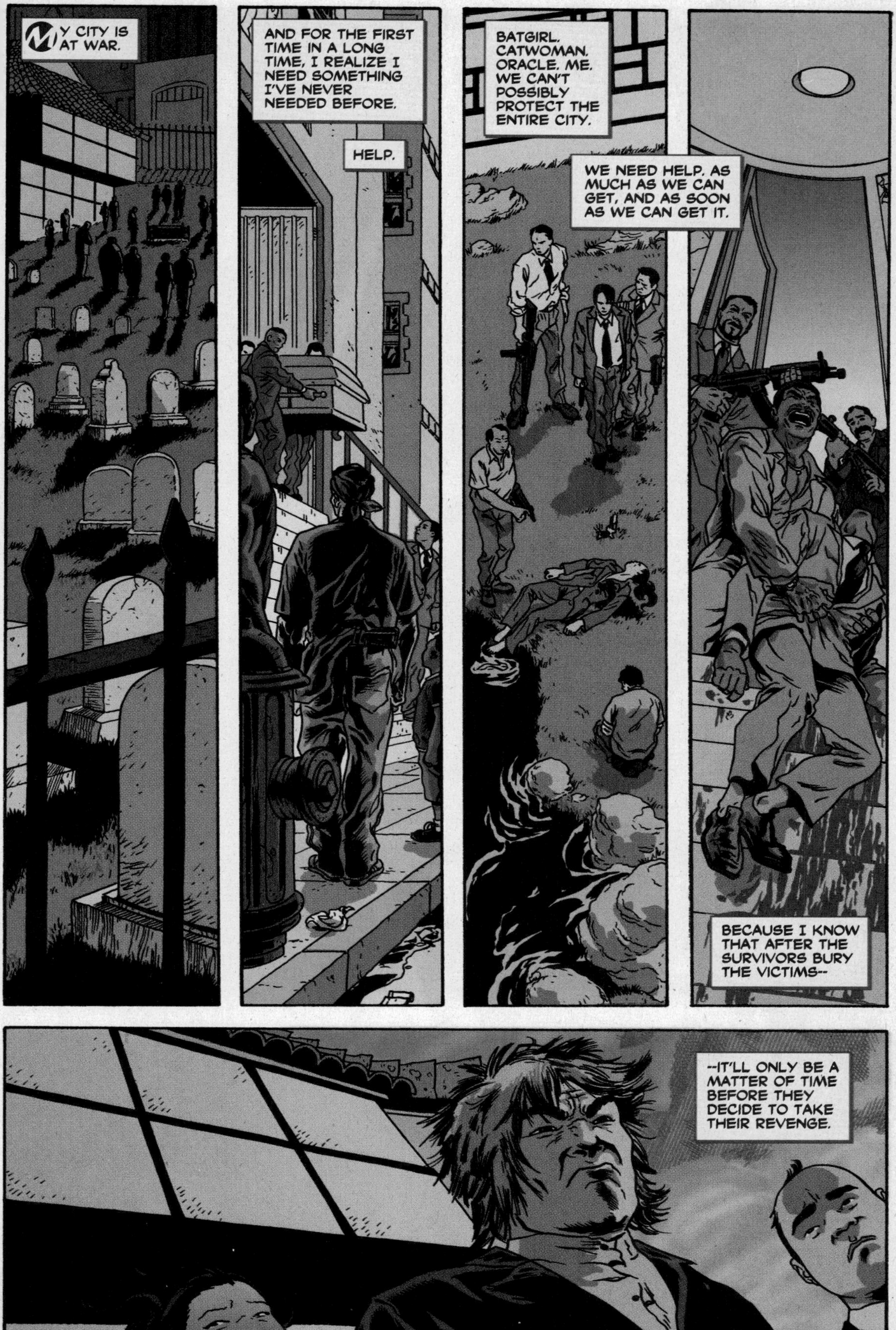
MY CITY IS AT WAR.
AND FOR THE FIRST TIME IN A LONG TIME, I REALIZE I NEED SOMETHING I'VE NEVER NEEDED BEFORE.
HELP.
BATGIRL, CATWOMAN, ORACLE, ME. WE CAN'T POSSIBLY PROTECT THE ENTIRE CITY.
WE NEED HELP, AS MUCH AS WE CAN GET, AND AS SOON AS WE CAN GET IT.
BECAUSE I KNOW THAT AFTER THE SURVIVORS BURY THE VICTIMS--
--IT'LL ONLY BE A MATTER OF TIME BEFORE THEY DECIDE TO TAKE THEIR REVENGE.

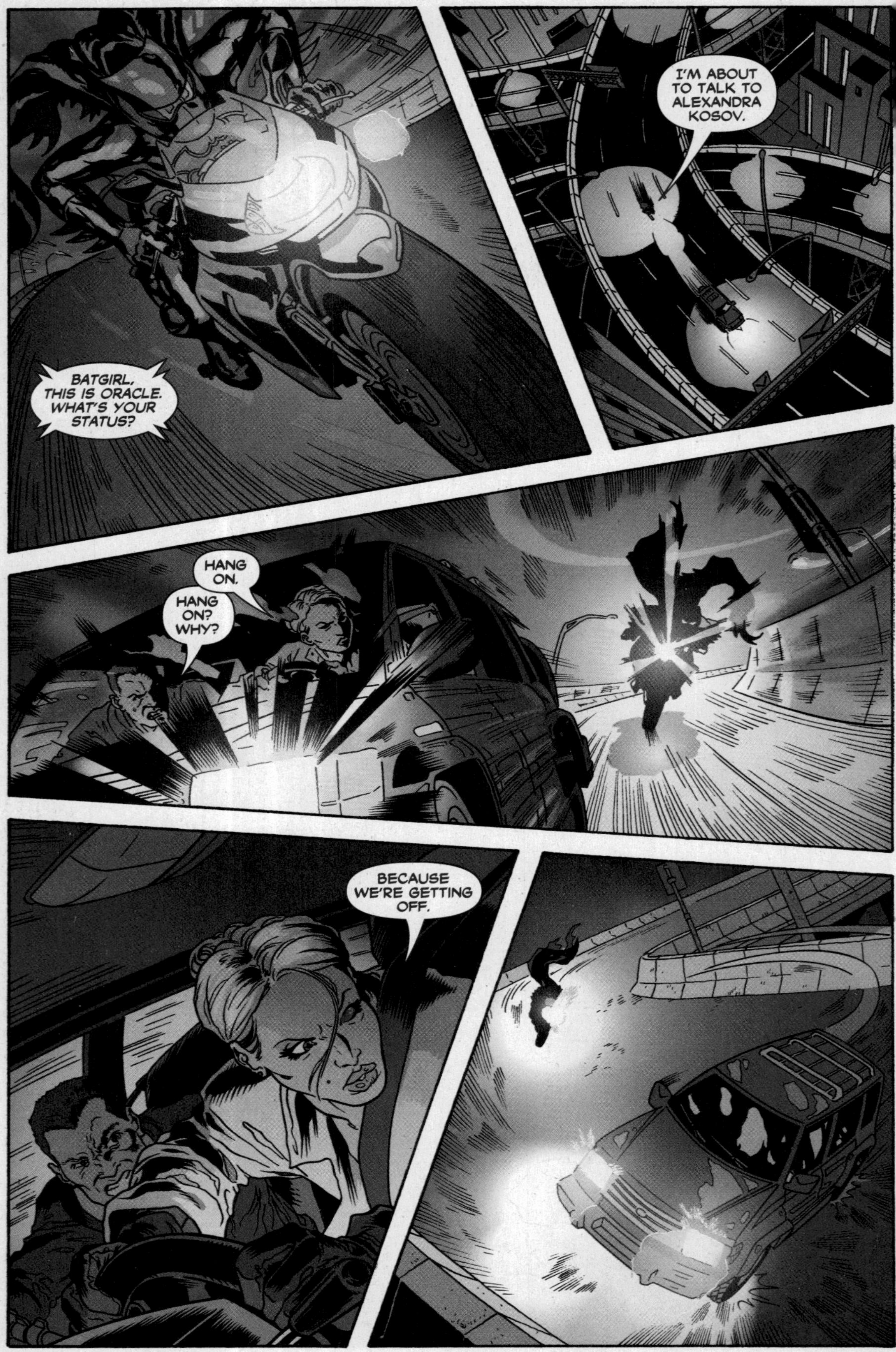
BATGIRL, THIS IS ORACLE. WHAT'S YOUR STATUS?
I'M ABOUT TO TALK TO ALEXANDRA KOSOV.
HANG ON.
HANG ON? WHY?
BECAUSE WE'RE GETTING OFF.

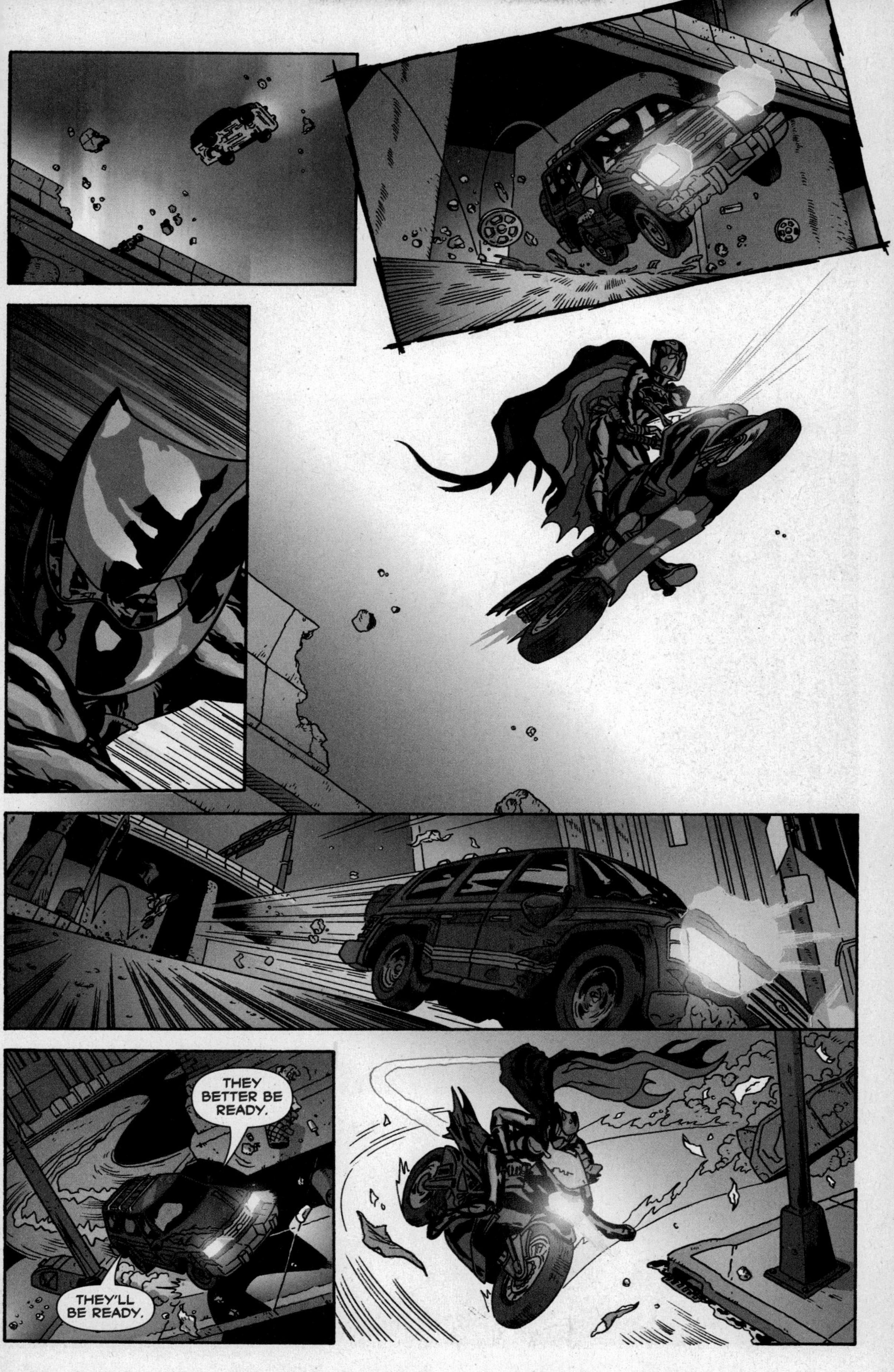
THEY BETTER BE READY.
THEY'LL BE READY.

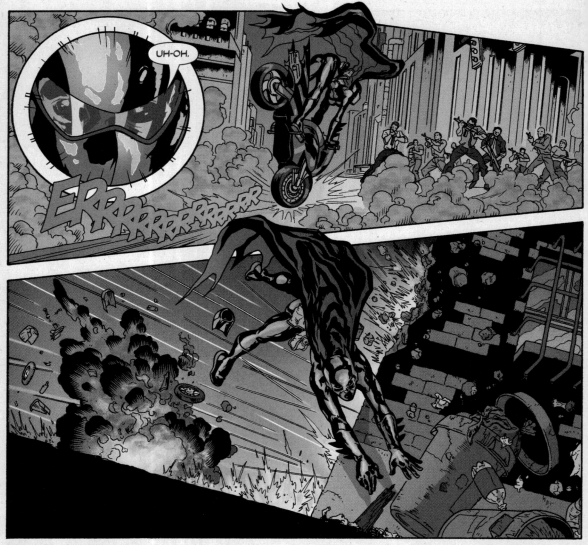

UH-OH.

ERRRRRRRRRRR

BATGIRL, IT'S ME AGAIN. WE NEED SOMEONE TO GET UP TO THE HILL AND--

ORACLE, I'M KINDA BUSY RIGHT NOW.

DOING WHAT?

STAYING ALIVE.

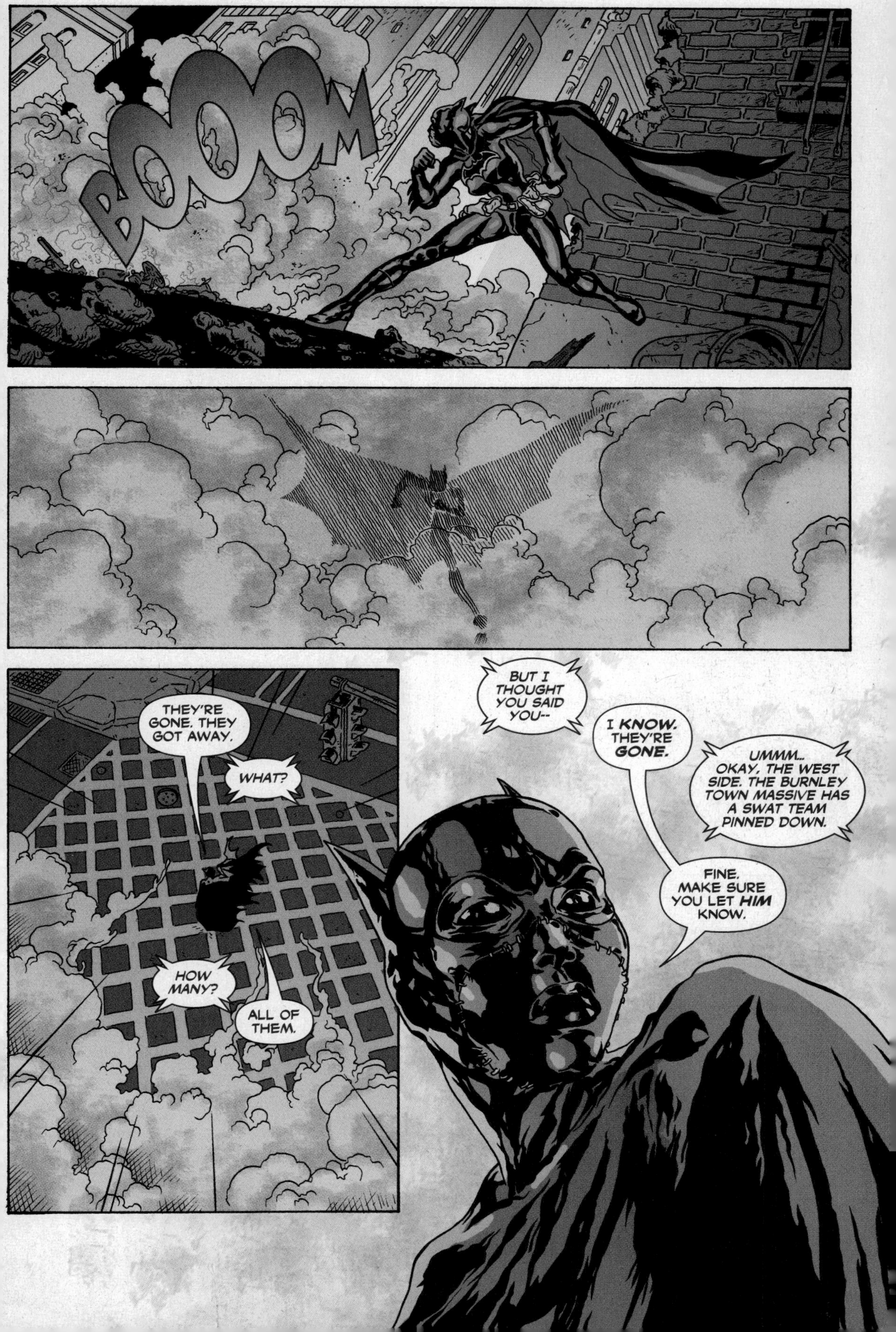
BOOOOM
THEY'RE GONE. THEY GOT AWAY.
WHAT?
HOW MANY?
ALL OF THEM.
BUT I THOUGHT YOU SAID YOU--
I KNOW. THEY'RE GONE.
UMMM... OKAY, THE WEST SIDE. THE BURNLEY TOWN MASSIVE HAS A SWAT TEAM PINNED DOWN.
FINE. MAKE SURE YOU LET HIM KNOW.

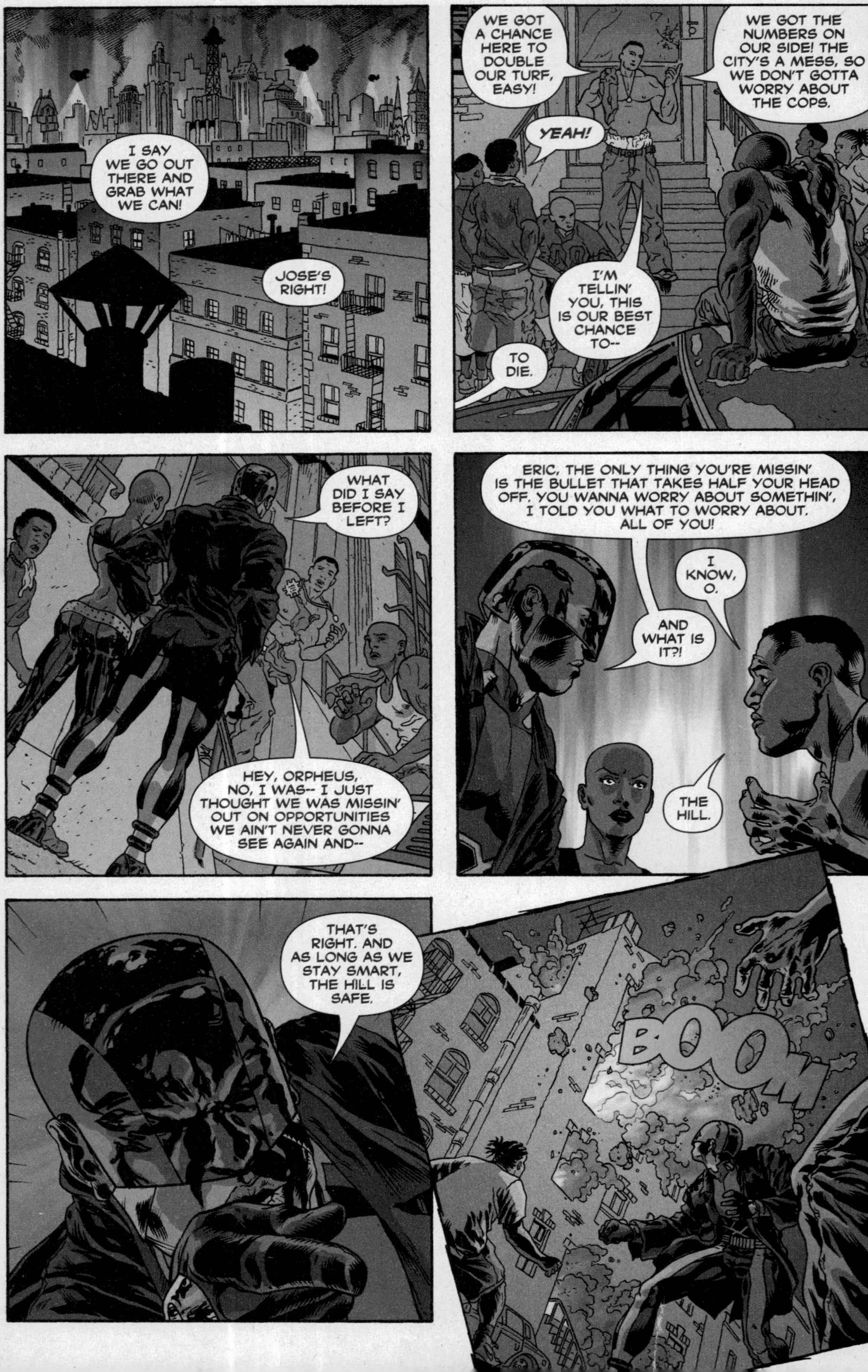
I SAY WE GO OUT THERE AND GRAB WHAT WE CAN!
JOSE'S RIGHT!
WE GOT A CHANCE HERE TO DOUBLE OUR TURF, EASY!
WE GOT THE NUMBERS ON OUR SIDE! THE CITY'S A MESS, SO WE DON'T GOTTA WORRY ABOUT THE COPS.
YEAH!
I'M TELLIN' YOU, THIS IS OUR BEST CHANCE TO--
TO DIE.
WHAT DID I SAY BEFORE I LEFT?
HEY, ORPHEUS, NO, I WAS-- I JUST THOUGHT WE WAS MISSIN' OUT ON OPPORTUNITIES WE AIN'T NEVER GONNA SEE AGAIN AND--
ERIC, THE ONLY THING YOU'RE MISSIN' IS THE BULLET THAT TAKES HALF YOUR HEAD OFF. YOU WANNA WORRY ABOUT SOMETHIN', I TOLD YOU WHAT TO WORRY ABOUT. ALL OF YOU!
I KNOW, O.
AND WHAT IS IT?!
THE HILL.
THAT'S RIGHT. AND AS LONG AS WE STAY SMART, THE HILL IS SAFE.
BOOM

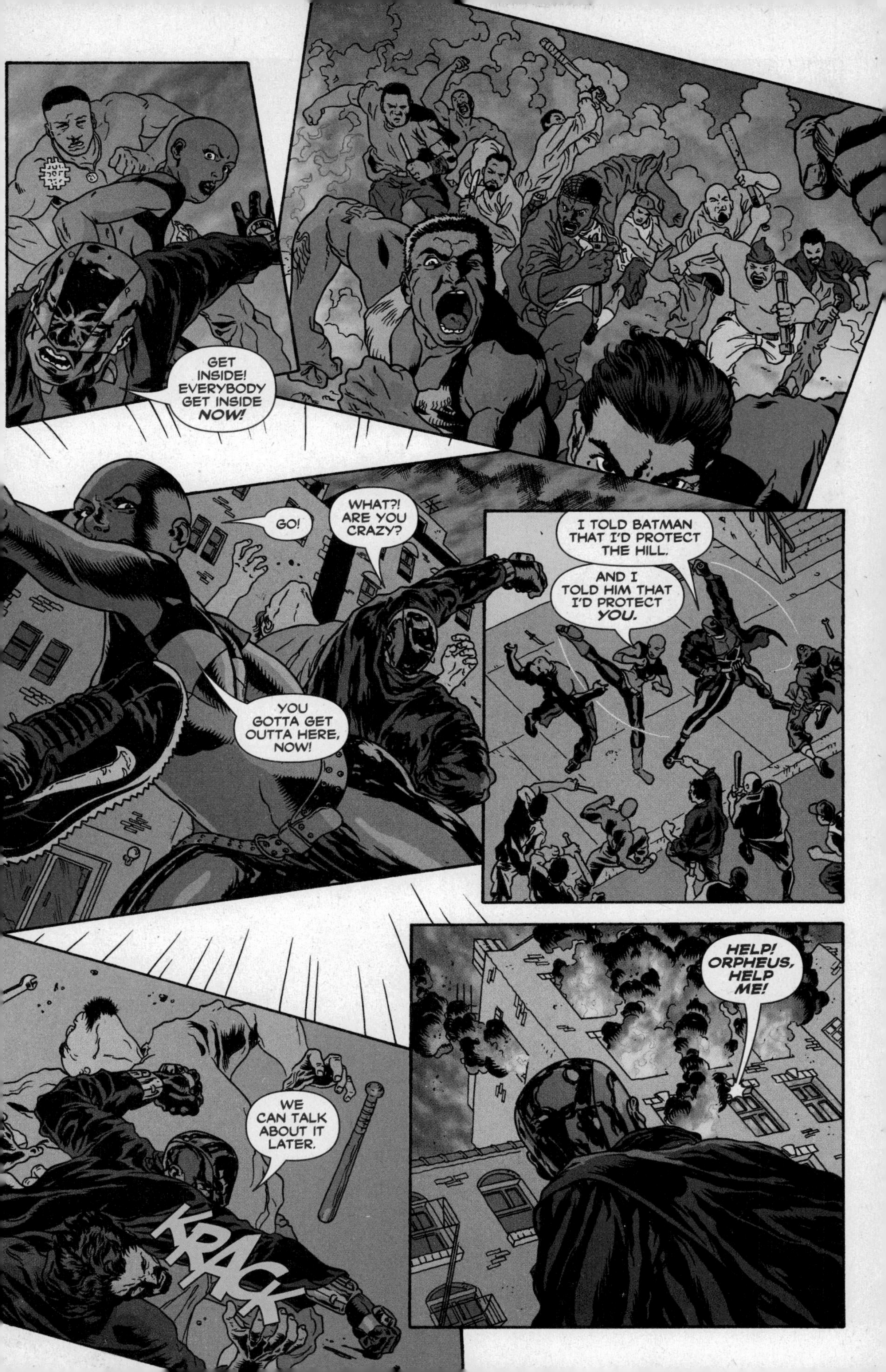
GET INSIDE! EVERYBODY GET INSIDE NOW!
GO!
WHAT?! ARE YOU CRAZY?
YOU GOTTA GET OUTTA HERE, NOW!
I TOLD BATMAN THAT I'D PROTECT THE HILL.
AND I TOLD HIM THAT I'D PROTECT YOU.
WE CAN TALK ABOUT IT LATER.
KRACK
HELP! ORPHEUS, HELP ME!

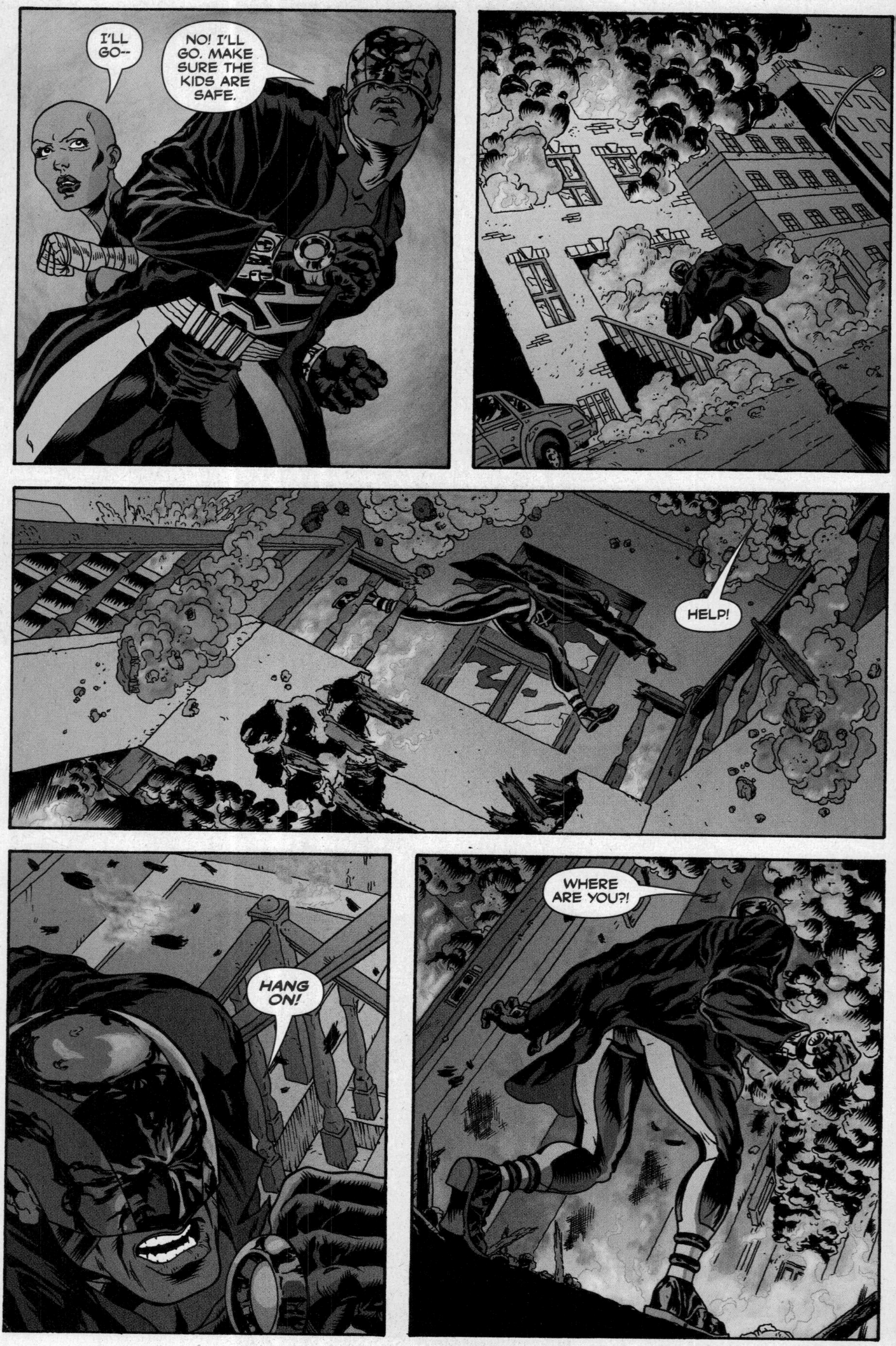
I'LL GO--
NO! I'LL GO. MAKE SURE THE KIDS ARE SAFE.
HELP!
HANG ON!
WHERE ARE YOU?!

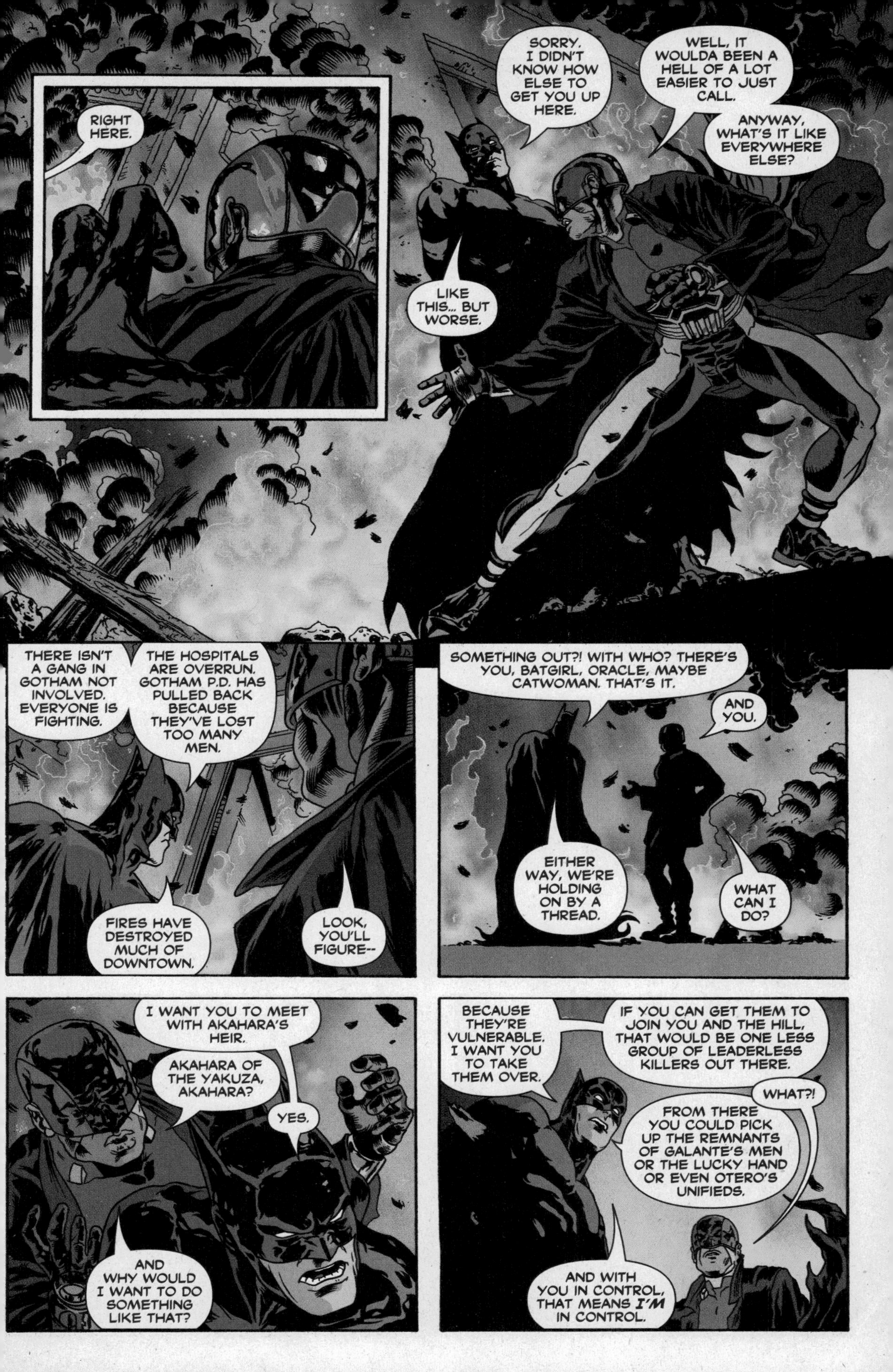
RIGHT HERE.
SORRY. I DIDN'T KNOW HOW ELSE TO GET YOU UP HERE.
WELL, IT WOULDA BEEN A HELL OF A LOT EASIER TO JUST CALL.
ANYWAY, WHAT'S IT LIKE EVERYWHERE ELSE?
LIKE THIS... BUT WORSE.
THERE ISN'T A GANG IN GOTHAM NOT INVOLVED. EVERYONE IS FIGHTING.
THE HOSPITALS ARE OVERRUN. GOTHAM P.D. HAS PULLED BACK BECAUSE THEY'VE LOST TOO MANY MEN.
FIRES HAVE DESTROYED MUCH OF DOWNTOWN.
LOOK, YOU'LL FIGURE--
SOMETHING OUT?! WITH WHO? THERE'S YOU, BATGIRL, ORACLE, MAYBE CATWOMAN. THAT'S IT.
AND YOU.
EITHER WAY, WE'RE HOLDING ON BY A THREAD.
WHAT CAN I DO?
I WANT YOU TO MEET WITH AKAHARA'S HEIR.
AKAHARA OF THE YAKUZA, AKAHARA?
YES.
AND WHY WOULD I WANT TO DO SOMETHING LIKE THAT?
BECAUSE THEY'RE VULNERABLE. I WANT YOU TO TAKE THEM OVER.
IF YOU CAN GET THEM TO JOIN YOU AND THE HILL, THAT WOULD BE ONE LESS GROUP OF LEADERLESS KILLERS OUT THERE.
WHAT?!
FROM THERE YOU COULD PICK UP THE REMNANTS OF GALANTE'S MEN OR THE LUCKY HAND OR EVEN OTERO'S UNIFIEDS.
AND WITH YOU IN CONTROL, THAT MEANS *I'M* IN CONTROL.

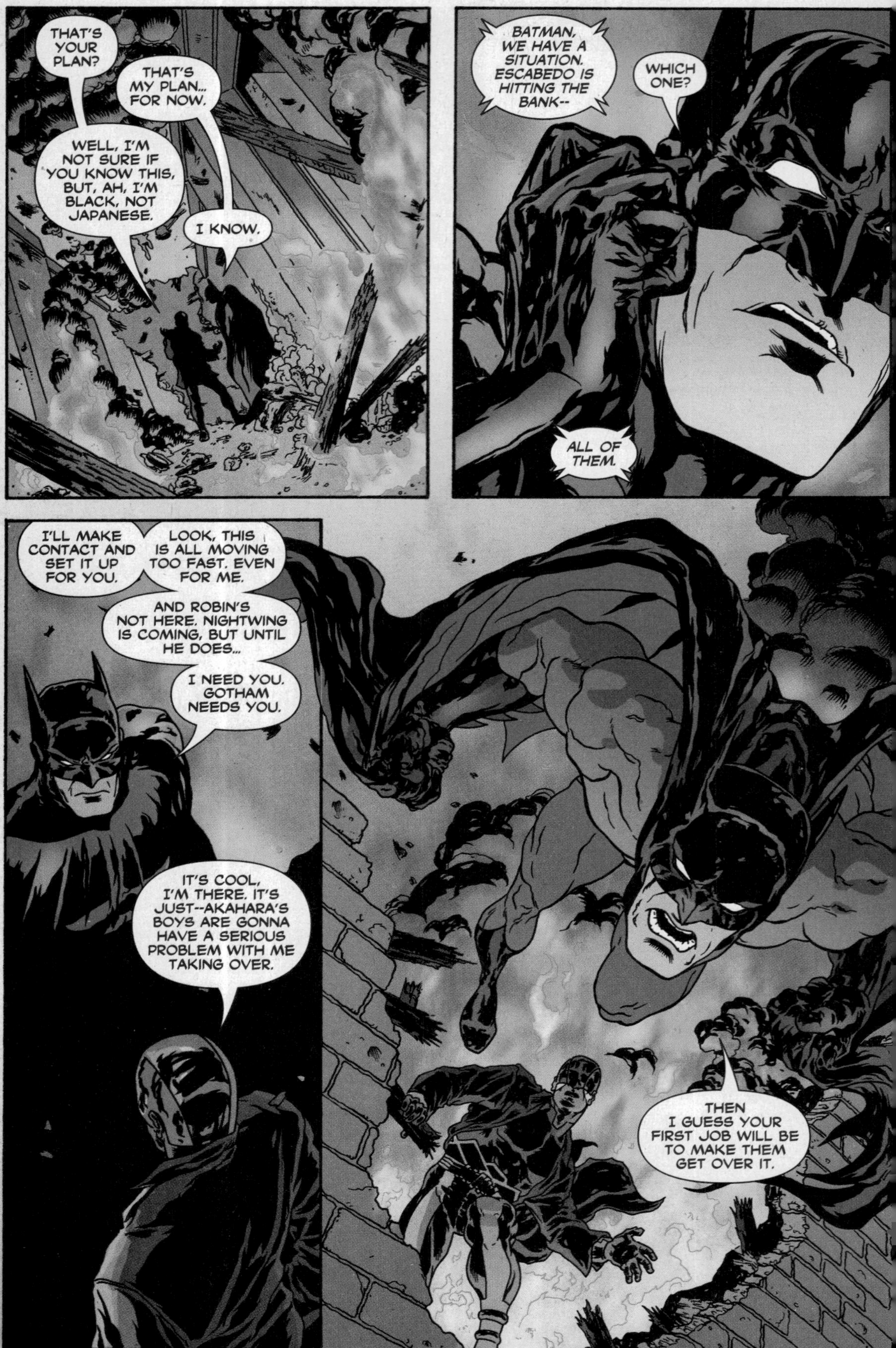
THAT'S YOUR PLAN?
THAT'S MY PLAN... FOR NOW.
WELL, I'M NOT SURE IF YOU KNOW THIS, BUT, AH, I'M BLACK, NOT JAPANESE.
I KNOW.
BATMAN, WE HAVE A SITUATION. ESCABEDO IS HITTING THE BANK--
WHICH ONE?
ALL OF THEM.
I'LL MAKE CONTACT AND SET IT UP FOR YOU.
LOOK, THIS IS ALL MOVING TOO FAST. EVEN FOR ME.
AND ROBIN'S NOT HERE. NIGHTWING IS COMING, BUT UNTIL HE DOES...
I NEED YOU. GOTHAM NEEDS YOU.
IT'S COOL, I'M THERE. IT'S JUST--AKAHARA'S BOYS ARE GONNA HAVE A SERIOUS PROBLEM WITH ME TAKING OVER.
THEN I GUESS YOUR FIRST JOB WILL BE TO MAKE THEM GET OVER IT.

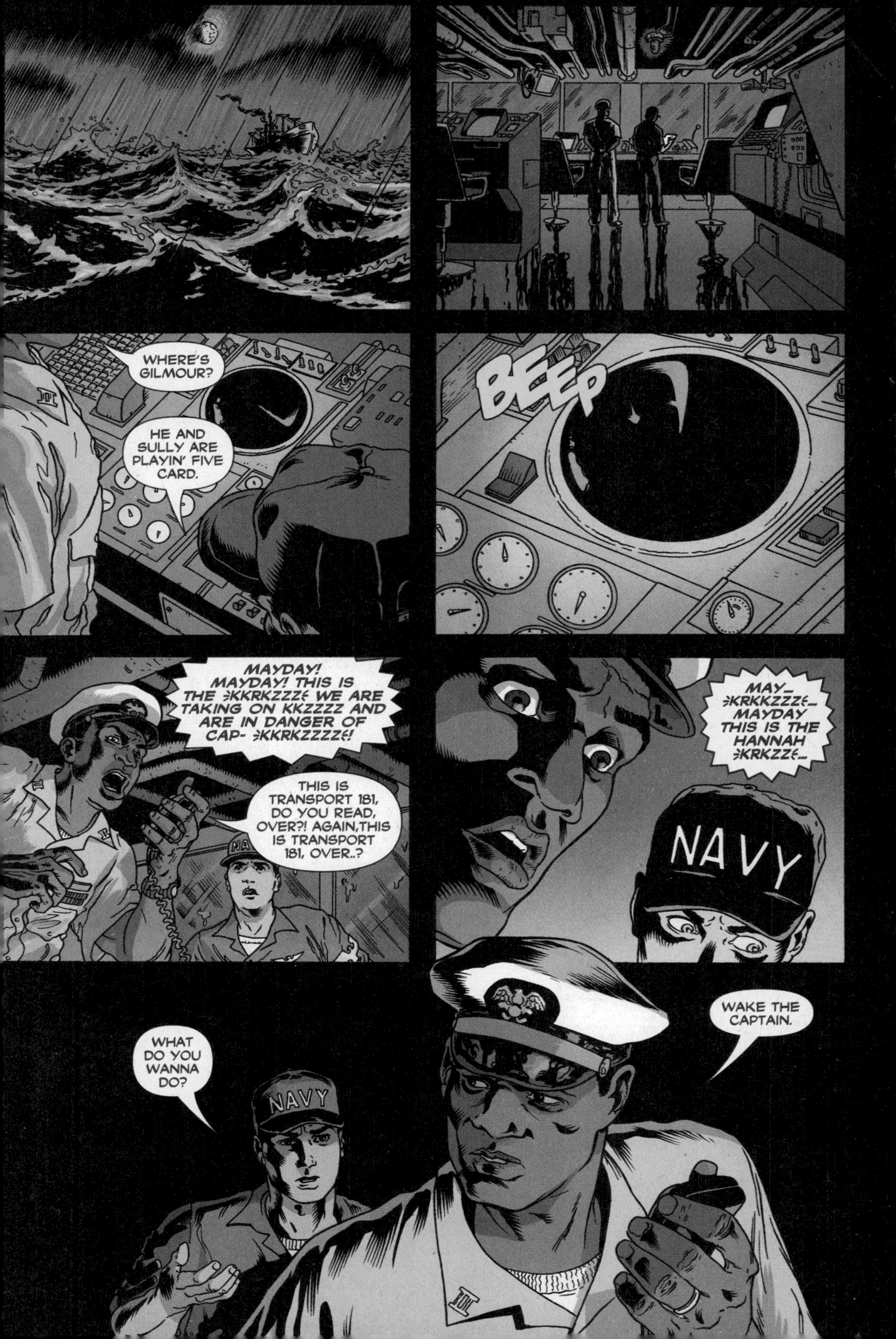
WHERE'S GILMOUR?
HE AND SULLY ARE PLAYIN' FIVE CARD.
BEEP
MAYDAY! MAYDAY! THIS IS THE KKRKZZZ WE ARE TAKING ON KKZZZZ AND ARE IN DANGER OF CAP- KKRKZZZZ!
THIS IS TRANSPORT 181, DO YOU READ, OVER?! AGAIN,THIS IS TRANSPORT 181, OVER..?
MAY.. KRKKZZZ.. MAYDAY THIS IS THE HANNAH KRKZZ..
NAVY
WHAT DO YOU WANNA DO?
WAKE THE CAPTAIN.
NAVY

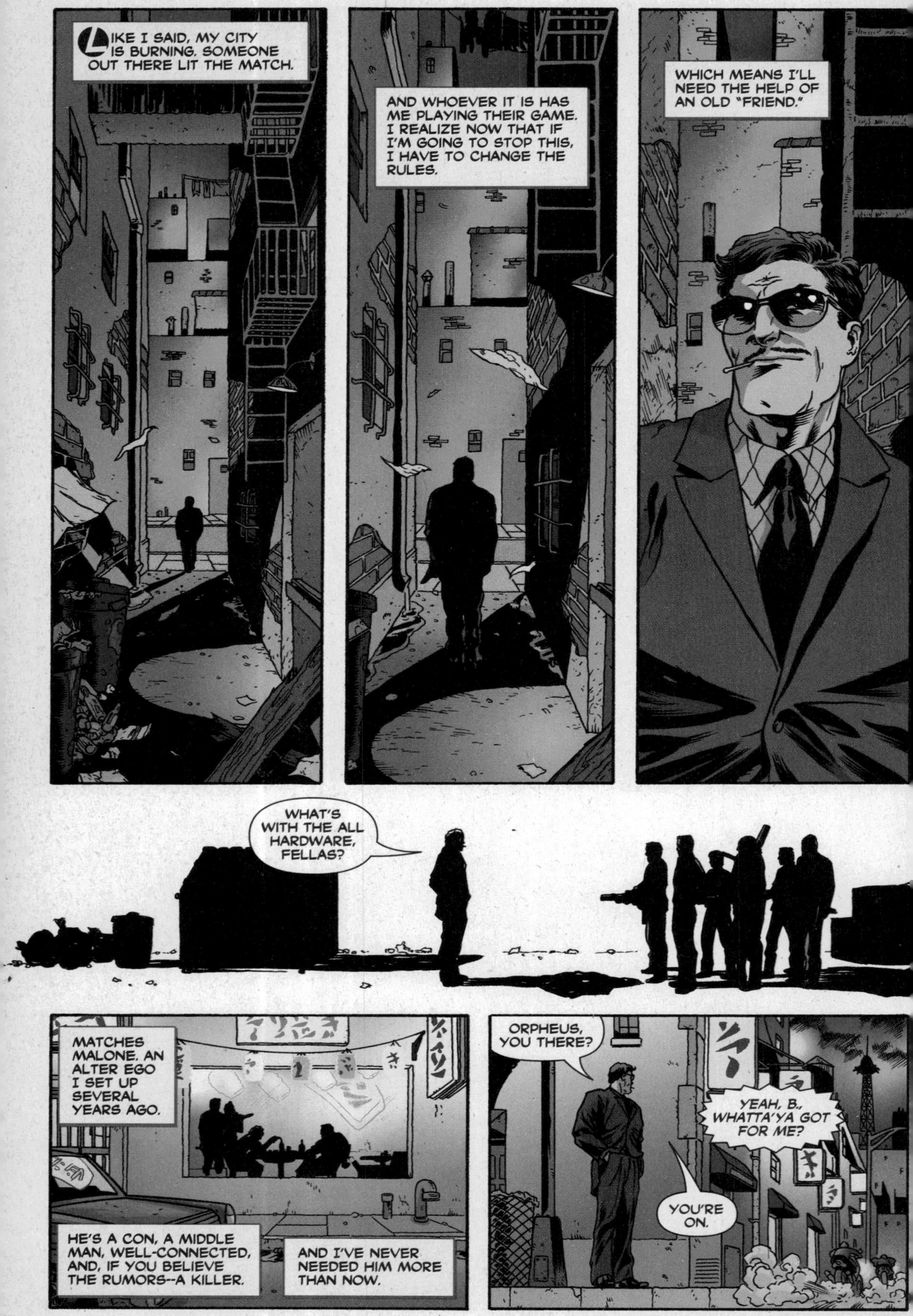
LIKE I SAID, MY CITY IS BURNING. SOMEONE OUT THERE LIT THE MATCH.
AND WHOEVER IT IS HAS ME PLAYING THEIR GAME. I REALIZE NOW THAT IF I'M GOING TO STOP THIS, I HAVE TO CHANGE THE RULES.
WHICH MEANS I'LL NEED THE HELP OF AN OLD "FRIEND."
WHAT'S WITH THE ALL HARDWARE, FELLAS?
MATCHES MALONE. AN ALTER EGO I SET UP SEVERAL YEARS AGO.
HE'S A CON, A MIDDLE MAN, WELL-CONNECTED, AND, IF YOU BELIEVE THE RUMORS--A KILLER.
AND I'VE NEVER NEEDED HIM MORE THAN NOW.
ORPHEUS, YOU THERE?
YEAH, B., WHATTA'YA GOT FOR ME?
YOU'RE ON.

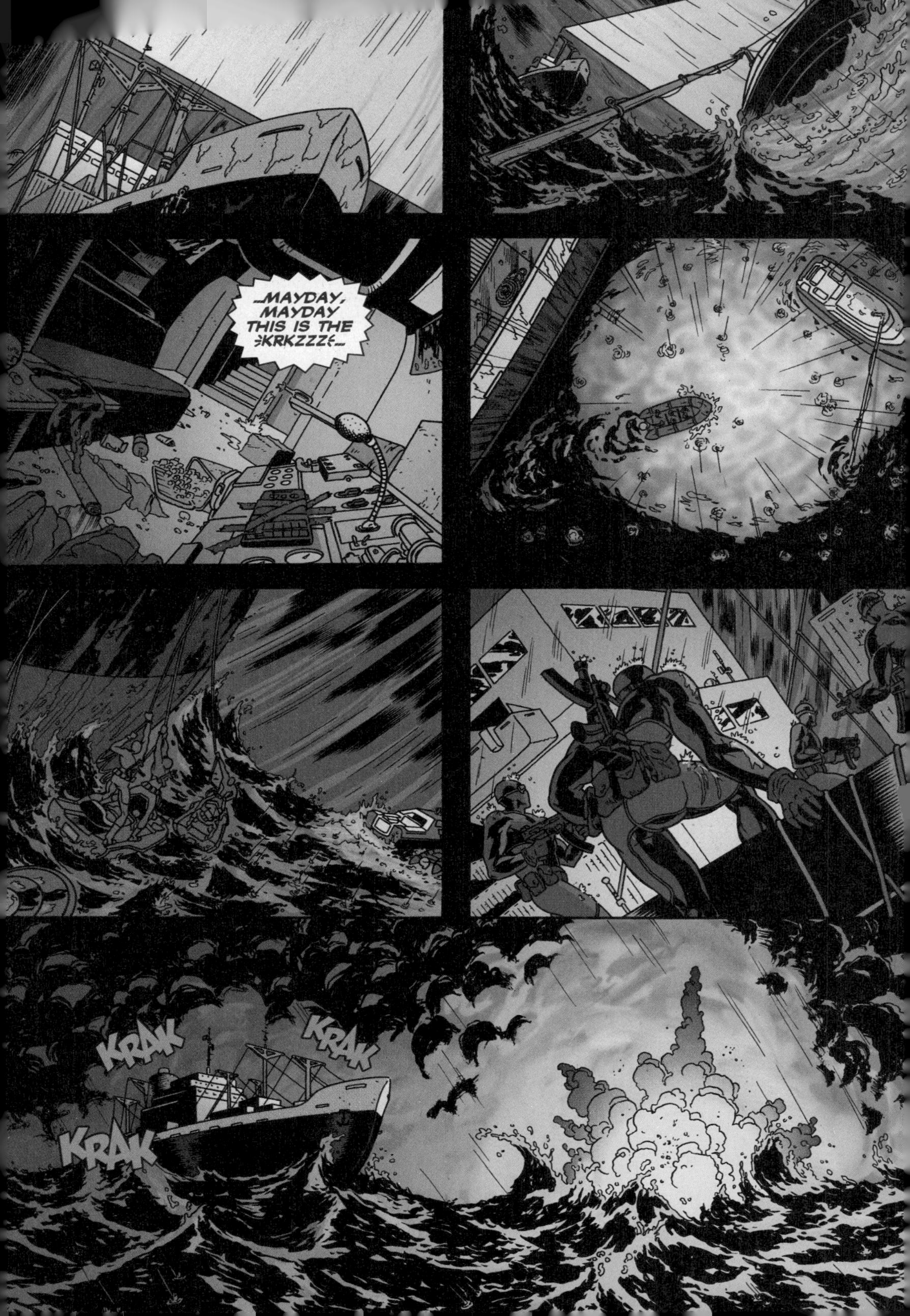

--MAYDAY, MAYDAY THIS IS THE ⸗KRKZZZ⸗--
KRAK
KRAK
KRAK

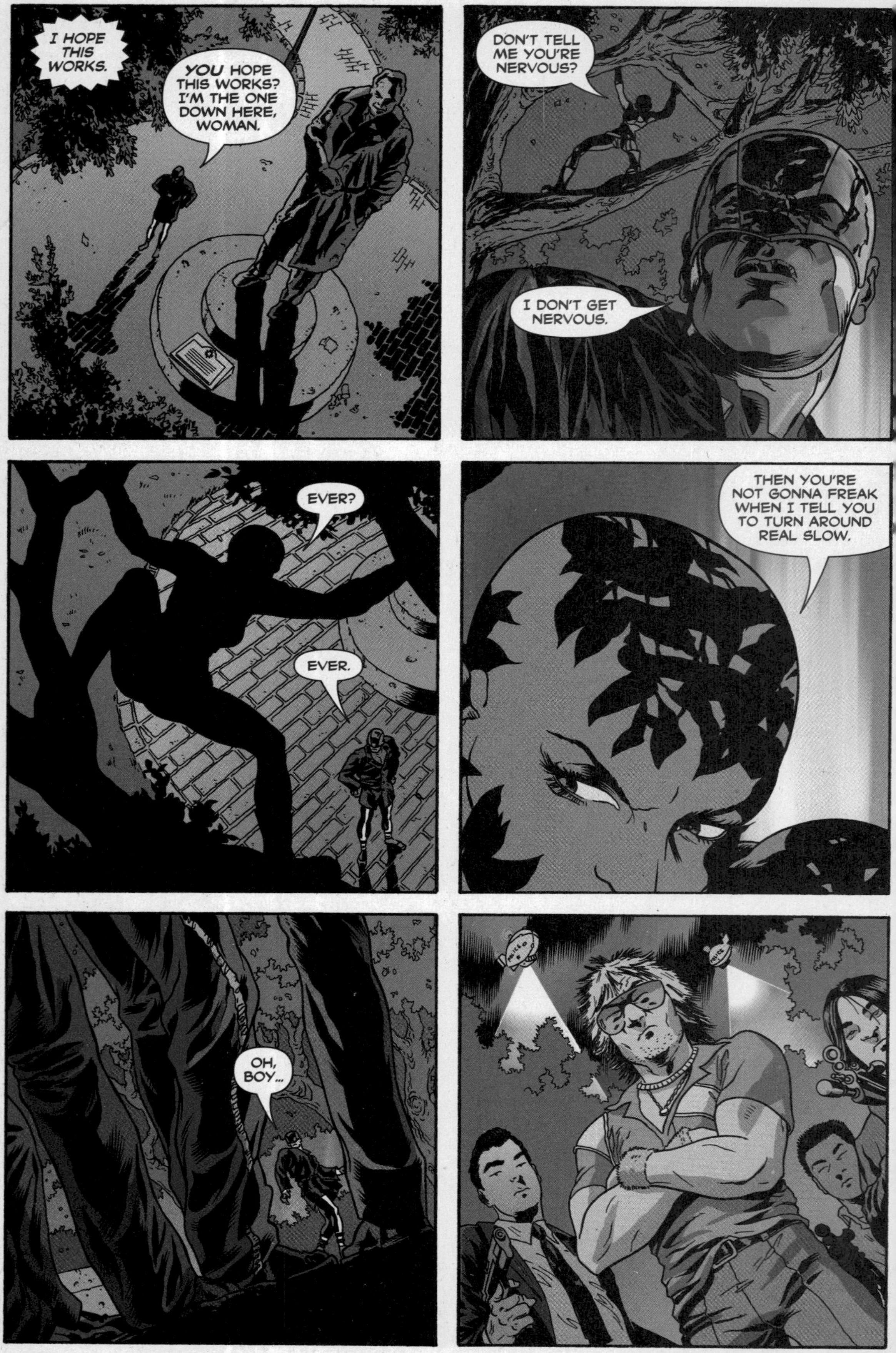
I HOPE THIS WORKS.
YOU HOPE THIS WORKS? I'M THE ONE DOWN HERE, WOMAN.
DON'T TELL ME YOU'RE NERVOUS?
I DON'T GET NERVOUS.
EVER?
EVER.
THEN YOU'RE NOT GONNA FREAK WHEN I TELL YOU TO TURN AROUND REAL SLOW.
OH, BOY...

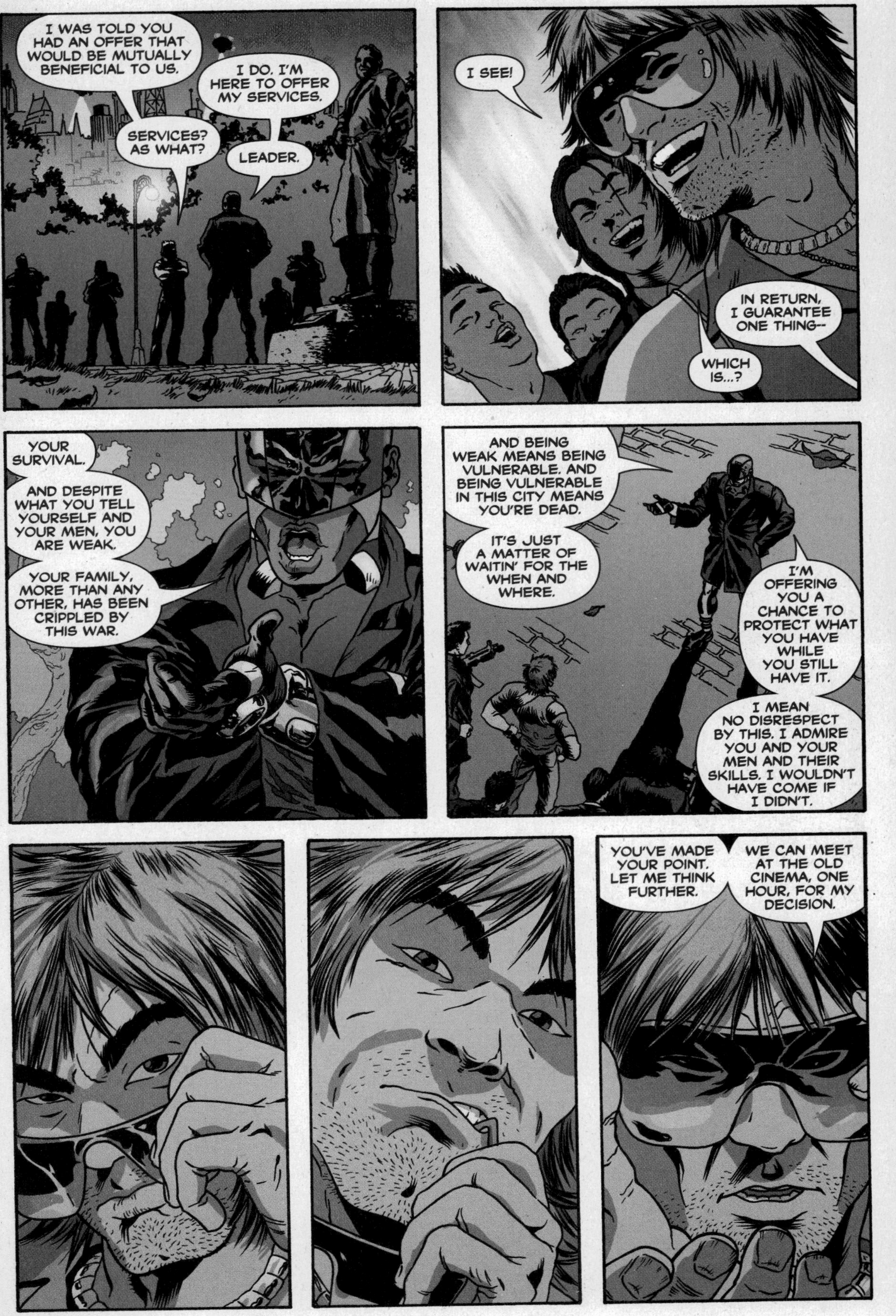
I WAS TOLD YOU HAD AN OFFER THAT WOULD BE MUTUALLY BENEFICIAL TO US.
I DO. I'M HERE TO OFFER MY SERVICES.
SERVICES? AS WHAT?
LEADER.
I SEE!
IN RETURN, I GUARANTEE ONE THING--
WHICH IS...?
YOUR SURVIVAL.
AND DESPITE WHAT YOU TELL YOURSELF AND YOUR MEN, YOU ARE WEAK.
YOUR FAMILY, MORE THAN ANY OTHER, HAS BEEN CRIPPLED BY THIS WAR.
AND BEING WEAK MEANS BEING VULNERABLE. AND BEING VULNERABLE IN THIS CITY MEANS YOU'RE DEAD.
IT'S JUST A MATTER OF WAITIN' FOR THE WHEN AND WHERE.
I'M OFFERING YOU A CHANCE TO PROTECT WHAT YOU HAVE WHILE YOU STILL HAVE IT.
I MEAN NO DISRESPECT BY THIS. I ADMIRE YOU AND YOUR MEN AND THEIR SKILLS. I WOULDN'T HAVE COME IF I DIDN'T.
YOU'VE MADE YOUR POINT. LET ME THINK FURTHER.
WE CAN MEET AT THE OLD CINEMA, ONE HOUR, FOR MY DECISION.

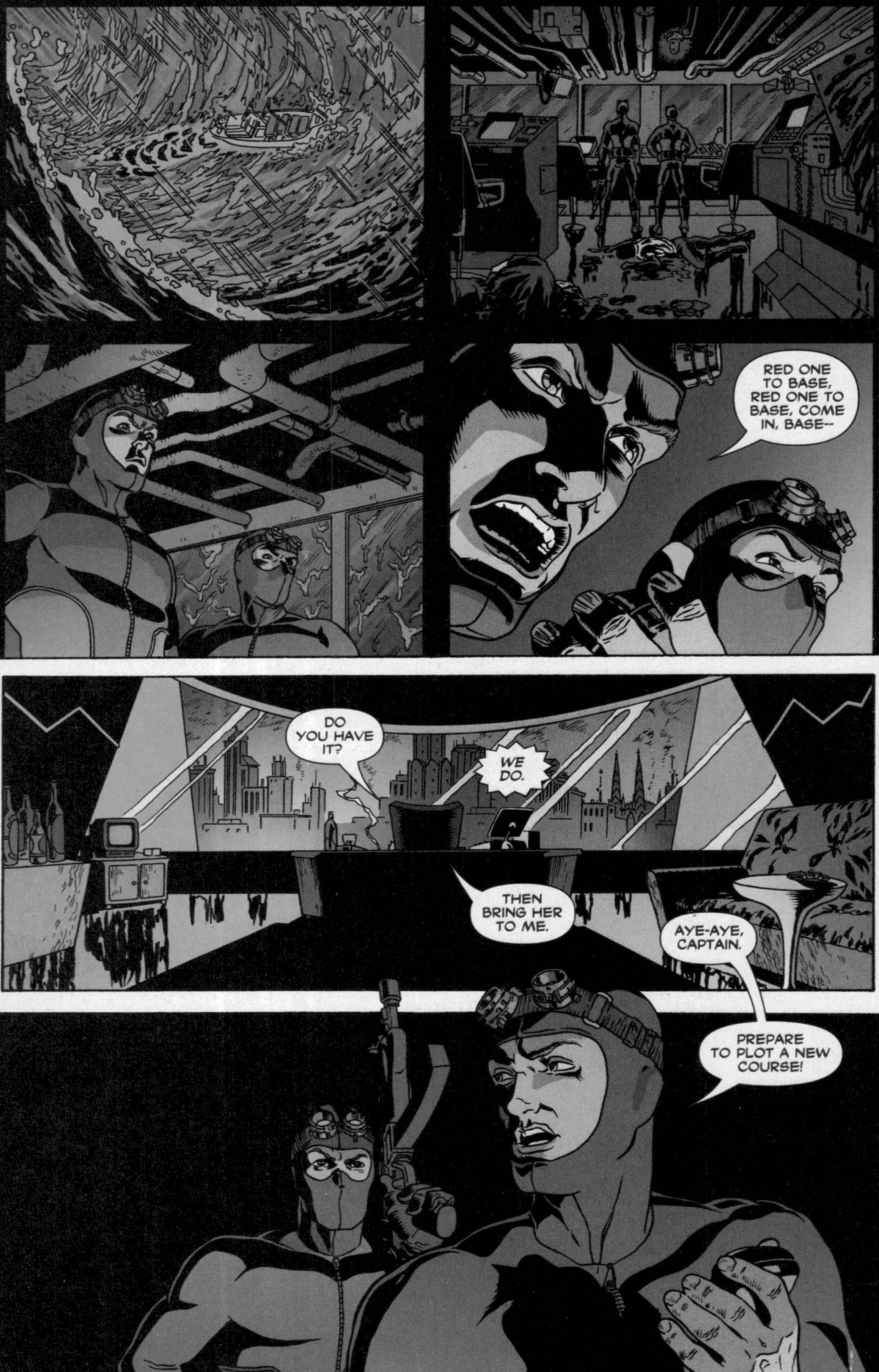
RED ONE TO BASE, RED ONE TO BASE, COME IN, BASE--
DO YOU HAVE IT?
WE DO.
THEN BRING HER TO ME.
AYE-AYE, CAPTAIN.
PREPARE TO PLOT A NEW COURSE!

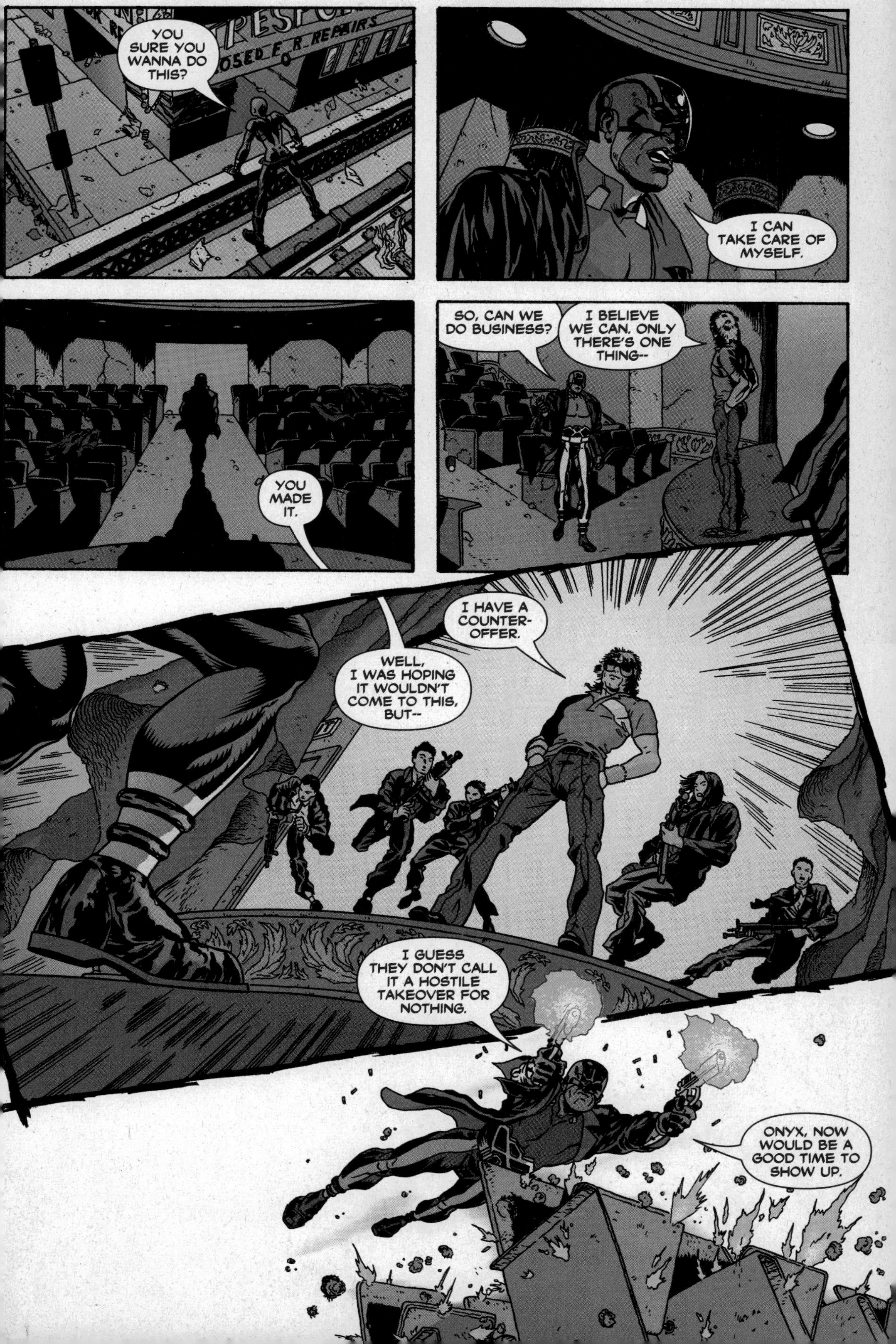
YOU SURE YOU WANNA DO THIS?
I CAN TAKE CARE OF MYSELF.
YOU MADE IT.
SO, CAN WE DO BUSINESS?
I BELIEVE WE CAN. ONLY THERE'S ONE THING--
WELL, I WAS HOPING IT WOULDN'T COME TO THIS, BUT--
I HAVE A COUNTER-OFFER.
I GUESS THEY DON'T CALL IT A HOSTILE TAKEOVER FOR NOTHING.
ONYX, NOW WOULD BE A GOOD TIME TO SHOW UP.

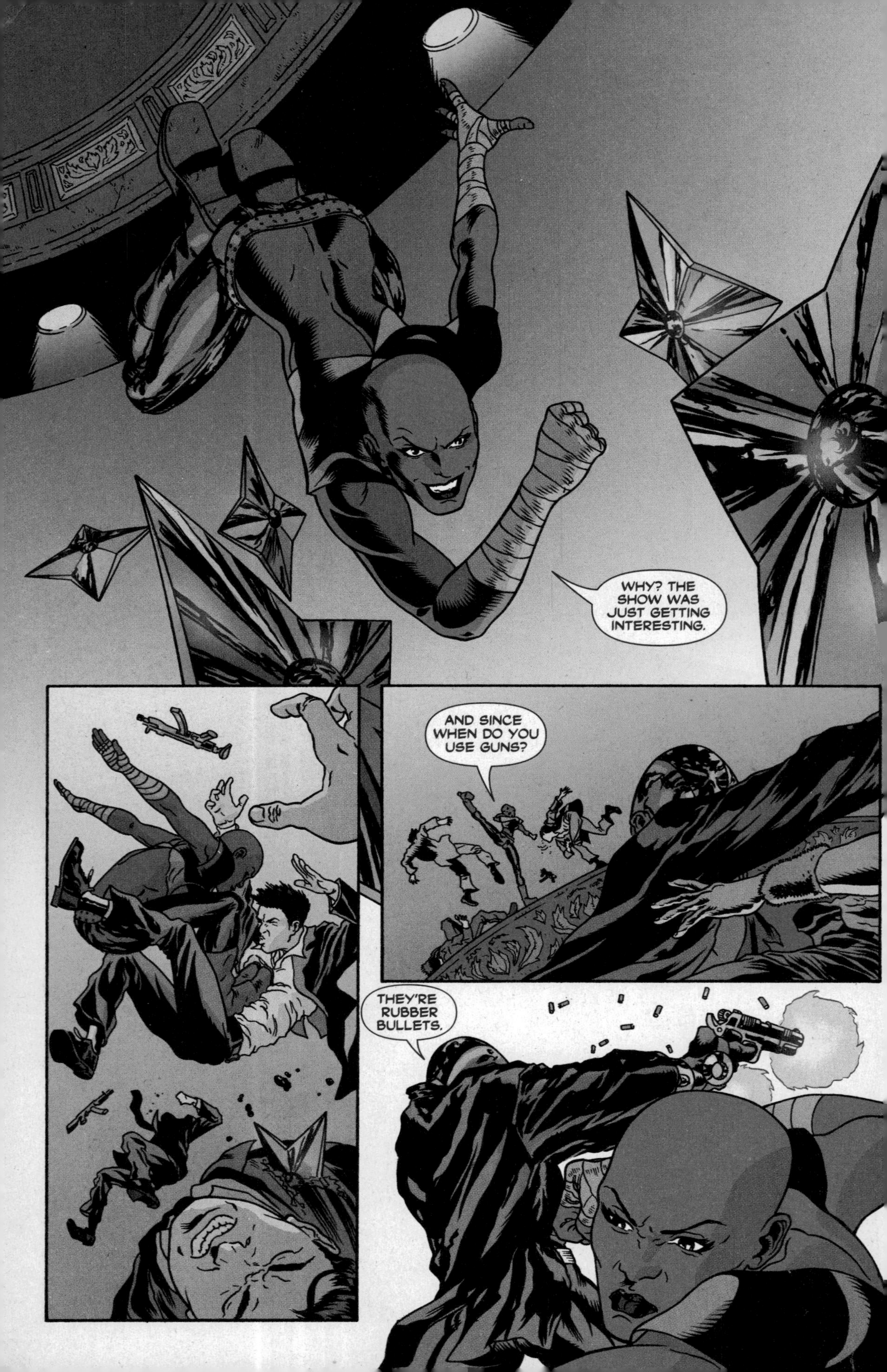
WHY? THE SHOW WAS JUST GETTING INTERESTING.
AND SINCE WHEN DO YOU USE GUNS?
THEY'RE RUBBER BULLETS.

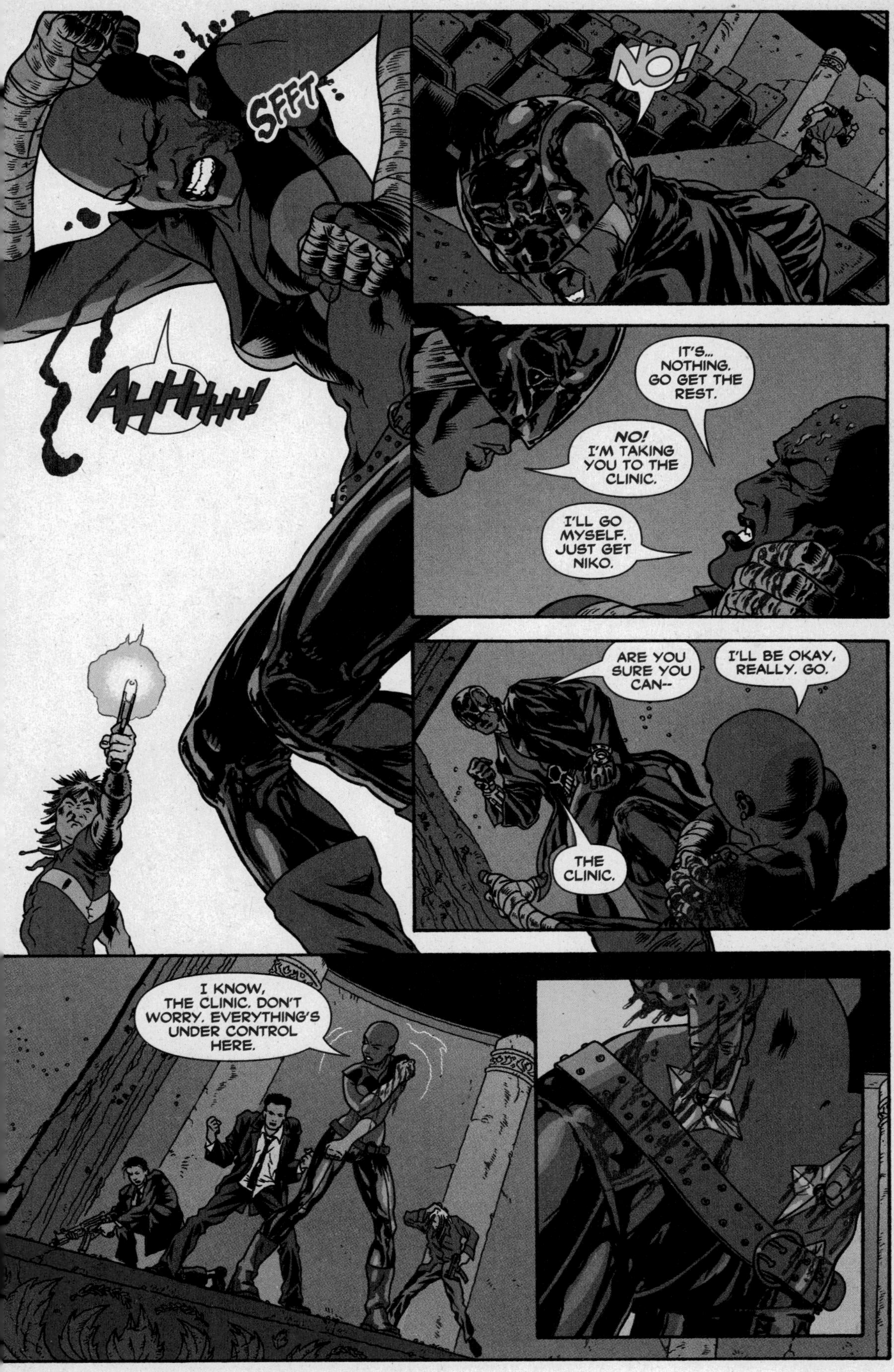
SFFT
AHHHHH!
NO!
IT'S... NOTHING. GO GET THE REST.
NO! I'M TAKING YOU TO THE CLINIC.
I'LL GO MYSELF. JUST GET NIKO.
ARE YOU SURE YOU CAN--
I'LL BE OKAY, REALLY. GO.
THE CLINIC.
I KNOW, THE CLINIC. DON'T WORRY. EVERYTHING'S UNDER CONTROL HERE.

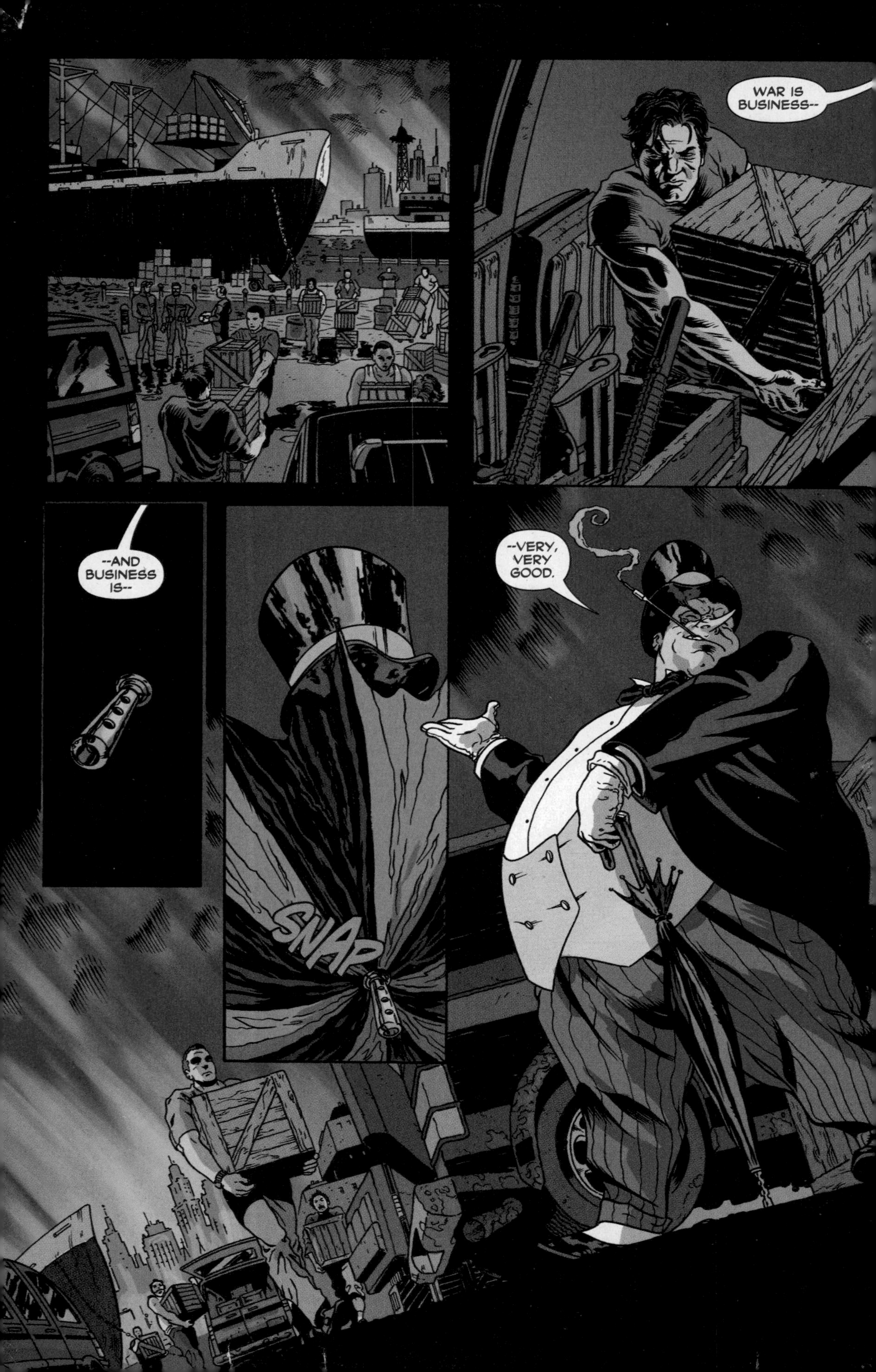
WAR IS BUSINESS--
--AND BUSINESS IS--
SNAP
--VERY, VERY GOOD.

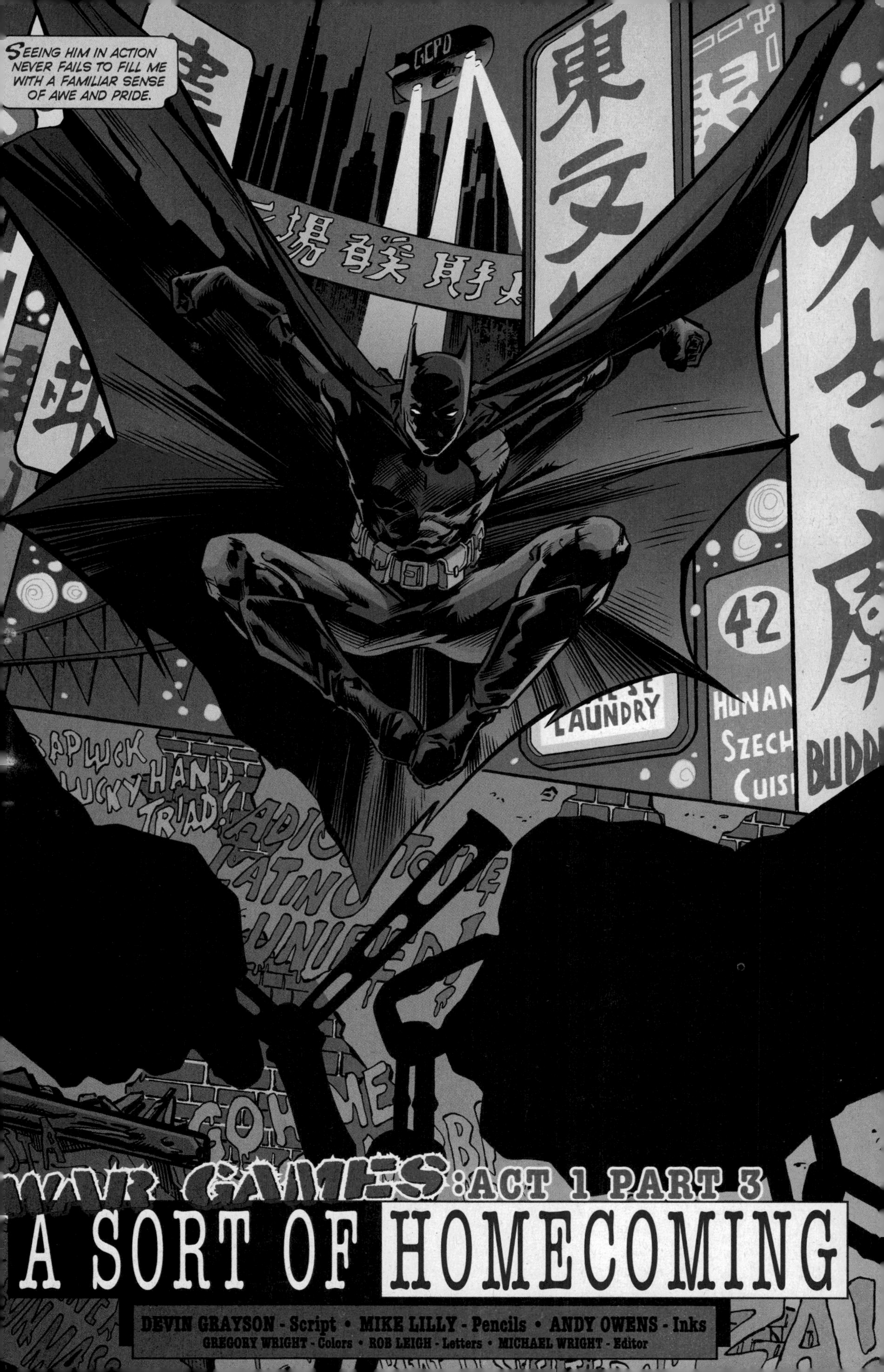
SEEING HIM IN ACTION NEVER FAILS TO FILL ME WITH A FAMILIAR SENSE OF AWE AND PRIDE.
GCPD
LAUNDRY
42
WAR GAMES: ACT 1 PART 3
A SORT OF HOMECOMING
DEVIN GRAYSON - Script • MIKE LILLY - Pencils • ANDY OWENS - Inks
GREGORY WRIGHT - Colors • ROB LEIGH - Letters • MICHAEL WRIGHT - Editor

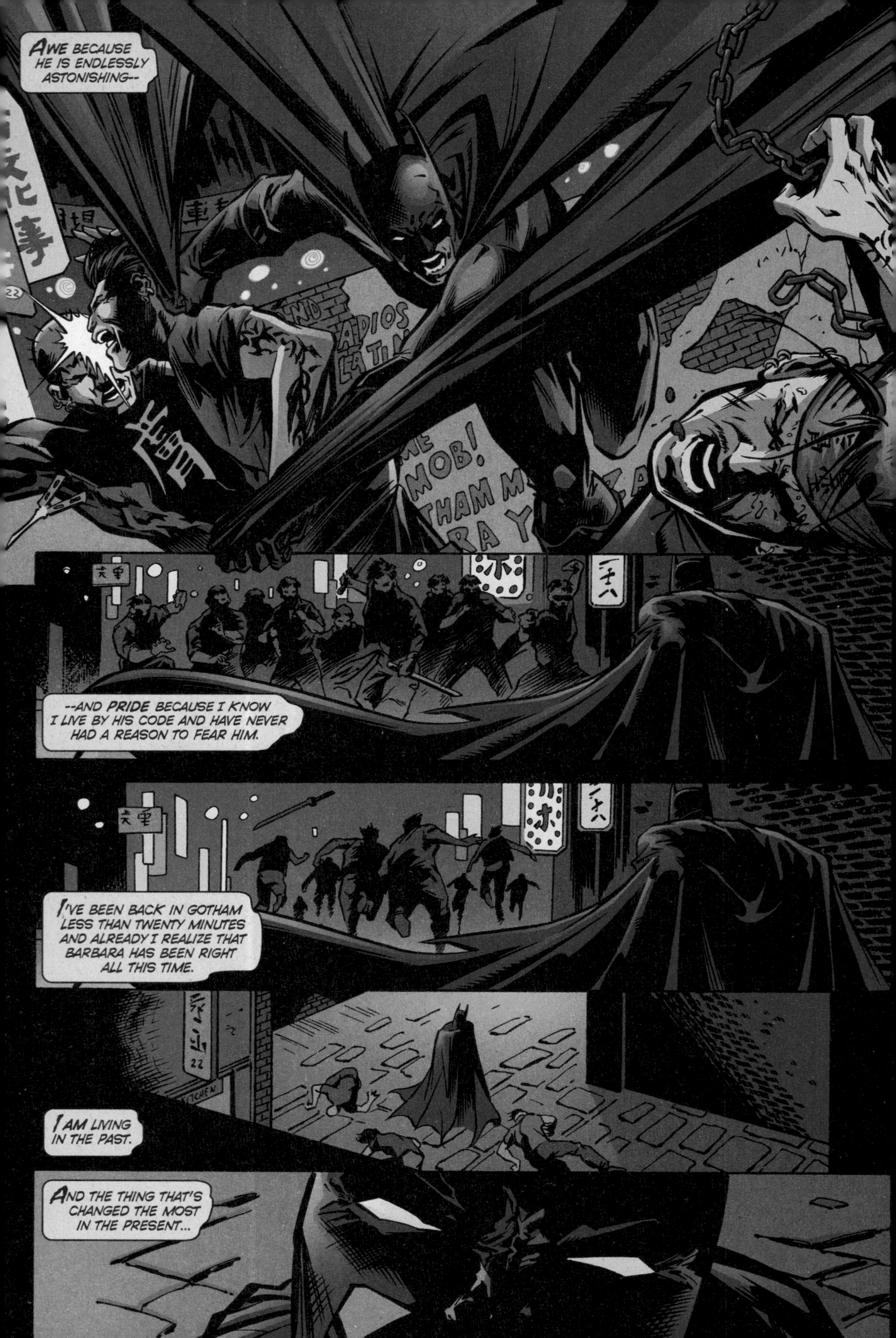
AWE BECAUSE HE IS ENDLESSLY ASTONISHING--
ADIOS
MOB!
--AND PRIDE BECAUSE I KNOW I LIVE BY HIS CODE AND HAVE NEVER HAD A REASON TO FEAR HIM.
I'VE BEEN BACK IN GOTHAM LESS THAN TWENTY MINUTES AND ALREADY I REALIZE THAT BARBARA HAS BEEN RIGHT ALL THIS TIME.
I AM LIVING IN THE PAST.
AND THE THING THAT'S CHANGED THE MOST IN THE PRESENT...

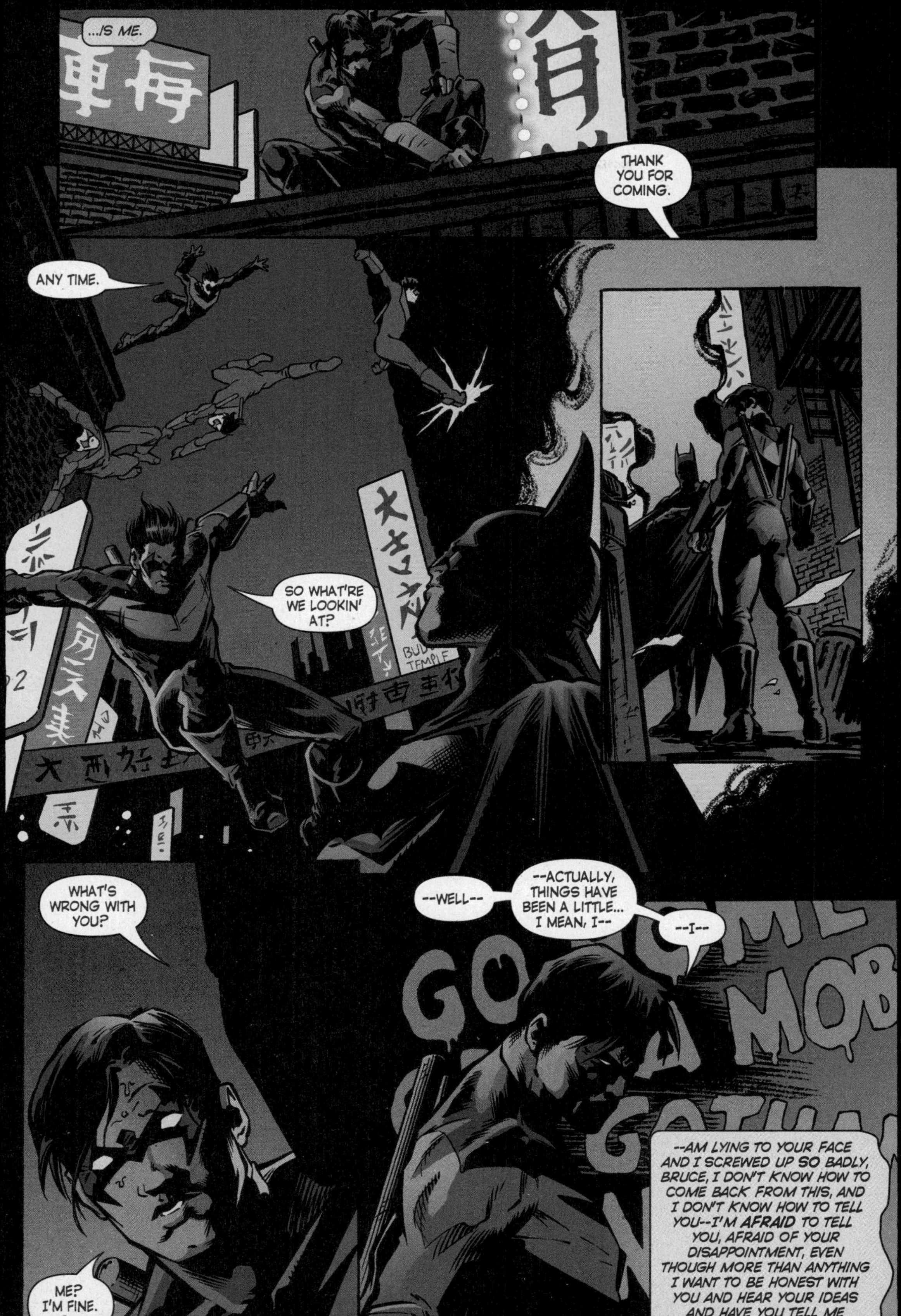

...IS ME.
THANK YOU FOR COMING.
ANY TIME.
SO WHAT'RE WE LOOKIN' AT?
WHAT'S WRONG WITH YOU?
ME? I'M FINE. I--
--WELL--
--ACTUALLY, THINGS HAVE BEEN A LITTLE... I MEAN, I--
--I--
--AM LYING TO YOUR FACE AND I SCREWED UP SO BADLY, BRUCE, I DON'T KNOW HOW TO COME BACK FROM THIS, AND I DON'T KNOW HOW TO TELL YOU--I'M AFRAID TO TELL YOU, AFRAID OF YOUR DISAPPOINTMENT, EVEN THOUGH MORE THAN ANYTHING I WANT TO BE HONEST WITH YOU AND HEAR YOUR IDEAS AND HAVE YOU TELL ME SOMETHING I COULD DO THAT WOULD MAKE UP FOR--

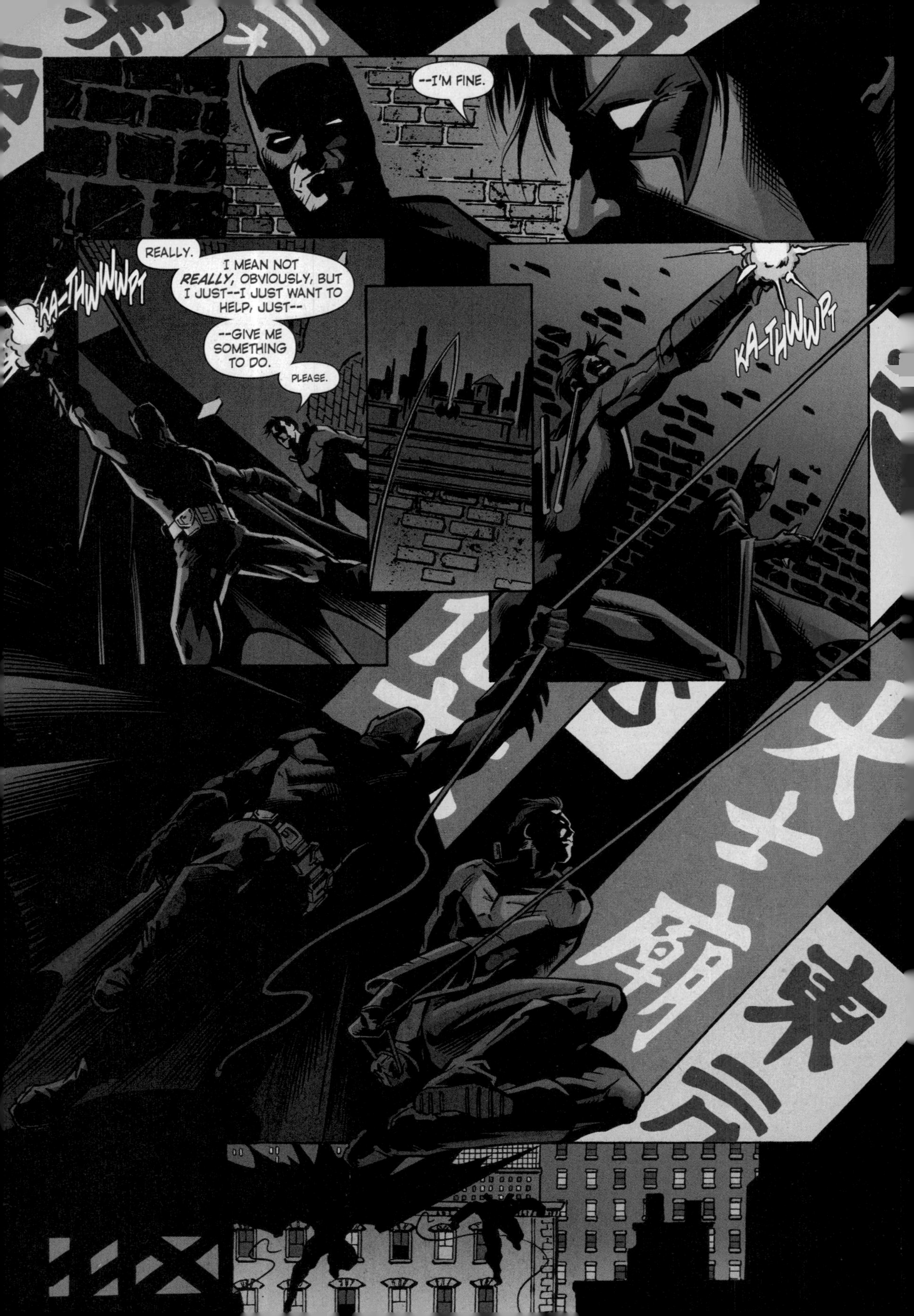
--I'M FINE.
REALLY.
I MEAN NOT *REALLY*, OBVIOUSLY, BUT I JUST--I JUST WANT TO HELP, JUST--
--GIVE ME SOMETHING TO DO.
PLEASE.
KA-THWWWP!
KA-THWWP!

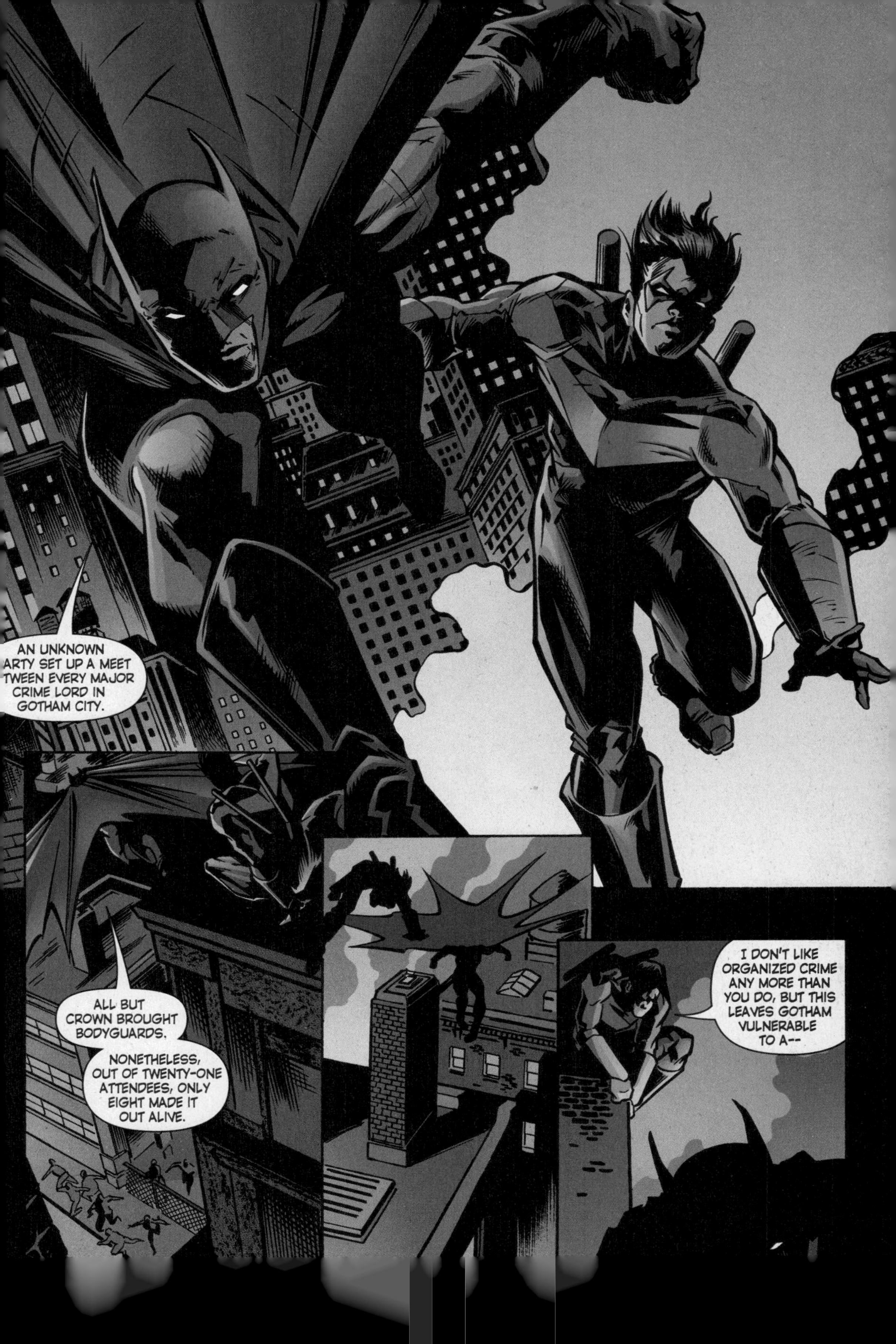
AN UNKNOWN
ARTY SET UP A MEET
TWEEN EVERY MAJOR
CRIME LORD IN
GOTHAM CITY.
ALL BUT
CROWN BROUGHT
BODYGUARDS.
NONETHELESS,
OUT OF TWENTY-ONE
ATTENDEES, ONLY
EIGHT MADE IT
OUT ALIVE.
I DON'T LIKE
ORGANIZED CRIME
ANY MORE THAN
YOU DO, BUT THIS
LEAVES GOTHAM
VULNERABLE
TO A--

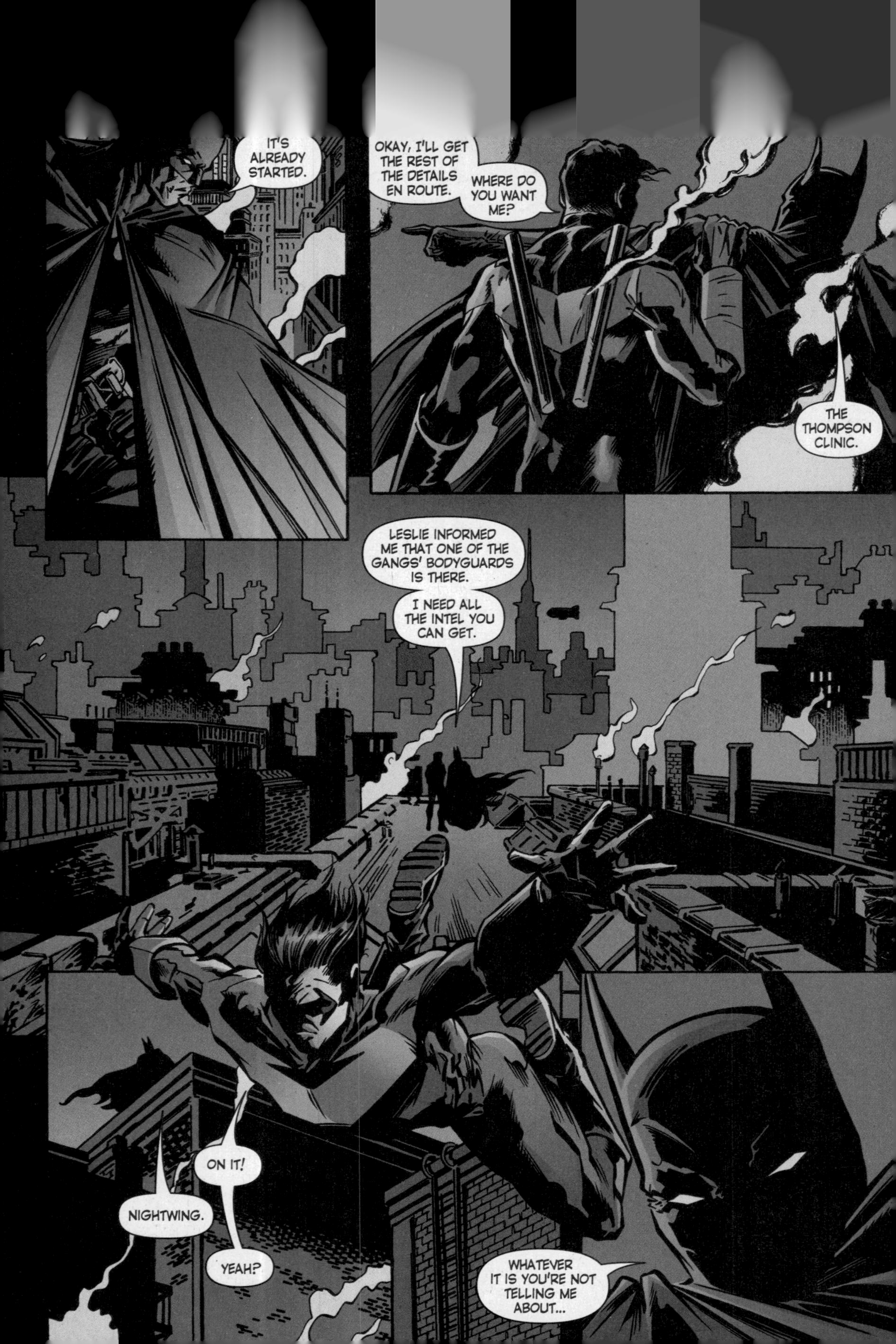
IT'S ALREADY STARTED.
OKAY, I'LL GET THE REST OF THE DETAILS EN ROUTE.
WHERE DO YOU WANT ME?
THE THOMPSON CLINIC.
LESLIE INFORMED ME THAT ONE OF THE GANGS' BODYGUARDS IS THERE.
I NEED ALL THE INTEL YOU CAN GET.
ON IT!
NIGHTWING.
YEAH?
WHATEVER IT IS YOU'RE NOT TELLING ME ABOUT...

mejor fuerte
para las noticias
locales en Gotham!

ARTURO RODRIGUEZ › LUNES A VIERNES

WLAT
88.5 fm

"...MAKE SURE IT DOESN'T FOLLOW YOU HERE."

BASTA!

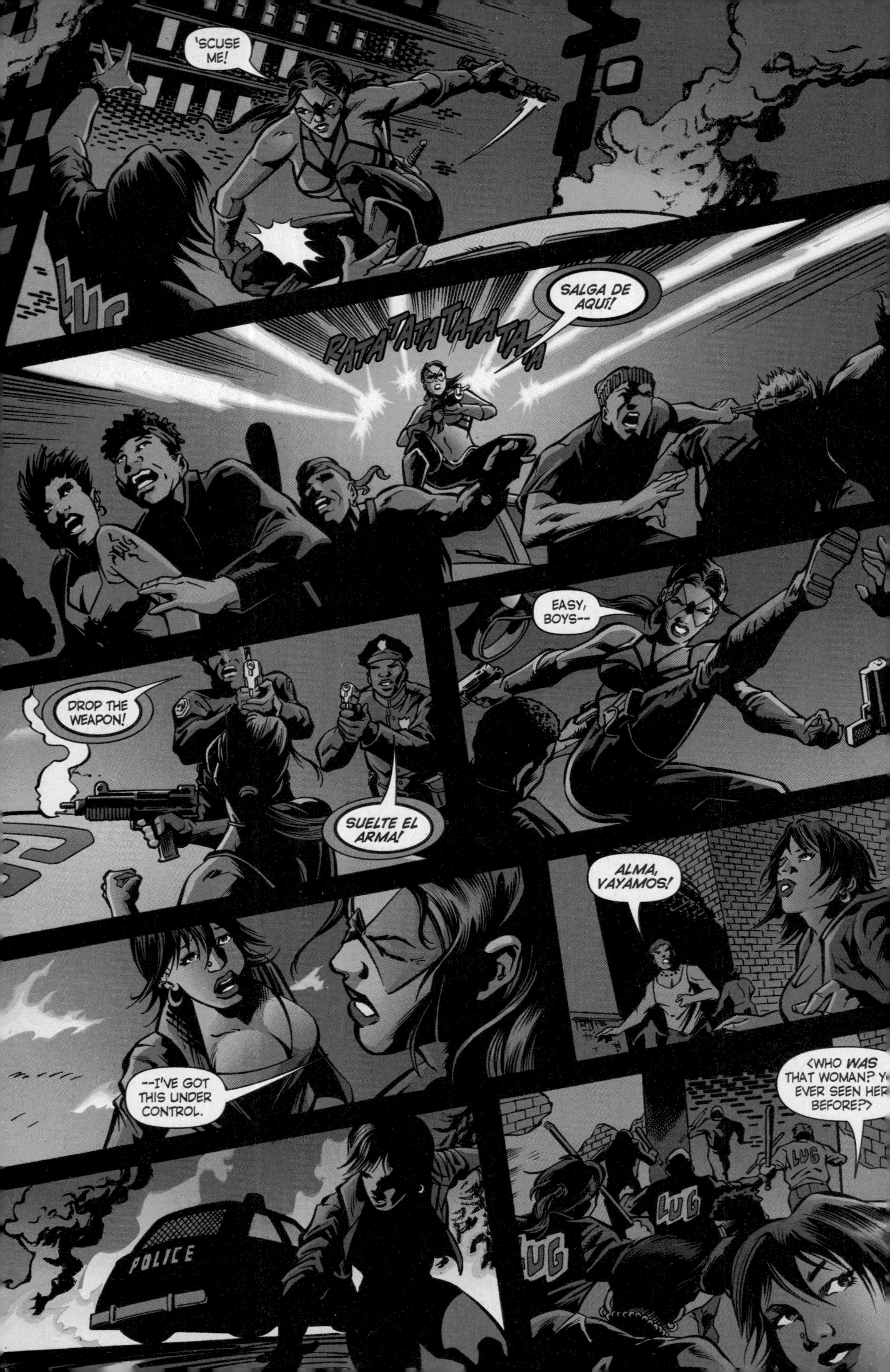
'SCUSE ME!
SALGA DE AQUÍ!
RATATATATATATATA
EASY, BOYS--
DROP THE WEAPON!
SUELTE EL ARMA!
ALMA, VAYAMOS!
--I'VE GOT THIS UNDER CONTROL.
<WHO WAS THAT WOMAN? YO EVER SEEN HER BEFORE?>
LUG
LUG
LUG
POLICE

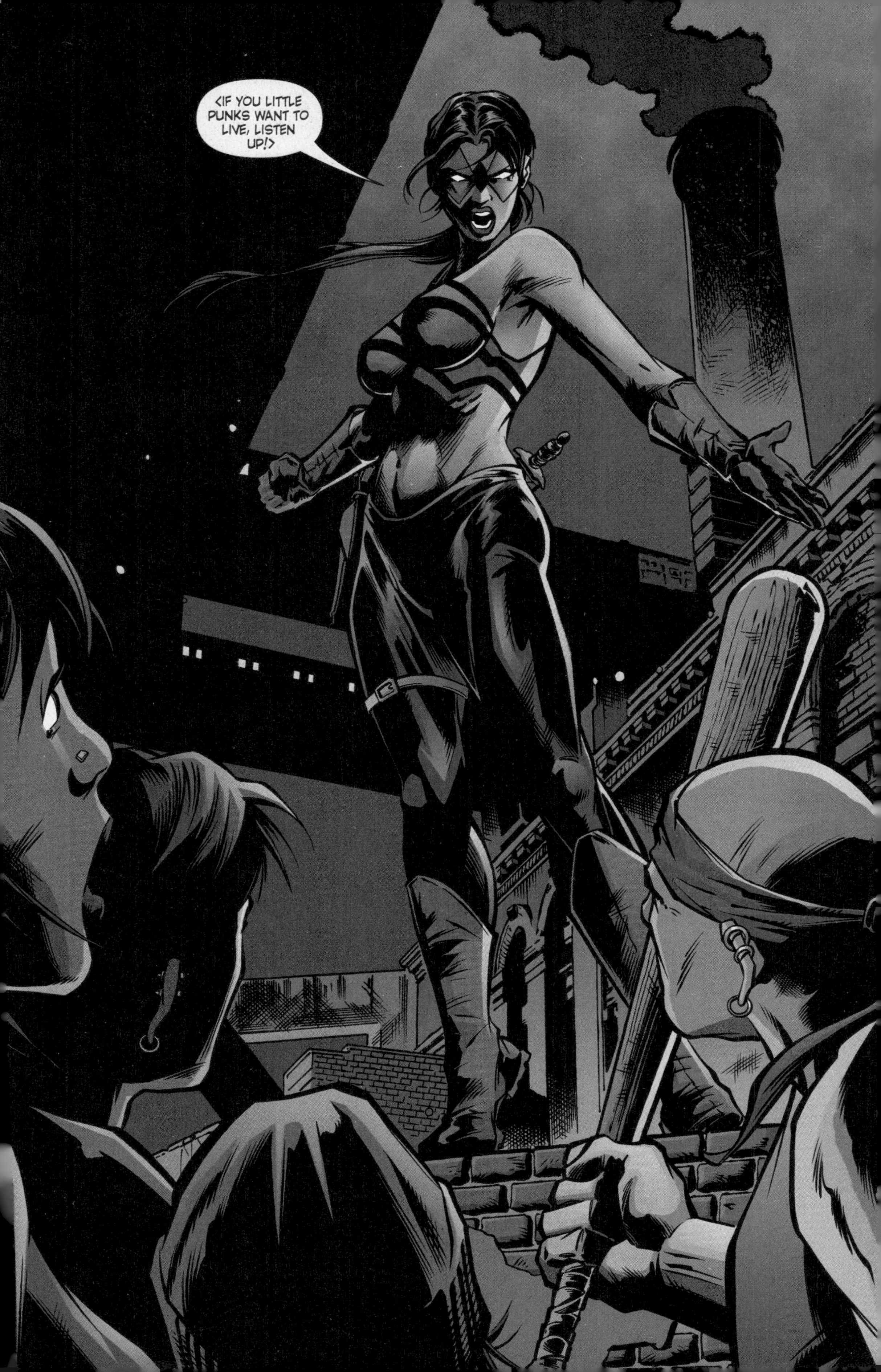
<IF YOU LITTLE PUNKS WANT TO LIVE, LISTEN UP!>

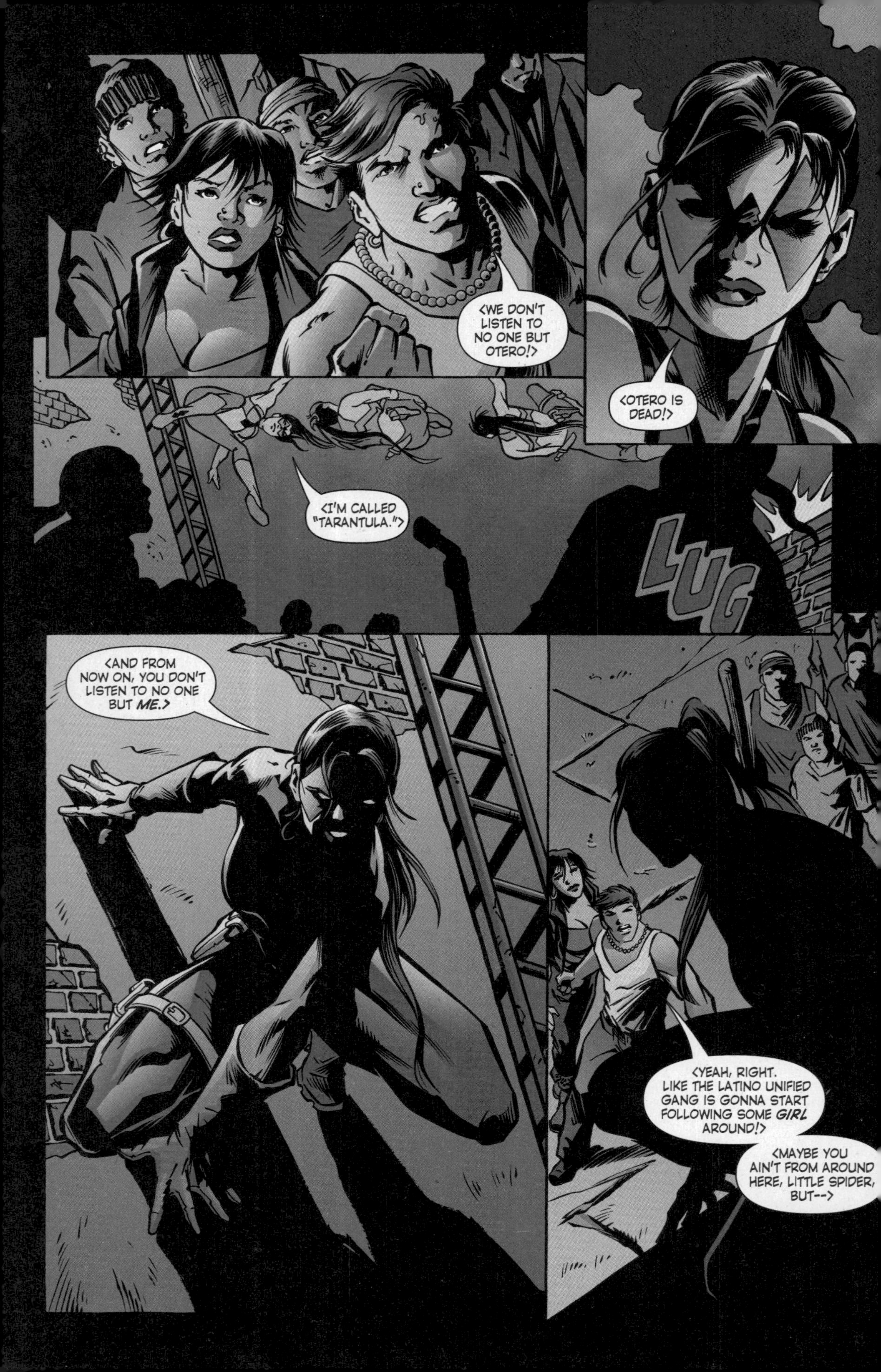
<WE DON'T LISTEN TO NO ONE BUT OTERO!>
<OTERO IS DEAD!>
<I'M CALLED "TARANTULA.">
LUG
<AND FROM NOW ON, YOU DON'T LISTEN TO NO ONE BUT *ME*.>
<YEAH, RIGHT. LIKE THE LATINO UNIFIED GANG IS GONNA START FOLLOWING SOME *GIRL* AROUND!>
<MAYBE YOU AIN'T FROM AROUND HERE, LITTLE SPIDER, BUT-->

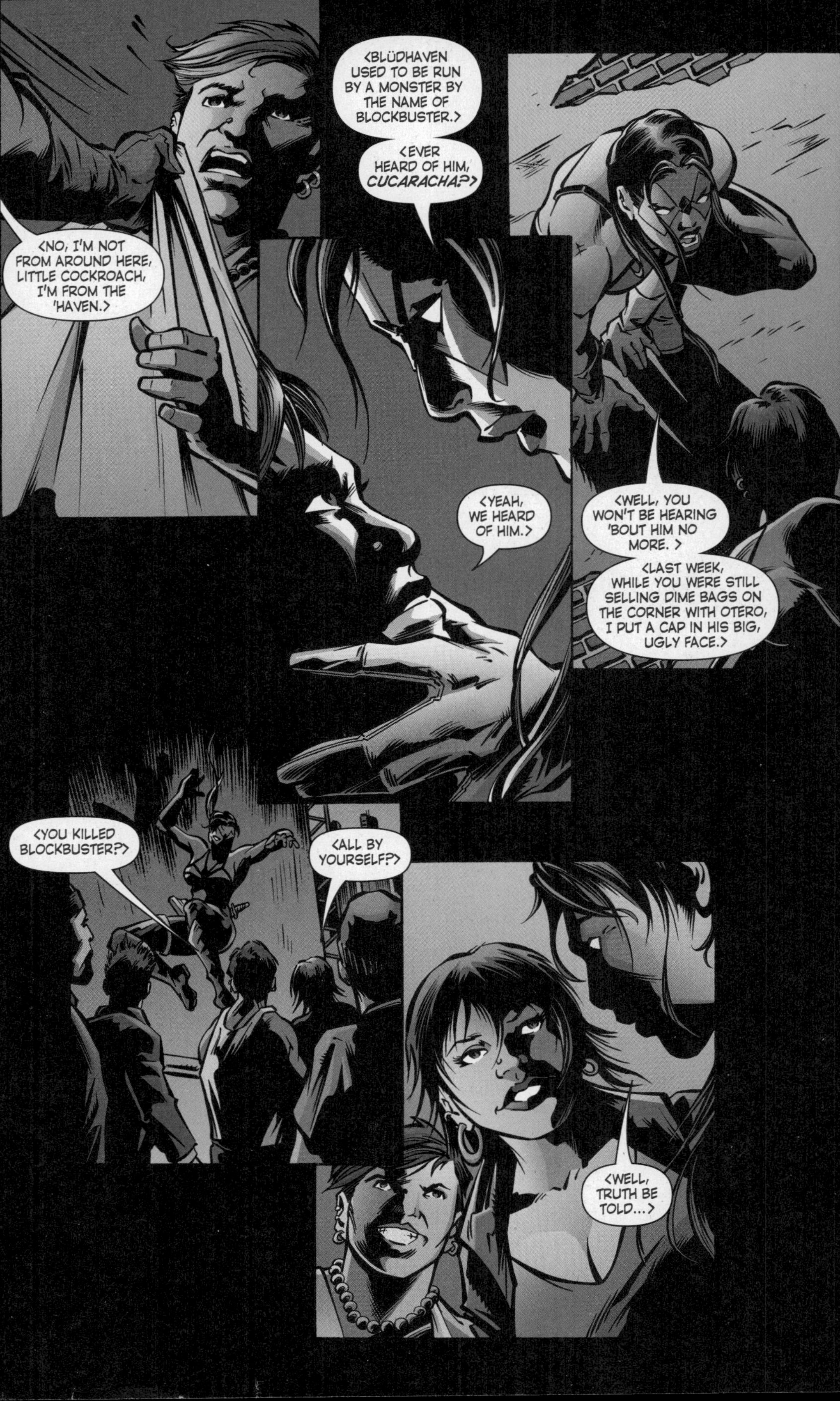
<NO, I'M NOT FROM AROUND HERE, LITTLE COCKROACH, I'M FROM THE 'HAVEN.>
<BLÜDHAVEN USED TO BE RUN BY A MONSTER BY THE NAME OF BLOCKBUSTER.>
<EVER HEARD OF HIM, *CUCARACHA*?>
<YEAH, WE HEARD OF HIM.>
<WELL, YOU WON'T BE HEARING 'BOUT HIM NO MORE. >
<LAST WEEK, WHILE YOU WERE STILL SELLING DIME BAGS ON THE CORNER WITH OTERO, I PUT A CAP IN HIS BIG, UGLY FACE.>
<YOU KILLED BLOCKBUSTER?>
<ALL BY YOURSELF?>
<WELL, TRUTH BE TOLD...>

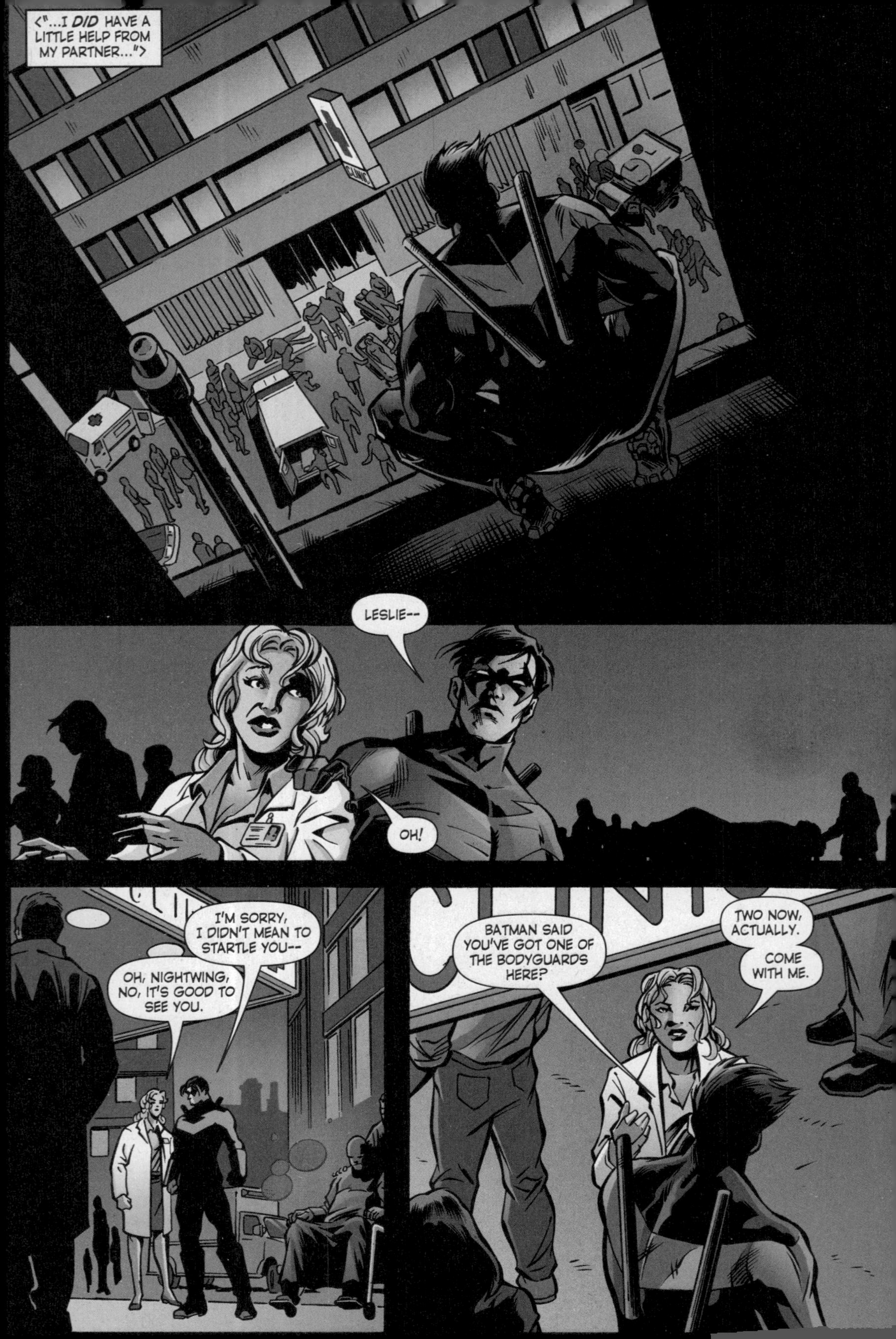

<"...I *DID* HAVE A LITTLE HELP FROM MY PARTNER...">
CLINIC
LESLIE--
OH!
I'M SORRY, I DIDN'T MEAN TO STARTLE YOU--
OH, NIGHTWING, NO, IT'S GOOD TO SEE YOU.
BATMAN SAID YOU'VE GOT ONE OF THE BODYGUARDS HERE?
TWO NOW, ACTUALLY.
COME WITH ME.

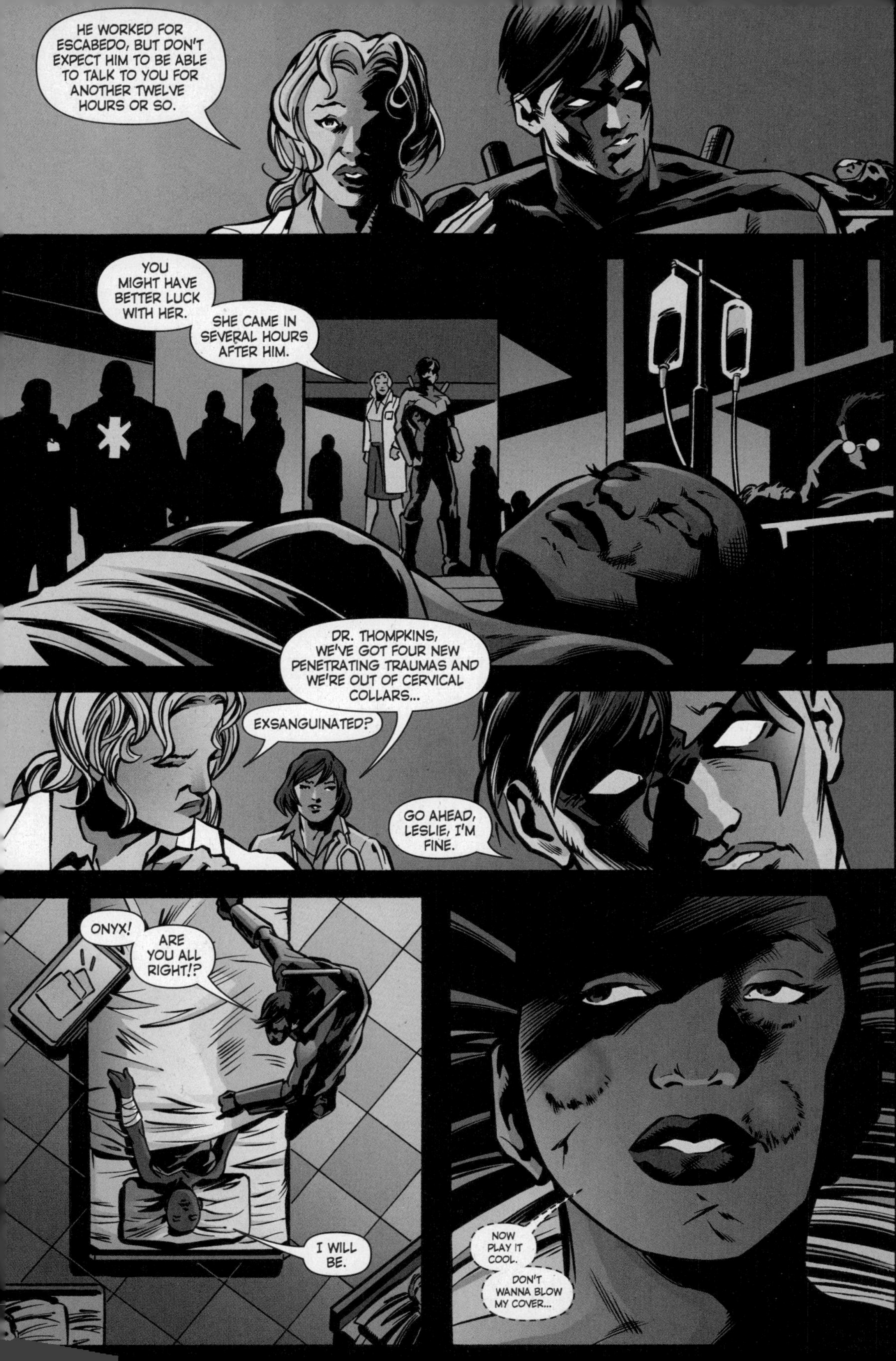
HE WORKED FOR ESCABEDO, BUT DON'T EXPECT HIM TO BE ABLE TO TALK TO YOU FOR ANOTHER TWELVE HOURS OR SO.
YOU MIGHT HAVE BETTER LUCK WITH HER.
SHE CAME IN SEVERAL HOURS AFTER HIM.
DR. THOMPKINS, WE'VE GOT FOUR NEW PENETRATING TRAUMAS AND WE'RE OUT OF CERVICAL COLLARS...
EXSANGUINATED?
GO AHEAD, LESLIE, I'M FINE.
ONYX!
ARE YOU ALL RIGHT!?
I WILL BE.
NOW PLAY IT COOL.
DON'T WANNA BLOW MY COVER...

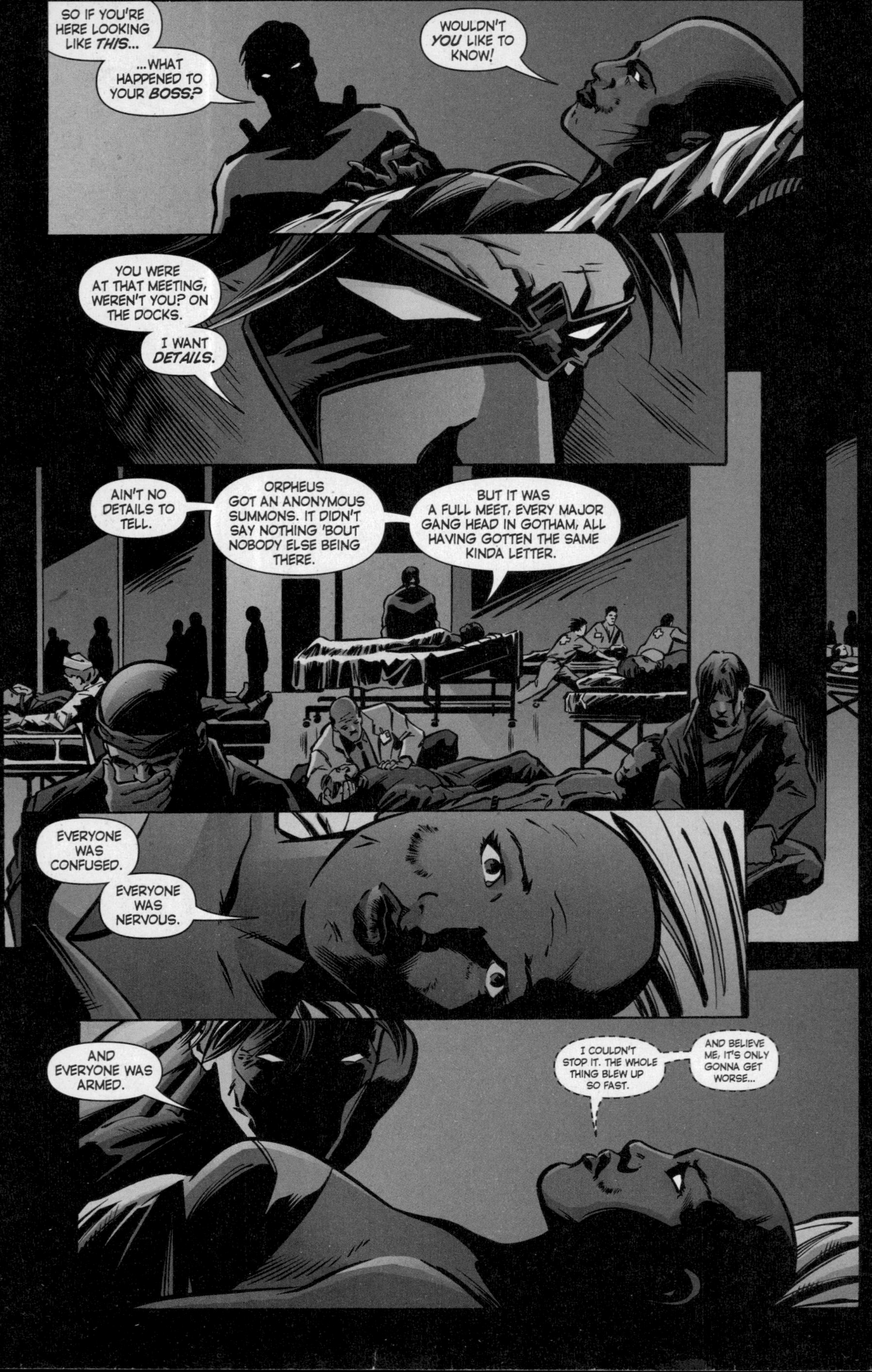
SO IF YOU'RE HERE LOOKING LIKE *THIS*...
...WHAT HAPPENED TO YOUR *BOSS?*
WOULDN'T *YOU* LIKE TO KNOW!
YOU WERE AT THAT MEETING, WEREN'T YOU? ON THE DOCKS.
I WANT *DETAILS*.
AIN'T NO DETAILS TO TELL.
ORPHEUS GOT AN ANONYMOUS SUMMONS. IT DIDN'T SAY NOTHING 'BOUT NOBODY ELSE BEING THERE.
BUT IT WAS A FULL MEET, EVERY MAJOR GANG HEAD IN GOTHAM, ALL HAVING GOTTEN THE SAME KINDA LETTER.
EVERYONE WAS CONFUSED.
EVERYONE WAS NERVOUS.
AND EVERYONE WAS ARMED.
I COULDN'T STOP IT. THE WHOLE THING BLEW UP SO FAST.
AND BELIEVE ME, IT'S ONLY GONNA GET WORSE...

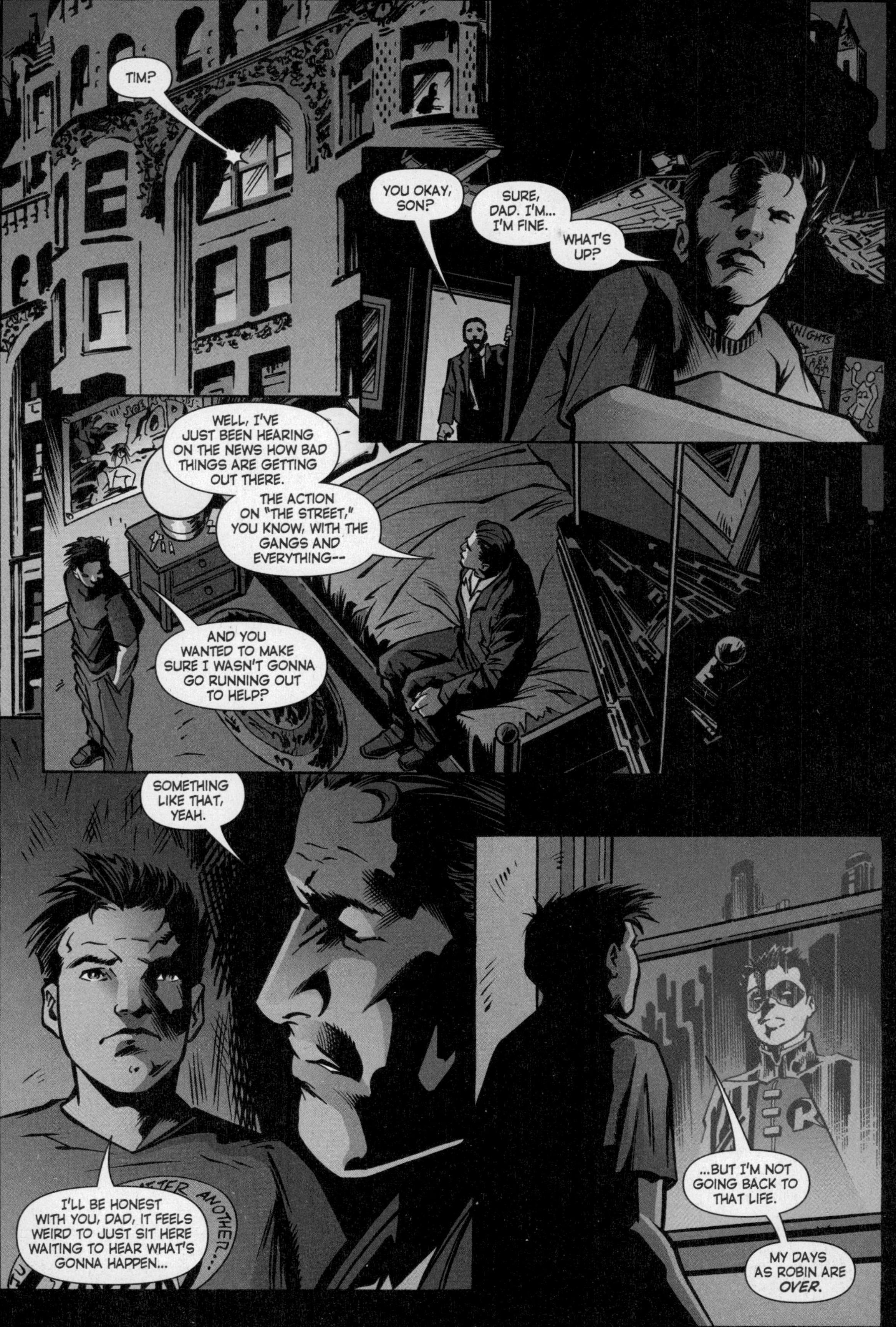
TIM?
YOU OKAY, SON?
SURE, DAD. I'M... I'M FINE.
WHAT'S UP?
KNIGHTS
WELL, I'VE JUST BEEN HEARING ON THE NEWS HOW BAD THINGS ARE GETTING OUT THERE.
THE ACTION ON "THE STREET," YOU KNOW, WITH THE GANGS AND EVERYTHING--
AND YOU WANTED TO MAKE SURE I WASN'T GONNA GO RUNNING OUT TO HELP?
SOMETHING LIKE THAT, YEAH.
I'LL BE HONEST WITH YOU, DAD, IT FEELS WEIRD TO JUST SIT HERE WAITING TO HEAR WHAT'S GONNA HAPPEN...
...BUT I'M NOT GOING BACK TO THAT LIFE.
MY DAYS AS ROBIN ARE *OVER*.

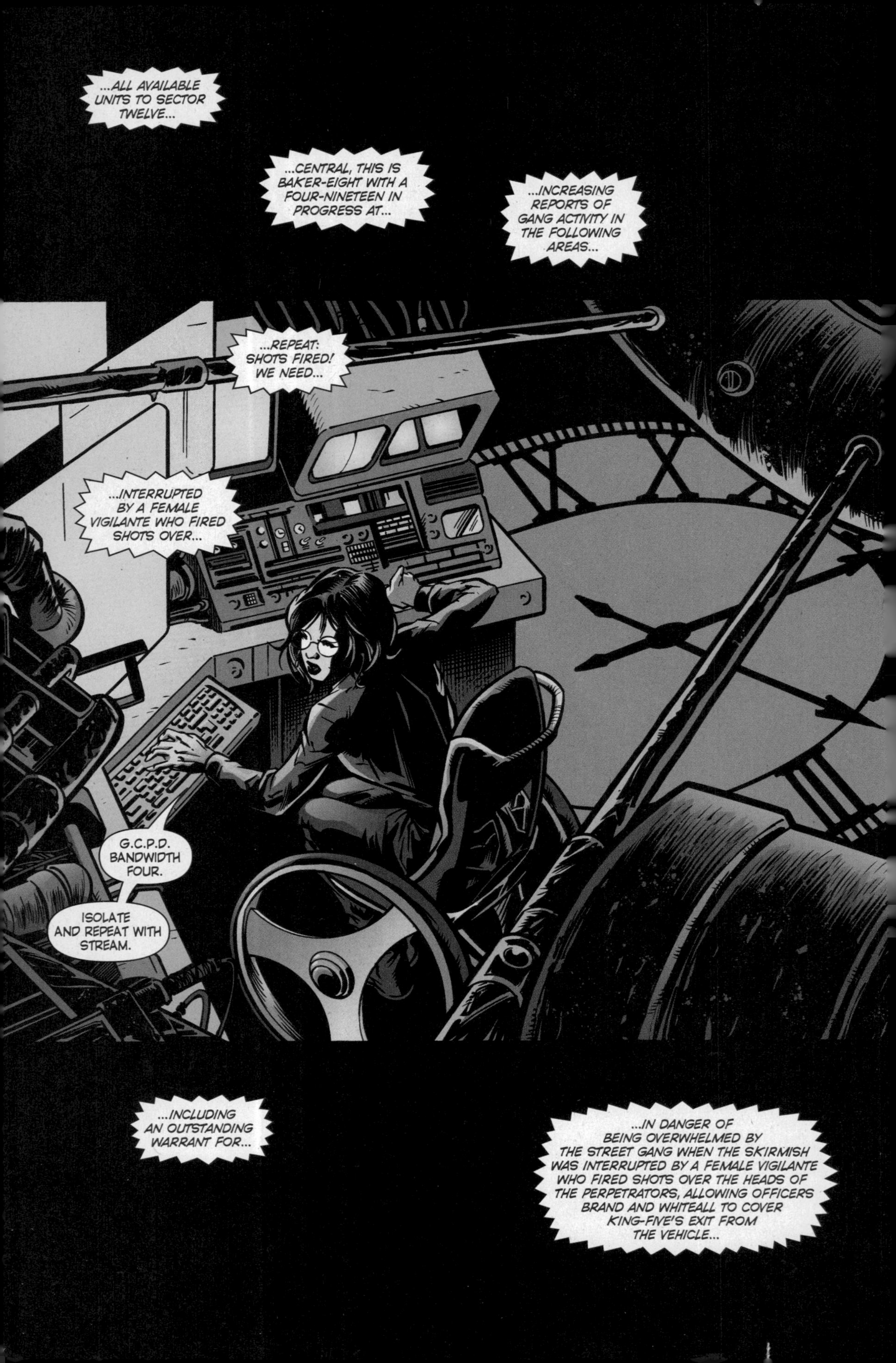
...ALL AVAILABLE UNITS TO SECTOR TWELVE...
...CENTRAL, THIS IS BAKER-EIGHT WITH A FOUR-NINETEEN IN PROGRESS AT...
...INCREASING REPORTS OF GANG ACTIVITY IN THE FOLLOWING AREAS...
...REPEAT: SHOTS FIRED! WE NEED...
...INTERRUPTED BY A FEMALE VIGILANTE WHO FIRED SHOTS OVER...
G.C.P.D. BANDWIDTH FOUR.
ISOLATE AND REPEAT WITH STREAM.
...INCLUDING AN OUTSTANDING WARRANT FOR...
...IN DANGER OF BEING OVERWHELMED BY THE STREET GANG WHEN THE SKIRMISH WAS INTERRUPTED BY A FEMALE VIGILANTE WHO FIRED SHOTS OVER THE HEADS OF THE PERPETRATORS, ALLOWING OFFICERS BRAND AND WHITEALL TO COVER KING-FIVE'S EXIT FROM THE VEHICLE...

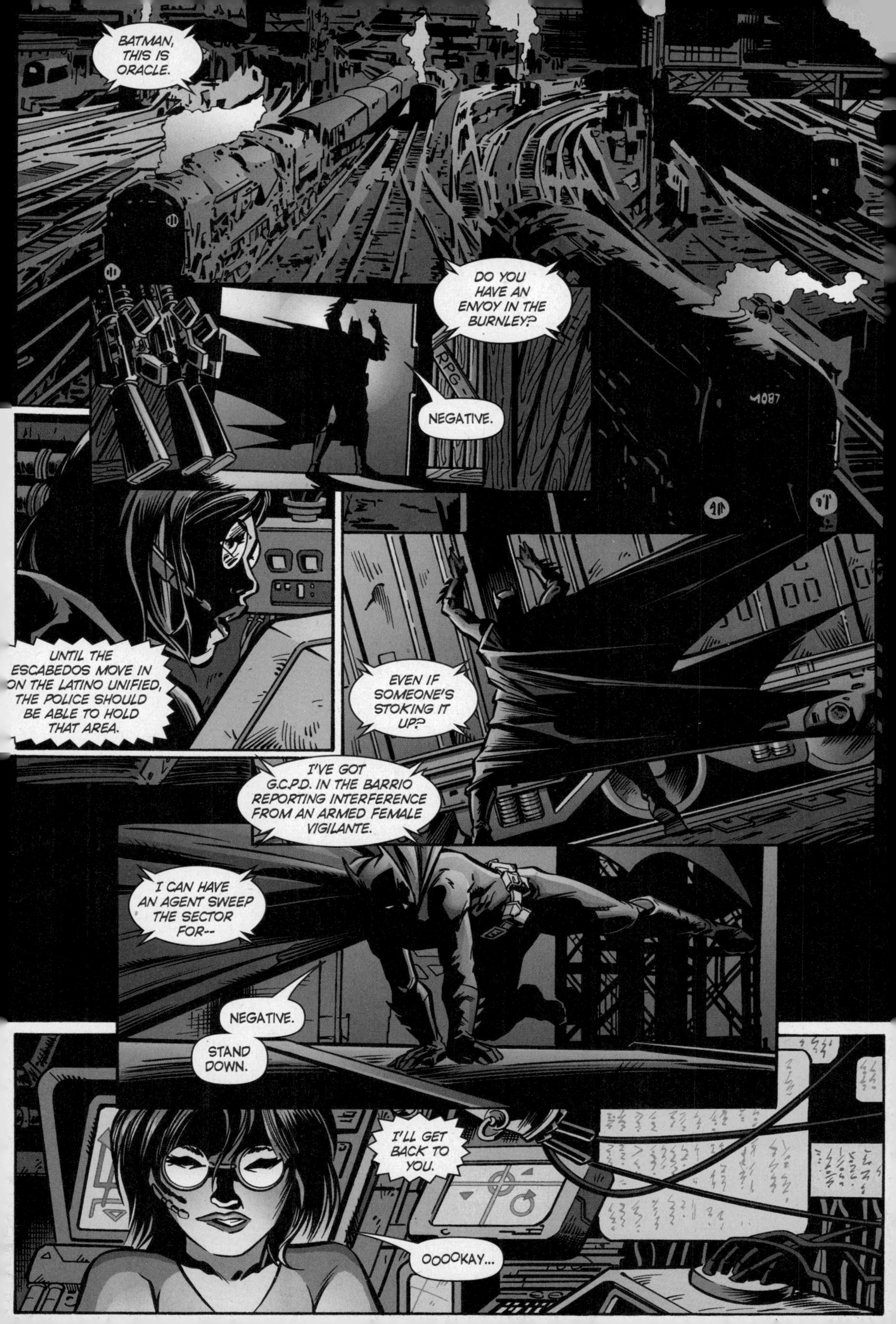
BATMAN, THIS IS ORACLE.
DO YOU HAVE AN ENVOY IN THE BURNLEY?
NEGATIVE.
UNTIL THE ESCABEDOS MOVE IN ON THE LATINO UNIFIED, THE POLICE SHOULD BE ABLE TO HOLD THAT AREA.
EVEN IF SOMEONE'S STOKING IT UP?
I'VE GOT G.C.P.D. IN THE BARRIO REPORTING INTERFERENCE FROM AN ARMED FEMALE VIGILANTE.
I CAN HAVE AN AGENT SWEEP THE SECTOR FOR--
NEGATIVE.
STAND DOWN.
I'LL GET BACK TO YOU.
OOOOKAY...

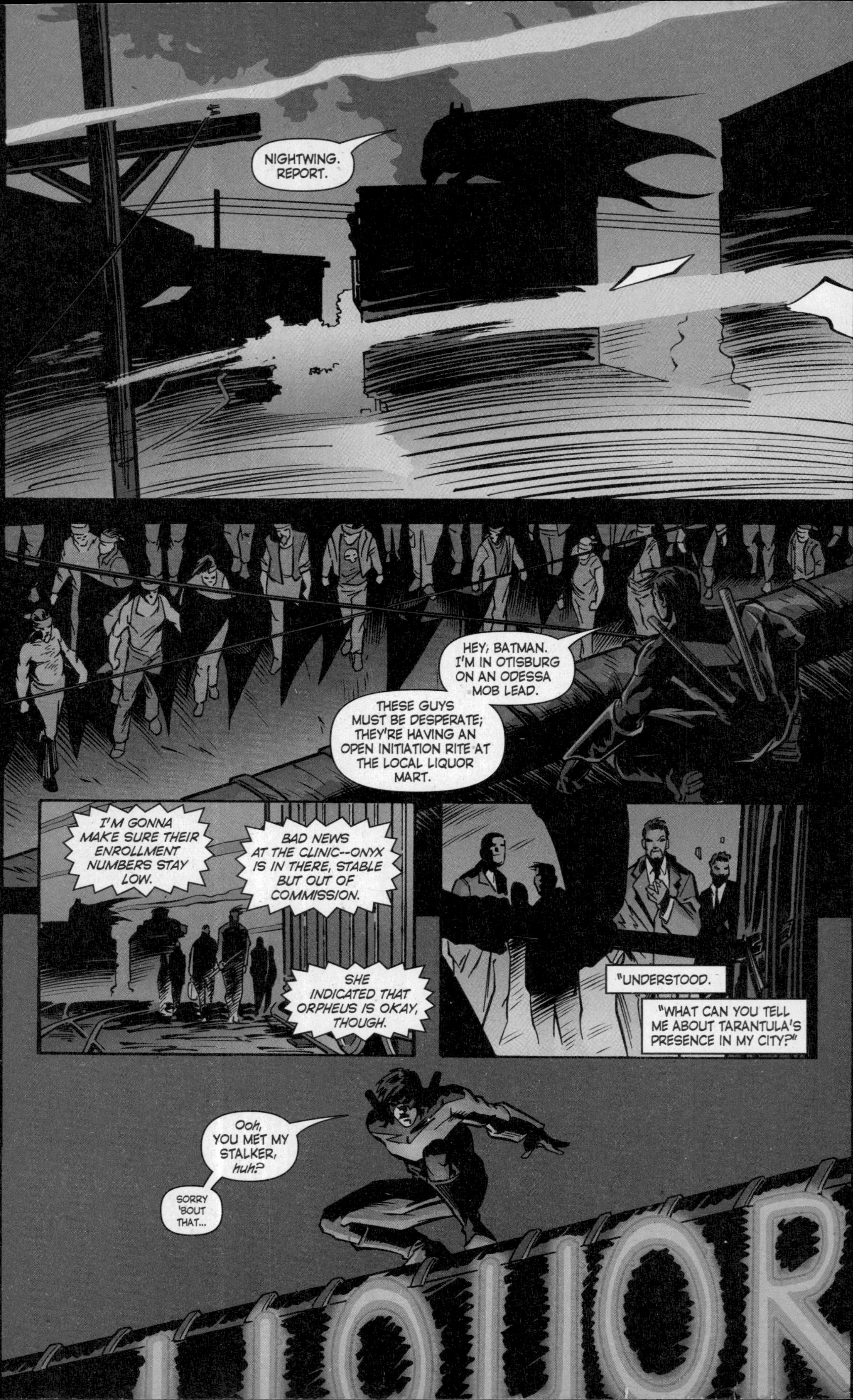
NIGHTWING. REPORT.
HEY, BATMAN. I'M IN OTISBURG ON AN ODESSA MOB LEAD.
THESE GUYS MUST BE DESPERATE; THEY'RE HAVING AN OPEN INITIATION RITE AT THE LOCAL LIQUOR MART.
I'M GONNA MAKE SURE THEIR ENROLLMENT NUMBERS STAY LOW.
BAD NEWS AT THE CLINIC--ONYX IS IN THERE, STABLE BUT OUT OF COMMISSION.
SHE INDICATED THAT ORPHEUS IS OKAY, THOUGH.
"UNDERSTOOD.
"WHAT CAN YOU TELL ME ABOUT TARANTULA'S PRESENCE IN MY CITY?"
Ooh, YOU MET MY STALKER, huh?
SORRY 'BOUT THAT...
LIQUOR

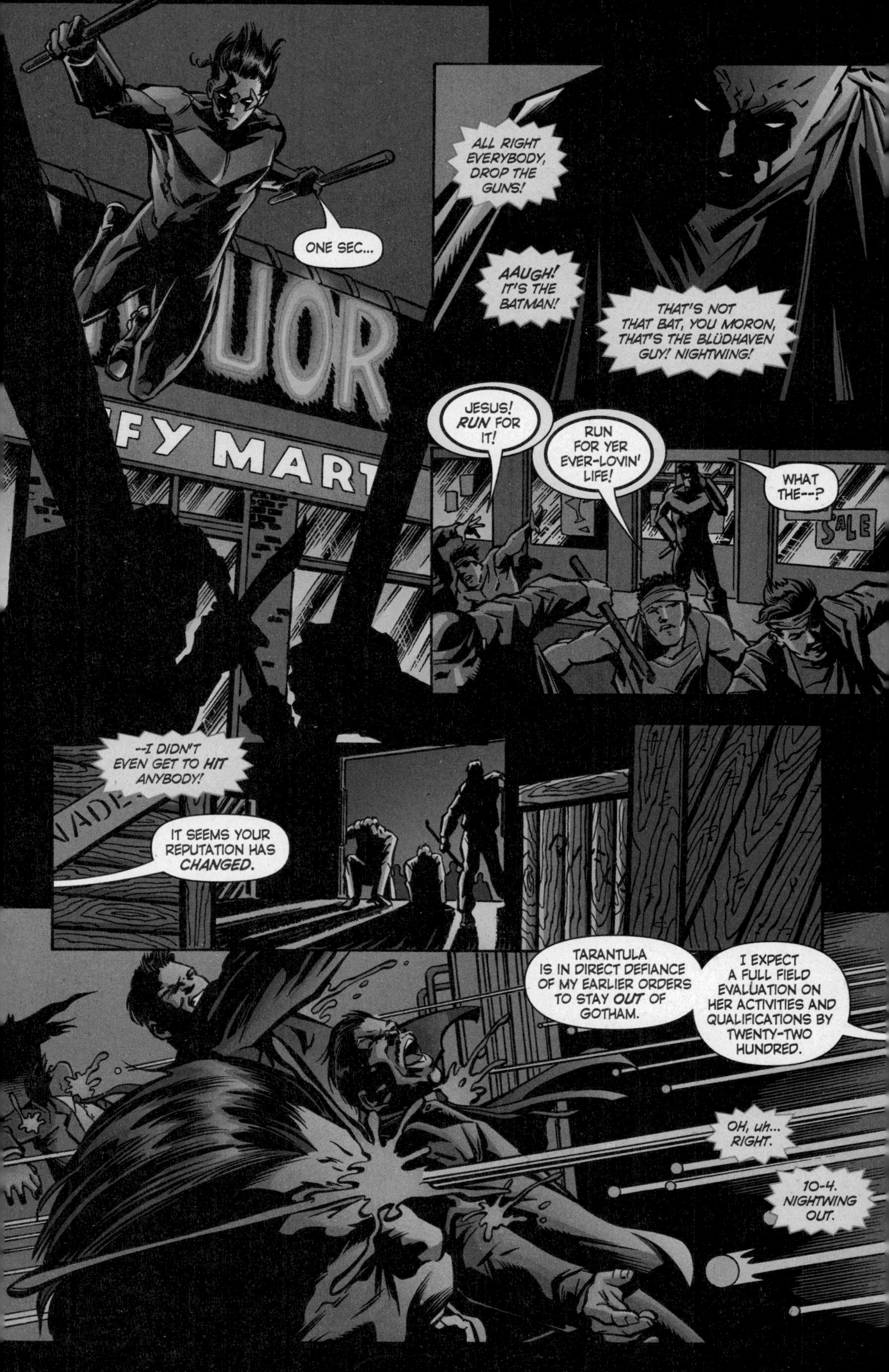
ONE SEC...
UOR
FY MART
ALL RIGHT EVERYBODY, DROP THE GUNS!
AAUGH! IT'S THE BATMAN!
THAT'S NOT THAT BAT, YOU MORON, THAT'S THE BLÜDHAVEN GUY! NIGHTWING!
JESUS! RUN FOR IT!
RUN FOR YER EVER-LOVIN' LIFE!
WHAT THE--?
SALE
--I DIDN'T EVEN GET TO HIT ANYBODY!
IT SEEMS YOUR REPUTATION HAS CHANGED.
TARANTULA IS IN DIRECT DEFIANCE OF MY EARLIER ORDERS TO STAY OUT OF GOTHAM.
I EXPECT A FULL FIELD EVALUATION ON HER ACTIVITIES AND QUALIFICATIONS BY TWENTY-TWO HUNDRED.
OH, uh... RIGHT.
10-4. NIGHTWING OUT.

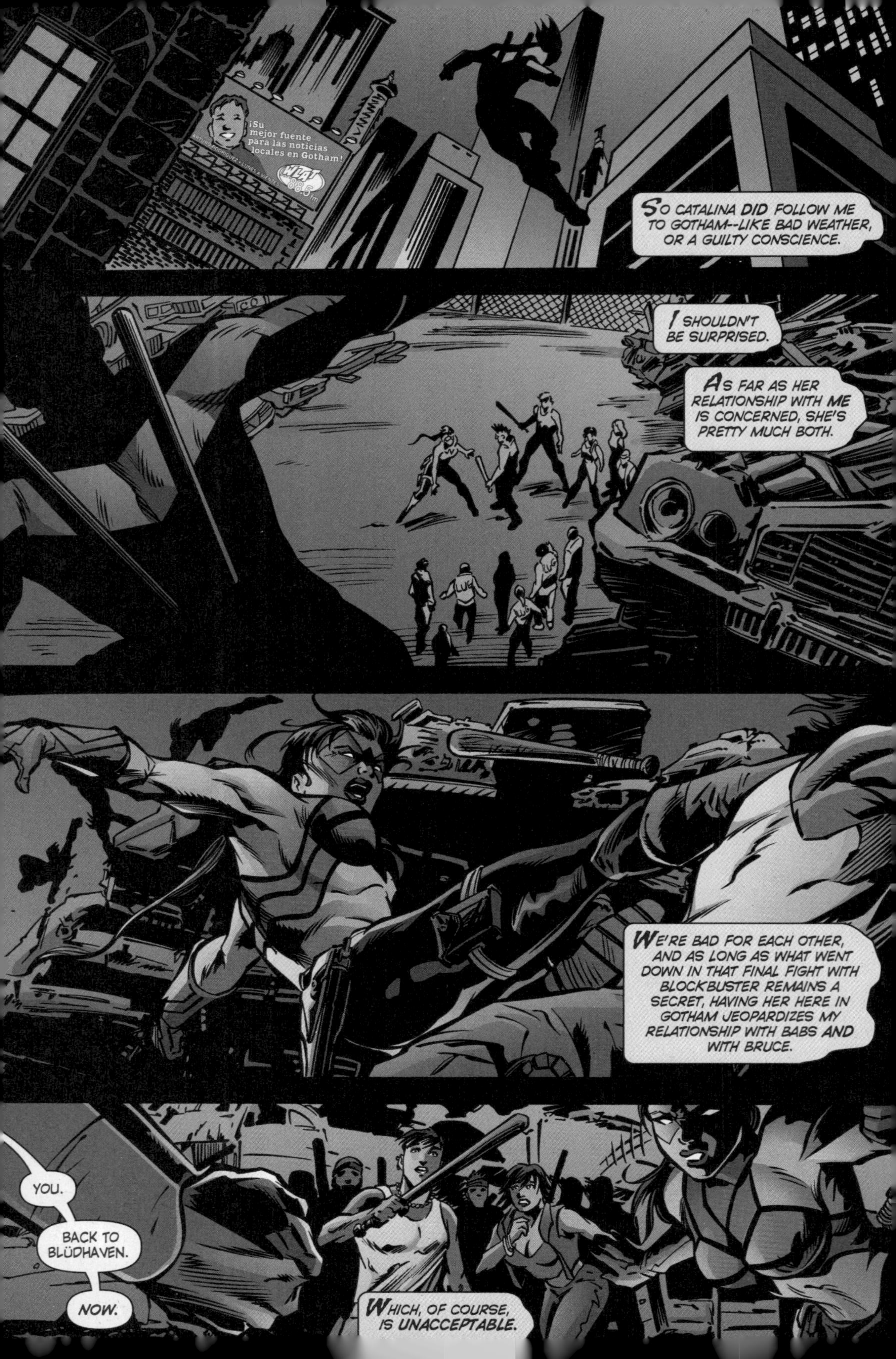
¡Su mejor fuente para las noticias locales en Gotham!
SO CATALINA DID FOLLOW ME TO GOTHAM--LIKE BAD WEATHER, OR A GUILTY CONSCIENCE.
I SHOULDN'T BE SURPRISED.
AS FAR AS HER RELATIONSHIP WITH ME IS CONCERNED, SHE'S PRETTY MUCH BOTH.
WE'RE BAD FOR EACH OTHER, AND AS LONG AS WHAT WENT DOWN IN THAT FINAL FIGHT WITH BLOCKBUSTER REMAINS A SECRET, HAVING HER HERE IN GOTHAM JEOPARDIZES MY RELATIONSHIP WITH BABS AND WITH BRUCE.
YOU.
BACK TO BLÜDHAVEN.
NOW.
WHICH, OF COURSE, IS UNACCEPTABLE.

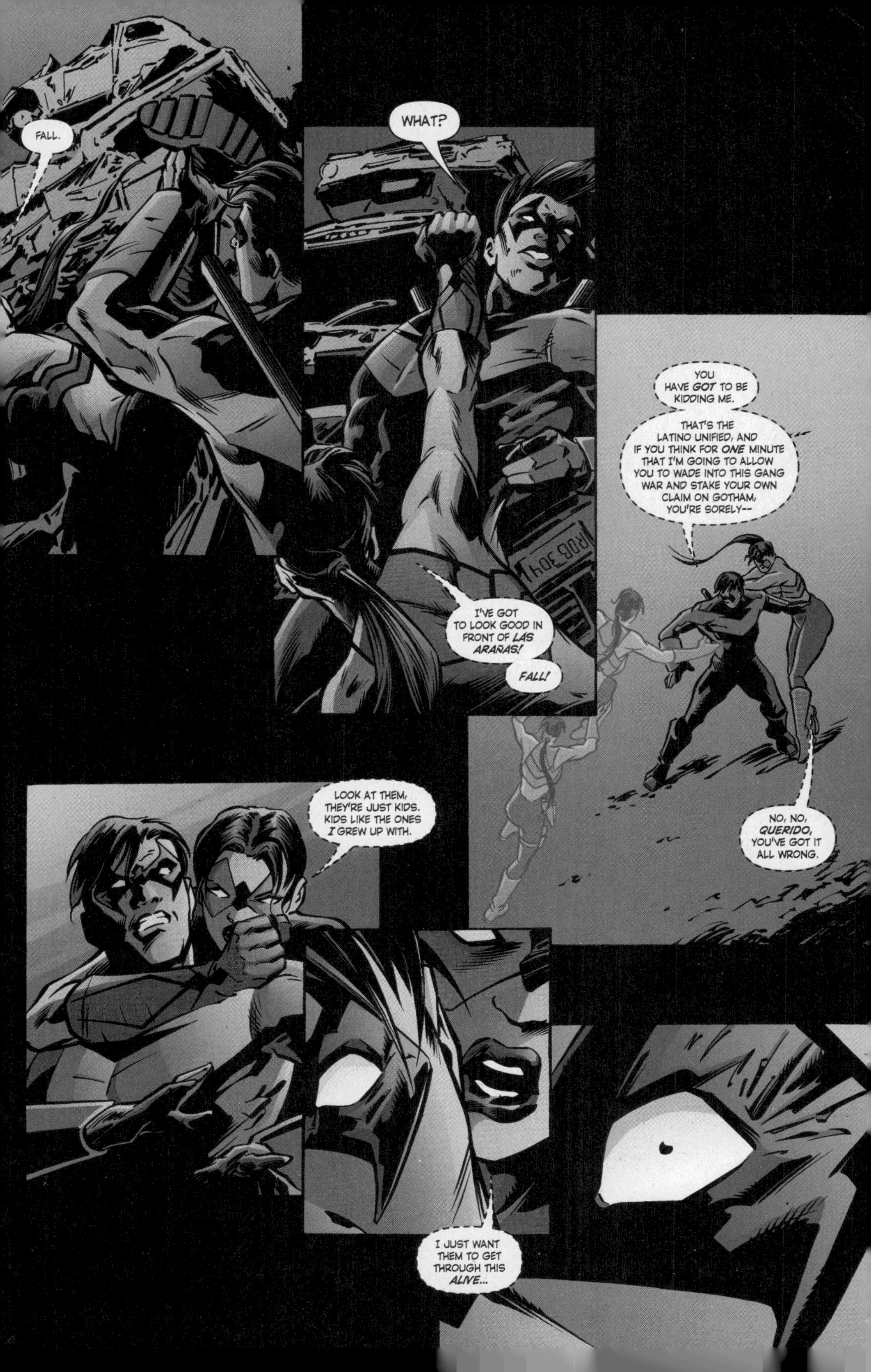
FALL.
WHAT?
I'VE GOT TO LOOK GOOD IN FRONT OF *LAS ARAÑAS!*
*FALL!*
YOU HAVE *GOT* TO BE KIDDING ME.
THAT'S THE LATINO UNIFIED, AND IF YOU THINK FOR *ONE* MINUTE THAT I'M GOING TO ALLOW YOU TO WADE INTO THIS GANG WAR AND STAKE YOUR OWN CLAIM ON GOTHAM, YOU'RE SORELY--
NO, NO, *QUERIDO,* YOU'VE GOT IT ALL WRONG.
LOOK AT THEM, THEY'RE JUST KIDS. KIDS LIKE THE ONES *I* GREW UP WITH.
I JUST WANT THEM TO GET THROUGH THIS *ALIVE...*

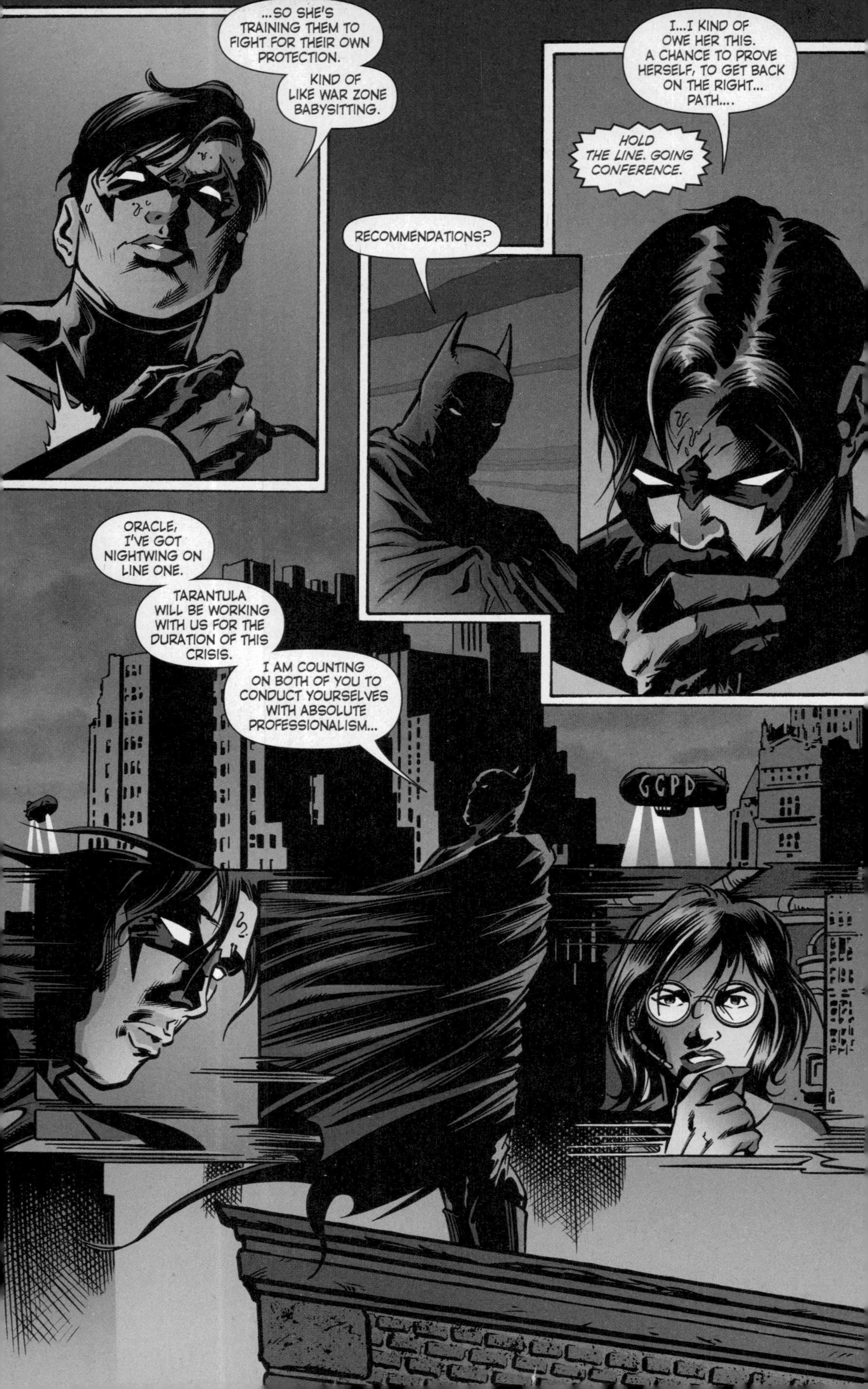
...SO SHE'S TRAINING THEM TO FIGHT FOR THEIR OWN PROTECTION.
KIND OF LIKE WAR ZONE BABYSITTING.
I...I KIND OF OWE HER THIS. A CHANCE TO PROVE HERSELF, TO GET BACK ON THE RIGHT... PATH....
HOLD THE LINE. GOING CONFERENCE.
RECOMMENDATIONS?
ORACLE, I'VE GOT NIGHTWING ON LINE ONE.
TARANTULA WILL BE WORKING WITH US FOR THE DURATION OF THIS CRISIS.
I AM COUNTING ON BOTH OF YOU TO CONDUCT YOURSELVES WITH ABSOLUTE PROFESSIONALISM...
GCPD

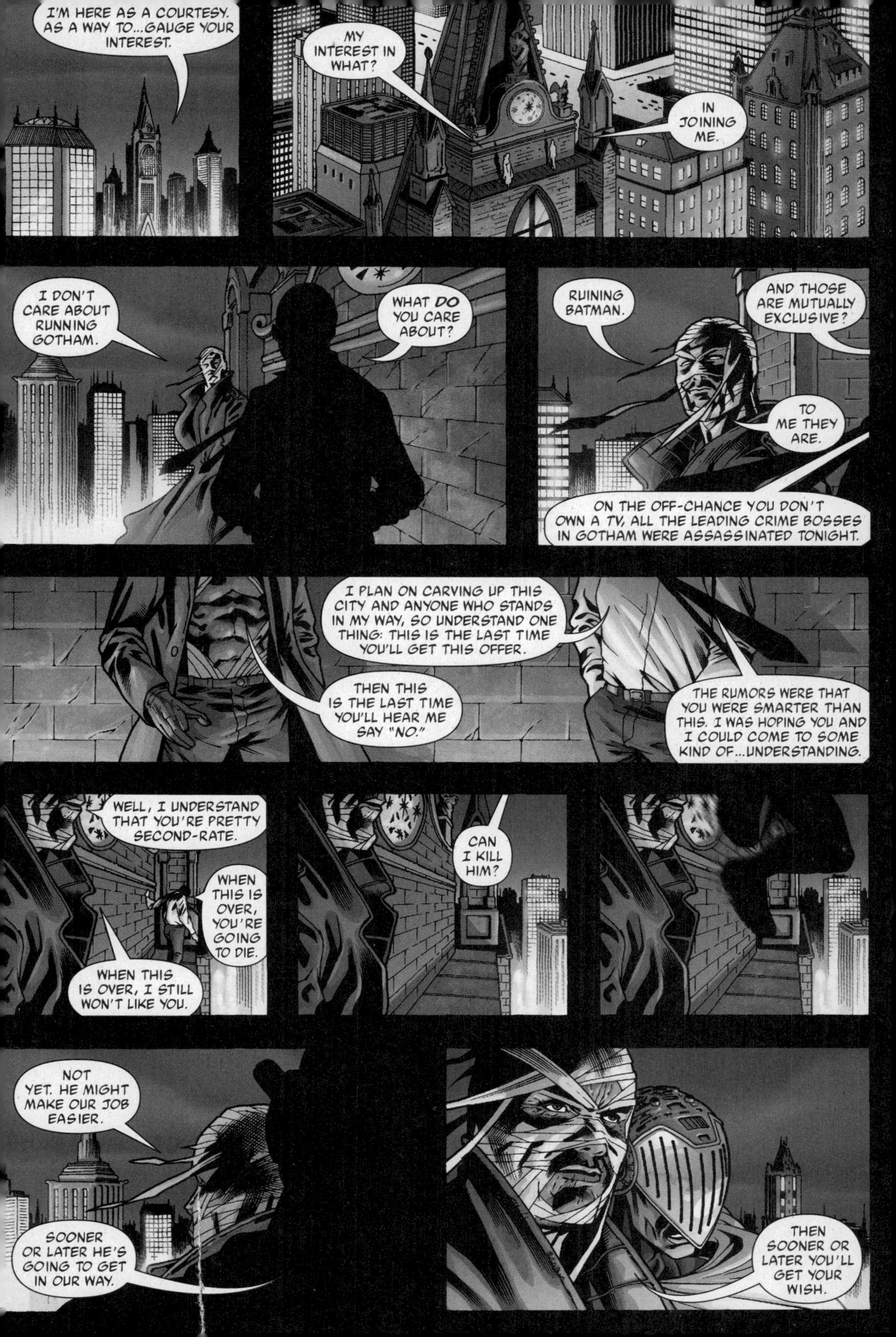

I'M HERE AS A COURTESY. AS A WAY TO...GAUGE YOUR INTEREST.
MY INTEREST IN WHAT?
IN JOINING ME.
I DON'T CARE ABOUT RUNNING GOTHAM.
WHAT DO YOU CARE ABOUT?
RUINING BATMAN.
AND THOSE ARE MUTUALLY EXCLUSIVE?
TO ME THEY ARE.
ON THE OFF-CHANCE YOU DON'T OWN A TV, ALL THE LEADING CRIME BOSSES IN GOTHAM WERE ASSASSINATED TONIGHT.
I PLAN ON CARVING UP THIS CITY AND ANYONE WHO STANDS IN MY WAY, SO UNDERSTAND ONE THING: THIS IS THE LAST TIME YOU'LL GET THIS OFFER.
THEN THIS IS THE LAST TIME YOU'LL HEAR ME SAY "NO."
THE RUMORS WERE THAT YOU WERE SMARTER THAN THIS. I WAS HOPING YOU AND I COULD COME TO SOME KIND OF...UNDERSTANDING.
WELL, I UNDERSTAND THAT YOU'RE PRETTY SECOND-RATE.
WHEN THIS IS OVER, YOU'RE GOING TO DIE.
WHEN THIS IS OVER, I STILL WON'T LIKE YOU.
CAN I KILL HIM?
NOT YET. HE MIGHT MAKE OUR JOB EASIER.
SOONER OR LATER HE'S GOING TO GET IN OUR WAY.
THEN SOONER OR LATER YOU'LL GET YOUR WISH.

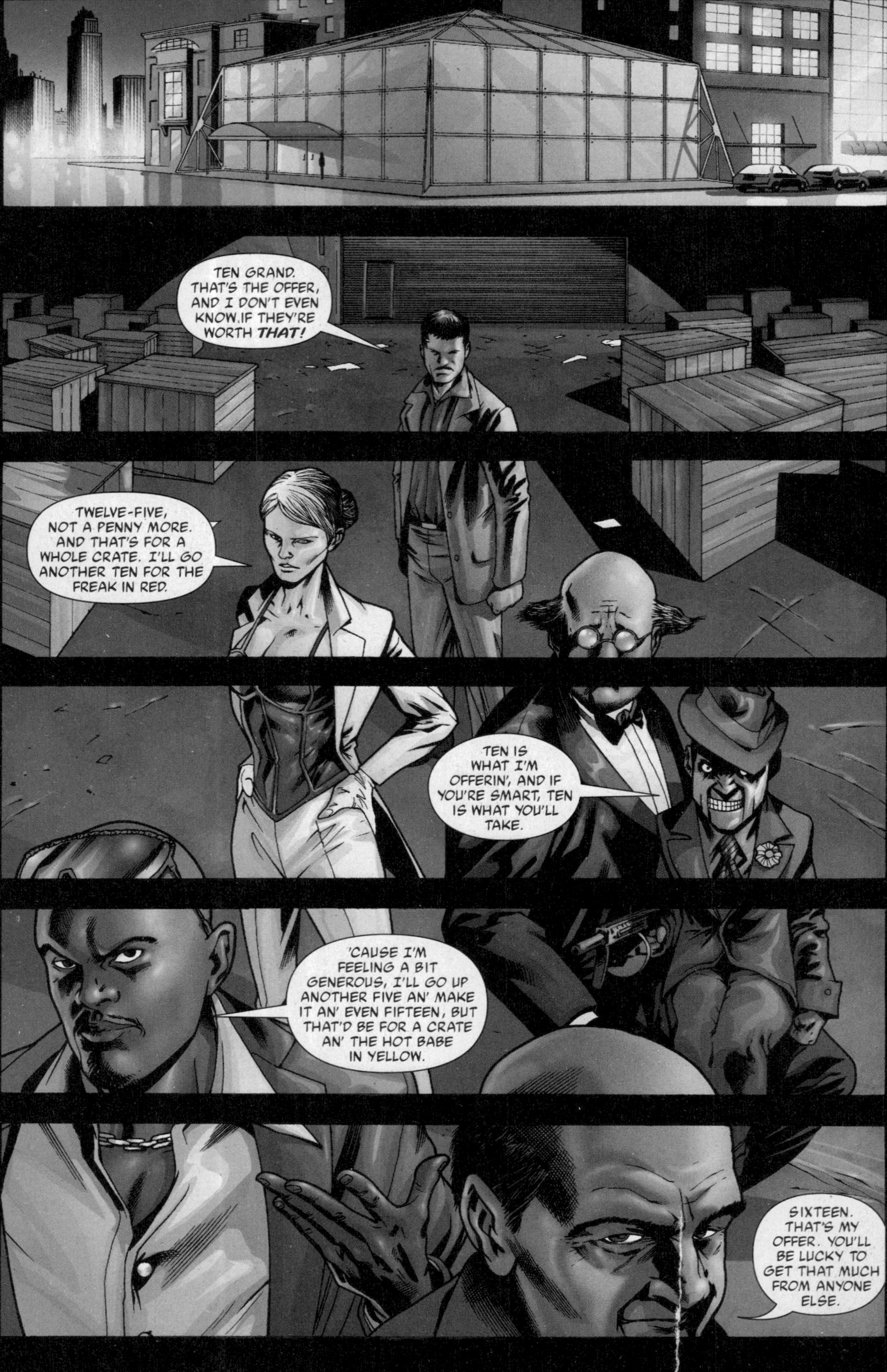
TEN GRAND. THAT'S THE OFFER, AND I DON'T EVEN KNOW IF THEY'RE WORTH **THAT!**
TWELVE-FIVE, NOT A PENNY MORE. AND THAT'S FOR A WHOLE CRATE. I'LL GO ANOTHER TEN FOR THE FREAK IN RED.
TEN IS WHAT I'M OFFERIN', AND IF YOU'RE SMART, TEN IS WHAT YOU'LL TAKE.
'CAUSE I'M FEELING A BIT GENEROUS, I'LL GO UP ANOTHER FIVE AN' MAKE IT AN' EVEN FIFTEEN, BUT THAT'D BE FOR A CRATE AN' THE HOT BABE IN YELLOW.
SIXTEEN. THAT'S MY OFFER. YOU'LL BE LUCKY TO GET THAT MUCH FROM ANYONE ELSE.

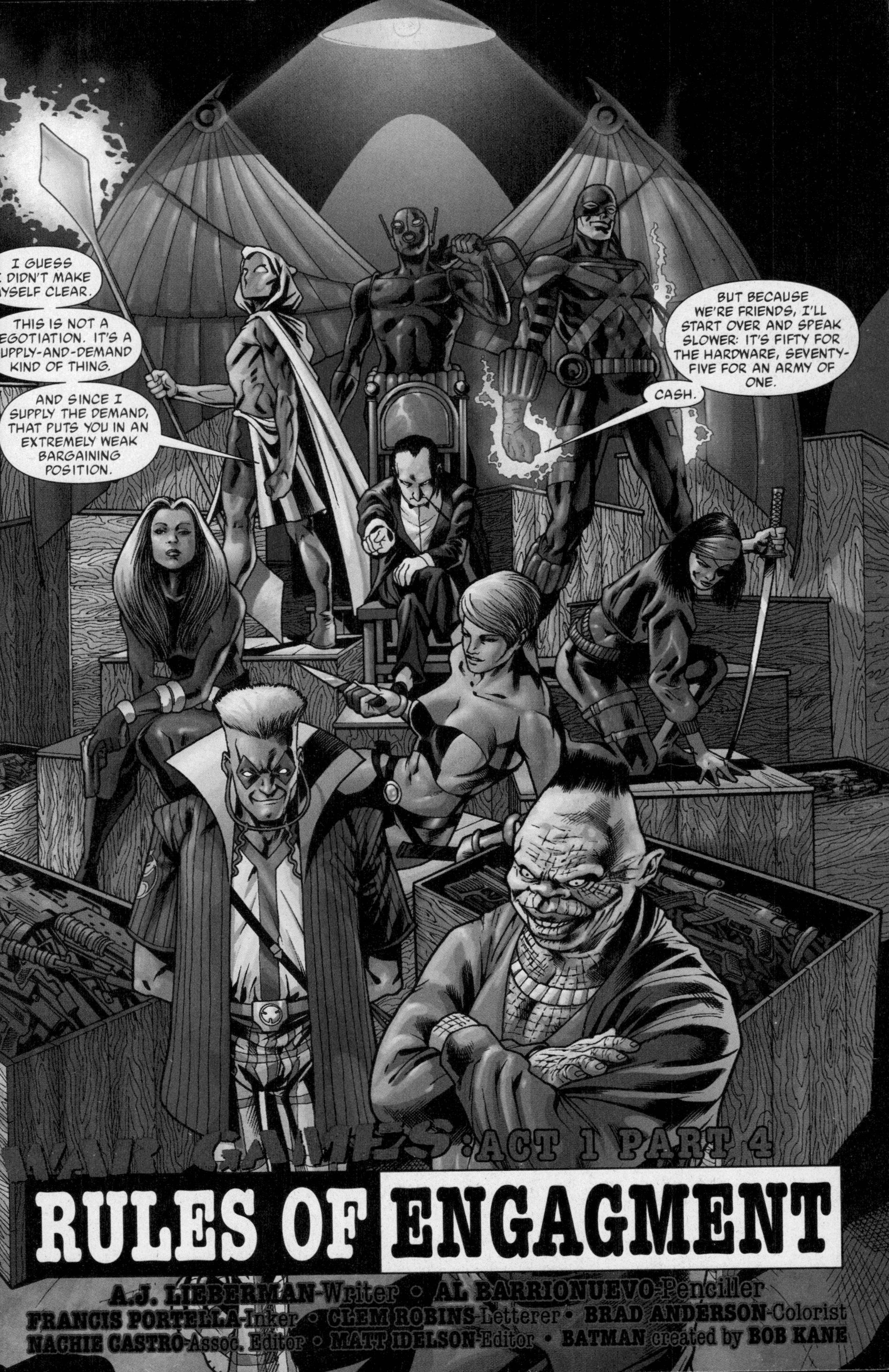
I GUESS DIDN'T MAKE YSELF CLEAR.
THIS IS NOT A EGOTIATION. IT'S A UPPLY-AND-DEMAND KIND OF THING.
AND SINCE I SUPPLY THE DEMAND, THAT PUTS YOU IN AN EXTREMELY WEAK BARGAINING POSITION.
BUT BECAUSE WE'RE FRIENDS, I'LL START OVER AND SPEAK SLOWER: IT'S FIFTY FOR THE HARDWARE, SEVENTY-FIVE FOR AN ARMY OF ONE.
CASH.
ACT 1 PART 4
RULES OF ENGAGMENT
A.J. LIEBERMAN-Writer • AL BARRIONUEVO-Penciller
FRANCIS PORTELLA-Inker • CLEM ROBINS-Letterer • BRAD ANDERSON-Colorist
NACHIE CASTRO-Assoc. Editor • MATT IDELSON-Editor • BATMAN created by BOB KANE

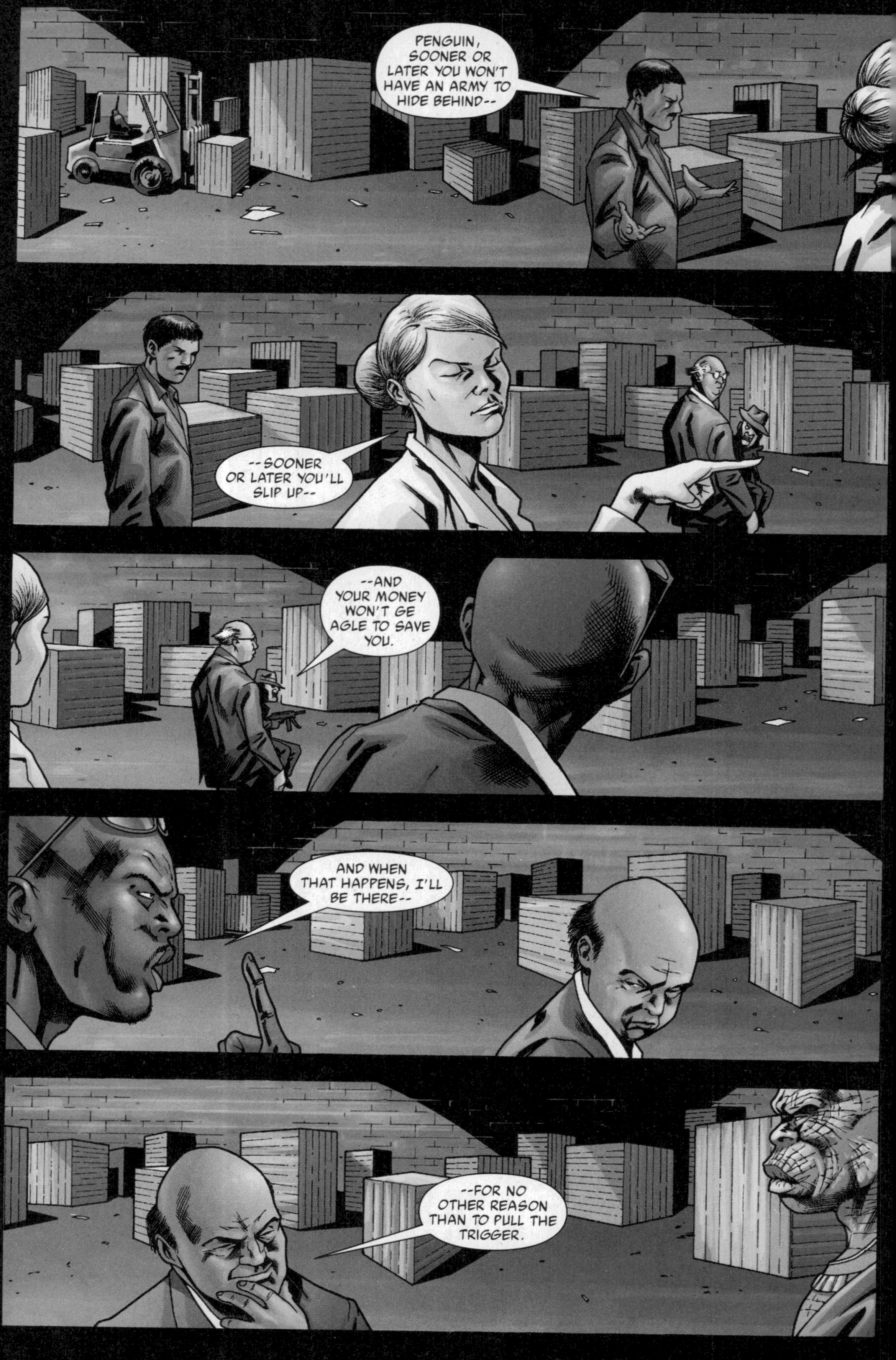
PENGUIN, SOONER OR LATER YOU WON'T HAVE AN ARMY TO HIDE BEHIND--
--SOONER OR LATER YOU'LL SLIP UP--
--AND YOUR MONEY WON'T GE AGLE TO SAVE YOU.
AND WHEN THAT HAPPENS, I'LL BE THERE--
--FOR NO OTHER REASON THAN TO PULL THE TRIGGER.

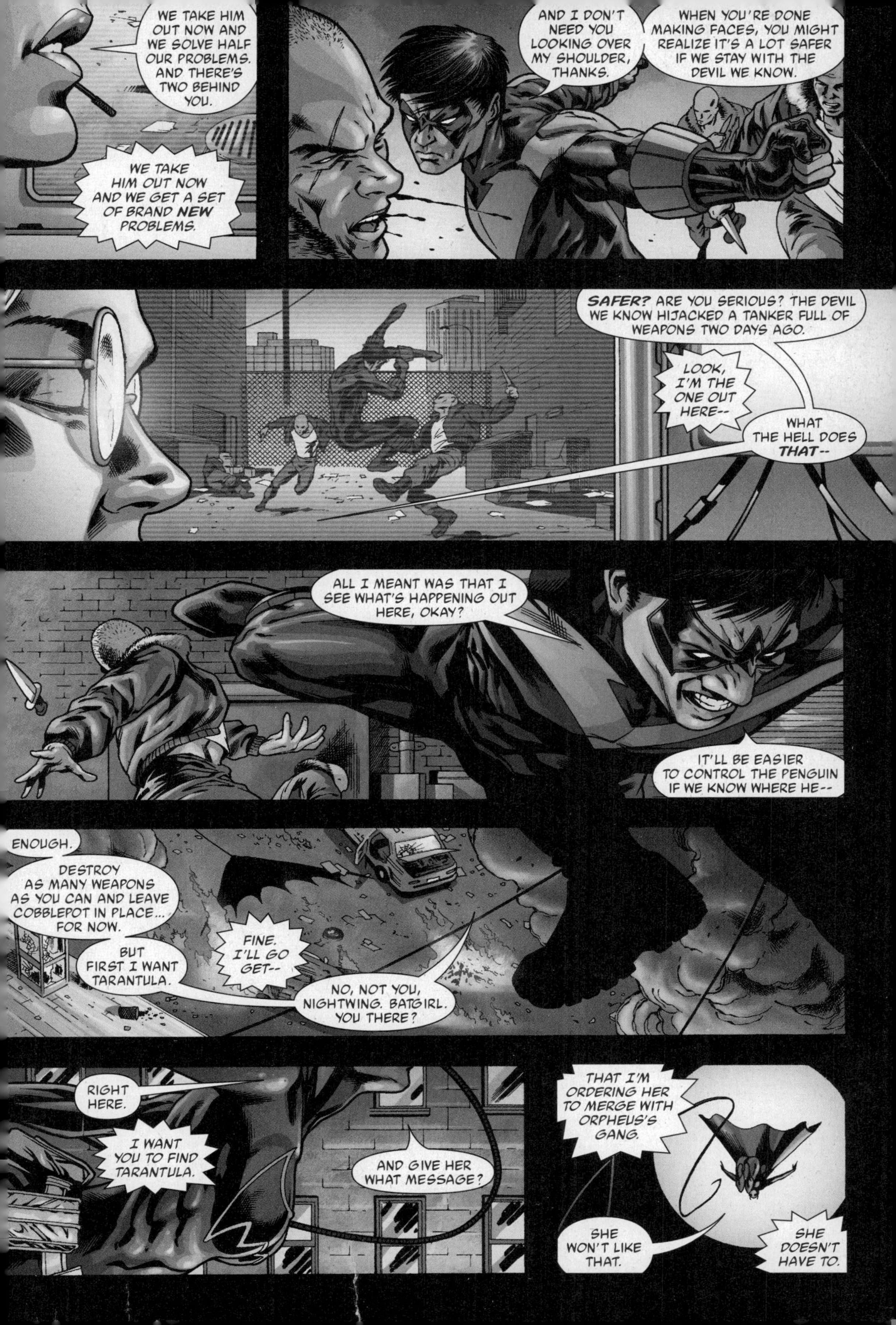
WE TAKE HIM OUT NOW AND WE SOLVE HALF OUR PROBLEMS. AND THERE'S TWO BEHIND YOU.
WE TAKE HIM OUT NOW AND WE GET A SET OF BRAND NEW PROBLEMS.
AND I DON'T NEED YOU LOOKING OVER MY SHOULDER, THANKS.
WHEN YOU'RE DONE MAKING FACES, YOU MIGHT REALIZE IT'S A LOT SAFER IF WE STAY WITH THE DEVIL WE KNOW.
SAFER? ARE YOU SERIOUS? THE DEVIL WE KNOW HIJACKED A TANKER FULL OF WEAPONS TWO DAYS AGO.
LOOK, I'M THE ONE OUT HERE--
WHAT THE HELL DOES THAT--
ALL I MEANT WAS THAT I SEE WHAT'S HAPPENING OUT HERE, OKAY?
IT'LL BE EASIER TO CONTROL THE PENGUIN IF WE KNOW WHERE HE--
ENOUGH.
DESTROY AS MANY WEAPONS AS YOU CAN AND LEAVE COBBLEPOT IN PLACE... FOR NOW.
BUT FIRST I WANT TARANTULA.
FINE. I'LL GO GET--
NO, NOT YOU, NIGHTWING. BATGIRL. YOU THERE?
RIGHT HERE.
I WANT YOU TO FIND TARANTULA.
AND GIVE HER WHAT MESSAGE?
THAT I'M ORDERING HER TO MERGE WITH ORPHEUS'S GANG.
SHE WON'T LIKE THAT.
SHE DOESN'T HAVE TO.

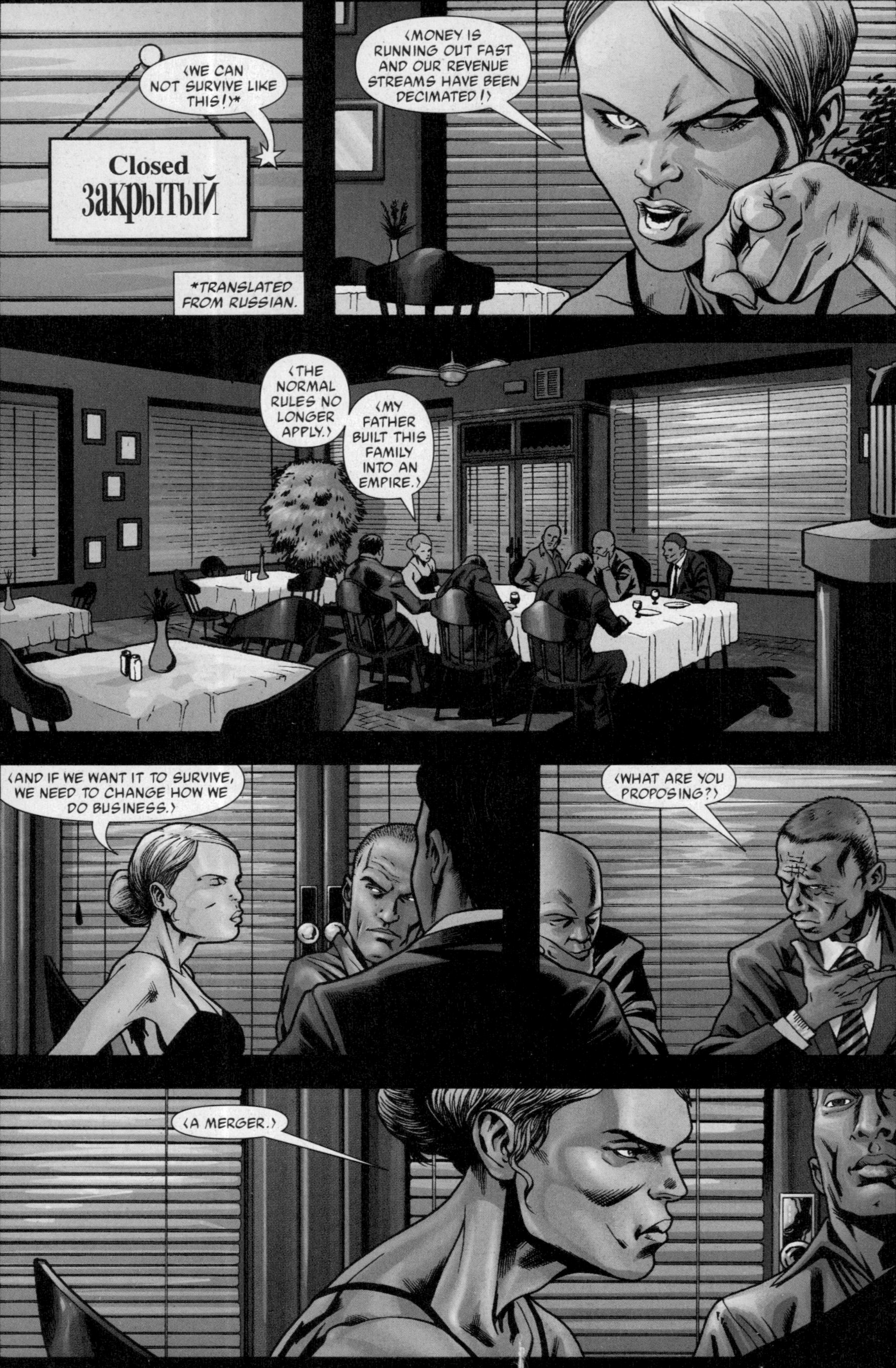
‹WE CAN NOT SURVIVE LIKE THIS!›*
Closed
ЗАКРЫТЫЙ
*TRANSLATED FROM RUSSIAN.
‹MONEY IS RUNNING OUT FAST AND OUR REVENUE STREAMS HAVE BEEN DECIMATED!›
‹THE NORMAL RULES NO LONGER APPLY.›
‹MY FATHER BUILT THIS FAMILY INTO AN EMPIRE.›
‹AND IF WE WANT IT TO SURVIVE, WE NEED TO CHANGE HOW WE DO BUSINESS.›
‹WHAT ARE YOU PROPOSING?›
‹A MERGER.›

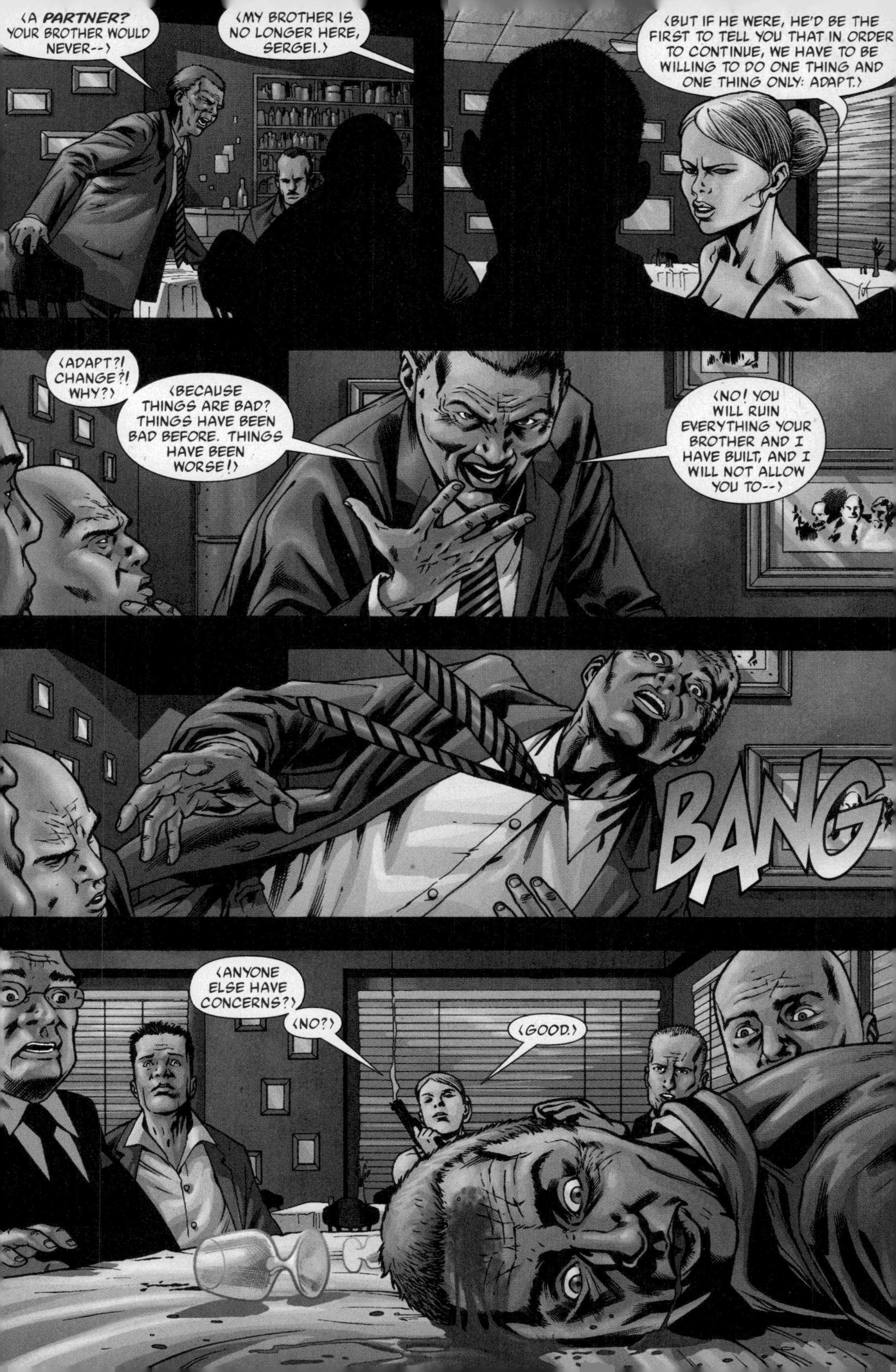

‹A PARTNER? YOUR BROTHER WOULD NEVER--›
‹MY BROTHER IS NO LONGER HERE, SERGEI.›
‹BUT IF HE WERE, HE'D BE THE FIRST TO TELL YOU THAT IN ORDER TO CONTINUE, WE HAVE TO BE WILLING TO DO ONE THING AND ONE THING ONLY: ADAPT.›
‹ADAPT?! CHANGE?! WHY?›
‹BECAUSE THINGS ARE BAD? THINGS HAVE BEEN BAD BEFORE. THINGS HAVE BEEN WORSE!›
‹NO! YOU WILL RUIN EVERYTHING YOUR BROTHER AND I HAVE BUILT, AND I WILL NOT ALLOW YOU TO--›
BANG
‹ANYONE ELSE HAVE CONCERNS?›
‹NO?›
‹GOOD.›

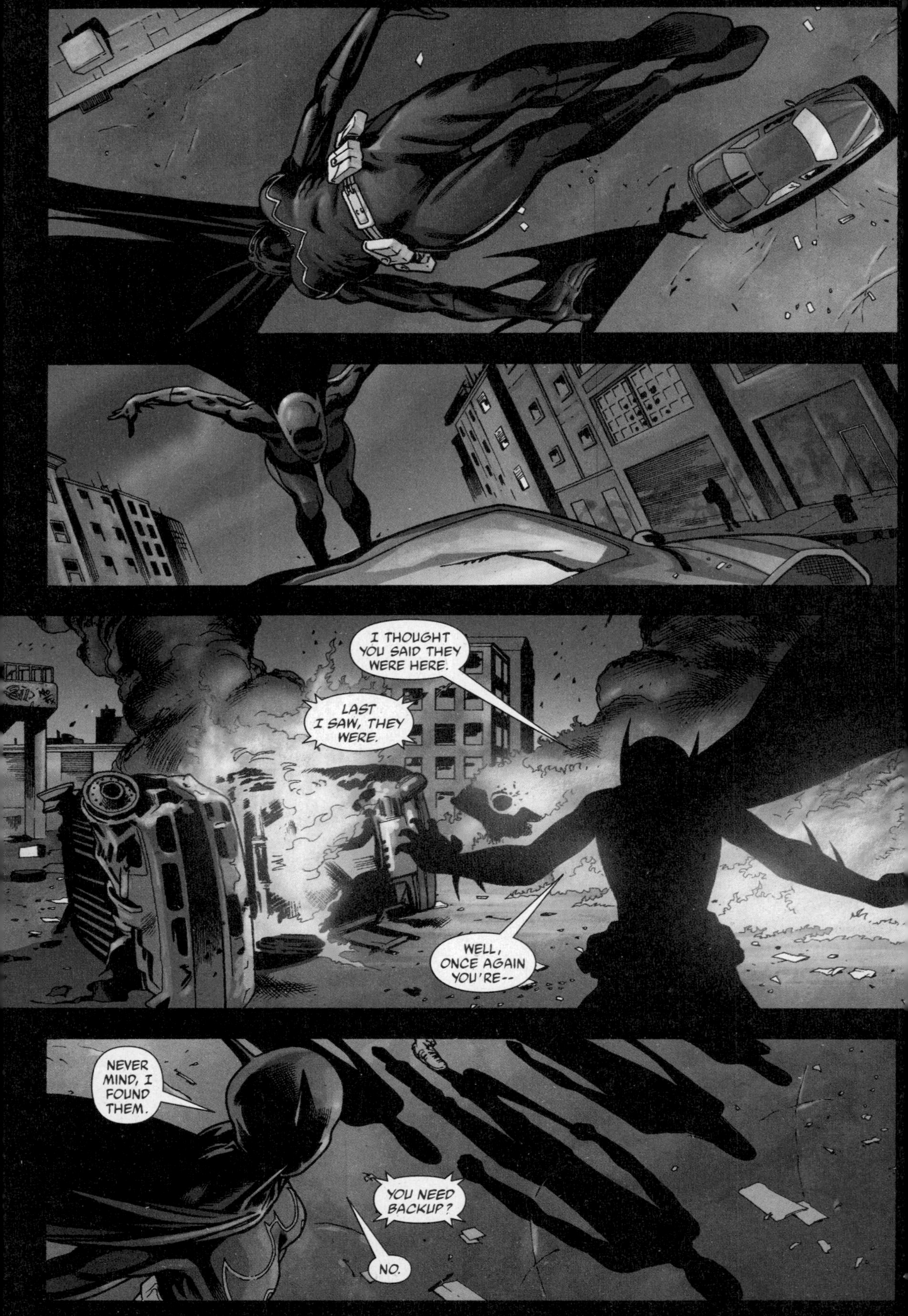
I THOUGHT YOU SAID THEY WERE HERE.
LAST I SAW, THEY WERE.
WELL, ONCE AGAIN YOU'RE--
NEVER MIND, I FOUND THEM.
YOU NEED BACKUP?
NO.

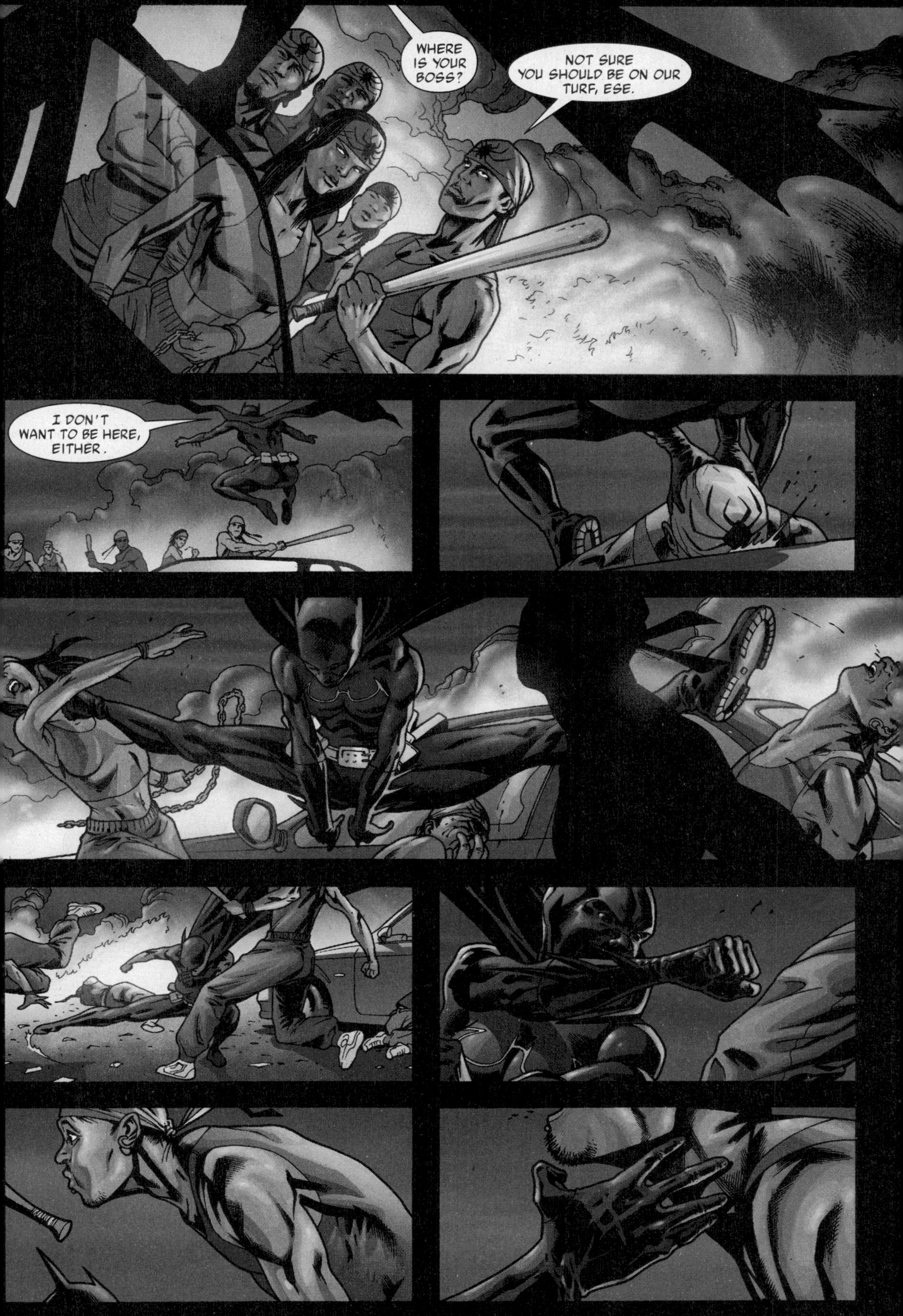
WHERE IS YOUR BOSS?
NOT SURE YOU SHOULD BE ON OUR TURF, ESE.
I DON'T WANT TO BE HERE, EITHER.

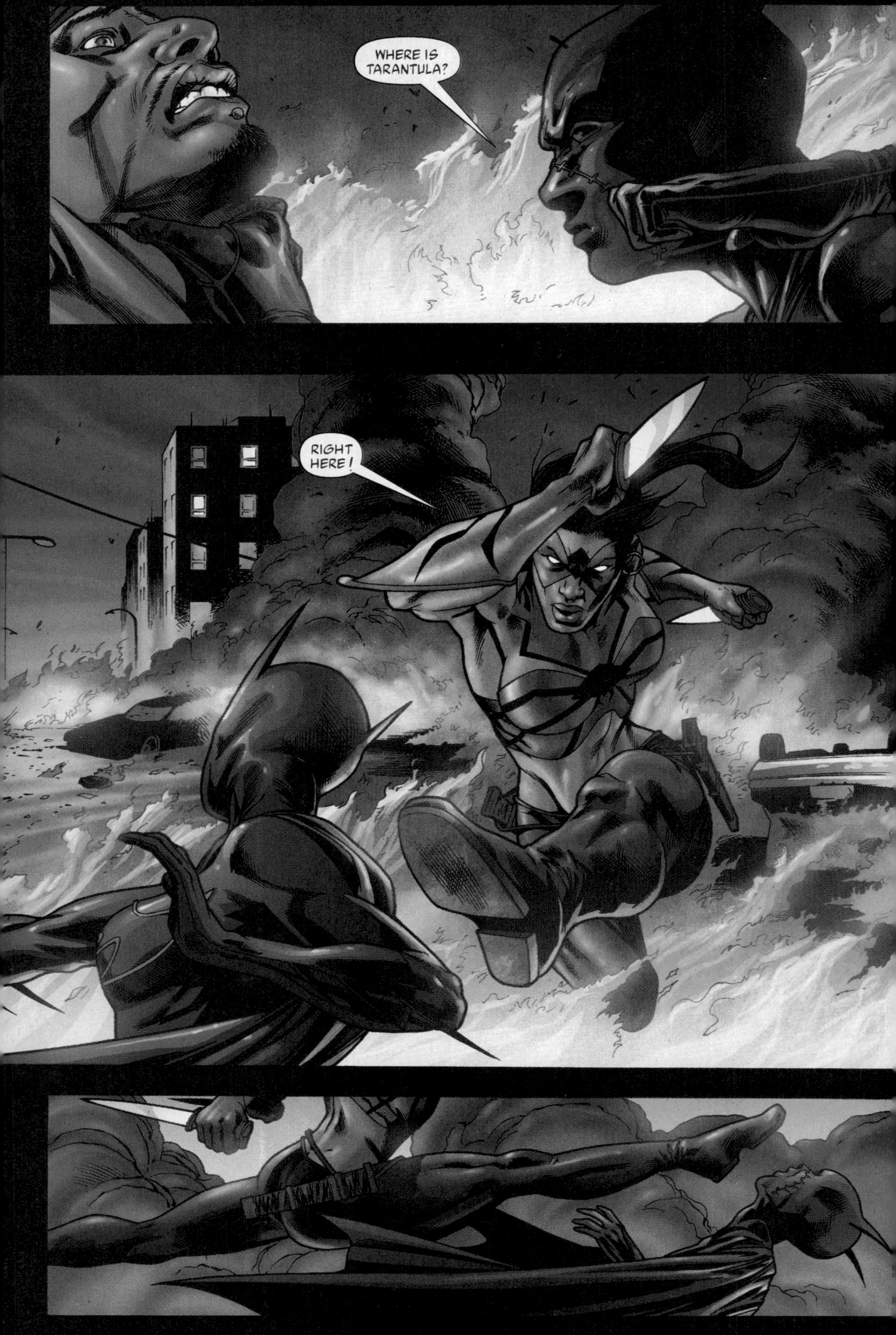
WHERE IS TARANTULA?
RIGHT HERE!

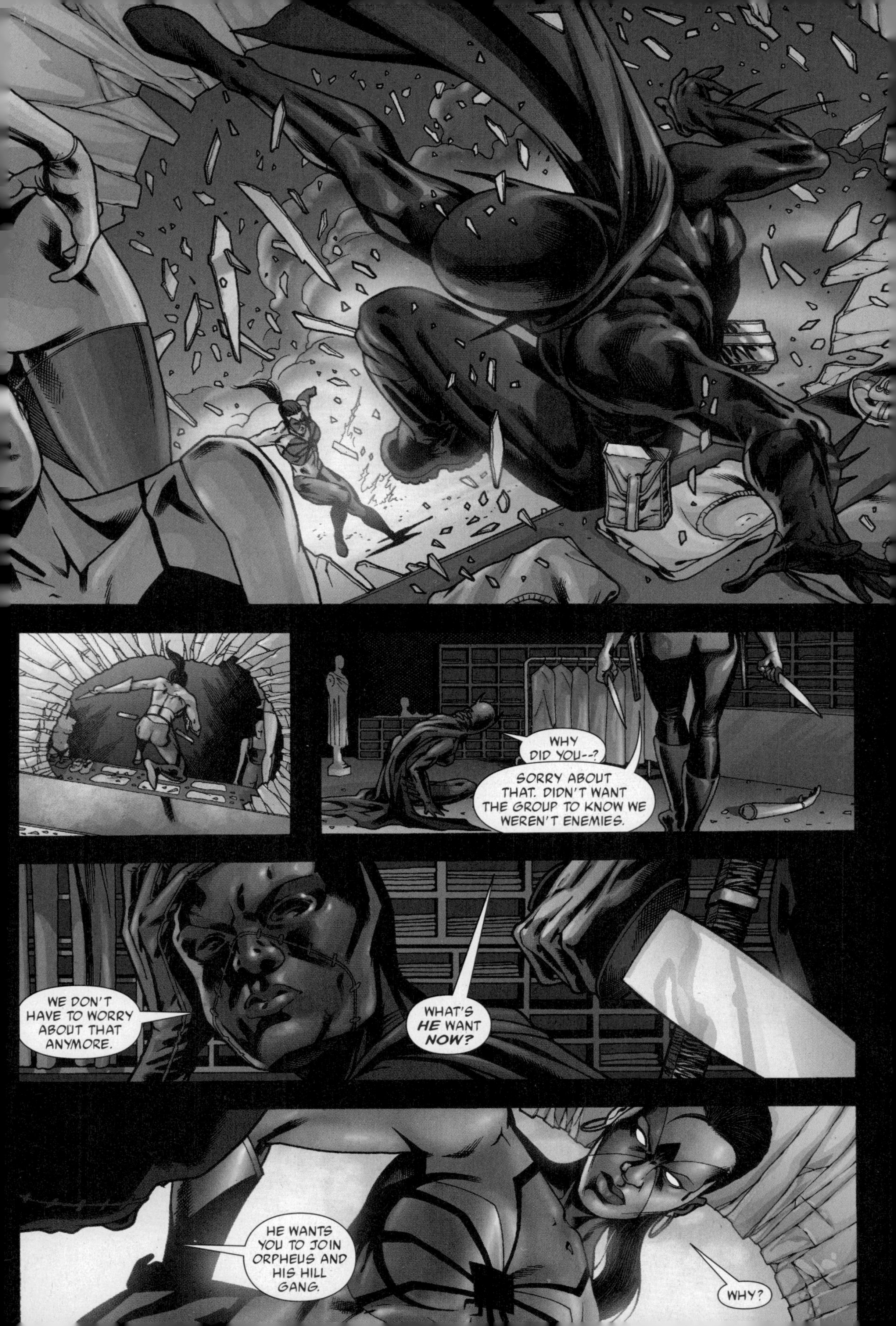
WHY DID YOU--?
SORRY ABOUT THAT. DIDN'T WANT THE GROUP TO KNOW WE WEREN'T ENEMIES.
WE DON'T HAVE TO WORRY ABOUT THAT ANYMORE.
WHAT'S HE WANT NOW?
HE WANTS YOU TO JOIN ORPHEUS AND HIS HILL GANG.
WHY?

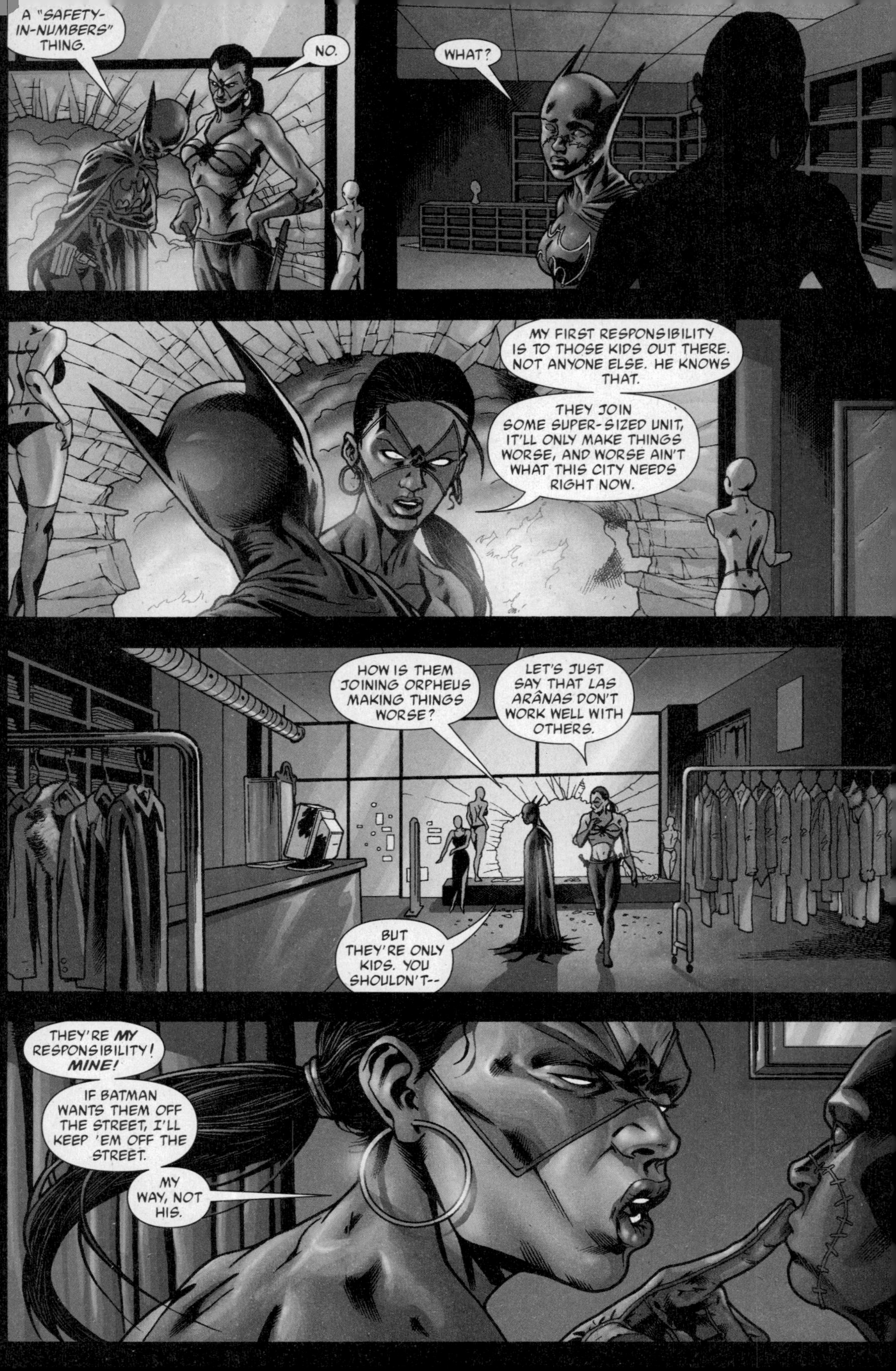

A "SAFETY-IN-NUMBERS" THING.
NO.
WHAT?
MY FIRST RESPONSIBILITY IS TO THOSE KIDS OUT THERE. NOT ANYONE ELSE. HE KNOWS THAT.
THEY JOIN SOME SUPER-SIZED UNIT, IT'LL ONLY MAKE THINGS WORSE, AND WORSE AIN'T WHAT THIS CITY NEEDS RIGHT NOW.
HOW IS THEM JOINING ORPHEUS MAKING THINGS WORSE?
LET'S JUST SAY THAT LAS ARÂNAS DON'T WORK WELL WITH OTHERS.
BUT THEY'RE ONLY KIDS. YOU SHOULDN'T--
THEY'RE *MY* RESPONSIBILITY! *MINE!*
IF BATMAN WANTS THEM OFF THE STREET, I'LL KEEP 'EM OFF THE STREET.
MY WAY, NOT HIS.

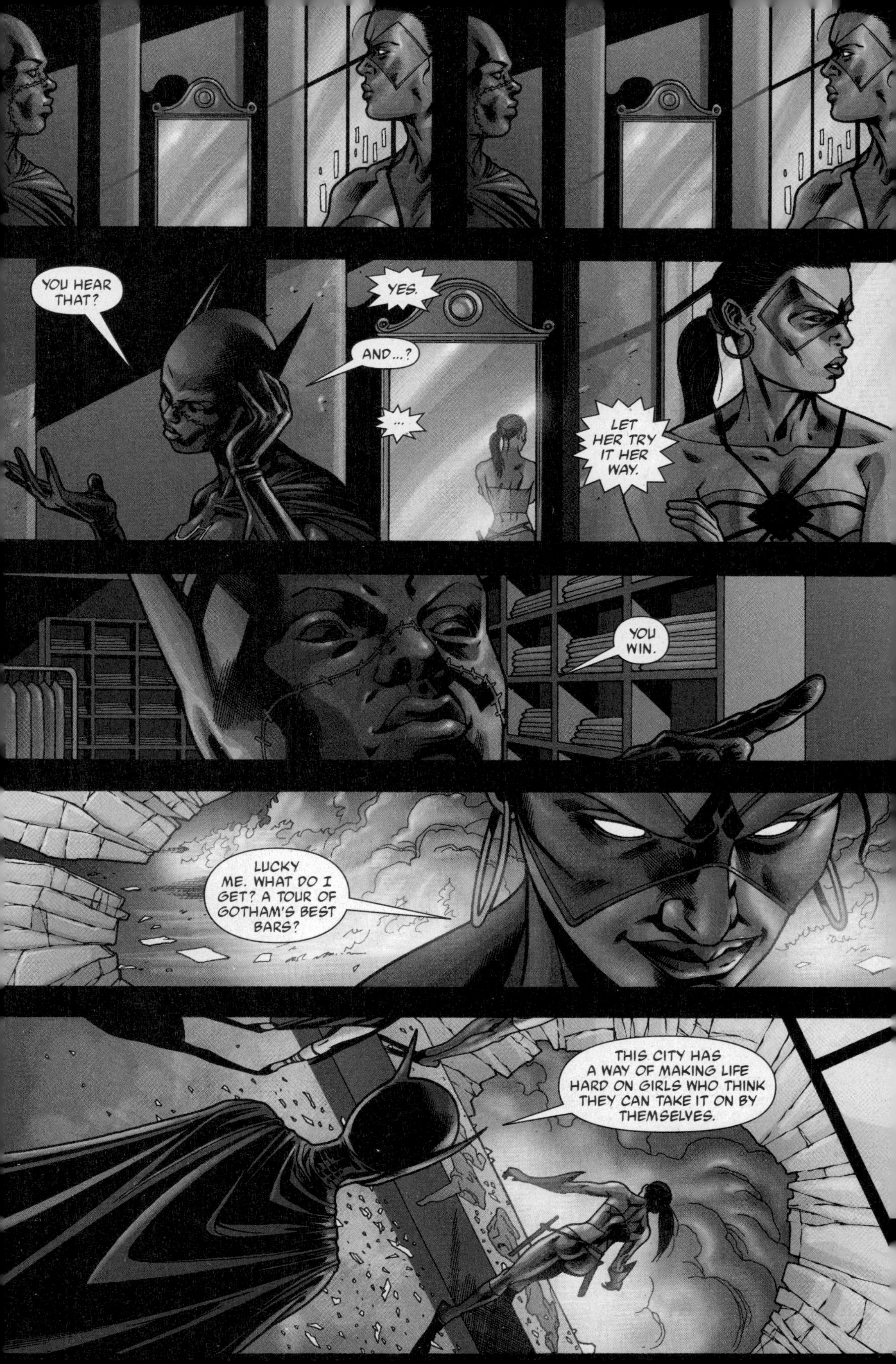
YOU HEAR THAT?
YES.
AND...?
...
LET HER TRY IT HER WAY.
YOU WIN.
LUCKY ME. WHAT DO I GET? A TOUR OF GOTHAM'S BEST BARS?
THIS CITY HAS A WAY OF MAKING LIFE HARD ON GIRLS WHO THINK THEY CAN TAKE IT ON BY THEMSELVES.

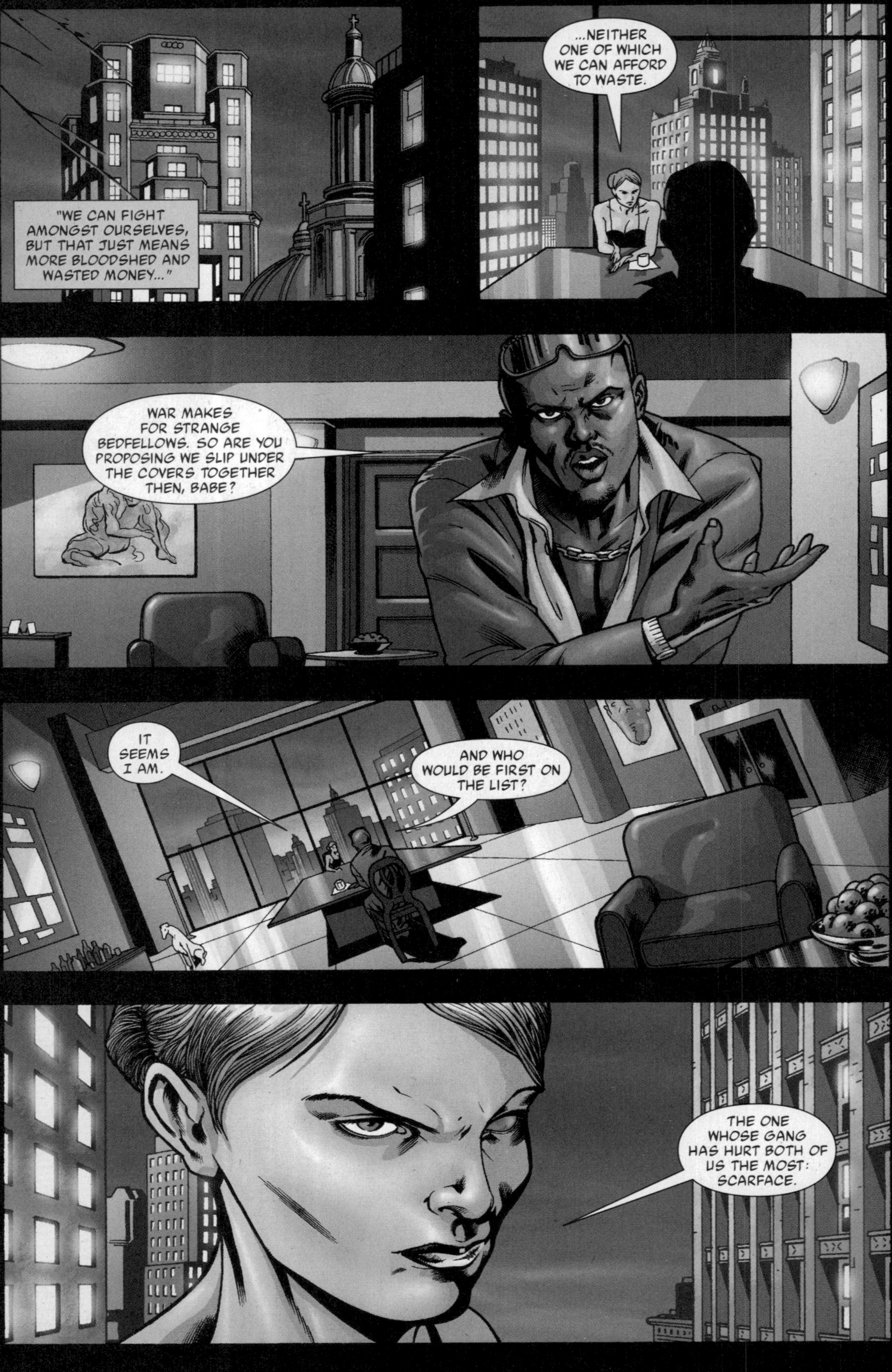
"WE CAN FIGHT AMONGST OURSELVES, BUT THAT JUST MEANS MORE BLOODSHED AND WASTED MONEY..."
...NEITHER ONE OF WHICH WE CAN AFFORD TO WASTE.
WAR MAKES FOR STRANGE BEDFELLOWS. SO ARE YOU PROPOSING WE SLIP UNDER THE COVERS TOGETHER THEN, BABE?
IT SEEMS I AM.
AND WHO WOULD BE FIRST ON THE LIST?
THE ONE WHOSE GANG HAS HURT BOTH OF US THE MOST: SCARFACE.

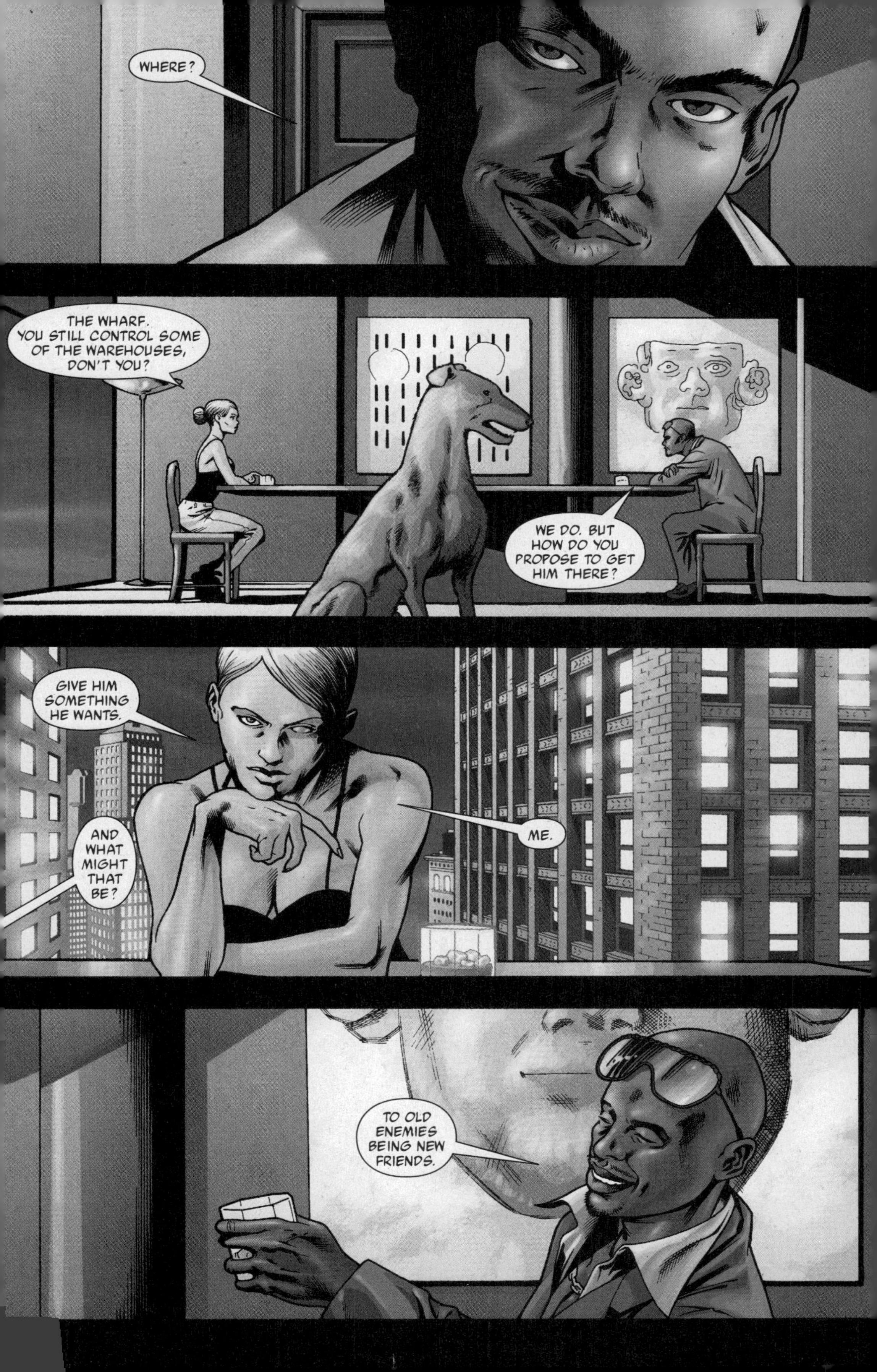
WHERE?
THE WHARF. YOU STILL CONTROL SOME OF THE WAREHOUSES, DON'T YOU?
WE DO. BUT HOW DO YOU PROPOSE TO GET HIM THERE?
GIVE HIM SOMETHING HE WANTS.
AND WHAT MIGHT THAT BE?
ME.
TO OLD ENEMIES BEING NEW FRIENDS.

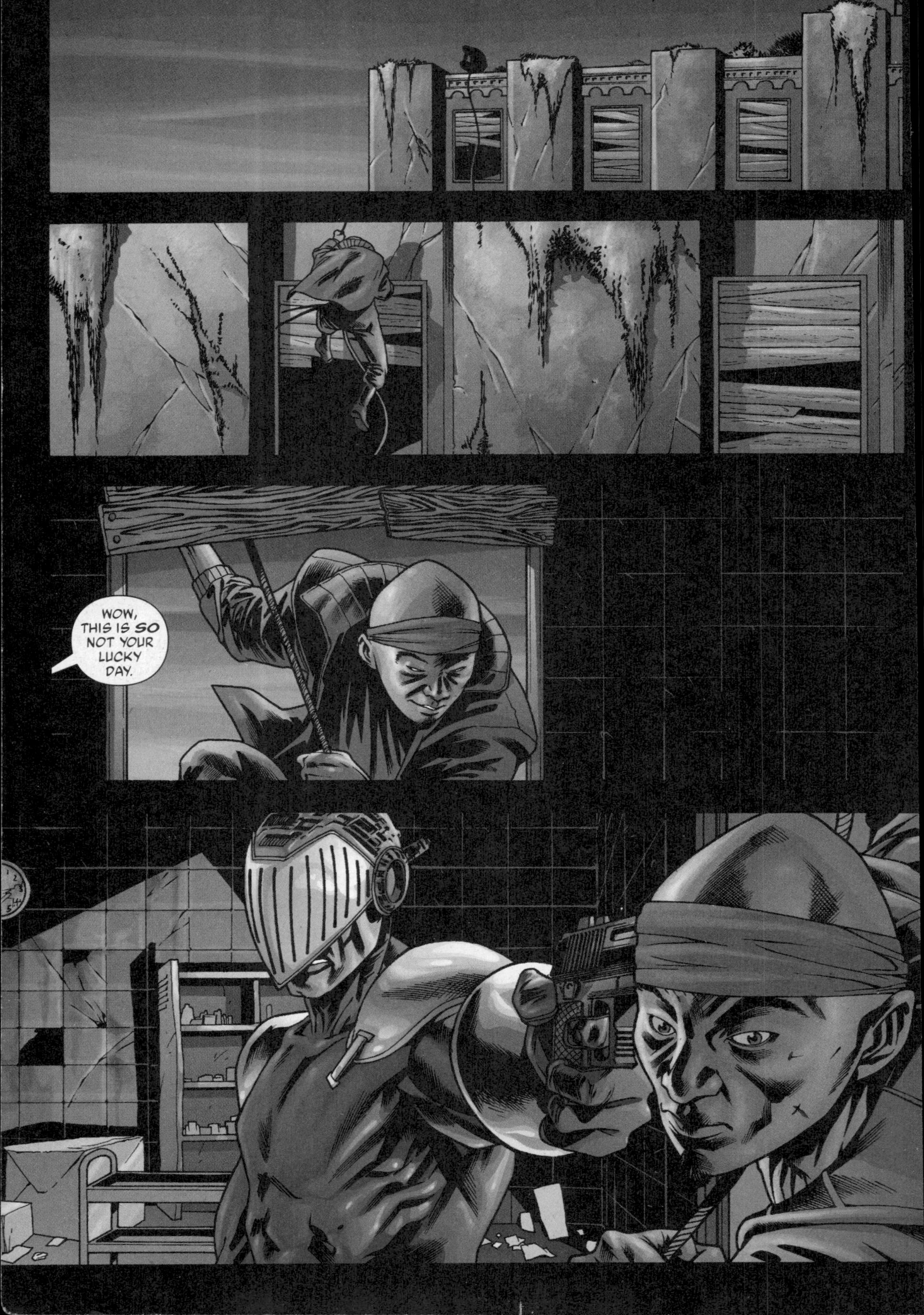
WOW, THIS IS SO NOT YOUR LUCKY DAY.

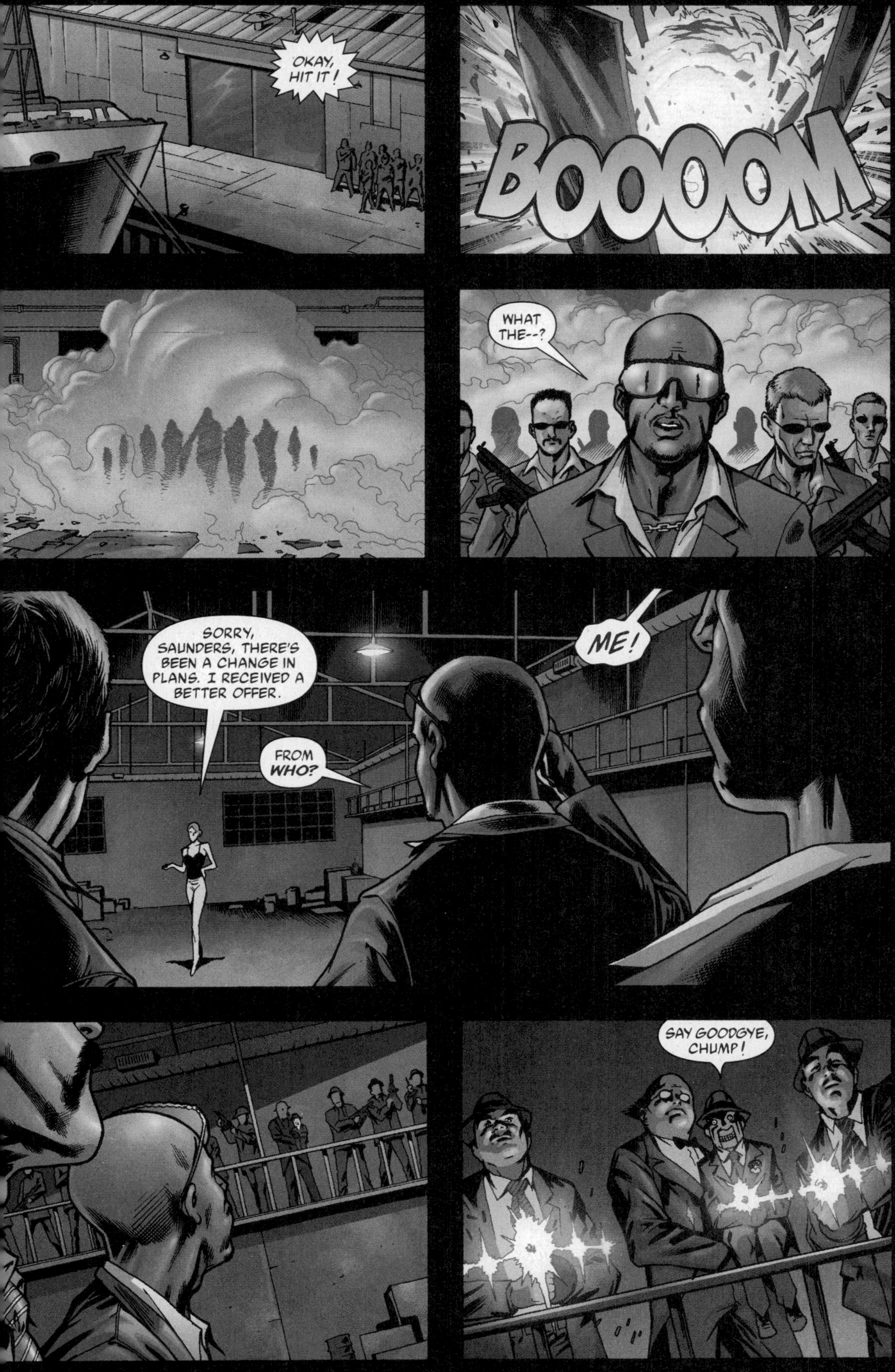

OKAY, HIT IT!
BOOOOM
WHAT THE--?
SORRY, SAUNDERS, THERE'S BEEN A CHANGE IN PLANS. I RECEIVED A BETTER OFFER.
FROM **WHO?**
*ME!*
SAY GOODGYE, CHUMP!

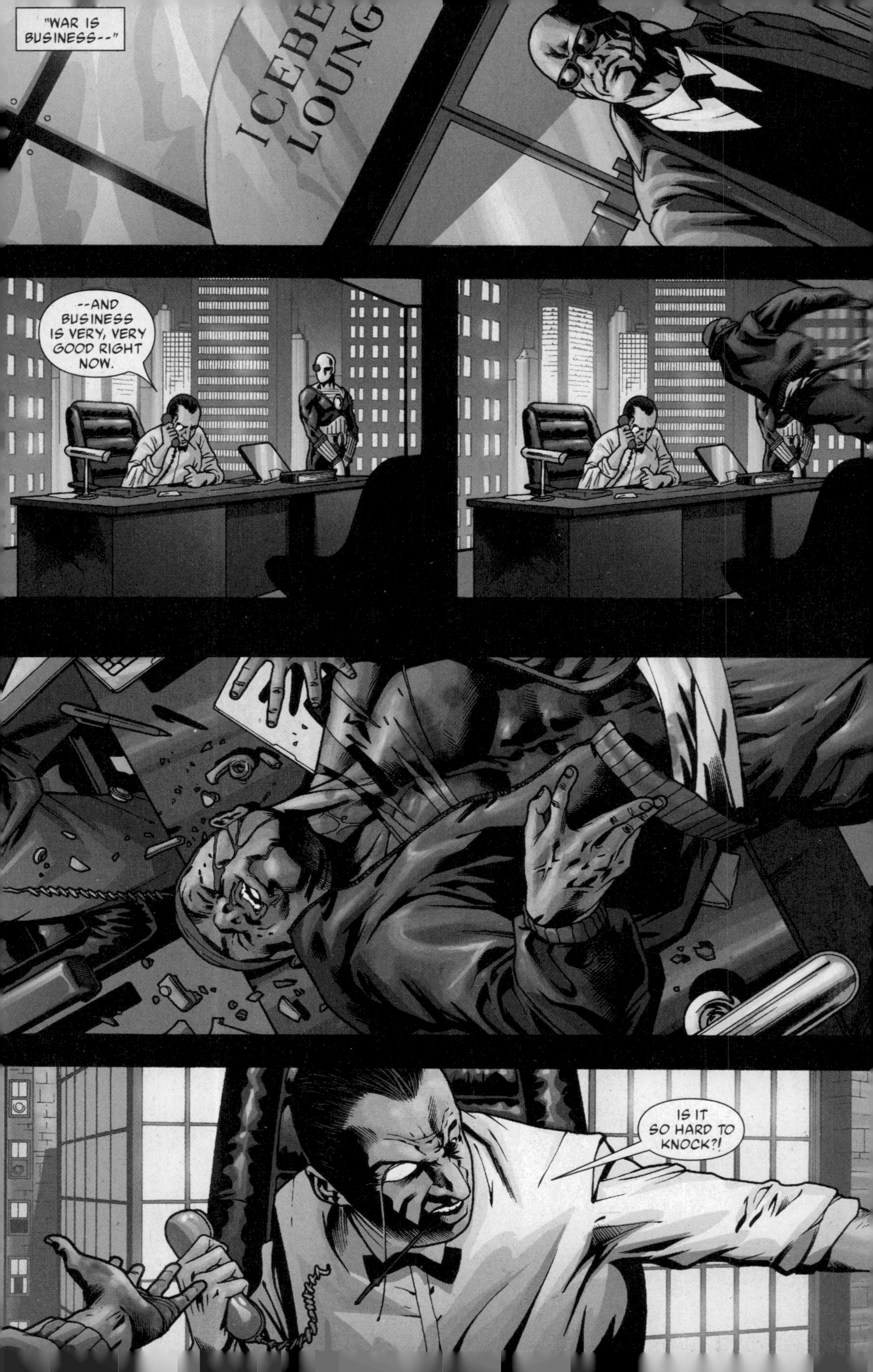
"WAR IS BUSINESS--"
ICEBE
LOUNG
--AND BUSINESS IS VERY, VERY GOOD RIGHT NOW.
IS IT SO HARD TO KNOCK?!

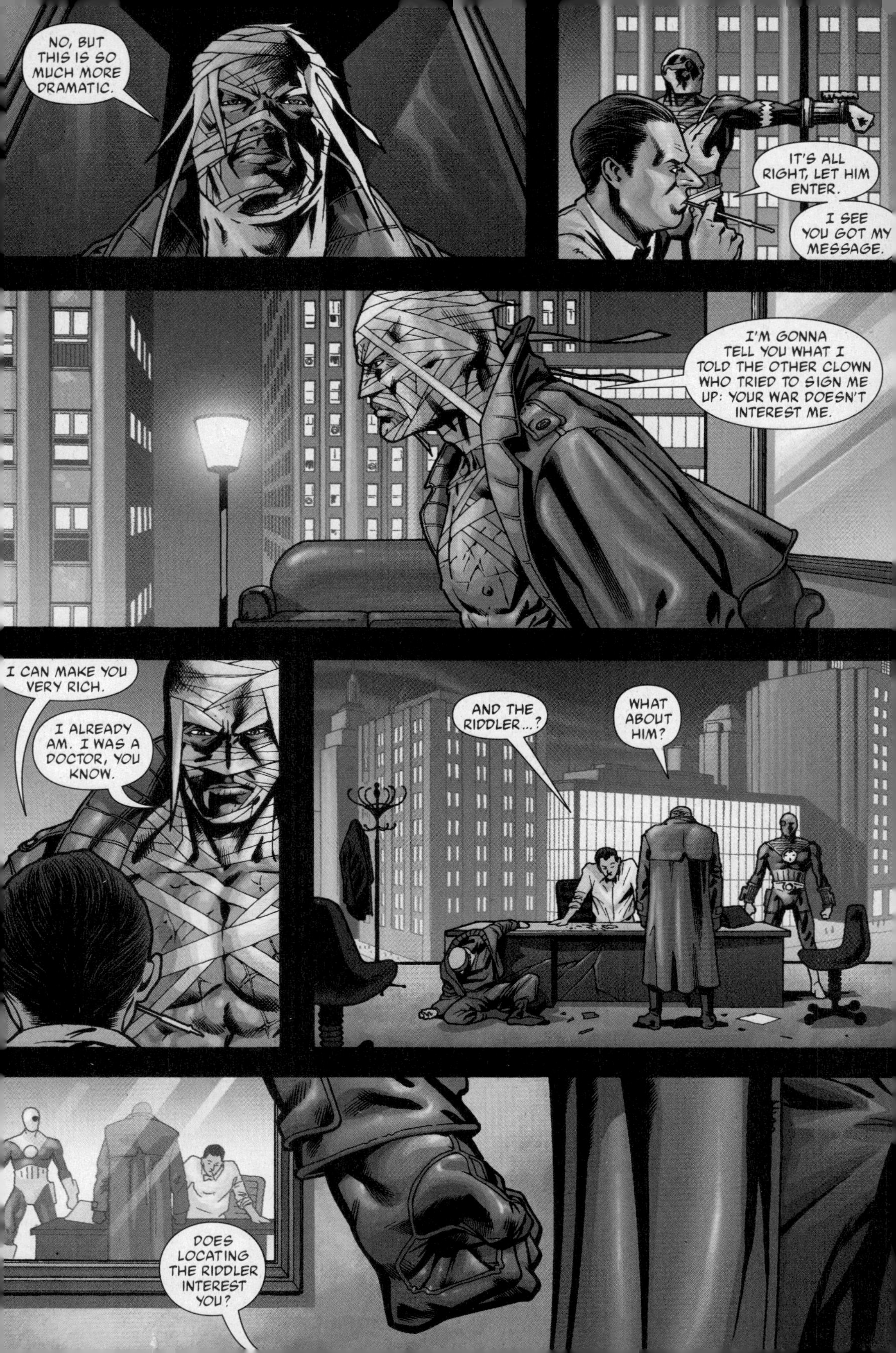
NO, BUT THIS IS SO MUCH MORE DRAMATIC.
IT'S ALL RIGHT, LET HIM ENTER.
I SEE YOU GOT MY MESSAGE.
I'M GONNA TELL YOU WHAT I TOLD THE OTHER CLOWN WHO TRIED TO SIGN ME UP: YOUR WAR DOESN'T INTEREST ME.
I CAN MAKE YOU VERY RICH.
I ALREADY AM. I WAS A DOCTOR, YOU KNOW.
AND THE RIDDLER...?
WHAT ABOUT HIM?
DOES LOCATING THE RIDDLER INTEREST YOU?

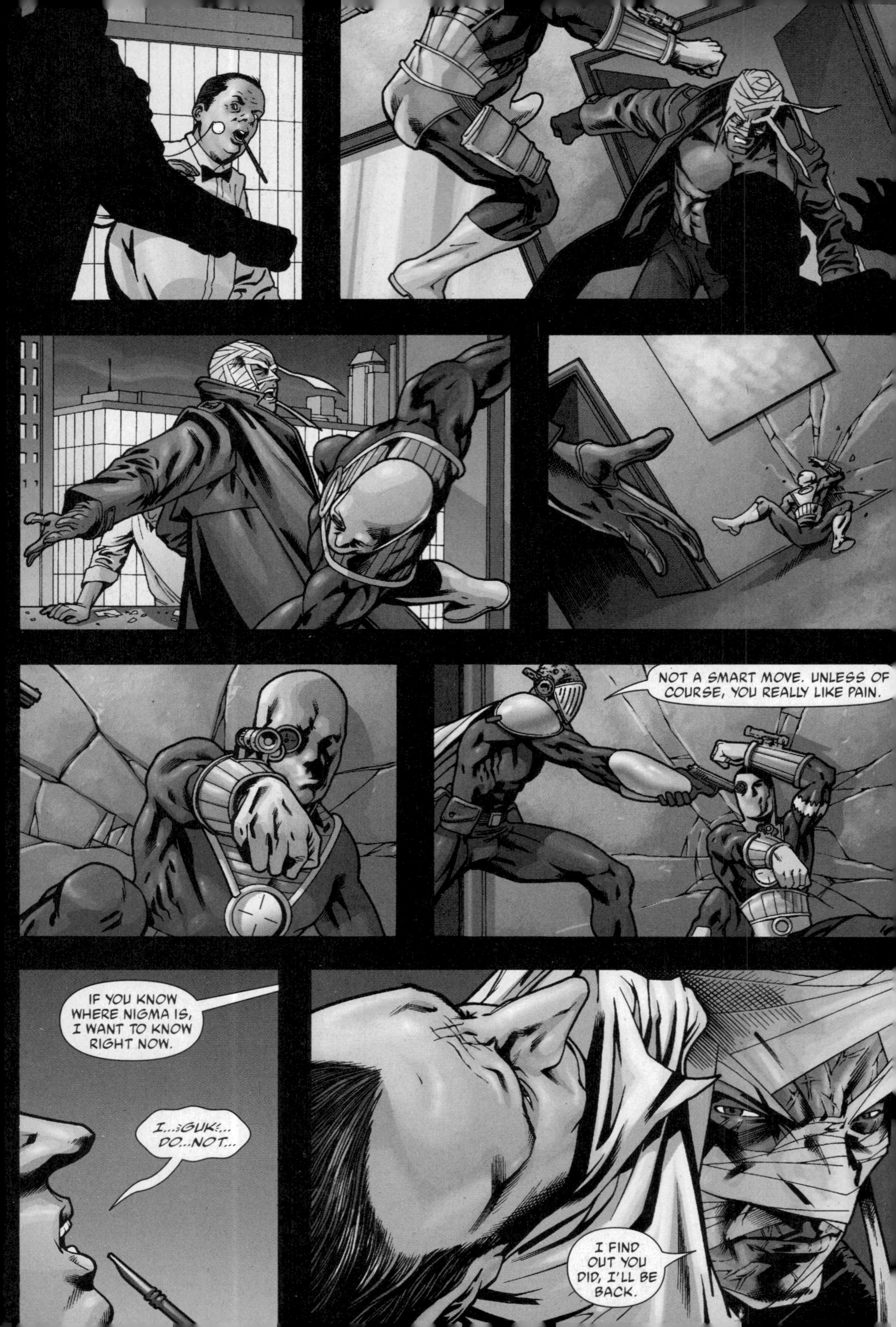
NOT A SMART MOVE. UNLESS OF COURSE, YOU REALLY LIKE PAIN.
IF YOU KNOW WHERE NIGMA IS, I WANT TO KNOW RIGHT NOW.
I...GUK... DO...NOT...
I FIND OUT YOU DID, I'LL BE BACK.

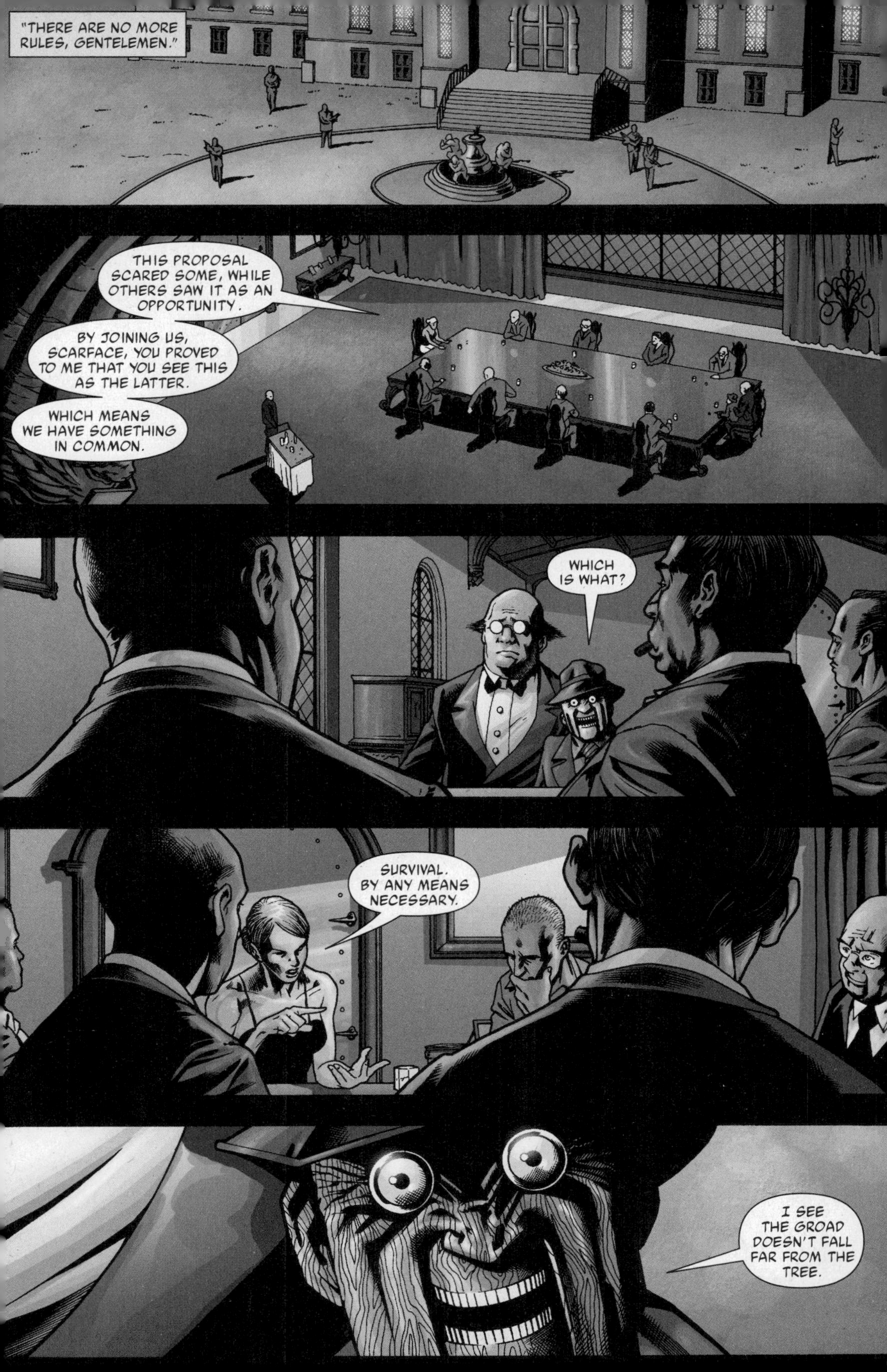
"THERE ARE NO MORE RULES, GENTELEMEN."
THIS PROPOSAL SCARED SOME, WHILE OTHERS SAW IT AS AN OPPORTUNITY.
BY JOINING US, SCARFACE, YOU PROVED TO ME THAT YOU SEE THIS AS THE LATTER.
WHICH MEANS WE HAVE SOMETHING IN COMMON.
WHICH IS WHAT?
SURVIVAL. BY ANY MEANS NECESSARY.
I SEE THE GROAD DOESN'T FALL FAR FROM THE TREE.

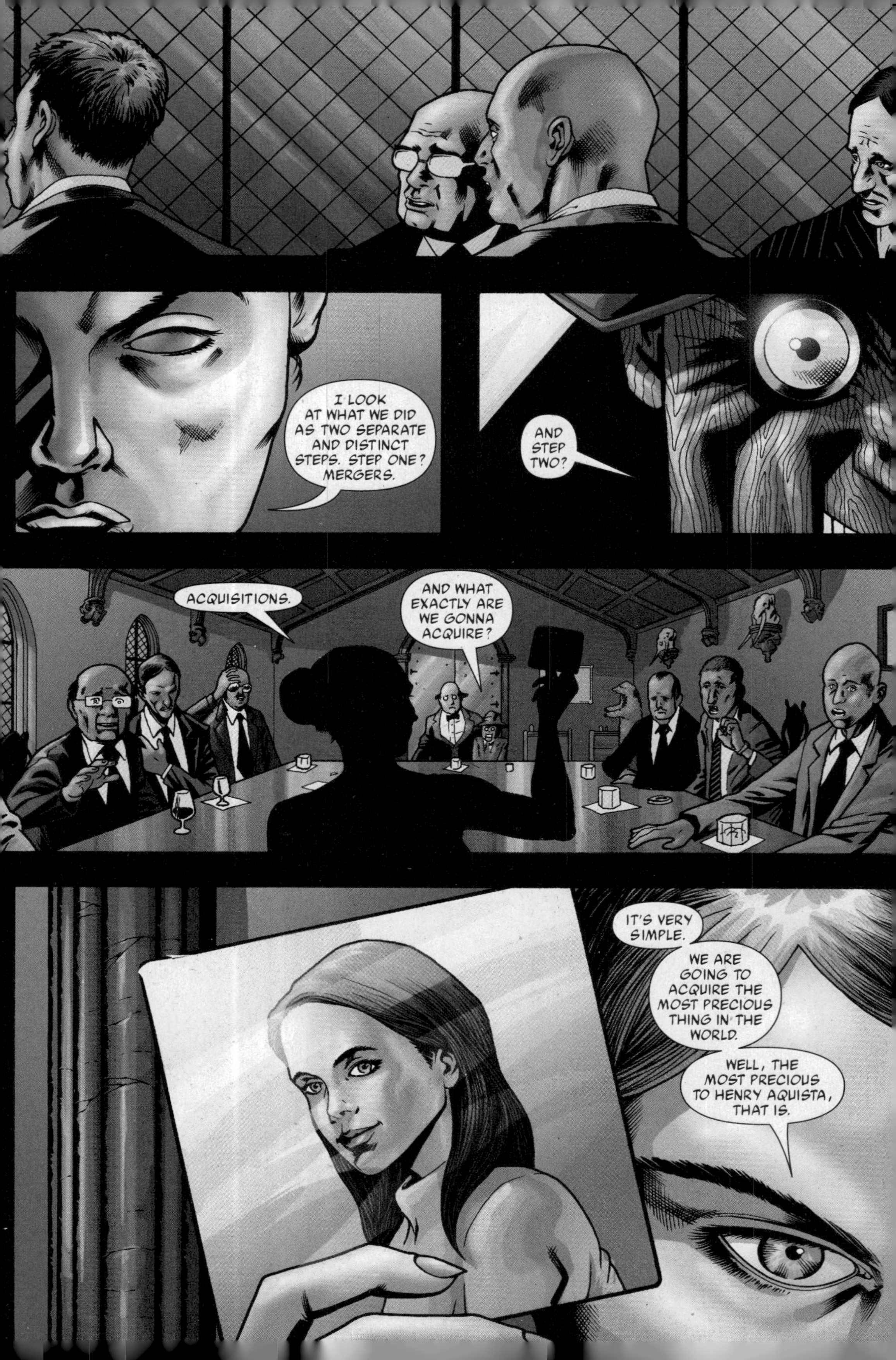
I LOOK AT WHAT WE DID AS TWO SEPARATE AND DISTINCT STEPS. STEP ONE? MERGERS.
AND STEP TWO?
ACQUISITIONS.
AND WHAT EXACTLY ARE WE GONNA ACQUIRE?
IT'S VERY SIMPLE.
WE ARE GOING TO ACQUIRE THE MOST PRECIOUS THING IN THE WORLD.
WELL, THE MOST PRECIOUS TO HENRY AQUISTA, THAT IS.

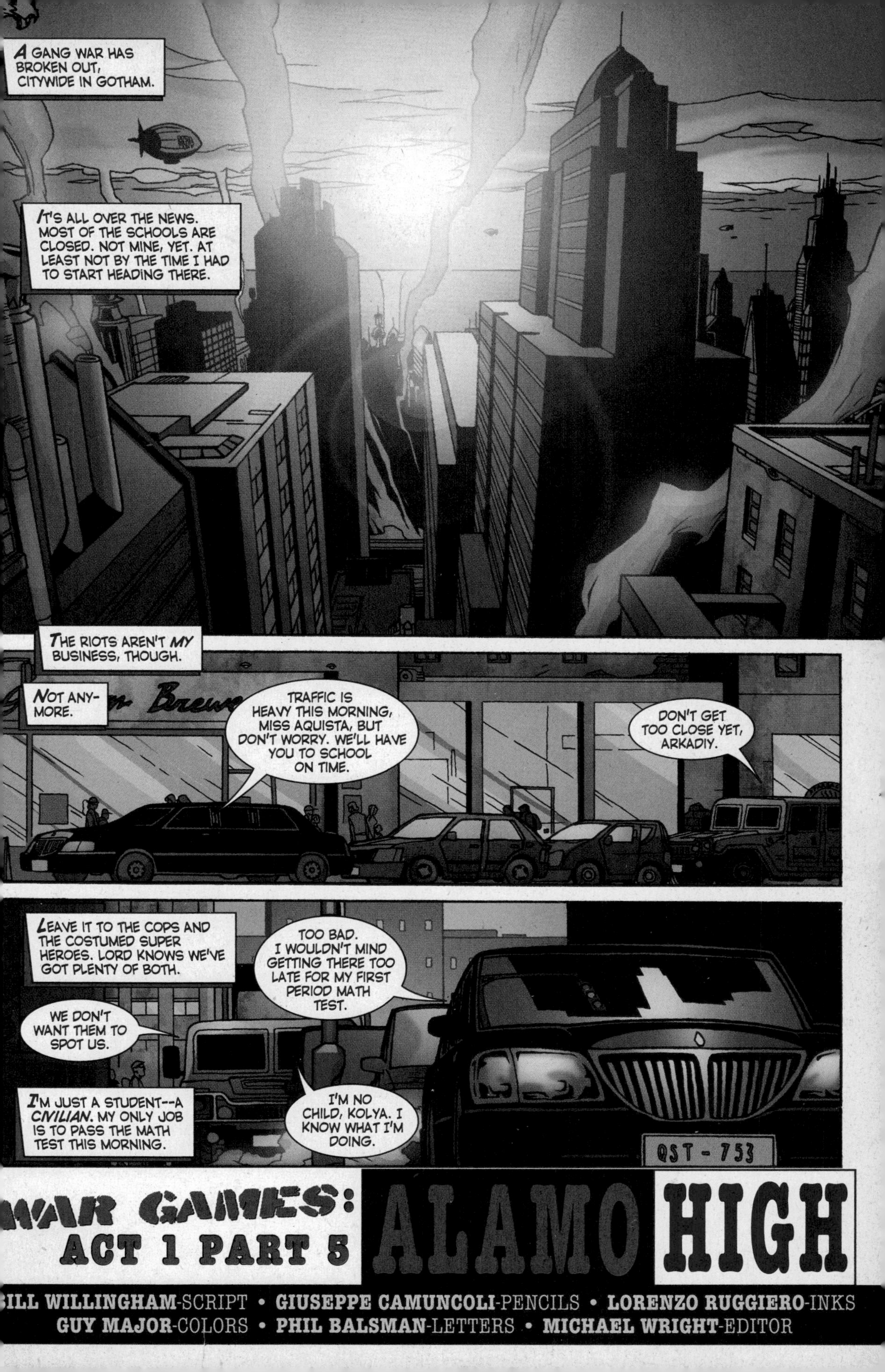
A GANG WAR HAS BROKEN OUT, CITYWIDE IN GOTHAM.
IT'S ALL OVER THE NEWS. MOST OF THE SCHOOLS ARE CLOSED. NOT MINE, YET. AT LEAST NOT BY THE TIME I HAD TO START HEADING THERE.
THE RIOTS AREN'T MY BUSINESS, THOUGH.
NOT ANY-MORE.
TRAFFIC IS HEAVY THIS MORNING, MISS AQUISTA, BUT DON'T WORRY. WE'LL HAVE YOU TO SCHOOL ON TIME.
DON'T GET TOO CLOSE YET, ARKADIY.
LEAVE IT TO THE COPS AND THE COSTUMED SUPER HEROES. LORD KNOWS WE'VE GOT PLENTY OF BOTH.
TOO BAD. I WOULDN'T MIND GETTING THERE TOO LATE FOR MY FIRST PERIOD MATH TEST.
WE DON'T WANT THEM TO SPOT US.
I'M JUST A STUDENT--A CIVILIAN. MY ONLY JOB IS TO PASS THE MATH TEST THIS MORNING.
I'M NO CHILD, KOLYA. I KNOW WHAT I'M DOING.
QST - 753
WAR GAMES: ACT 1 PART 5
ALAMO HIGH
BILL WILLINGHAM-SCRIPT • GIUSEPPE CAMUNCOLI-PENCILS • LORENZO RUGGIERO-INKS
GUY MAJOR-COLORS • PHIL BALSMAN-LETTERS • MICHAEL WRIGHT-EDITOR

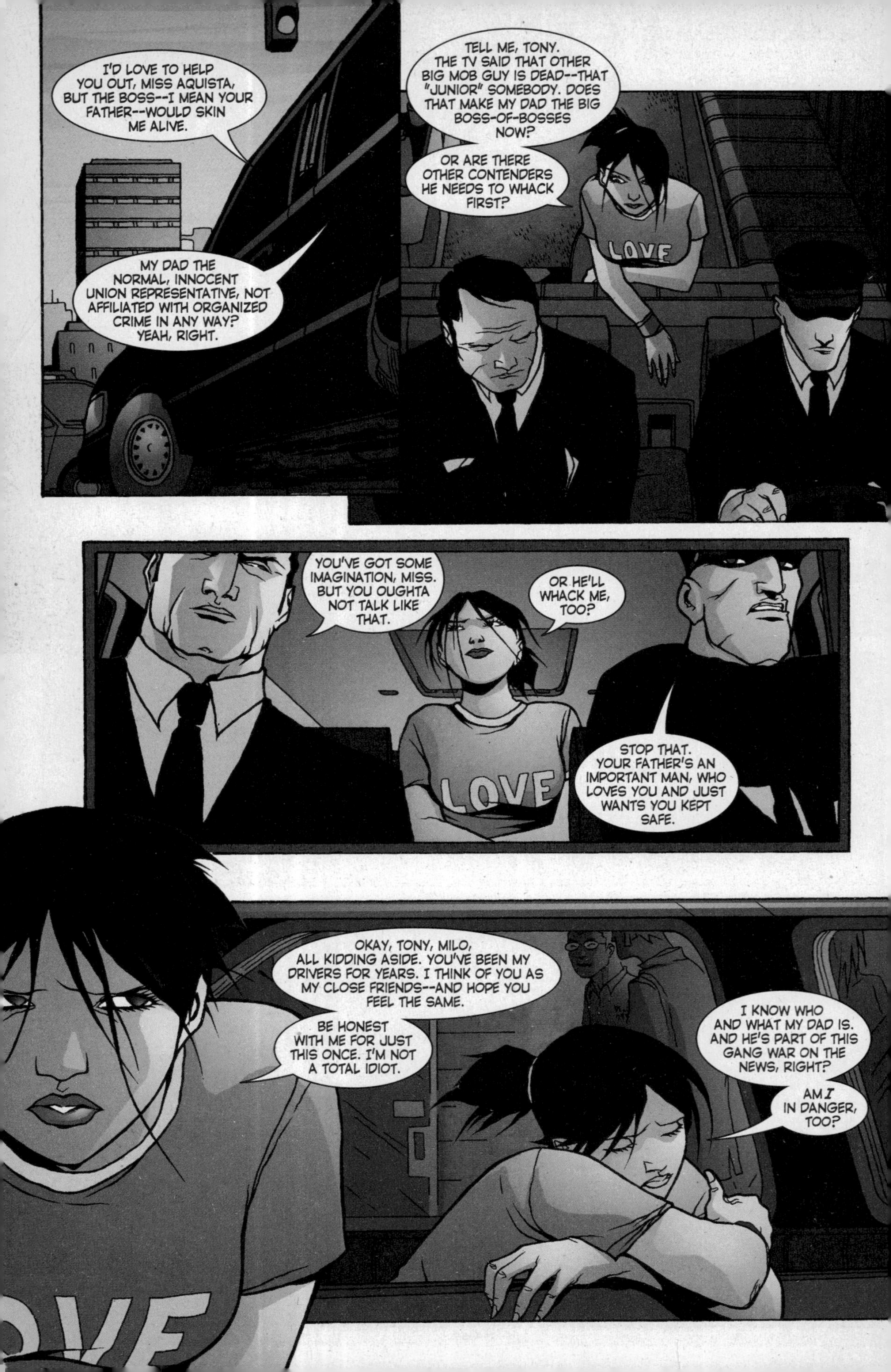
I'D LOVE TO HELP YOU OUT, MISS AQUISTA, BUT THE BOSS--I MEAN YOUR FATHER--WOULD SKIN ME ALIVE.
MY DAD THE NORMAL, INNOCENT UNION REPRESENTATIVE, NOT AFFILIATED WITH ORGANIZED CRIME IN ANY WAY? YEAH, RIGHT.
TELL ME, TONY. THE TV SAID THAT OTHER BIG MOB GUY IS DEAD--THAT "JUNIOR" SOMEBODY. DOES THAT MAKE MY DAD THE BIG BOSS-OF-BOSSES NOW?
OR ARE THERE OTHER CONTENDERS HE NEEDS TO WHACK FIRST?
LOVE
YOU'VE GOT SOME IMAGINATION, MISS. BUT YOU OUGHTA NOT TALK LIKE THAT.
OR HE'LL WHACK ME, TOO?
STOP THAT. YOUR FATHER'S AN IMPORTANT MAN, WHO LOVES YOU AND JUST WANTS YOU KEPT SAFE.
LOVE
OKAY, TONY, MILO, ALL KIDDING ASIDE. YOU'VE BEEN MY DRIVERS FOR YEARS. I THINK OF YOU AS MY CLOSE FRIENDS--AND HOPE YOU FEEL THE SAME.
BE HONEST WITH ME FOR JUST THIS ONCE. I'M NOT A TOTAL IDIOT.
I KNOW WHO AND WHAT MY DAD IS. AND HE'S PART OF THIS GANG WAR ON THE NEWS, RIGHT?
AM *I* IN DANGER, TOO?

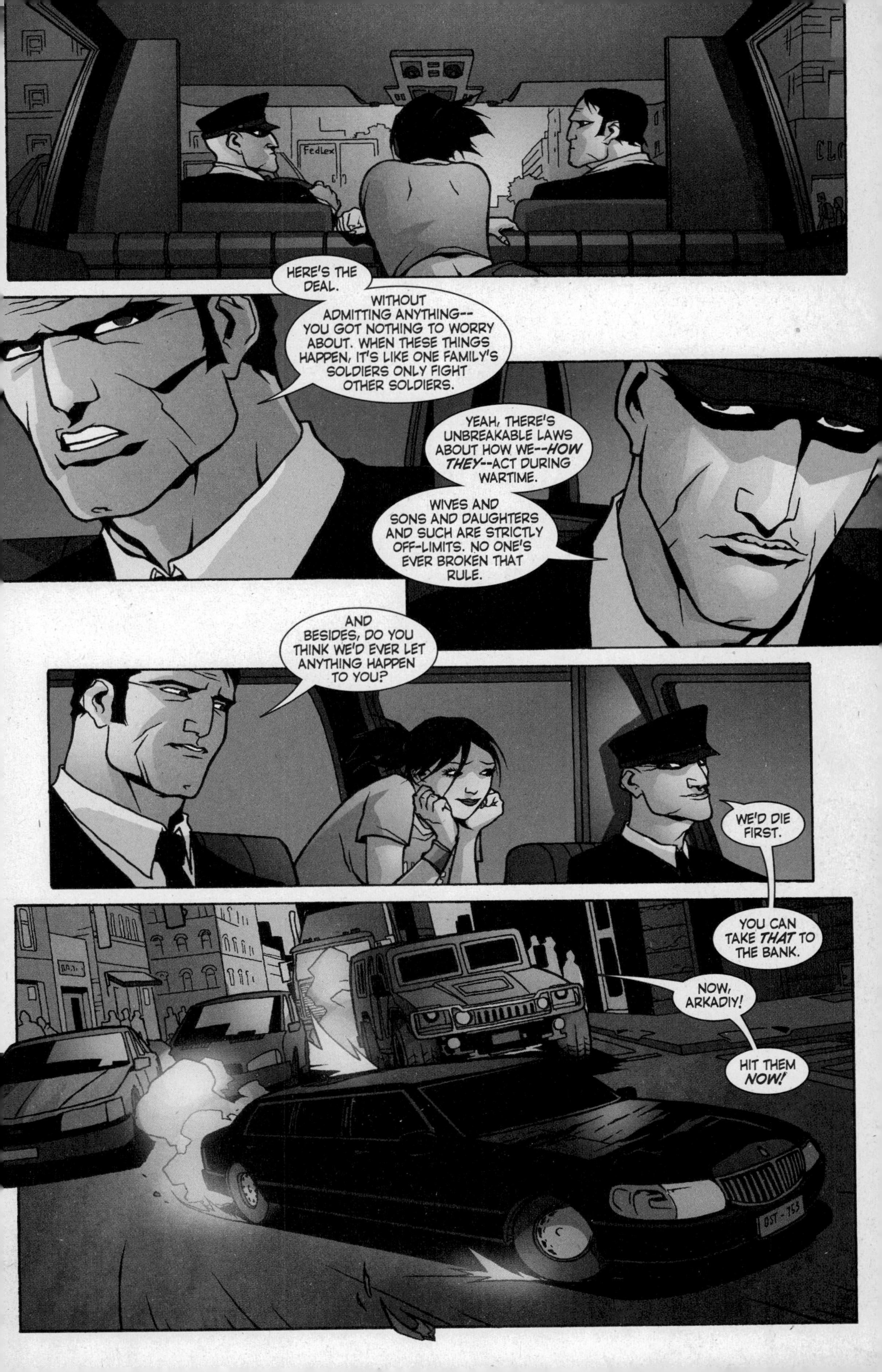
Fedlex
HERE'S THE DEAL.
WITHOUT ADMITTING ANYTHING-- YOU GOT NOTHING TO WORRY ABOUT. WHEN THESE THINGS HAPPEN, IT'S LIKE ONE FAMILY'S SOLDIERS ONLY FIGHT OTHER SOLDIERS.
YEAH, THERE'S UNBREAKABLE LAWS ABOUT HOW WE--*HOW THEY*--ACT DURING WARTIME.
WIVES AND SONS AND DAUGHTERS AND SUCH ARE STRICTLY OFF-LIMITS. NO ONE'S EVER BROKEN THAT RULE.
AND BESIDES, DO YOU THINK WE'D EVER LET ANYTHING HAPPEN TO YOU?
WE'D DIE FIRST.
YOU CAN TAKE *THAT* TO THE BANK.
NOW, ARKADIY!
HIT THEM *NOW!*

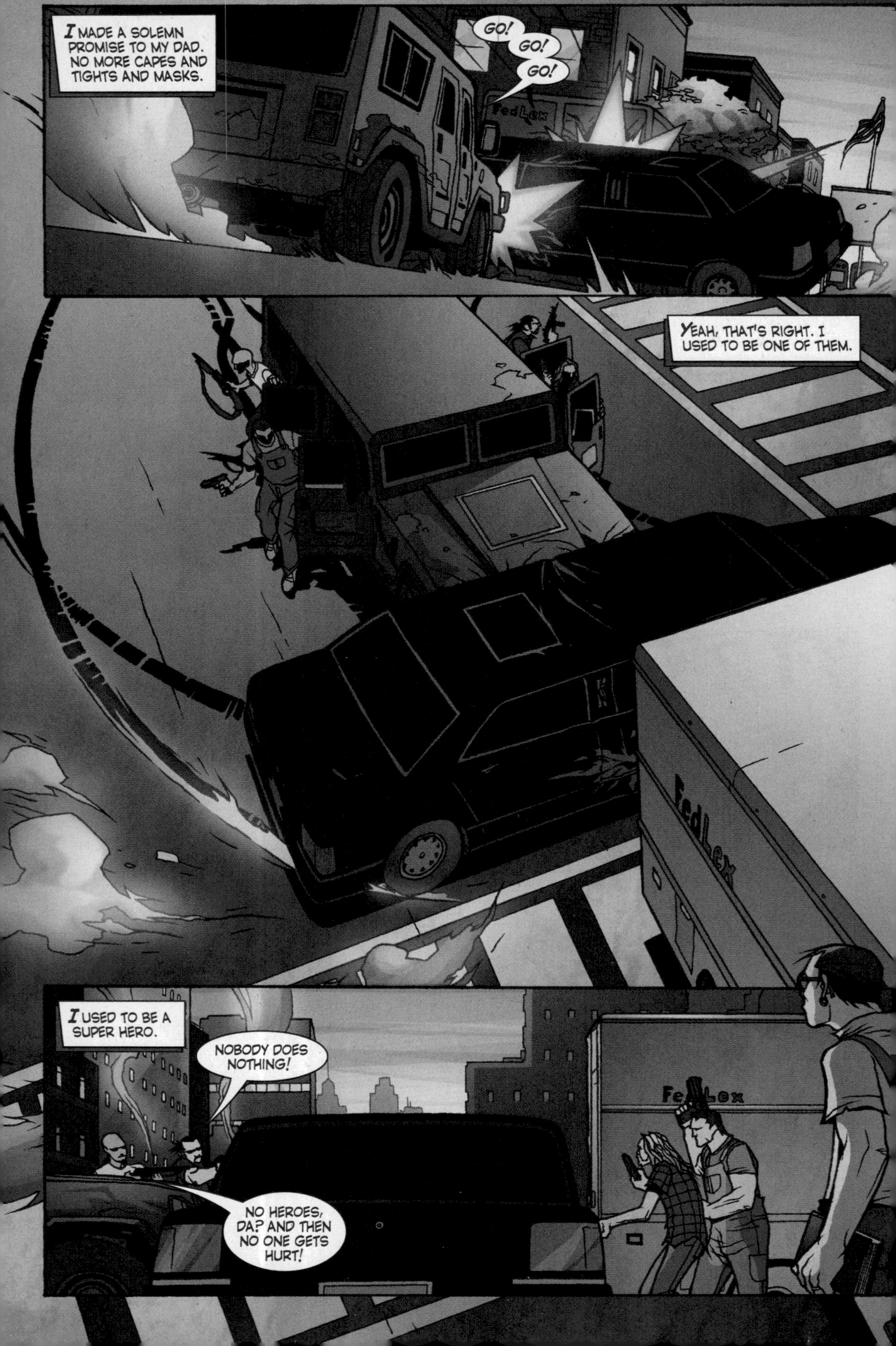
I MADE A SOLEMN PROMISE TO MY DAD. NO MORE CAPES AND TIGHTS AND MASKS.
GO!
GO!
GO!
FedLex
YEAH, THAT'S RIGHT. I USED TO BE ONE OF THEM.
FedLex
I USED TO BE A SUPER HERO.
NOBODY DOES NOTHING!
NO HEROES, DA? AND THEN NO ONE GETS HURT!
FedLex

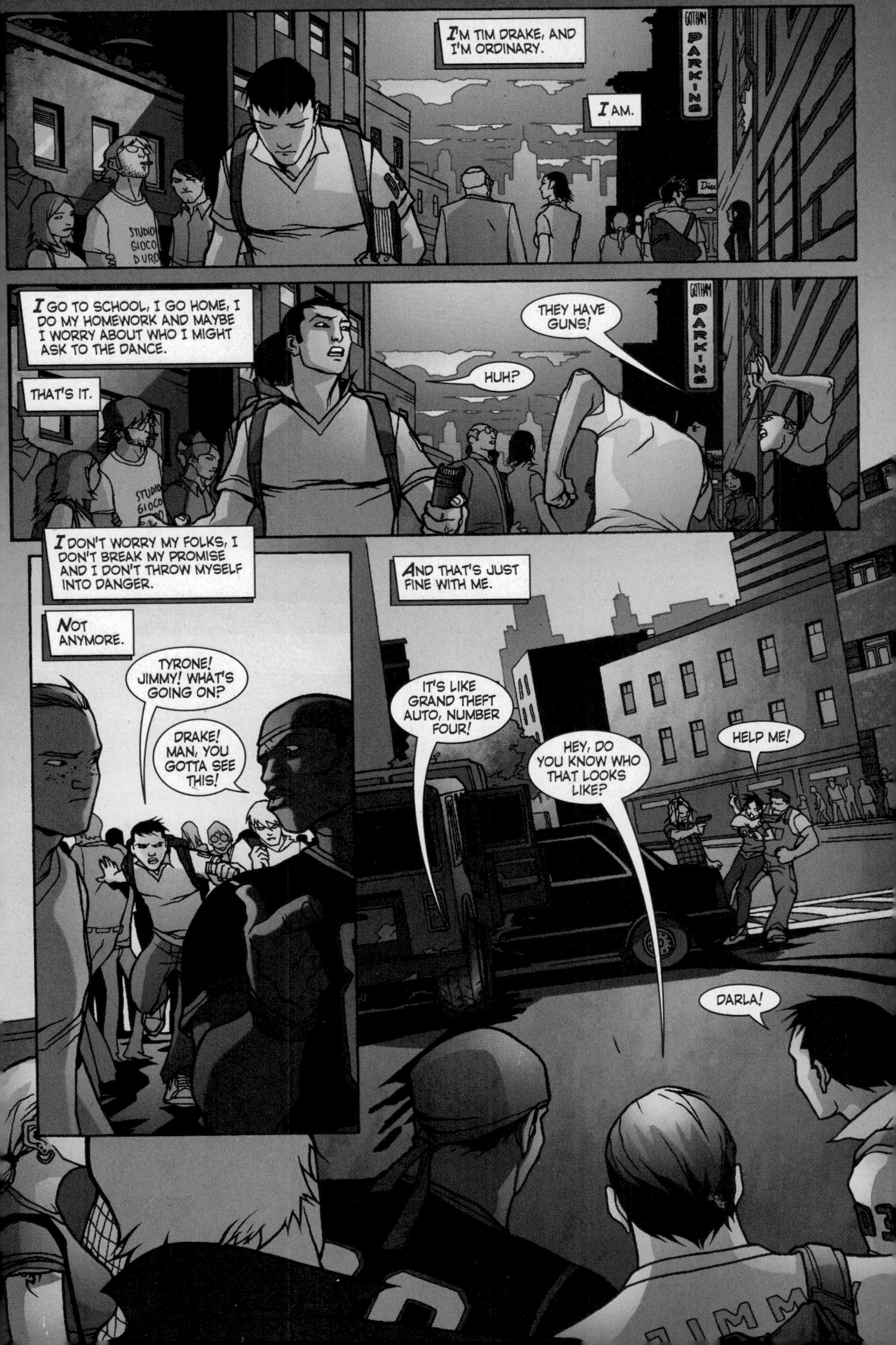
I'M TIM DRAKE, AND I'M ORDINARY.
I AM.
GOTHAM PARKING
STUDIO GIOCO DURO
I GO TO SCHOOL, I GO HOME, I DO MY HOMEWORK AND MAYBE I WORRY ABOUT WHO I MIGHT ASK TO THE DANCE.
THAT'S IT.
THEY HAVE GUNS!
HUH?
GOTHAM PARKING
I DON'T WORRY MY FOLKS, I DON'T BREAK MY PROMISE AND I DON'T THROW MYSELF INTO DANGER.
NOT ANYMORE.
AND THAT'S JUST FINE WITH ME.
TYRONE! JIMMY! WHAT'S GOING ON?
DRAKE! MAN, YOU GOTTA SEE THIS!
IT'S LIKE GRAND THEFT AUTO, NUMBER FOUR!
HEY, DO YOU KNOW WHO THAT LOOKS LIKE?
HELP ME!
DARLA!

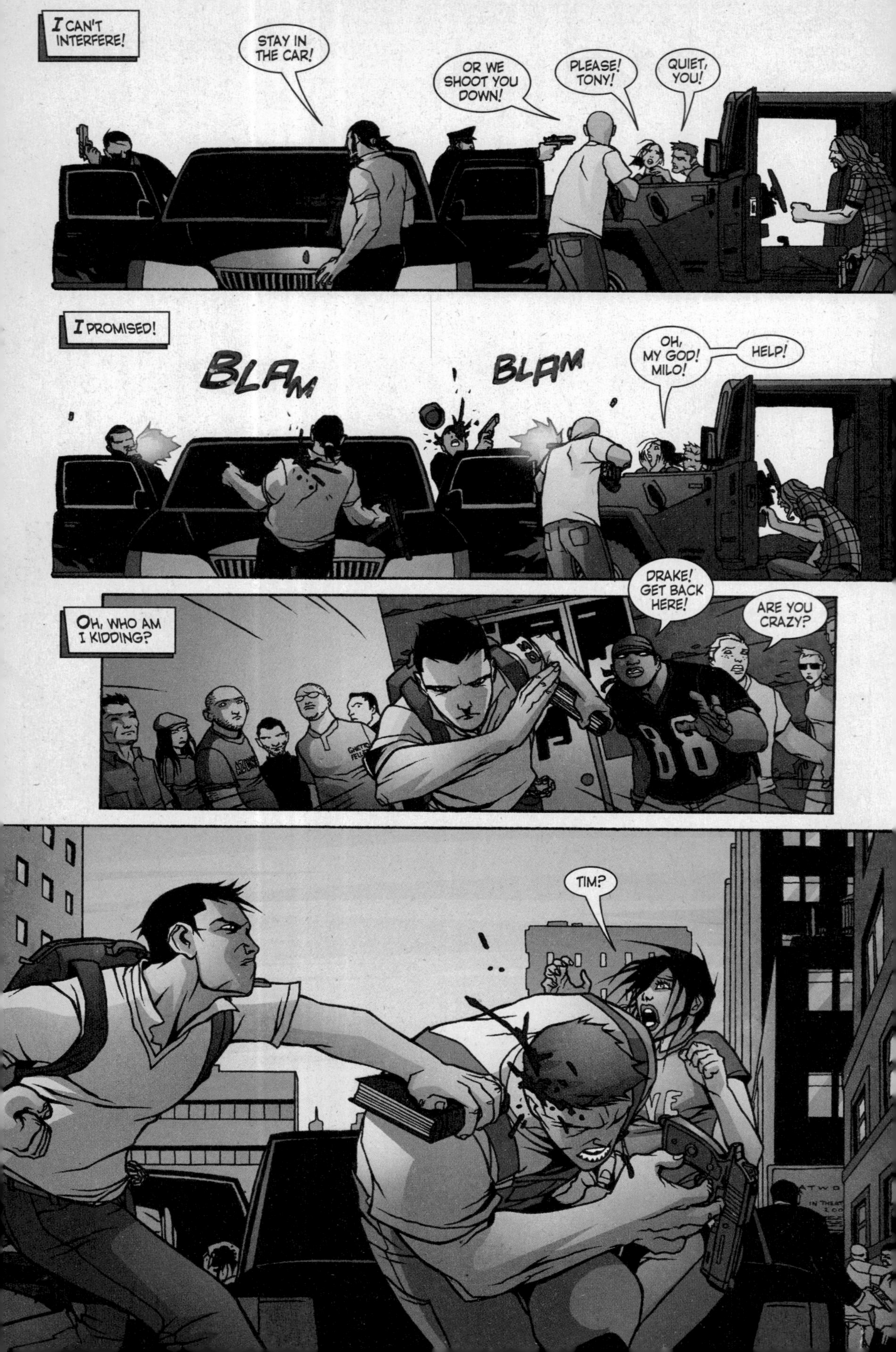
I CAN'T INTERFERE!
STAY IN THE CAR!
OR WE SHOOT YOU DOWN!
PLEASE! TONY!
QUIET, YOU!
I PROMISED!
BLAM
BLAM
OH, MY GOD! MILO!
HELP!
OH, WHO AM I KIDDING?
DRAKE! GET BACK HERE!
ARE YOU CRAZY?
TIM?

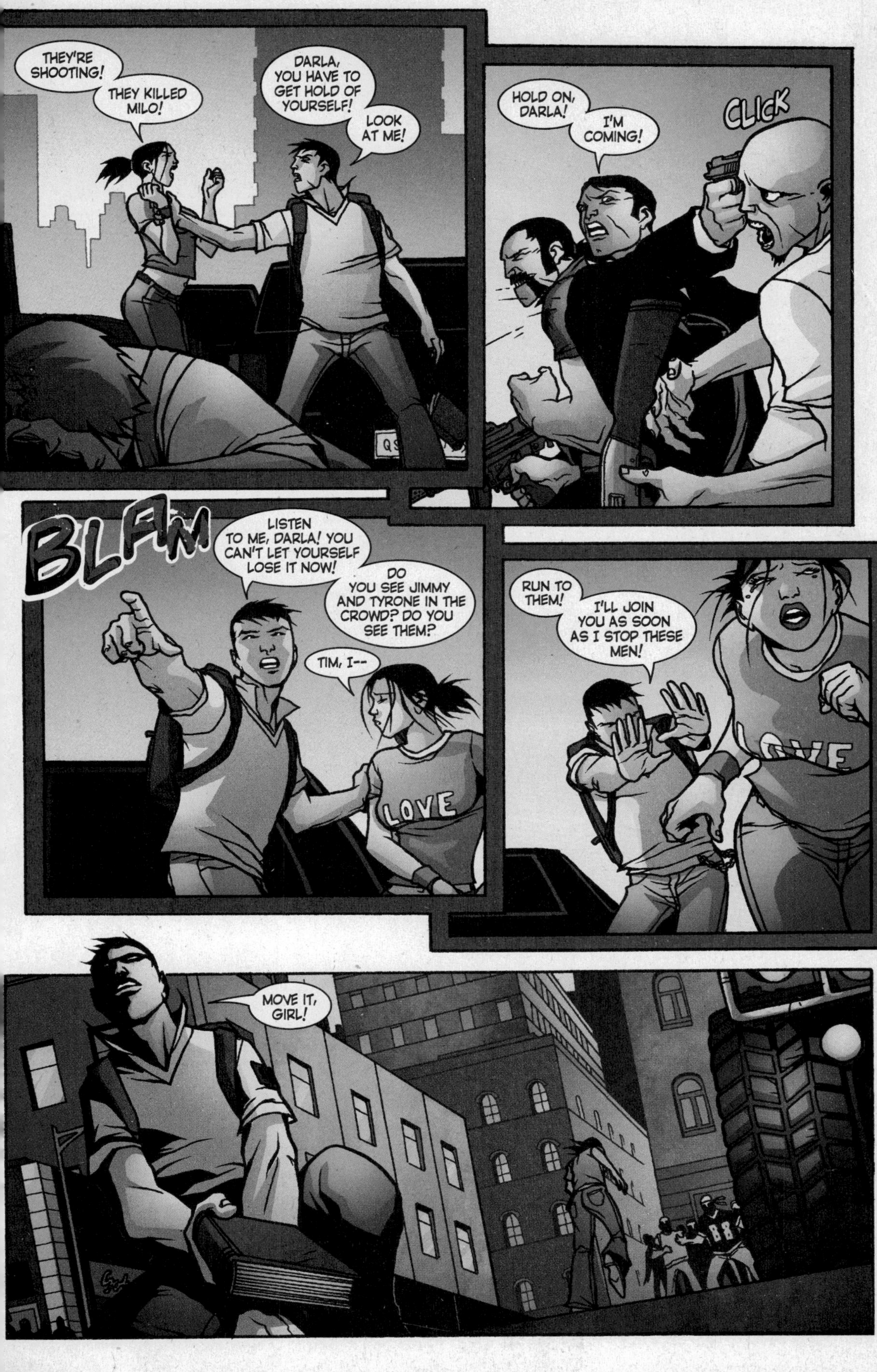
THEY'RE SHOOTING!
THEY KILLED MILO!
DARLA, YOU HAVE TO GET HOLD OF YOURSELF!
LOOK AT ME!
HOLD ON, DARLA!
I'M COMING!
CLICK
BLAM
LISTEN TO ME, DARLA! YOU CAN'T LET YOURSELF LOSE IT NOW!
DO YOU SEE JIMMY AND TYRONE IN THE CROWD? DO YOU SEE THEM?
TIM, I--
LOVE
RUN TO THEM!
I'LL JOIN YOU AS SOON AS I STOP THESE MEN!
MOVE IT, GIRL!

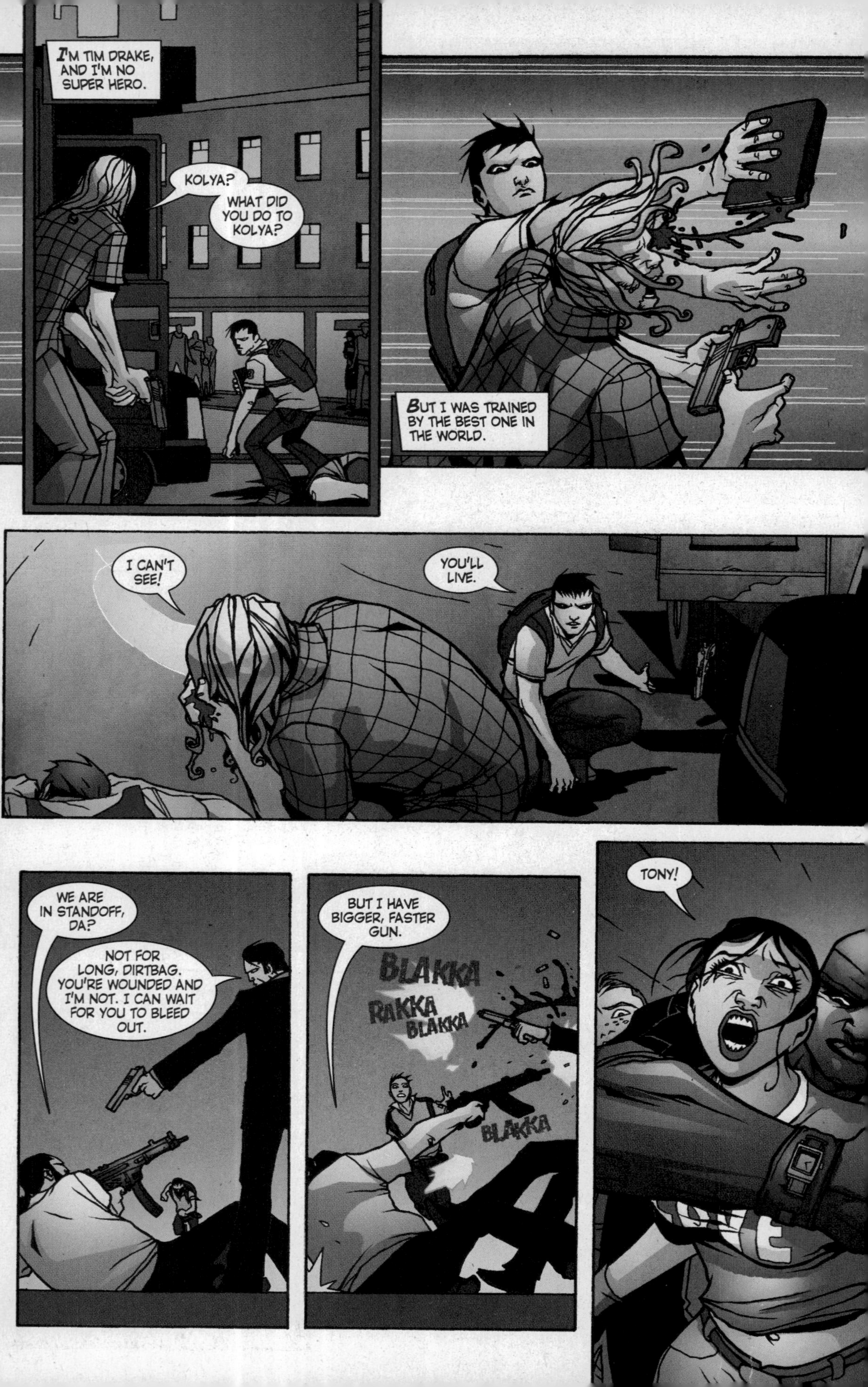
I'M TIM DRAKE, AND I'M NO SUPER HERO.
KOLYA?
WHAT DID YOU DO TO KOLYA?
BUT I WAS TRAINED BY THE BEST ONE IN THE WORLD.
I CAN'T SEE!
YOU'LL LIVE.
WE ARE IN STANDOFF, DA?
NOT FOR LONG, DIRTBAG. YOU'RE WOUNDED AND I'M NOT. I CAN WAIT FOR YOU TO BLEED OUT.
BUT I HAVE BIGGER, FASTER GUN.
BLAKKA
RAKKA
BLAKKA
BLAKKA
TONY!

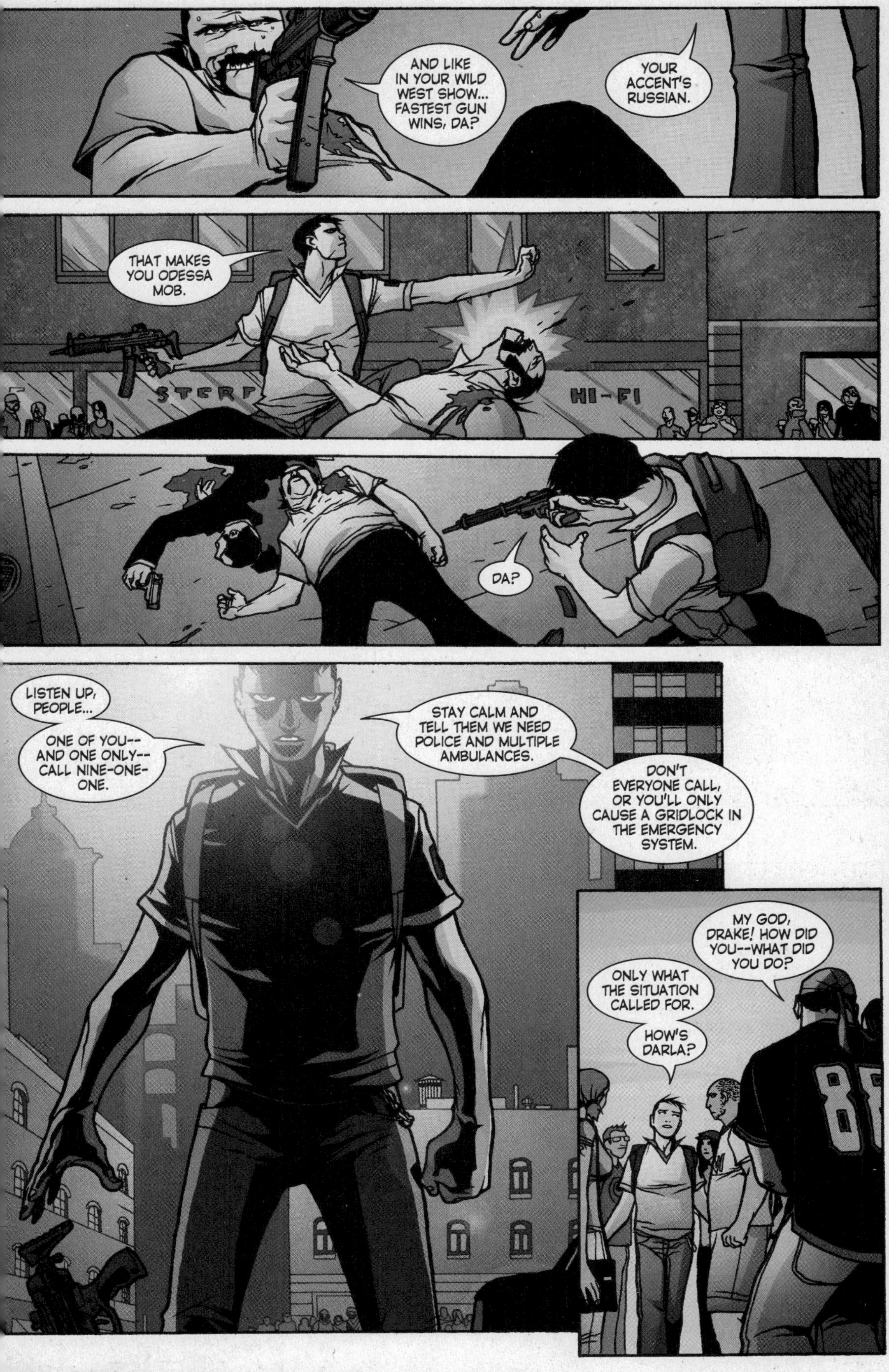
AND LIKE IN YOUR WILD WEST SHOW... FASTEST GUN WINS, DA?
YOUR ACCENT'S RUSSIAN.
THAT MAKES YOU ODESSA MOB.
STERP
HI-FI
DA?
LISTEN UP, PEOPLE...
ONE OF YOU--AND ONE ONLY--CALL NINE-ONE-ONE.
STAY CALM AND TELL THEM WE NEED POLICE AND MULTIPLE AMBULANCES.
DON'T EVERYONE CALL, OR YOU'LL ONLY CAUSE A GRIDLOCK IN THE EMERGENCY SYSTEM.
MY GOD, DRAKE! HOW DID YOU--WHAT DID YOU DO?
ONLY WHAT THE SITUATION CALLED FOR.
HOW'S DARLA?

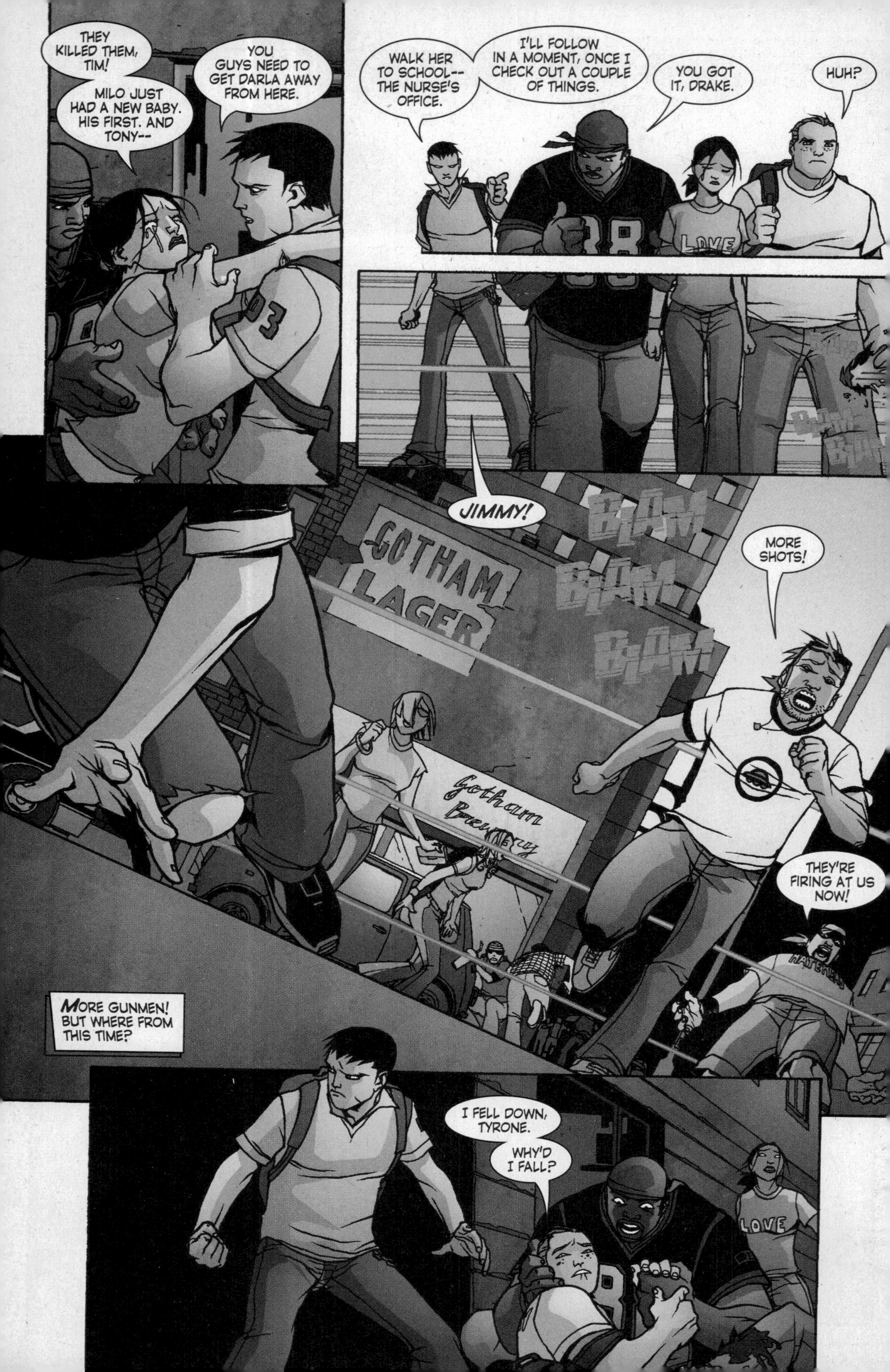
THEY KILLED THEM, TIM!
MILO JUST HAD A NEW BABY. HIS FIRST. AND TONY--
YOU GUYS NEED TO GET DARLA AWAY FROM HERE.
WALK HER TO SCHOOL-- THE NURSE'S OFFICE.
I'LL FOLLOW IN A MOMENT, ONCE I CHECK OUT A COUPLE OF THINGS.
YOU GOT IT, DRAKE.
HUH?
LOVE
JIMMY!
BLAM
BLAM
BLAM
GOTHAM LAGER
Gotham Brewery
MORE SHOTS!
THEY'RE FIRING AT US NOW!
MORE GUNMEN! BUT WHERE FROM THIS TIME?
I FELL DOWN, TYRONE.
WHY'D I FALL?
LOVE

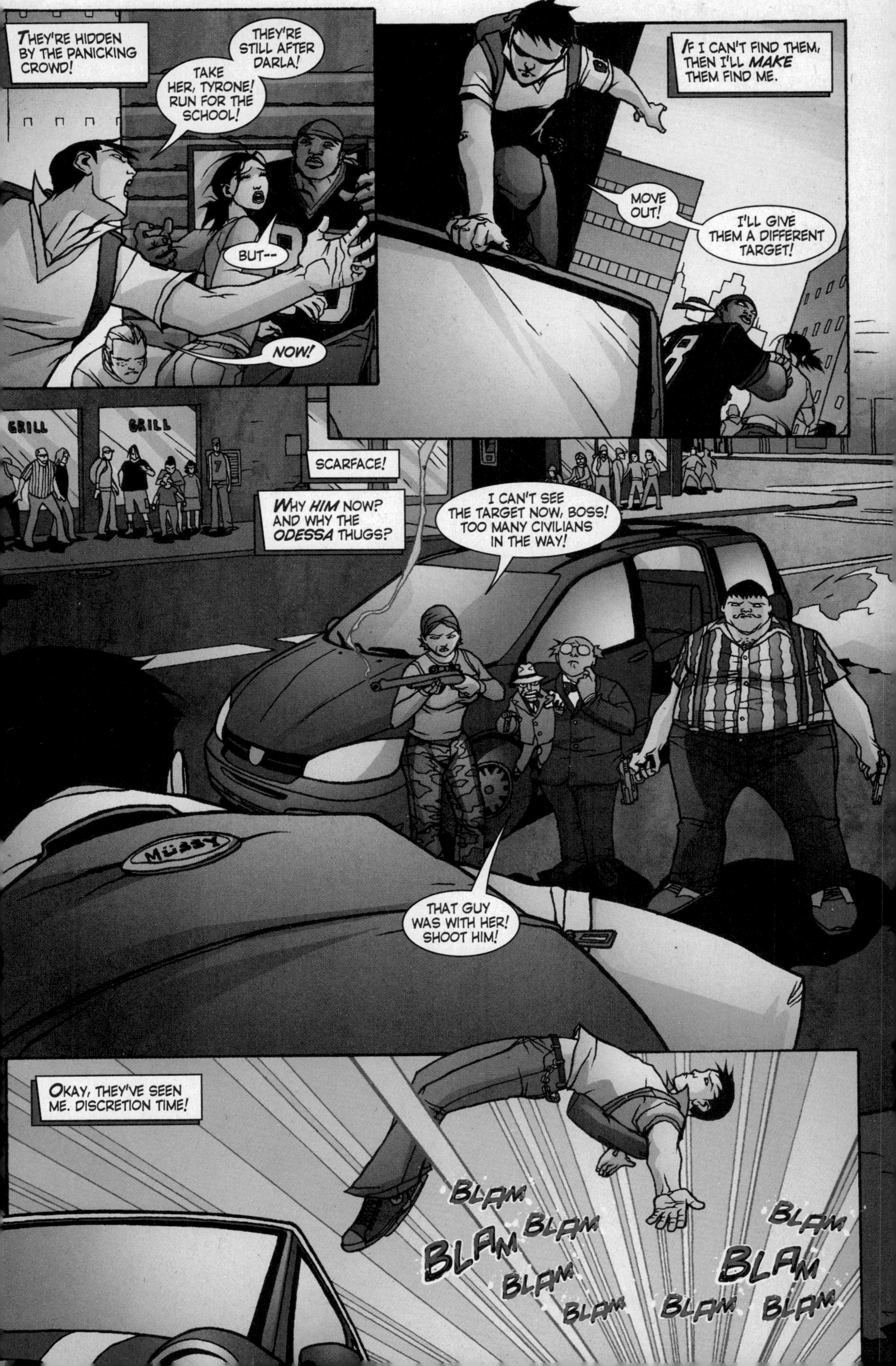
THEY'RE HIDDEN BY THE PANICKING CROWD!
THEY'RE STILL AFTER DARLA!
TAKE HER, TYRONE! RUN FOR THE SCHOOL!
BUT--
NOW!
IF I CAN'T FIND THEM, THEN I'LL MAKE THEM FIND ME.
MOVE OUT!
I'LL GIVE THEM A DIFFERENT TARGET!
GRILL
GRILL
SCARFACE!
WHY HIM NOW? AND WHY THE ODESSA THUGS?
I CAN'T SEE THE TARGET NOW, BOSS! TOO MANY CIVILIANS IN THE WAY!
THAT GUY WAS WITH HER! SHOOT HIM!
OKAY, THEY'VE SEEN ME. DISCRETION TIME!
BLAM BLAM BLAM BLAM BLAM BLAM BLAM BLAM BLAM

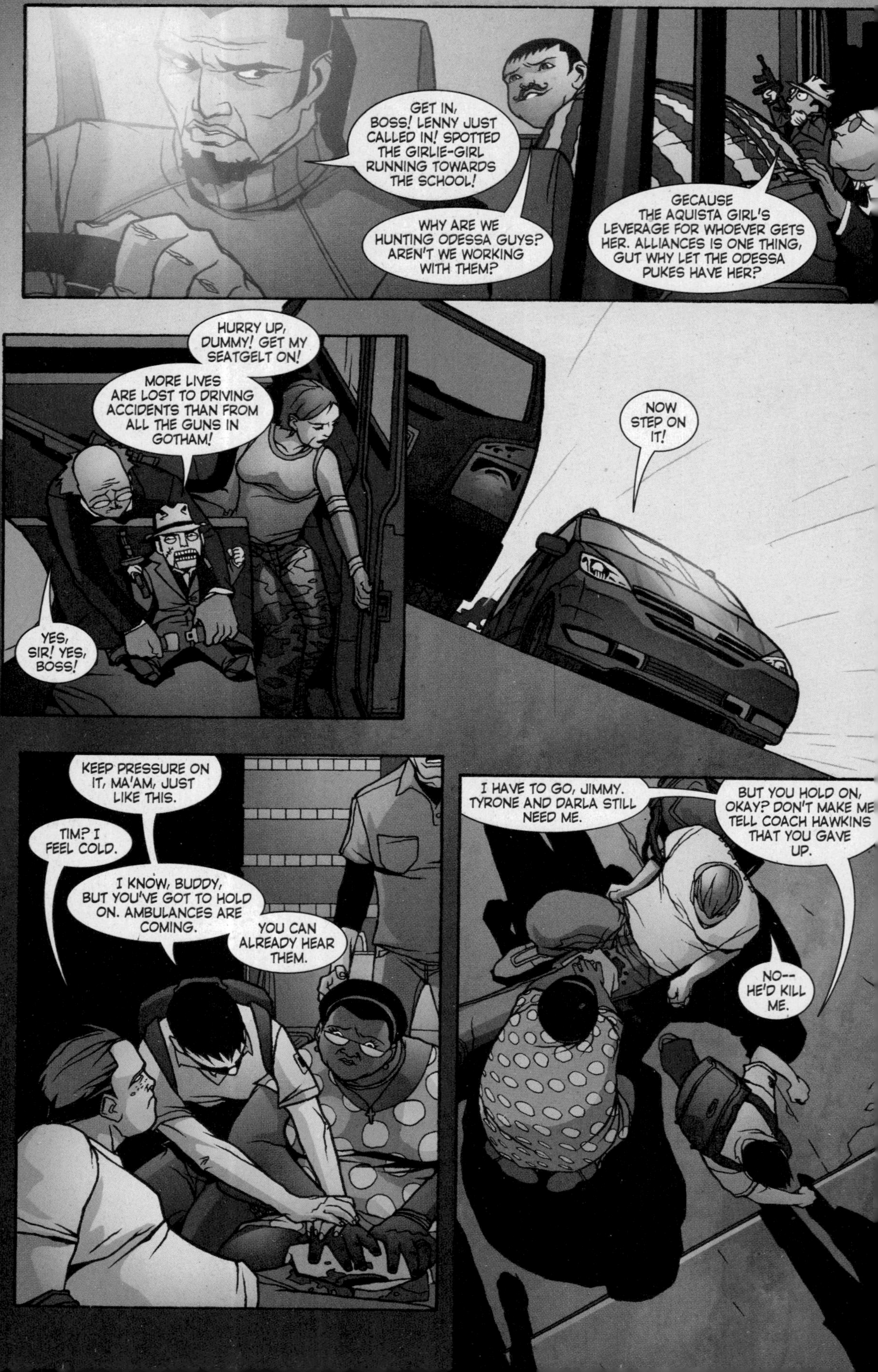
GET IN, BOSS! LENNY JUST CALLED IN! SPOTTED THE GIRLIE-GIRL RUNNING TOWARDS THE SCHOOL!
WHY ARE WE HUNTING ODESSA GUYS? AREN'T WE WORKING WITH THEM?
GECAUSE THE AQUISTA GIRL'S LEVERAGE FOR WHOEVER GETS HER. ALLIANCES IS ONE THING, GUT WHY LET THE ODESSA PUKES HAVE HER?
HURRY UP, DUMMY! GET MY SEATGELT ON!
MORE LIVES ARE LOST TO DRIVING ACCIDENTS THAN FROM ALL THE GUNS IN GOTHAM!
YES, SIR! YES, BOSS!
NOW STEP ON IT!
KEEP PRESSURE ON IT, MA'AM, JUST LIKE THIS.
TIM? I FEEL COLD.
I KNOW, BUDDY, BUT YOU'VE GOT TO HOLD ON. AMBULANCES ARE COMING.
YOU CAN ALREADY HEAR THEM.
I HAVE TO GO, JIMMY. TYRONE AND DARLA STILL NEED ME.
BUT YOU HOLD ON, OKAY? DON'T MAKE ME TELL COACH HAWKINS THAT YOU GAVE UP.
NO-- HE'D KILL ME.

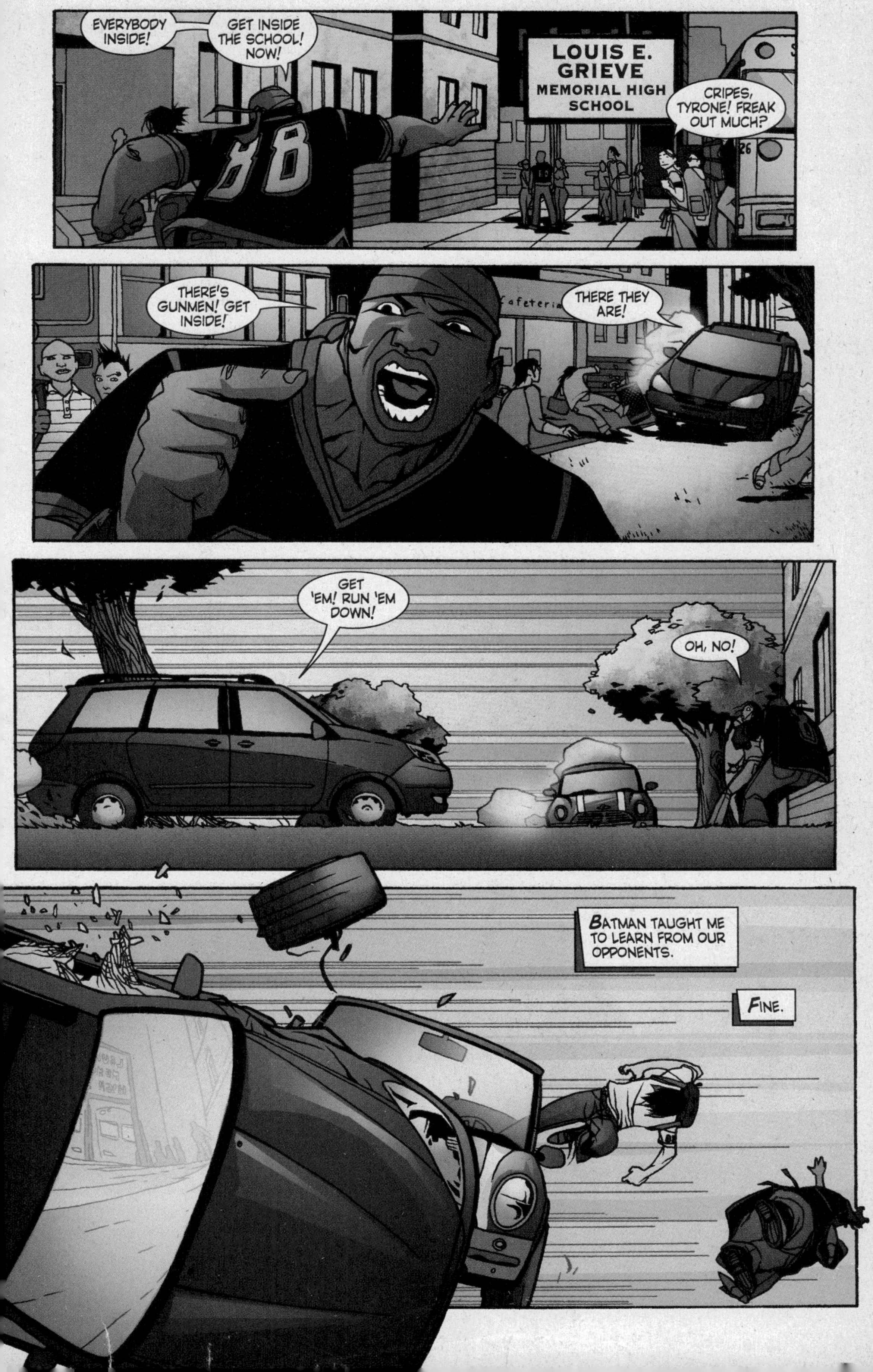
EVERYBODY INSIDE!
GET INSIDE THE SCHOOL! NOW!
LOUIS E. GRIEVE MEMORIAL HIGH SCHOOL
CRIPES, TYRONE! FREAK OUT MUCH?
THERE'S GUNMEN! GET INSIDE!
Cafeteria
THERE THEY ARE!
GET 'EM! RUN 'EM DOWN!
OH, NO!
BATMAN TAUGHT ME TO LEARN FROM OUR OPPONENTS.
FINE.

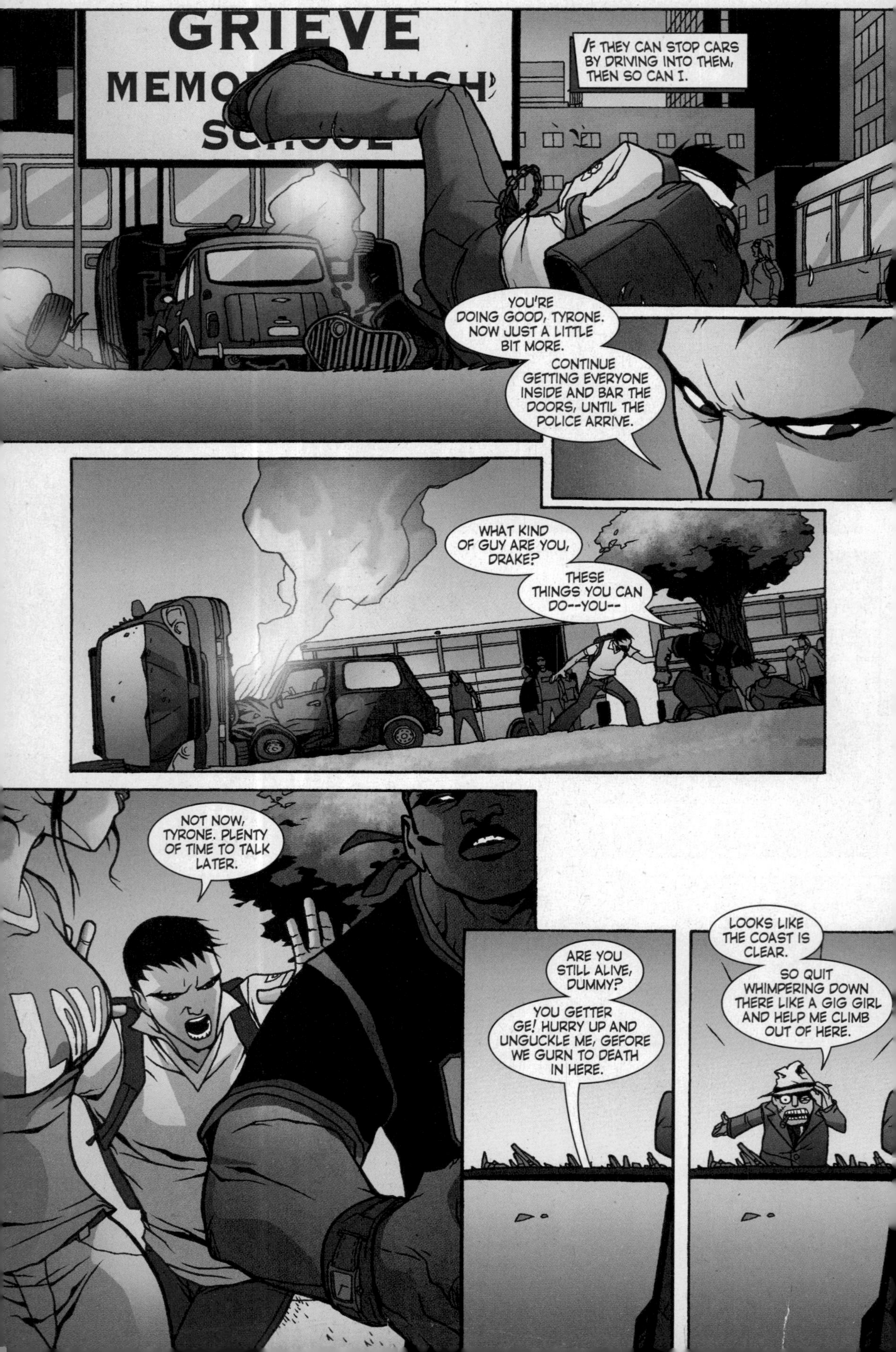
GRIEVE MEMORIAL HIGH SCHOOL
IF THEY CAN STOP CARS BY DRIVING INTO THEM, THEN SO CAN I.
YOU'RE DOING GOOD, TYRONE. NOW JUST A LITTLE BIT MORE.
CONTINUE GETTING EVERYONE INSIDE AND BAR THE DOORS, UNTIL THE POLICE ARRIVE.
WHAT KIND OF GUY ARE YOU, DRAKE?
THESE THINGS YOU CAN DO--YOU--
NOT NOW, TYRONE. PLENTY OF TIME TO TALK LATER.
ARE YOU STILL ALIVE, DUMMY?
YOU GETTER GE! HURRY UP AND UNGUCKLE ME, GEFORE WE GURN TO DEATH IN HERE.
LOOKS LIKE THE COAST IS CLEAR.
SO QUIT WHIMPERING DOWN THERE LIKE A GIG GIRL AND HELP ME CLIMB OUT OF HERE.

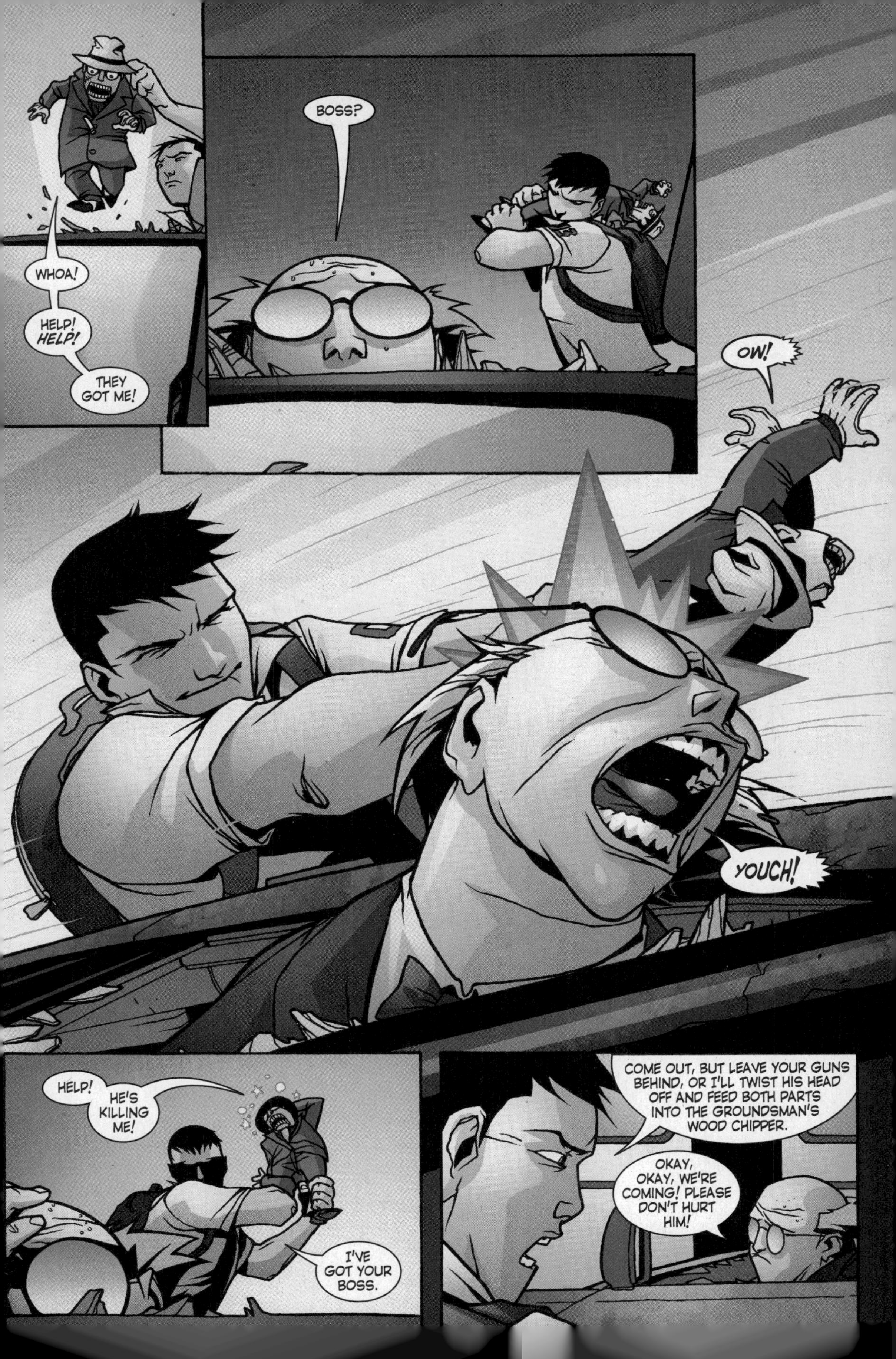

WHOA!
HELP! HELP!
THEY GOT ME!
BOSS?
OW!
YOUCH!
HELP!
HE'S KILLING ME!
I'VE GOT YOUR BOSS.
COME OUT, BUT LEAVE YOUR GUNS BEHIND, OR I'LL TWIST HIS HEAD OFF AND FEED BOTH PARTS INTO THE GROUNDSMAN'S WOOD CHIPPER.
OKAY, OKAY, WE'RE COMING! PLEASE DON'T HURT HIM!

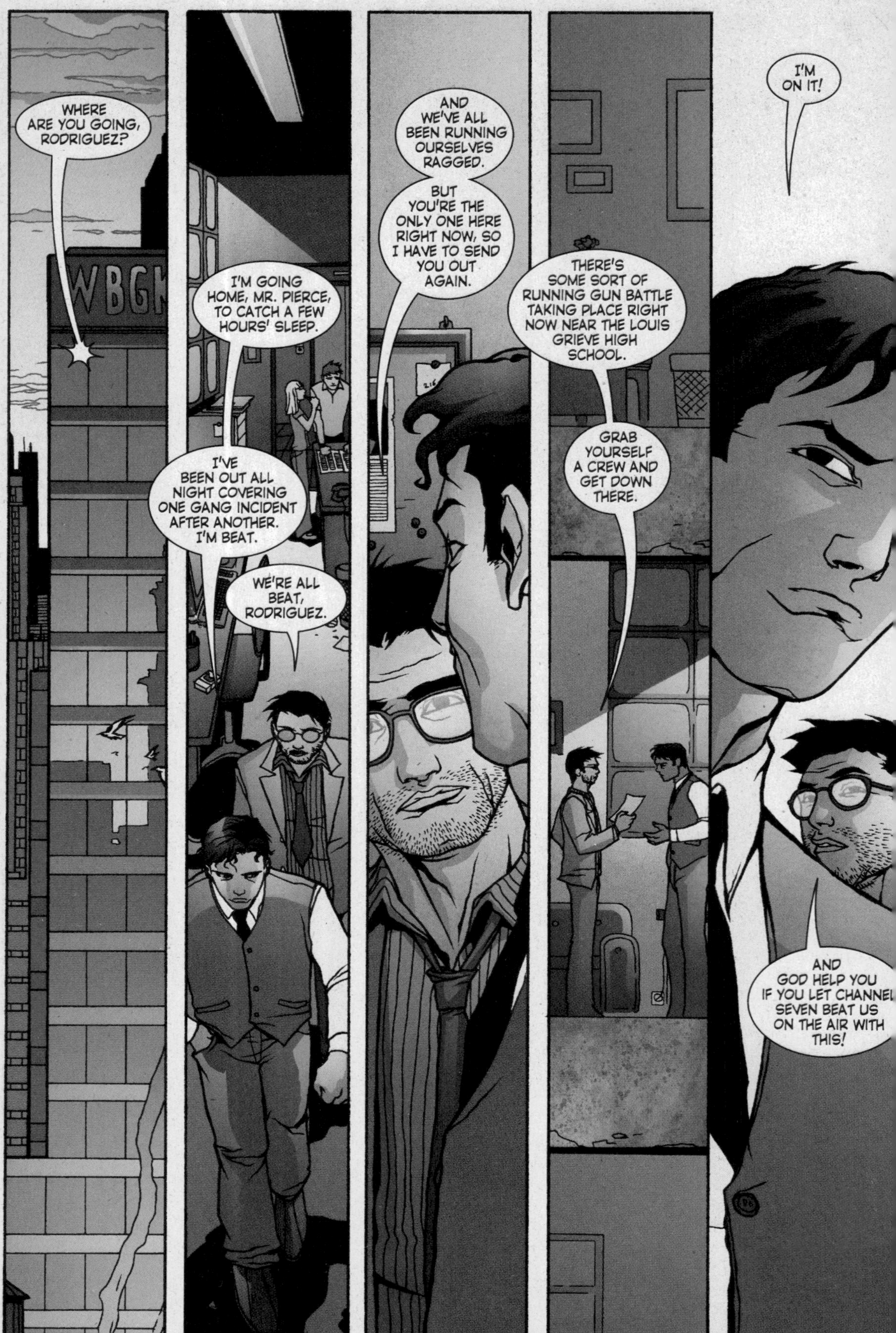
WHERE ARE YOU GOING, RODRIGUEZ?
WBGK
I'M GOING HOME, MR. PIERCE, TO CATCH A FEW HOURS' SLEEP.
I'VE BEEN OUT ALL NIGHT COVERING ONE GANG INCIDENT AFTER ANOTHER. I'M BEAT.
WE'RE ALL BEAT, RODRIGUEZ.
AND WE'VE ALL BEEN RUNNING OURSELVES RAGGED.
BUT YOU'RE THE ONLY ONE HERE RIGHT NOW, SO I HAVE TO SEND YOU OUT AGAIN.
THERE'S SOME SORT OF RUNNING GUN BATTLE TAKING PLACE RIGHT NOW NEAR THE LOUIS GRIEVE HIGH SCHOOL.
GRAB YOURSELF A CREW AND GET DOWN THERE.
I'M ON IT!
AND GOD HELP YOU IF YOU LET CHANNEL SEVEN BEAT US ON THE AIR WITH THIS!

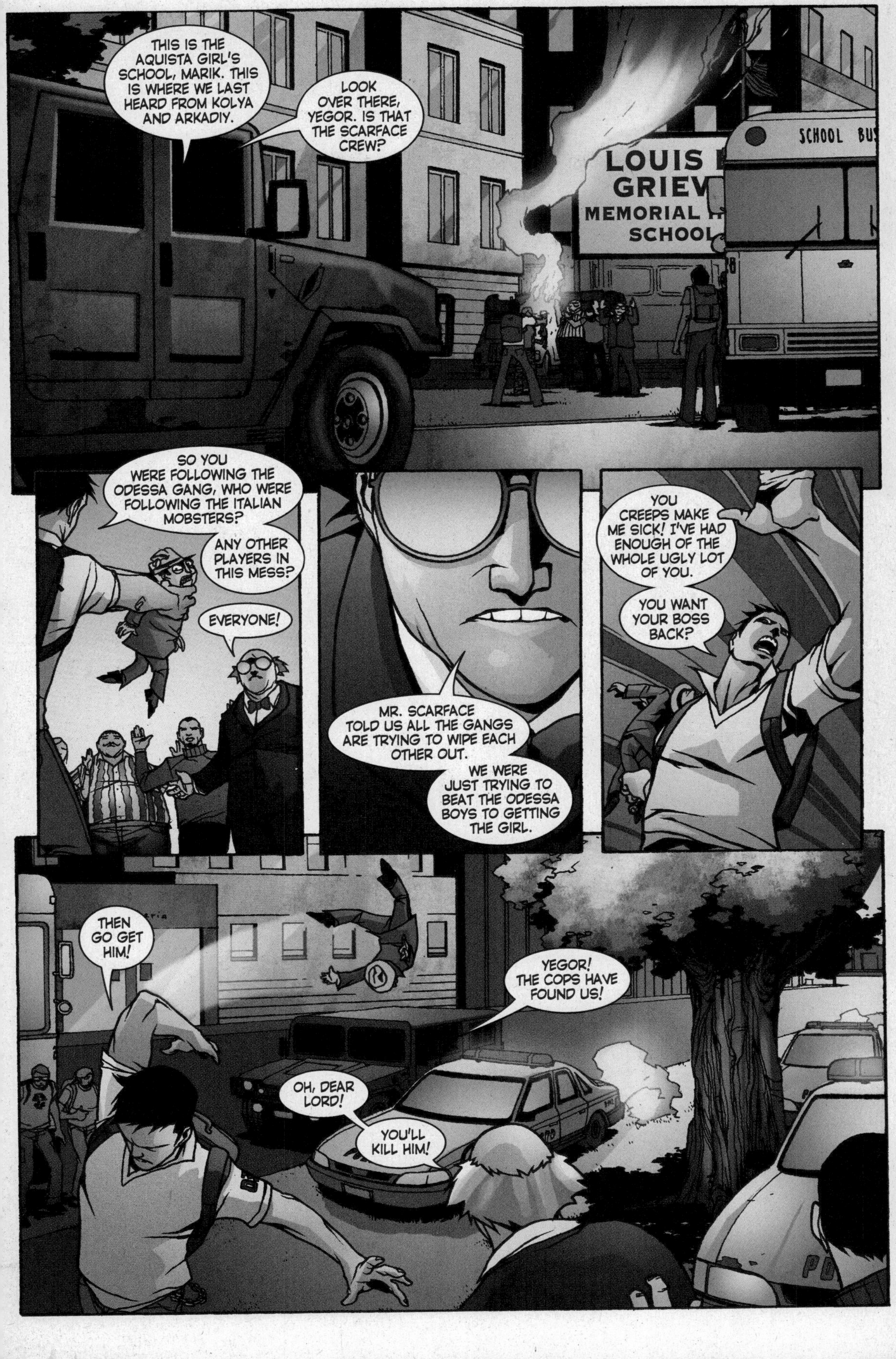
THIS IS THE AQUISTA GIRL'S SCHOOL, MARIK. THIS IS WHERE WE LAST HEARD FROM KOLYA AND ARKADIY.
LOOK OVER THERE, YEGOR. IS THAT THE SCARFACE CREW?
SCHOOL BUS
LOUIS
GRIEV
MEMORIAL
SCHOOL
SO YOU WERE FOLLOWING THE ODESSA GANG, WHO WERE FOLLOWING THE ITALIAN MOBSTERS?
ANY OTHER PLAYERS IN THIS MESS?
EVERYONE!
MR. SCARFACE TOLD US ALL THE GANGS ARE TRYING TO WIPE EACH OTHER OUT.
WE WERE JUST TRYING TO BEAT THE ODESSA BOYS TO GETTING THE GIRL.
YOU CREEPS MAKE ME SICK! I'VE HAD ENOUGH OF THE WHOLE UGLY LOT OF YOU.
YOU WANT YOUR BOSS BACK?
THEN GO GET HIM!
YEGOR! THE COPS HAVE FOUND US!
OH, DEAR LORD!
YOU'LL KILL HIM!

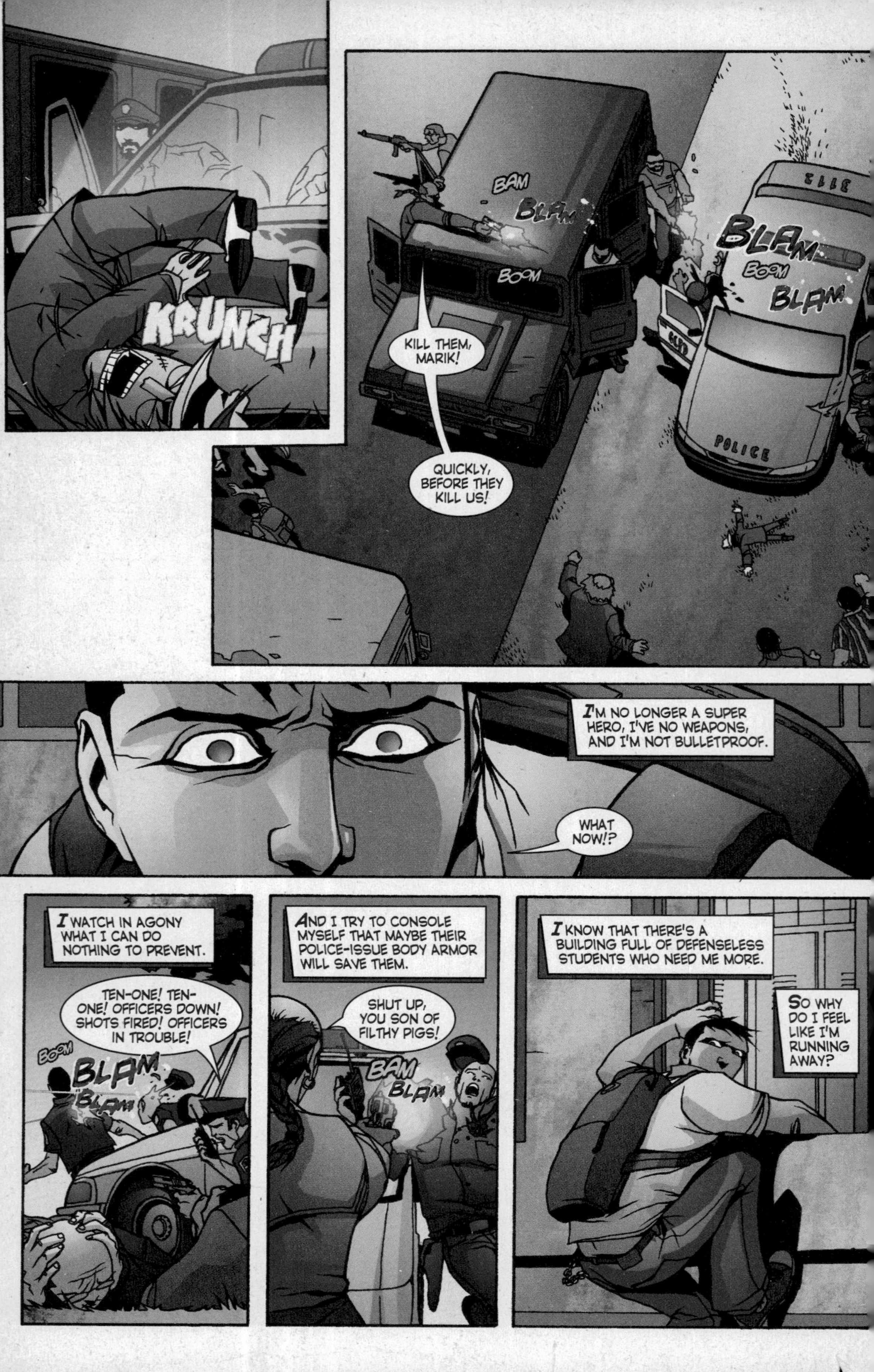
KRUNCH
BAM
BLAM
BOOM
KILL THEM, MARIK!
QUICKLY, BEFORE THEY KILL US!
3112
BLAM
BOOM
BLAM
POLICE
I'M NO LONGER A SUPER HERO, I'VE NO WEAPONS, AND I'M NOT BULLETPROOF.
WHAT NOW!?
I WATCH IN AGONY WHAT I CAN DO NOTHING TO PREVENT.
TEN-ONE! TEN-ONE! OFFICERS DOWN! SHOTS FIRED! OFFICERS IN TROUBLE!
BOOM
BLAM
BLAM
AND I TRY TO CONSOLE MYSELF THAT MAYBE THEIR POLICE-ISSUE BODY ARMOR WILL SAVE THEM.
SHUT UP, YOU SON OF FILTHY PIGS!
BAM
BLAM
I KNOW THAT THERE'S A BUILDING FULL OF DEFENSELESS STUDENTS WHO NEED ME MORE.
SO WHY DO I FEEL LIKE I'M RUNNING AWAY?

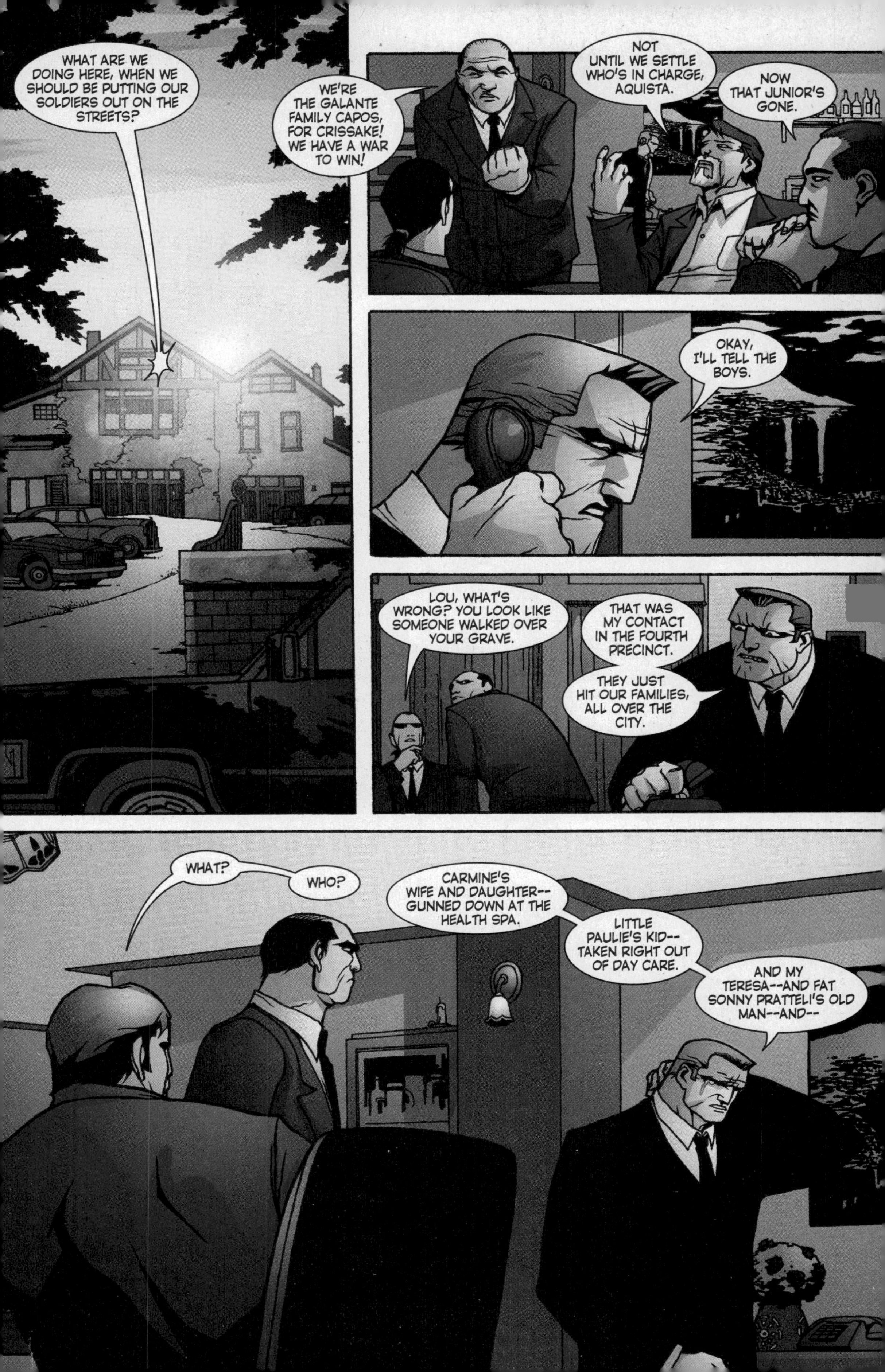
WHAT ARE WE DOING HERE, WHEN WE SHOULD BE PUTTING OUR SOLDIERS OUT ON THE STREETS?
WE'RE THE GALANTE FAMILY CAPOS, FOR CRISSAKE! WE HAVE A WAR TO WIN!
NOT UNTIL WE SETTLE WHO'S IN CHARGE, AQUISTA.
NOW THAT JUNIOR'S GONE.
OKAY, I'LL TELL THE BOYS.
LOU, WHAT'S WRONG? YOU LOOK LIKE SOMEONE WALKED OVER YOUR GRAVE.
THAT WAS MY CONTACT IN THE FOURTH PRECINCT.
THEY JUST HIT OUR FAMILIES, ALL OVER THE CITY.
WHAT?
WHO?
CARMINE'S WIFE AND DAUGHTER-- GUNNED DOWN AT THE HEALTH SPA.
LITTLE PAULIE'S KID-- TAKEN RIGHT OUT OF DAY CARE.
AND MY TERESA--AND FAT SONNY PRATTELI'S OLD MAN--AND--

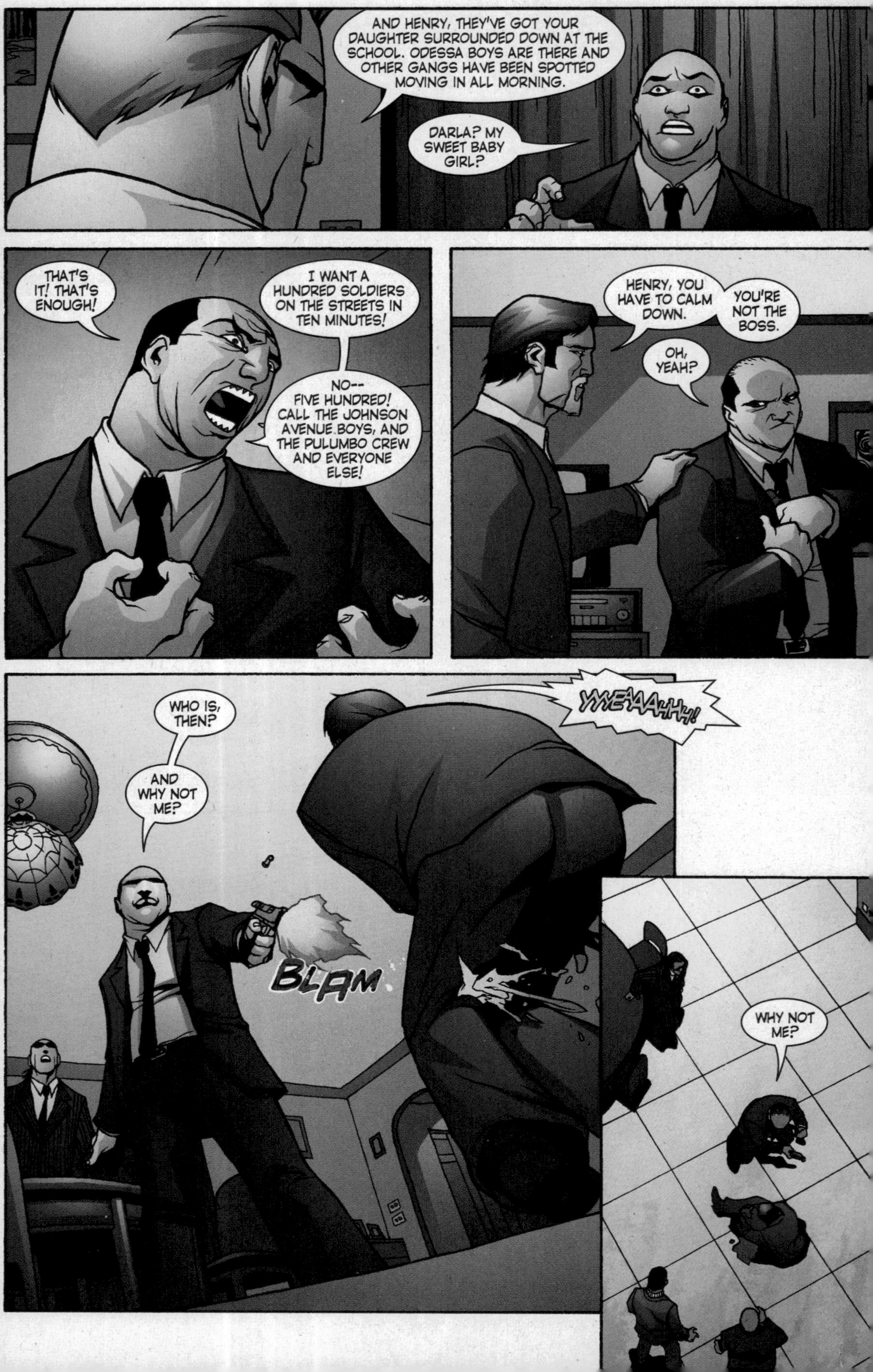
AND HENRY, THEY'VE GOT YOUR DAUGHTER SURROUNDED DOWN AT THE SCHOOL. ODESSA BOYS ARE THERE AND OTHER GANGS HAVE BEEN SPOTTED MOVING IN ALL MORNING.
DARLA? MY SWEET BABY GIRL?
THAT'S IT! THAT'S ENOUGH!
I WANT A HUNDRED SOLDIERS ON THE STREETS IN TEN MINUTES!
NO-- FIVE HUNDRED! CALL THE JOHNSON AVENUE BOYS, AND THE PULUMBO CREW AND EVERYONE ELSE!
HENRY, YOU HAVE TO CALM DOWN.
YOU'RE NOT THE BOSS.
OH, YEAH?
WHO IS, THEN?
AND WHY NOT ME?
YYYEAAAHHH!
BLAM
WHY NOT ME?

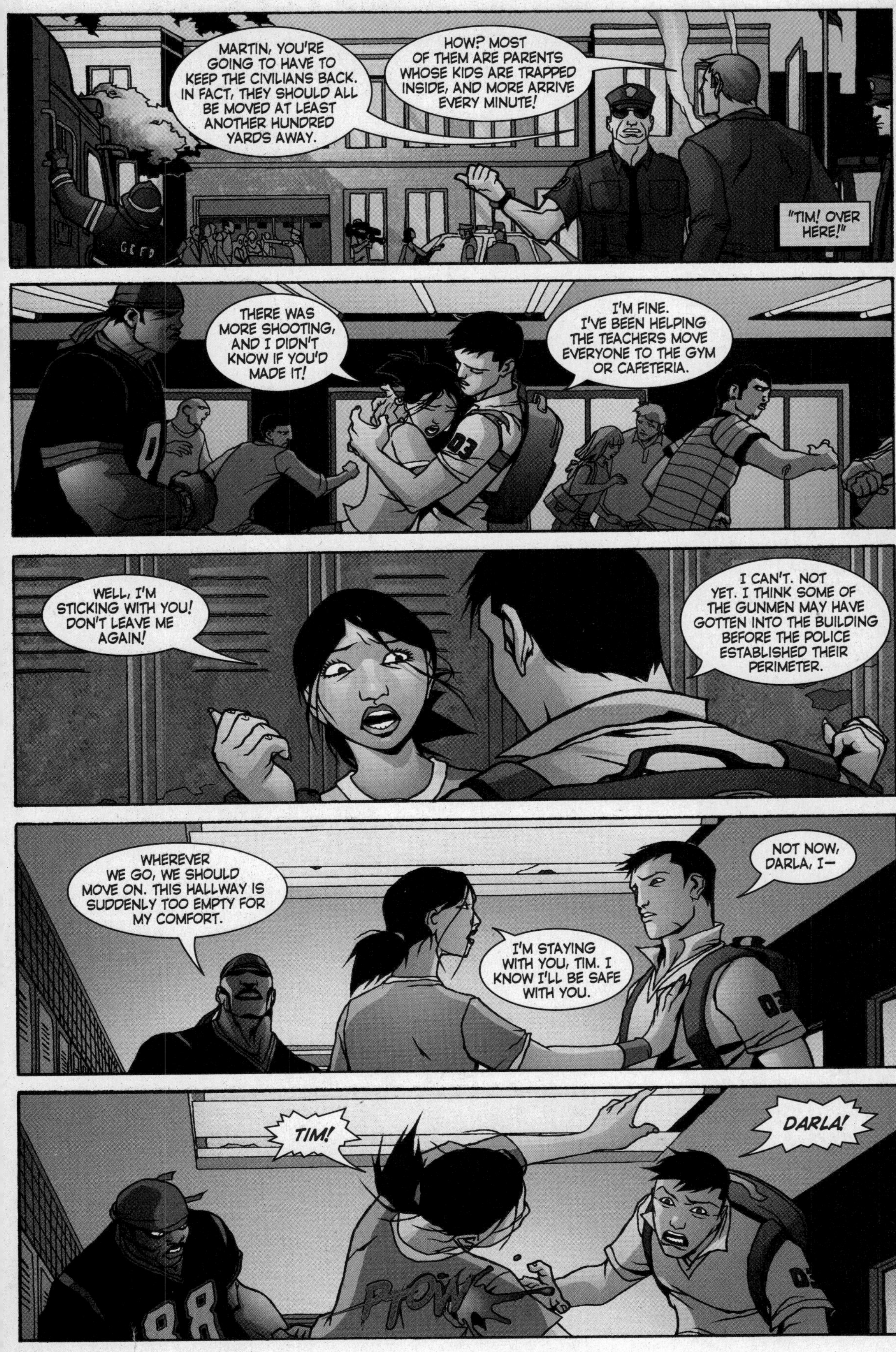
MARTIN, YOU'RE GOING TO HAVE TO KEEP THE CIVILIANS BACK. IN FACT, THEY SHOULD ALL BE MOVED AT LEAST ANOTHER HUNDRED YARDS AWAY.
HOW? MOST OF THEM ARE PARENTS WHOSE KIDS ARE TRAPPED INSIDE, AND MORE ARRIVE EVERY MINUTE!
GCFD
"TIM! OVER HERE!"
THERE WAS MORE SHOOTING, AND I DIDN'T KNOW IF YOU'D MADE IT!
I'M FINE. I'VE BEEN HELPING THE TEACHERS MOVE EVERYONE TO THE GYM OR CAFETERIA.
03
WELL, I'M STICKING WITH YOU! DON'T LEAVE ME AGAIN!
I CAN'T. NOT YET. I THINK SOME OF THE GUNMEN MAY HAVE GOTTEN INTO THE BUILDING BEFORE THE POLICE ESTABLISHED THEIR PERIMETER.
WHEREVER WE GO, WE SHOULD MOVE ON. THIS HALLWAY IS SUDDENLY TOO EMPTY FOR MY COMFORT.
I'M STAYING WITH YOU, TIM. I KNOW I'LL BE SAFE WITH YOU.
NOT NOW, DARLA, I—
TIM!
DARLA!
PTOW

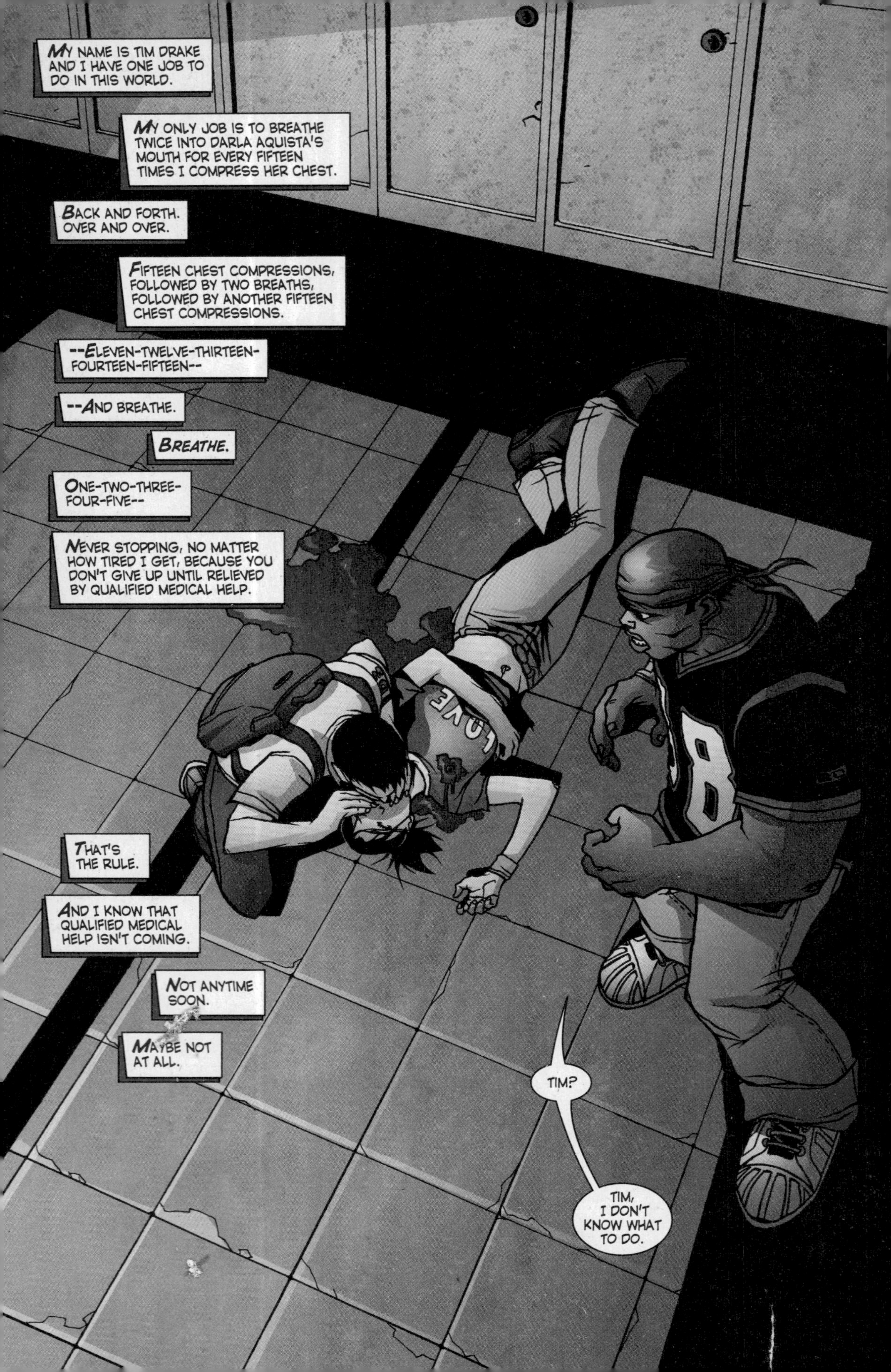
MY NAME IS TIM DRAKE AND I HAVE ONE JOB TO DO IN THIS WORLD.
MY ONLY JOB IS TO BREATHE TWICE INTO DARLA AQUISTA'S MOUTH FOR EVERY FIFTEEN TIMES I COMPRESS HER CHEST.
BACK AND FORTH. OVER AND OVER.
FIFTEEN CHEST COMPRESSIONS, FOLLOWED BY TWO BREATHS, FOLLOWED BY ANOTHER FIFTEEN CHEST COMPRESSIONS.
--ELEVEN-TWELVE-THIRTEEN-FOURTEEN-FIFTEEN--
--AND BREATHE.
BREATHE.
ONE-TWO-THREE-FOUR-FIVE--
NEVER STOPPING, NO MATTER HOW TIRED I GET, BECAUSE YOU DON'T GIVE UP UNTIL RELIEVED BY QUALIFIED MEDICAL HELP.
LOVE
THAT'S THE RULE.
AND I KNOW THAT QUALIFIED MEDICAL HELP ISN'T COMING.
NOT ANYTIME SOON.
MAYBE NOT AT ALL.
TIM?
TIM, I DON'T KNOW WHAT TO DO.

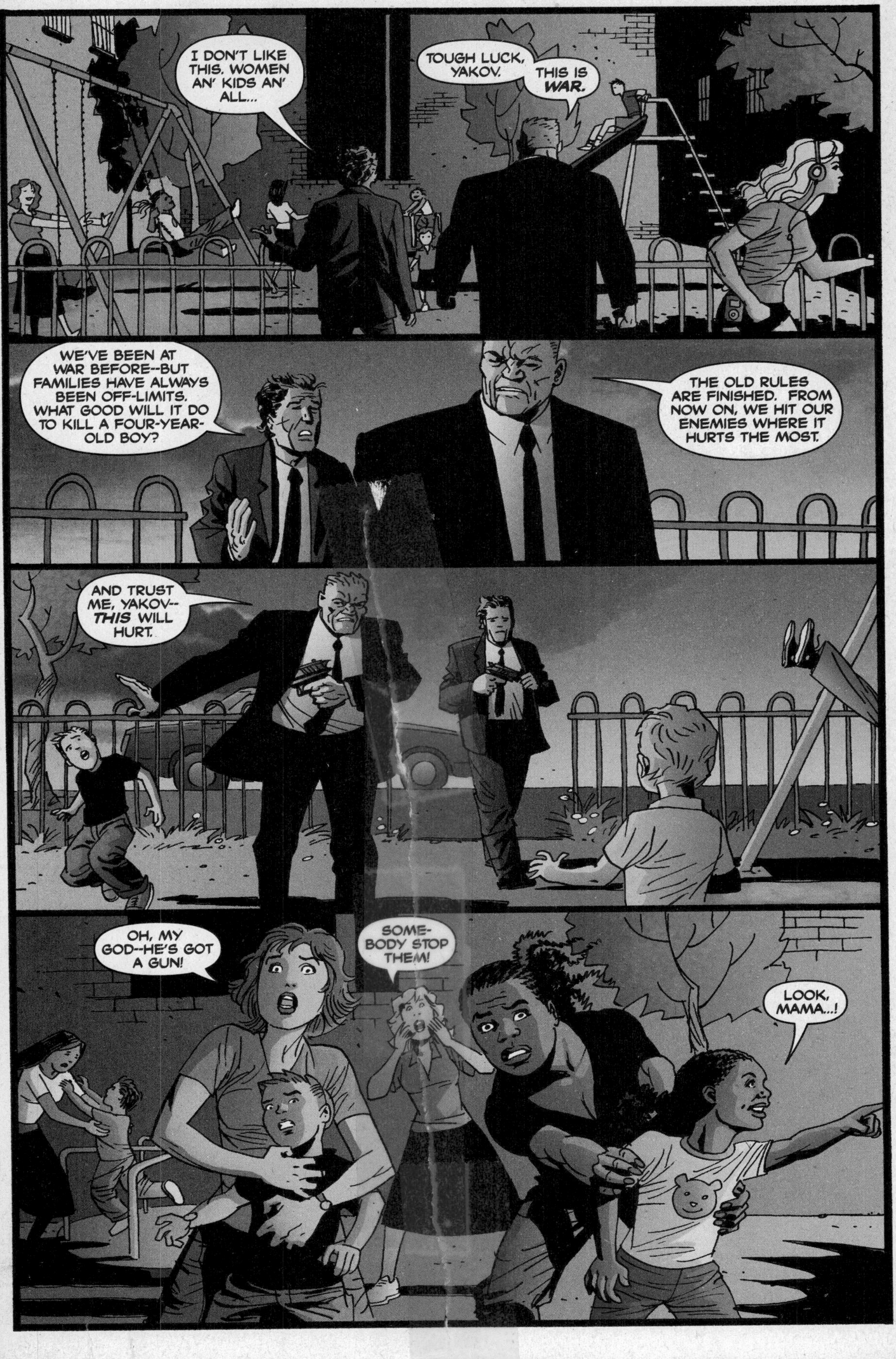
I DON'T LIKE THIS. WOMEN AN' KIDS AN' ALL...
TOUGH LUCK, YAKOV.
THIS IS *WAR.*
WE'VE BEEN AT WAR BEFORE--BUT FAMILIES HAVE ALWAYS BEEN OFF-LIMITS. WHAT GOOD WILL IT DO TO KILL A FOUR-YEAR-OLD BOY?
THE OLD RULES ARE FINISHED. FROM NOW ON, WE HIT OUR ENEMIES WHERE IT HURTS THE MOST.
AND TRUST ME, YAKOV-- *THIS* WILL HURT.
OH, MY GOD--HE'S GOT A GUN!
SOME-BODY STOP THEM!
LOOK, MAMA...!

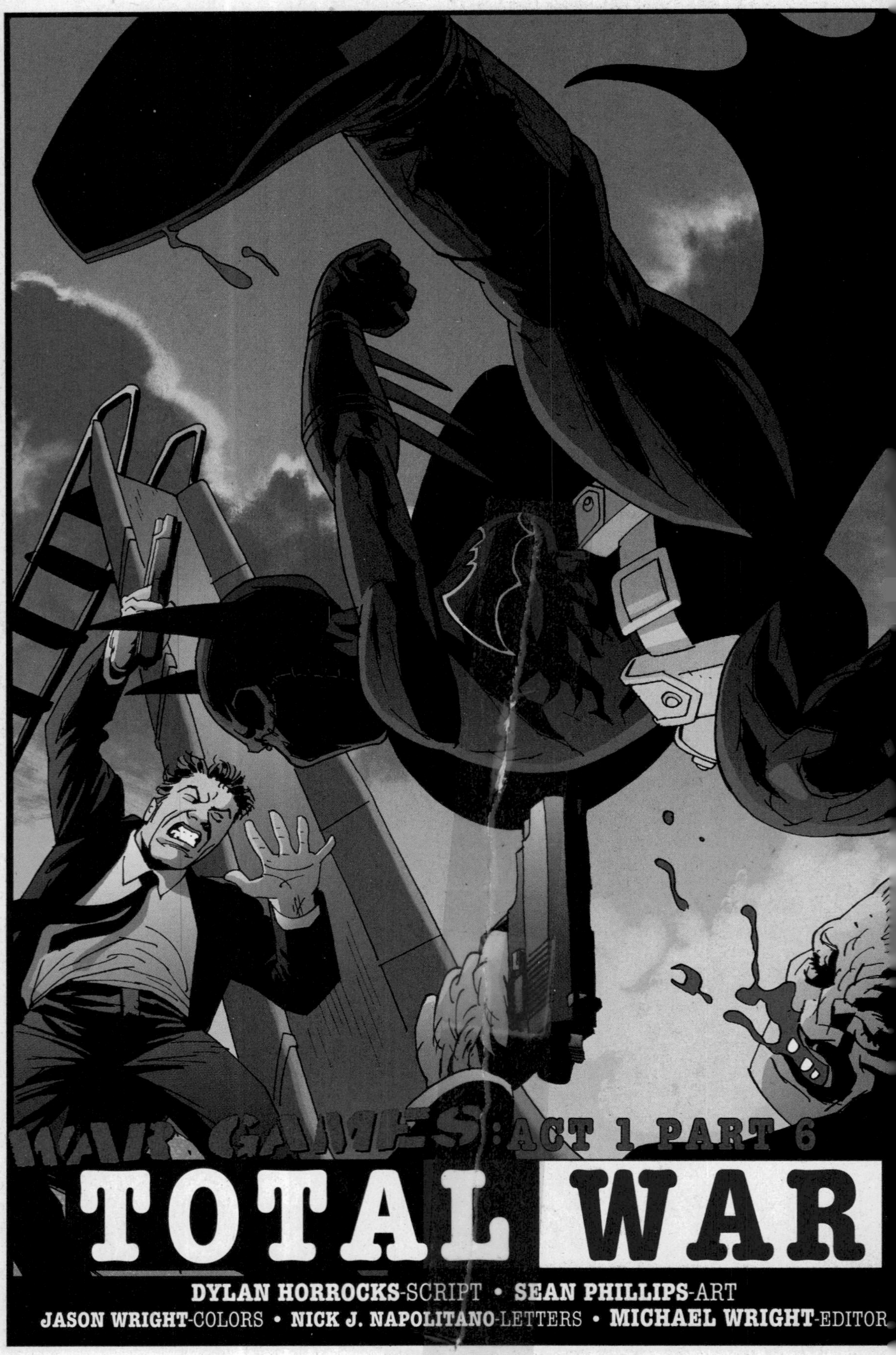
WAR GAMES: ACT 1 PART 6
TOTAL WAR
DYLAN HORROCKS-SCRIPT • SEAN PHILLIPS-ART
JASON WRIGHT-COLORS • NICK J. NAPOLITANO-LETTERS • MICHAEL WRIGHT-EDITOR

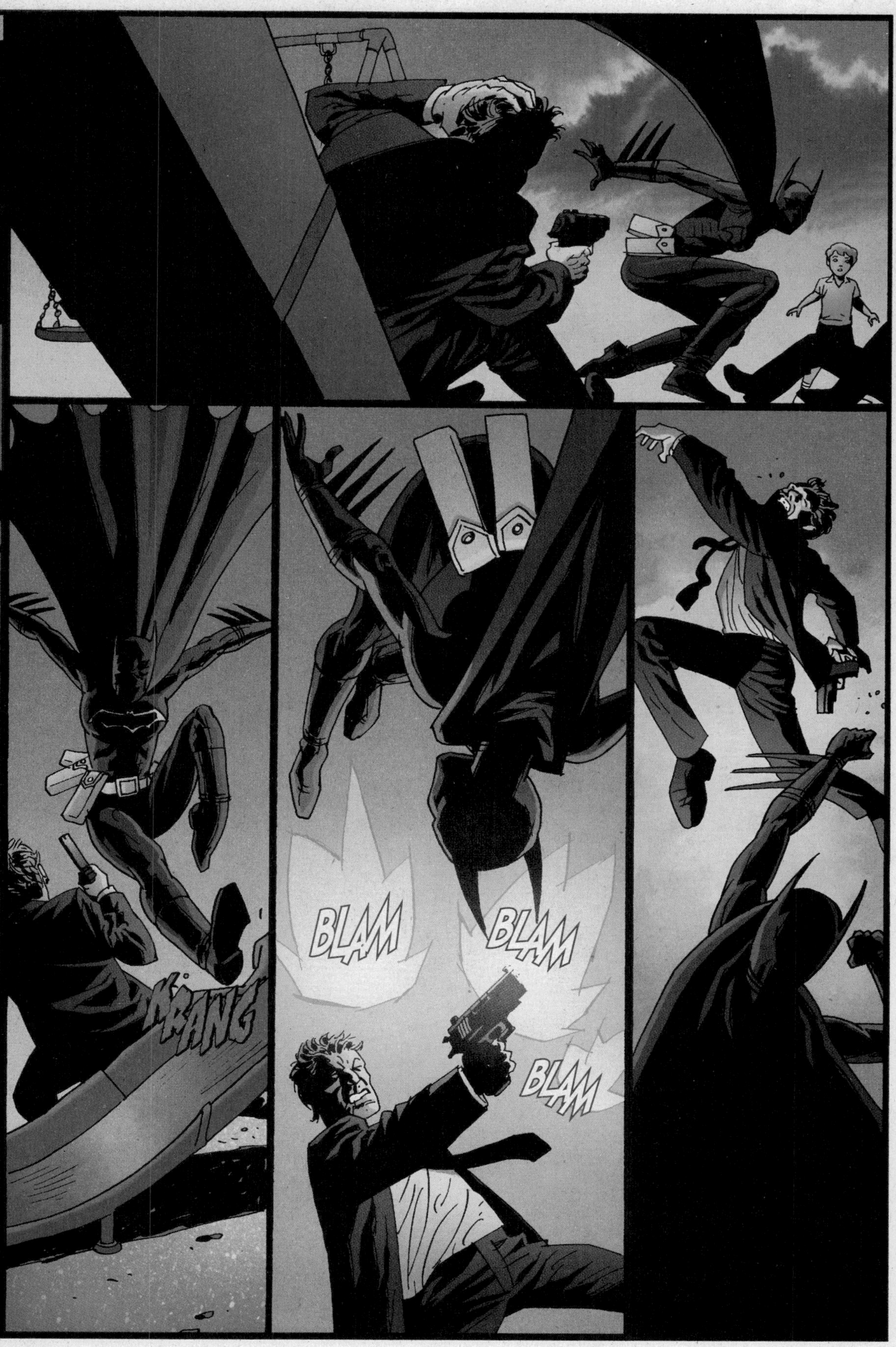
KRANG
BLAM
BLAM
BLAM

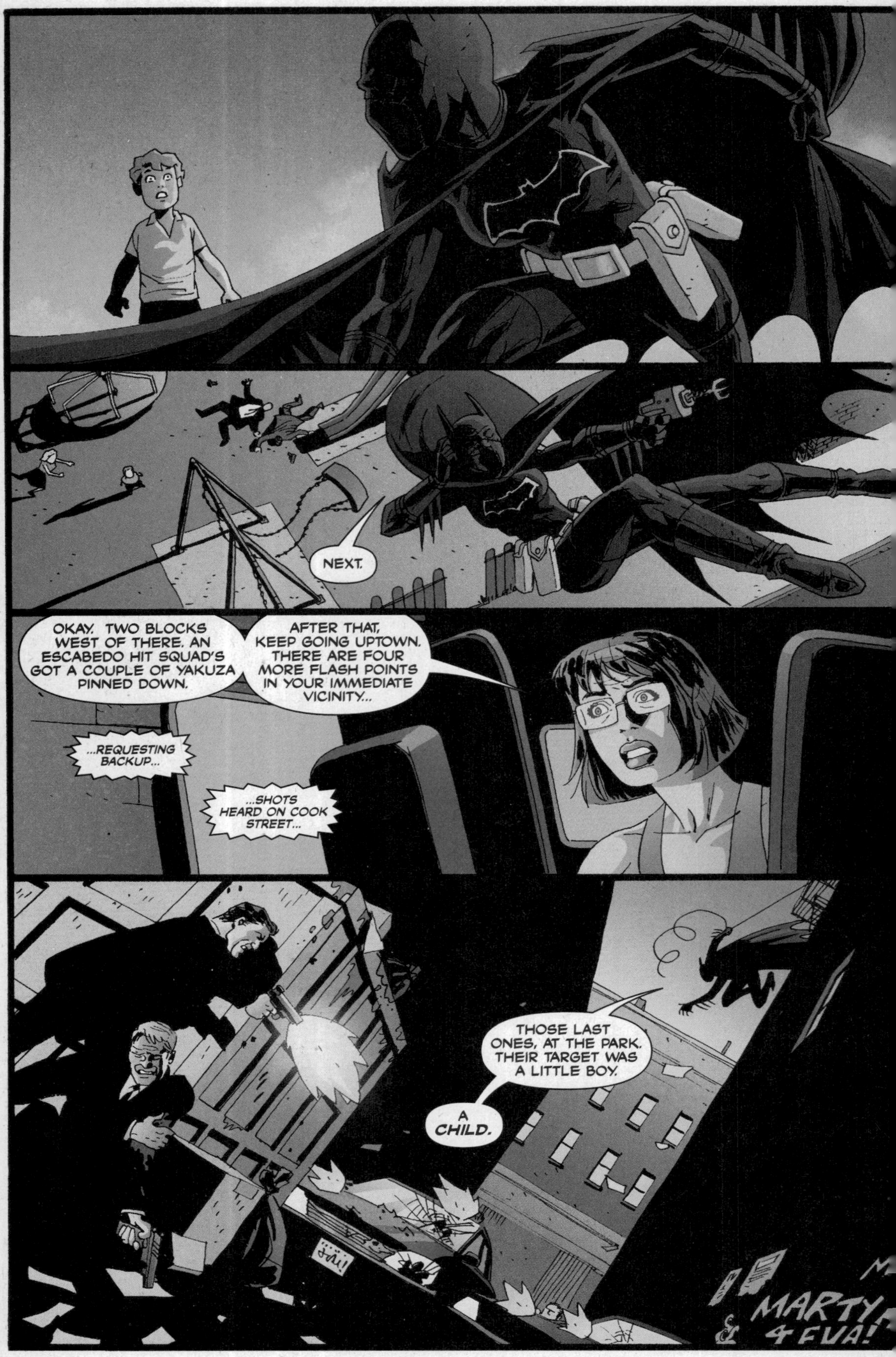
NEXT.
OKAY. TWO BLOCKS WEST OF THERE. AN ESCABEDO HIT SQUAD'S GOT A COUPLE OF YAKUZA PINNED DOWN.
AFTER THAT, KEEP GOING UPTOWN. THERE ARE FOUR MORE FLASH POINTS IN YOUR IMMEDIATE VICINITY...
...REQUESTING BACKUP...
...SHOTS HEARD ON COOK STREET...
THOSE LAST ONES, AT THE PARK. THEIR TARGET WAS A LITTLE BOY.
A CHILD.
MARTY
4 EVA!

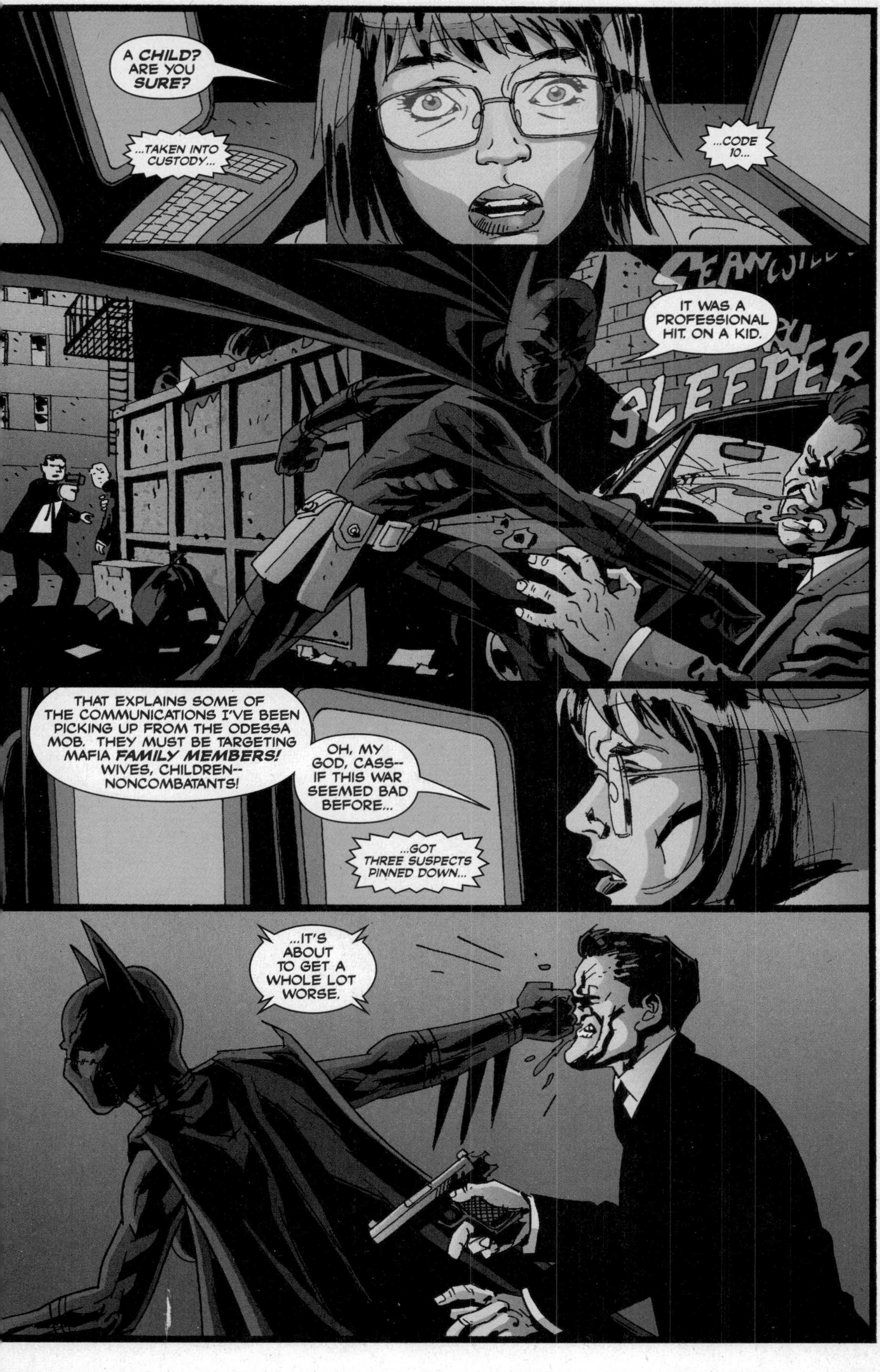
A CHILD? ARE YOU SURE?
...TAKEN INTO CUSTODY...
...CODE 10...
IT WAS A PROFESSIONAL HIT ON A KID.
SLEEPER
THAT EXPLAINS SOME OF THE COMMUNICATIONS I'VE BEEN PICKING UP FROM THE ODESSA MOB. THEY MUST BE TARGETING MAFIA FAMILY MEMBERS! WIVES, CHILDREN-- NONCOMBATANTS!
OH, MY GOD, CASS-- IF THIS WAR SEEMED BAD BEFORE...
...GOT THREE SUSPECTS PINNED DOWN...
...IT'S ABOUT TO GET A WHOLE LOT WORSE.

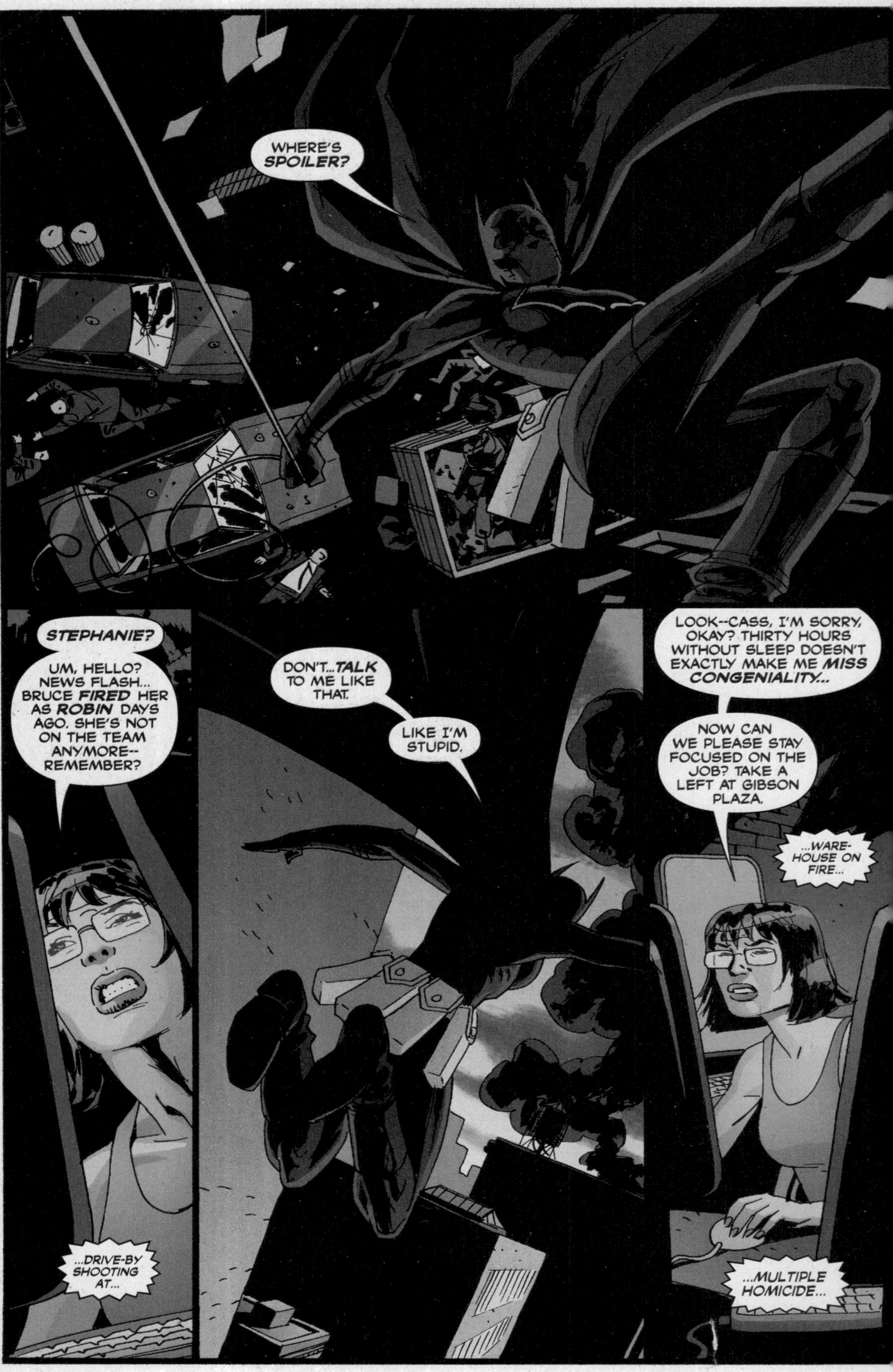

WHERE'S SPOILER?
STEPHANIE?
UM, HELLO? NEWS FLASH... BRUCE FIRED HER AS ROBIN DAYS AGO. SHE'S NOT ON THE TEAM ANYMORE--REMEMBER?
...DRIVE-BY SHOOTING AT...
DON'T...TALK TO ME LIKE THAT.
LIKE I'M STUPID.
LOOK--CASS, I'M SORRY, OKAY? THIRTY HOURS WITHOUT SLEEP DOESN'T EXACTLY MAKE ME MISS CONGENIALITY...
NOW CAN WE PLEASE STAY FOCUSED ON THE JOB? TAKE A LEFT AT GIBSON PLAZA.
...WARE-HOUSE ON FIRE...
...MULTIPLE HOMICIDE...

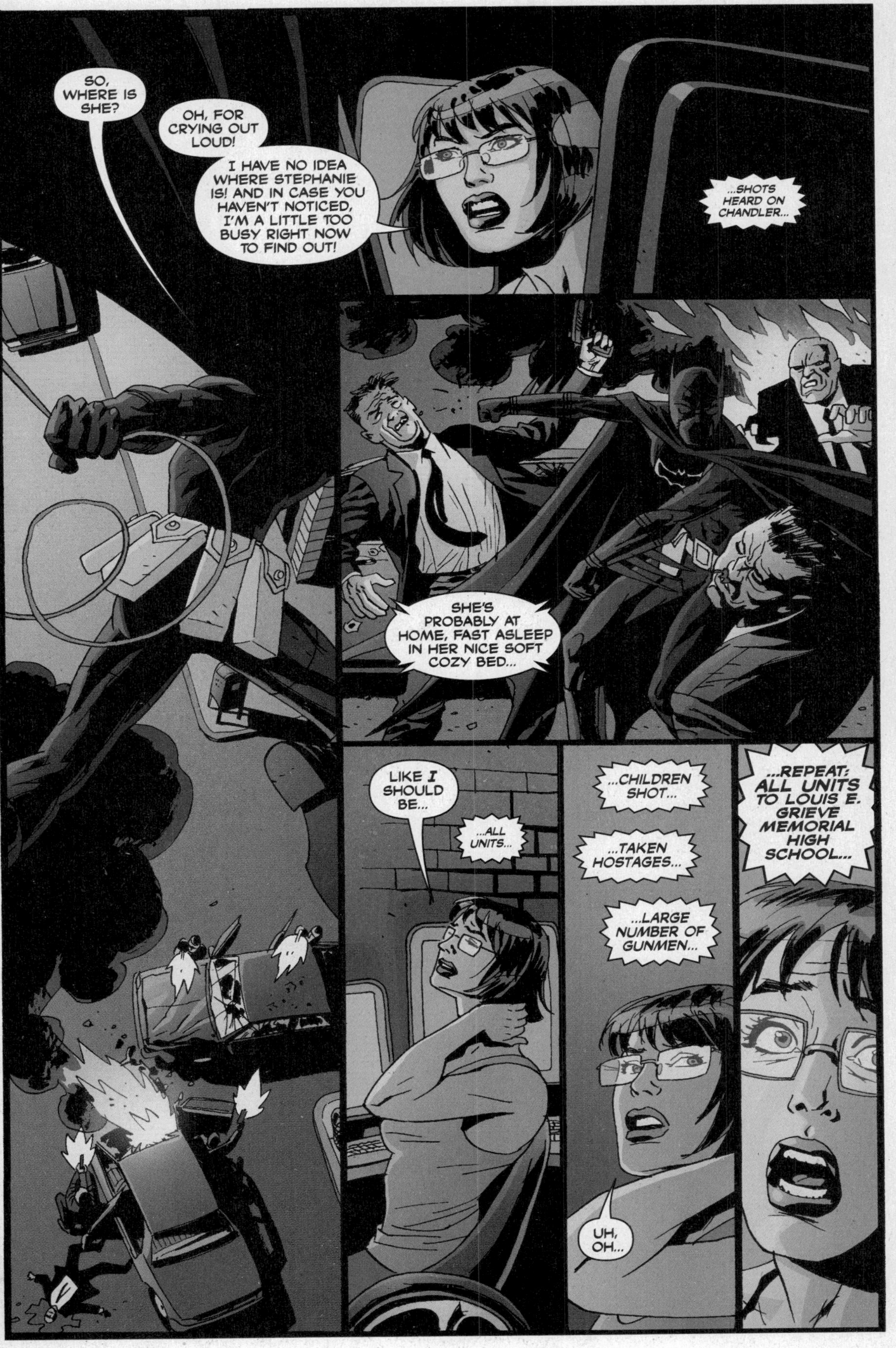

SO, WHERE IS SHE?
OH, FOR CRYING OUT LOUD!
I HAVE NO IDEA WHERE STEPHANIE IS! AND IN CASE YOU HAVEN'T NOTICED, I'M A LITTLE TOO BUSY RIGHT NOW TO FIND OUT!
...SHOTS HEARD ON CHANDLER...
SHE'S PROBABLY AT HOME, FAST ASLEEP IN HER NICE SOFT COZY BED...
LIKE I SHOULD BE...
...ALL UNITS...
...CHILDREN SHOT...
...TAKEN HOSTAGES...
...LARGE NUMBER OF GUNMEN...
UH, OH...
...REPEAT: ALL UNITS TO LOUIS E. GRIEVE MEMORIAL HIGH SCHOOL...

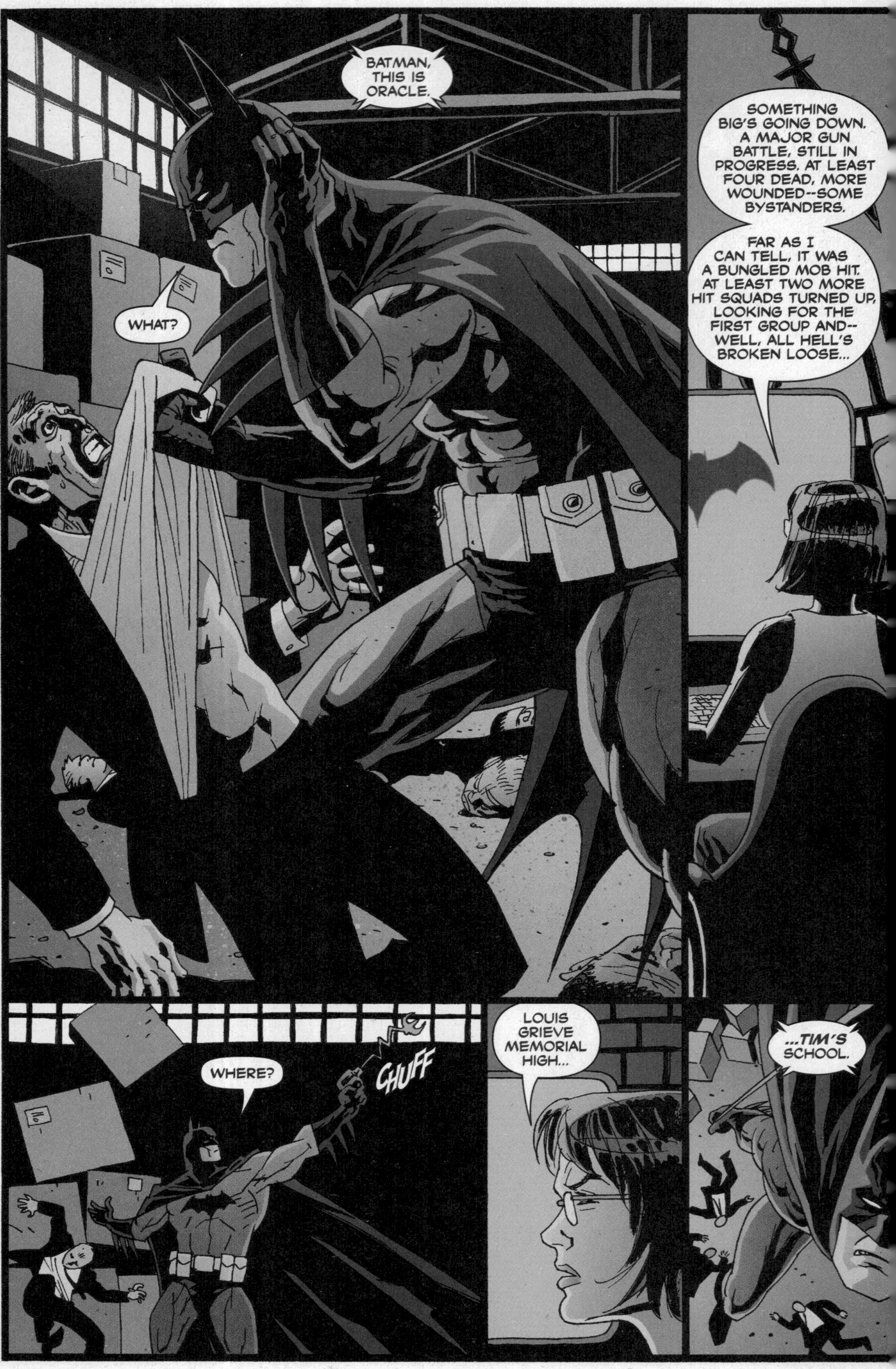
BATMAN, THIS IS ORACLE.
WHAT?
SOMETHING BIG'S GOING DOWN. A MAJOR GUN BATTLE, STILL IN PROGRESS. AT LEAST FOUR DEAD, MORE WOUNDED--SOME BYSTANDERS.
FAR AS I CAN TELL, IT WAS A BUNGLED MOB HIT. AT LEAST TWO MORE HIT SQUADS TURNED UP, LOOKING FOR THE FIRST GROUP AND--WELL, ALL HELL'S BROKEN LOOSE...
WHERE?
CHUFF
LOUIS GRIEVE MEMORIAL HIGH...
...TIM'S SCHOOL.

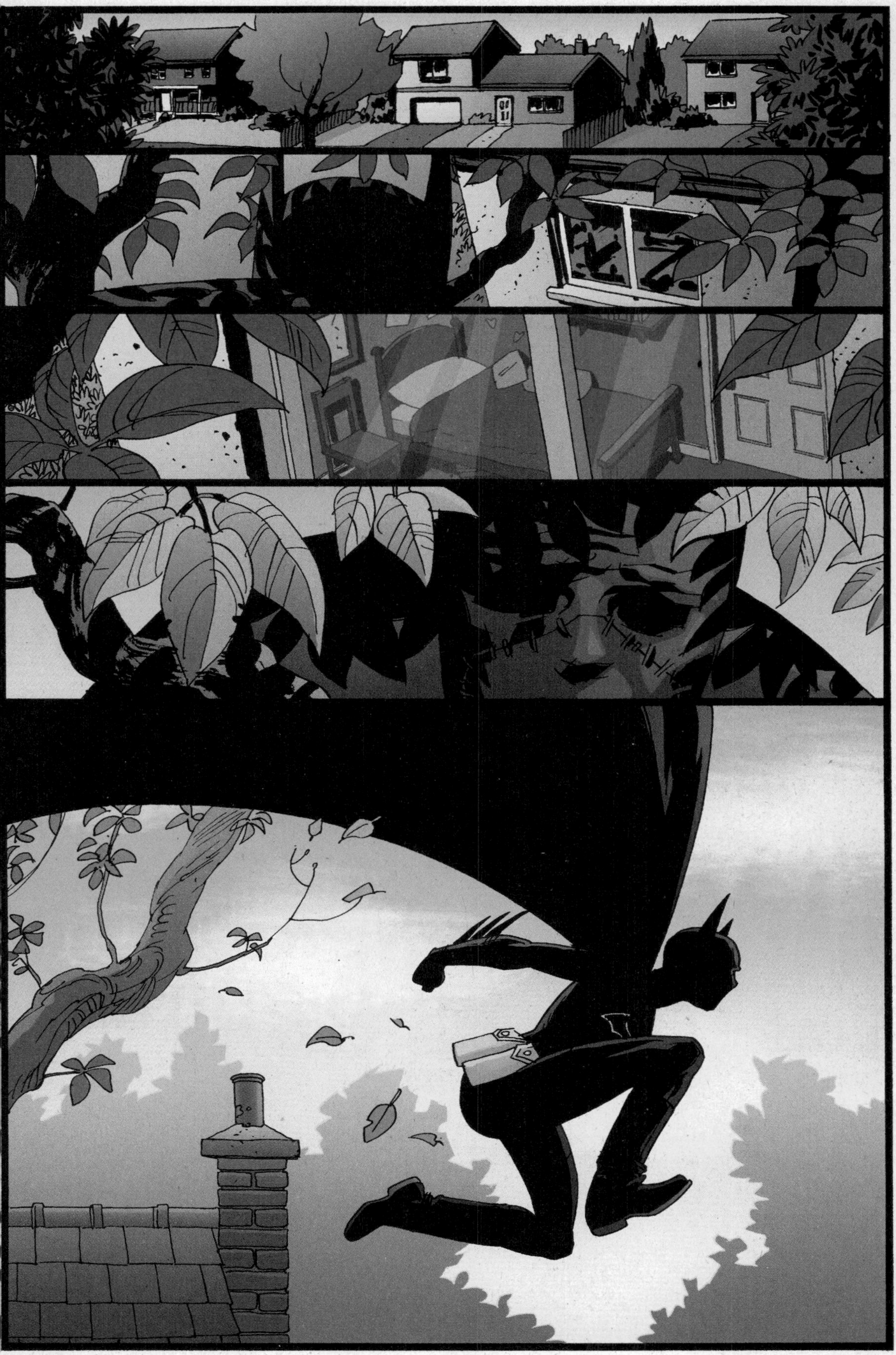

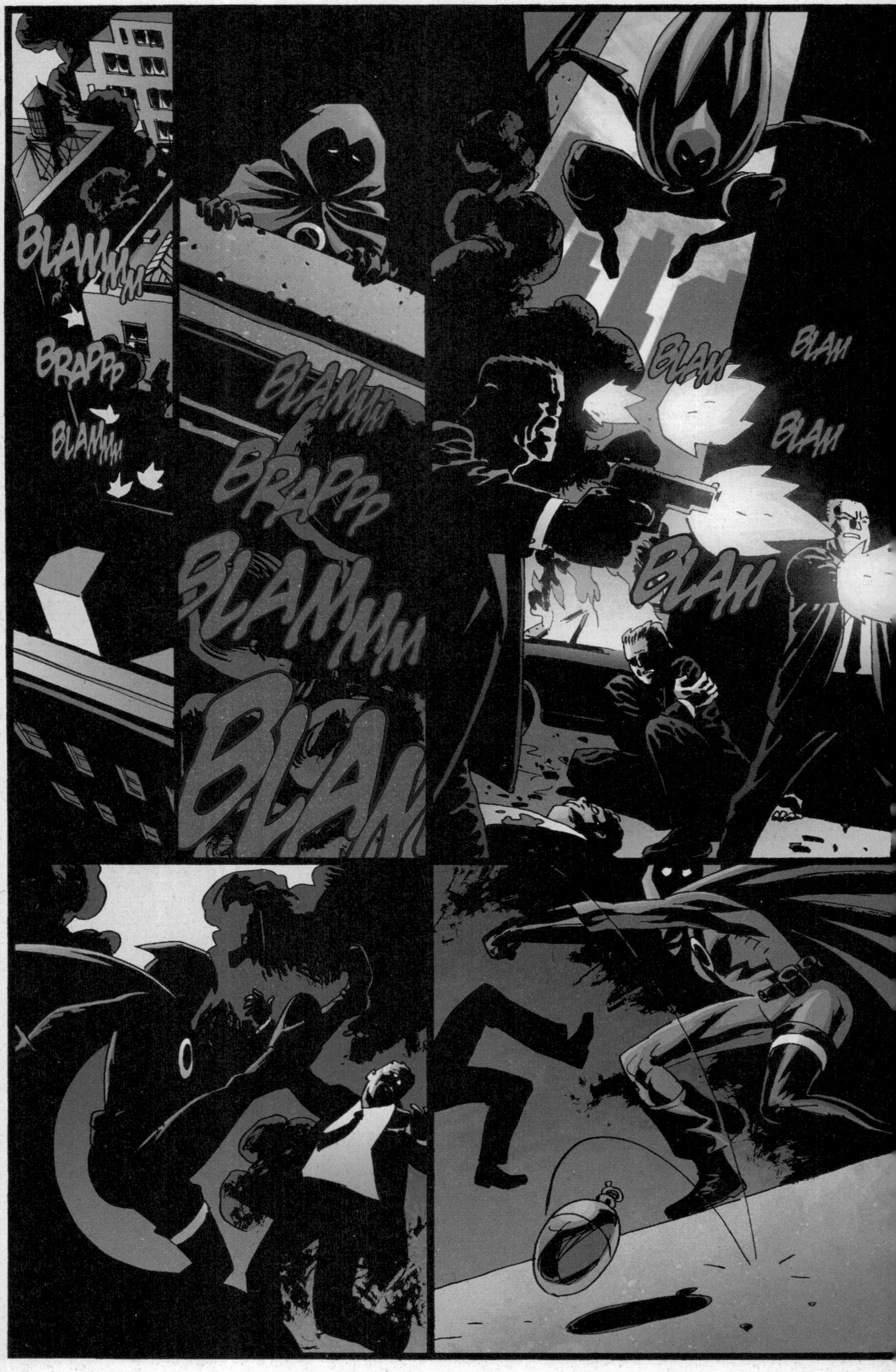

BLAMMMM
BRAPPP
BLAMMMM
BLAMMMM
BRAPPP
BLAMMMM
BLAM
BLAM
BLAM
BLAM
BLAM

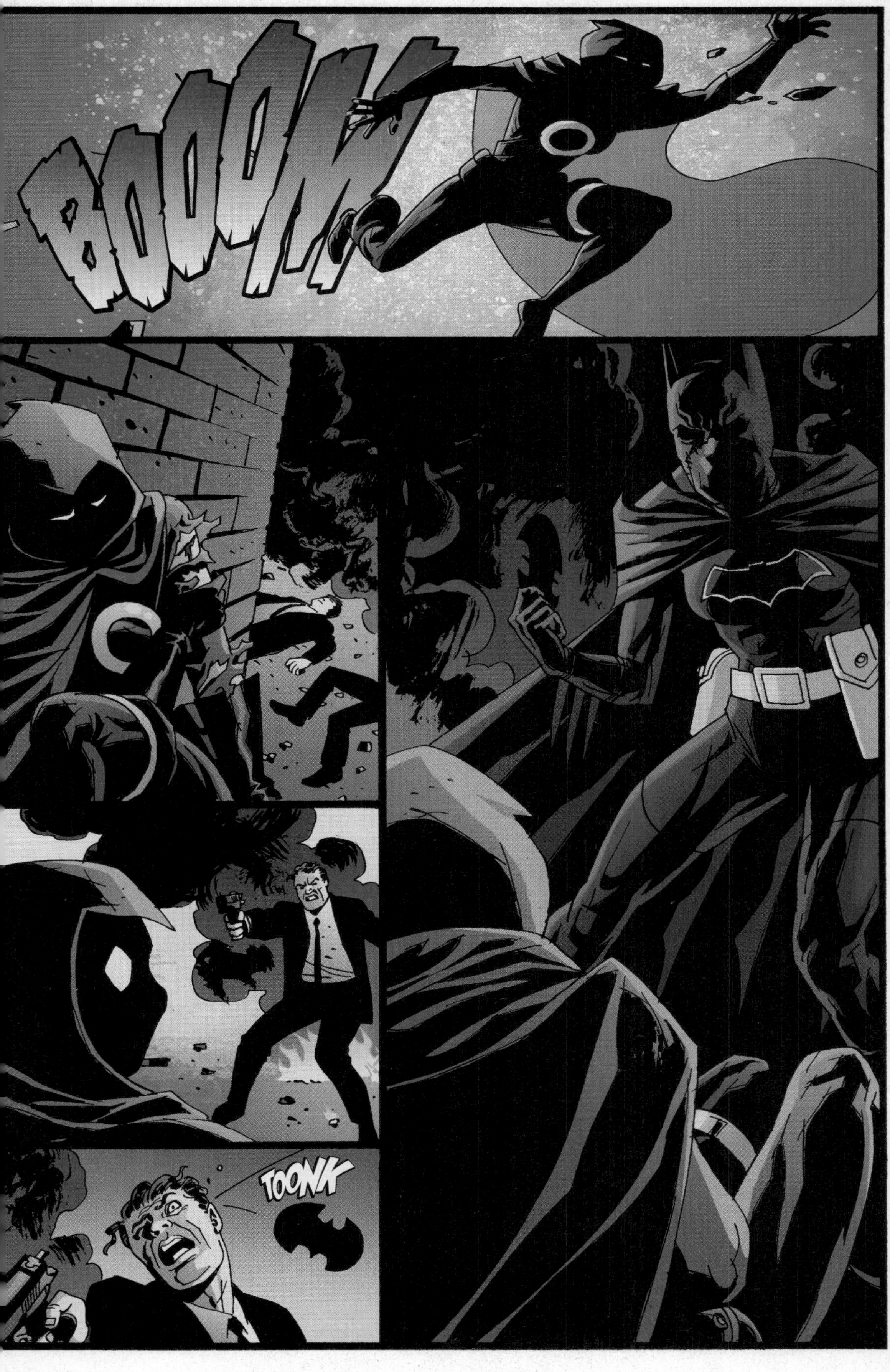

BOOOM
TOONK

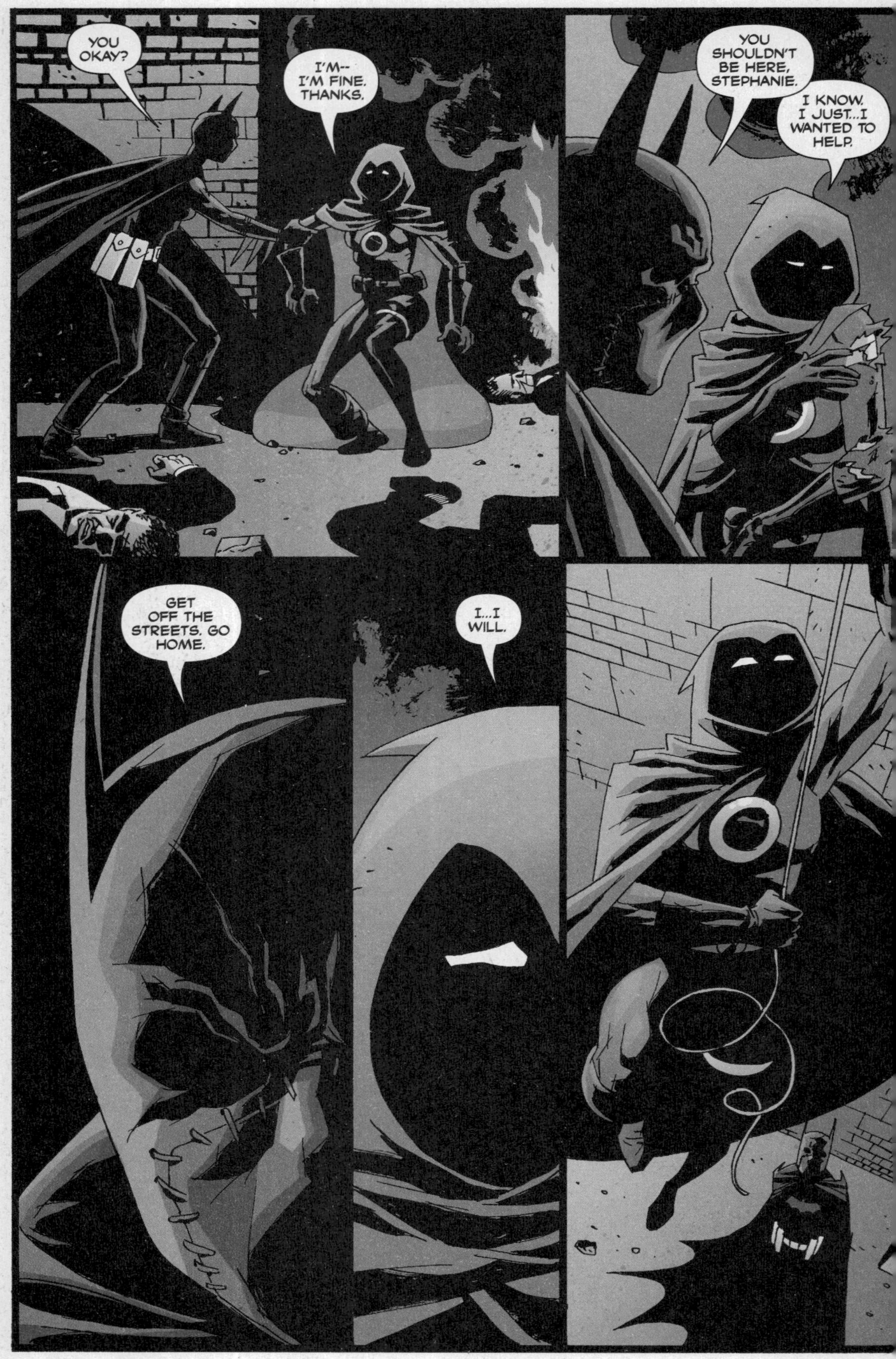
YOU OKAY?
I'M-- I'M FINE. THANKS.
YOU SHOULDN'T BE HERE, STEPHANIE.
I KNOW. I JUST...I WANTED TO HELP.
GET OFF THE STREETS. GO HOME.
I...I WILL.

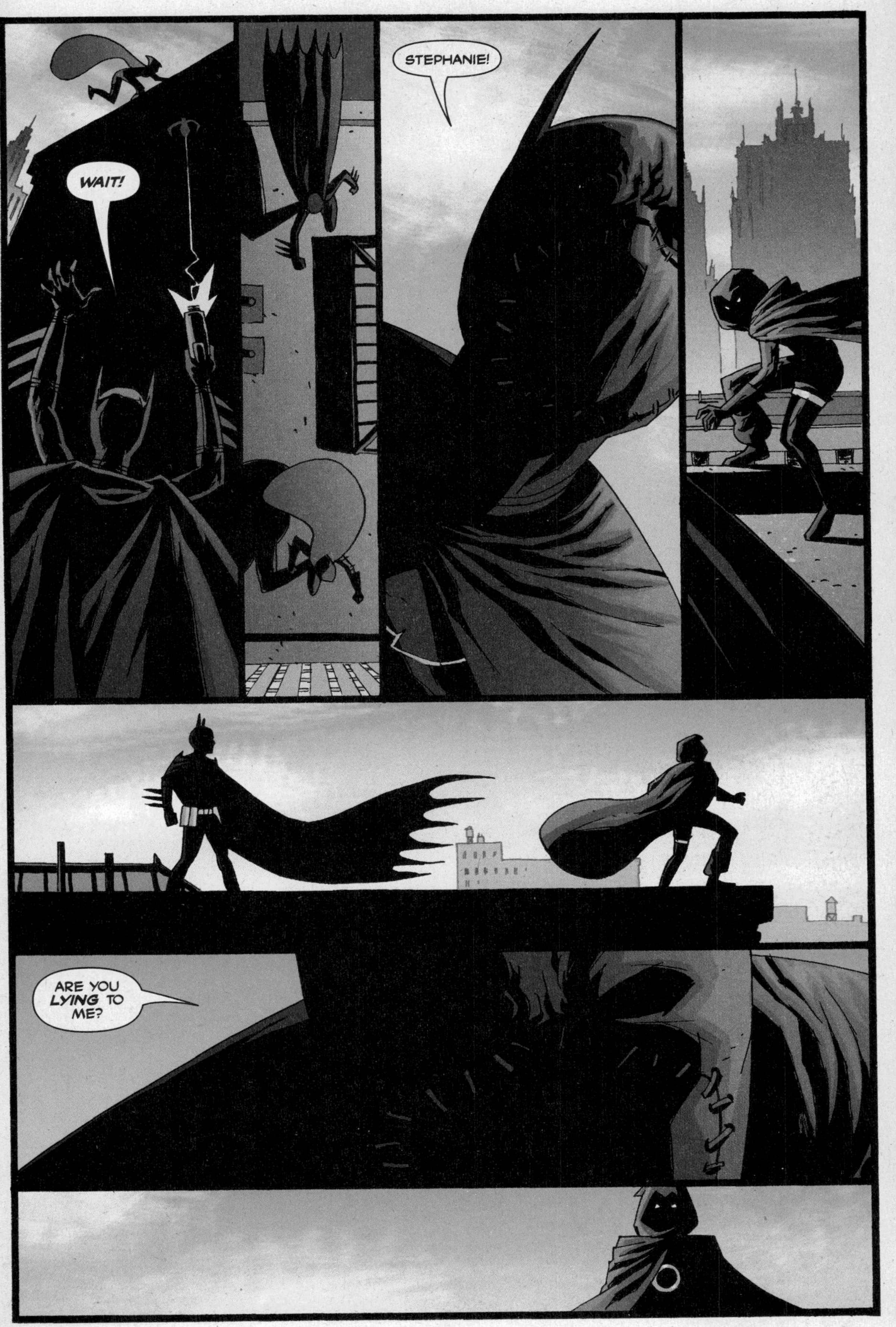
WAIT!
STEPHANIE!
ARE YOU LYING TO ME?

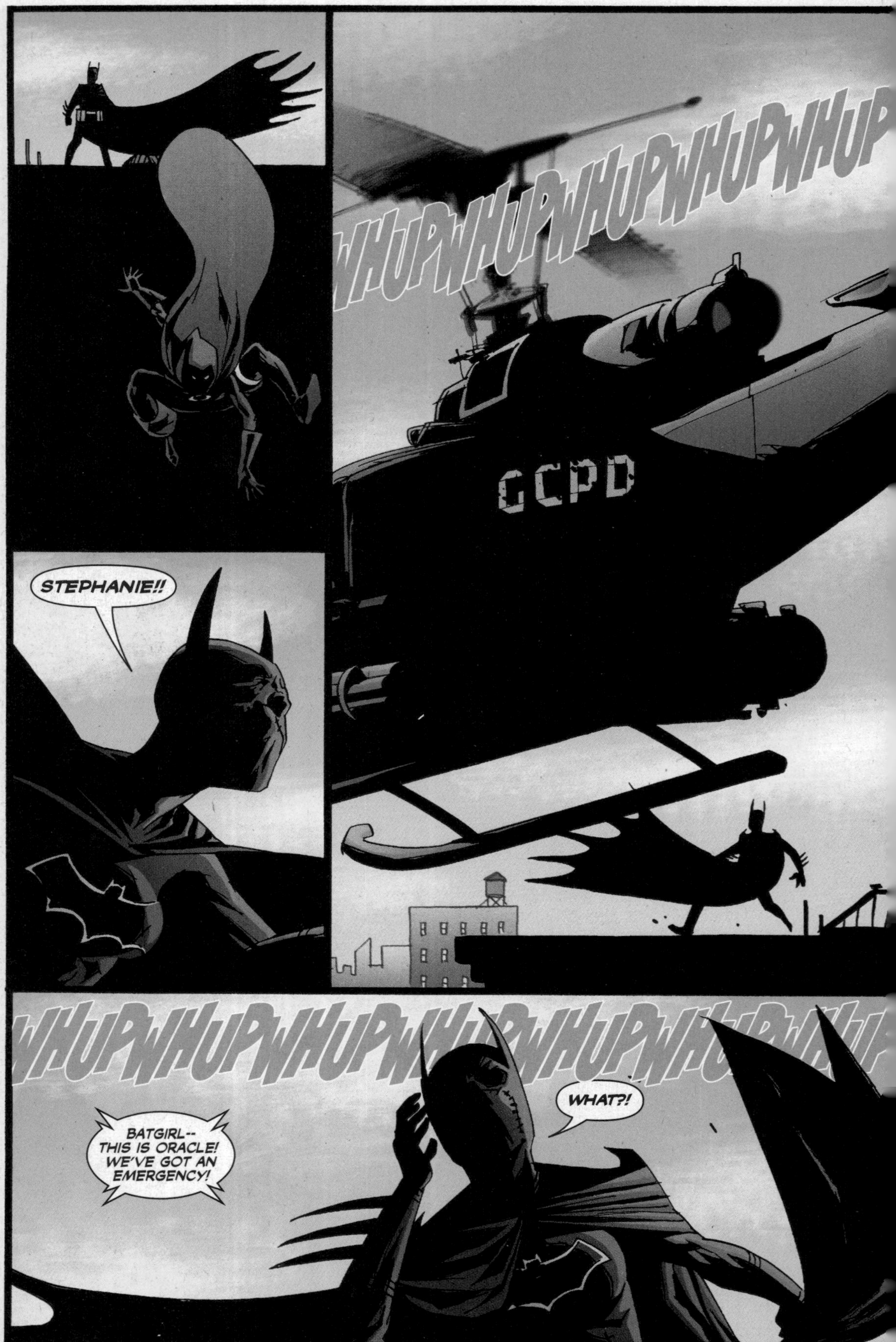
WHUPWHUPWHUPWHUPWHUPWHUPWHUP
GCPD
STEPHANIE!!
WHUPWHUPWHUPWHUPWHUPWHUPWHUP
BATGIRL-- THIS IS ORACLE! WE'VE GOT AN EMERGENCY!
WHAT?!

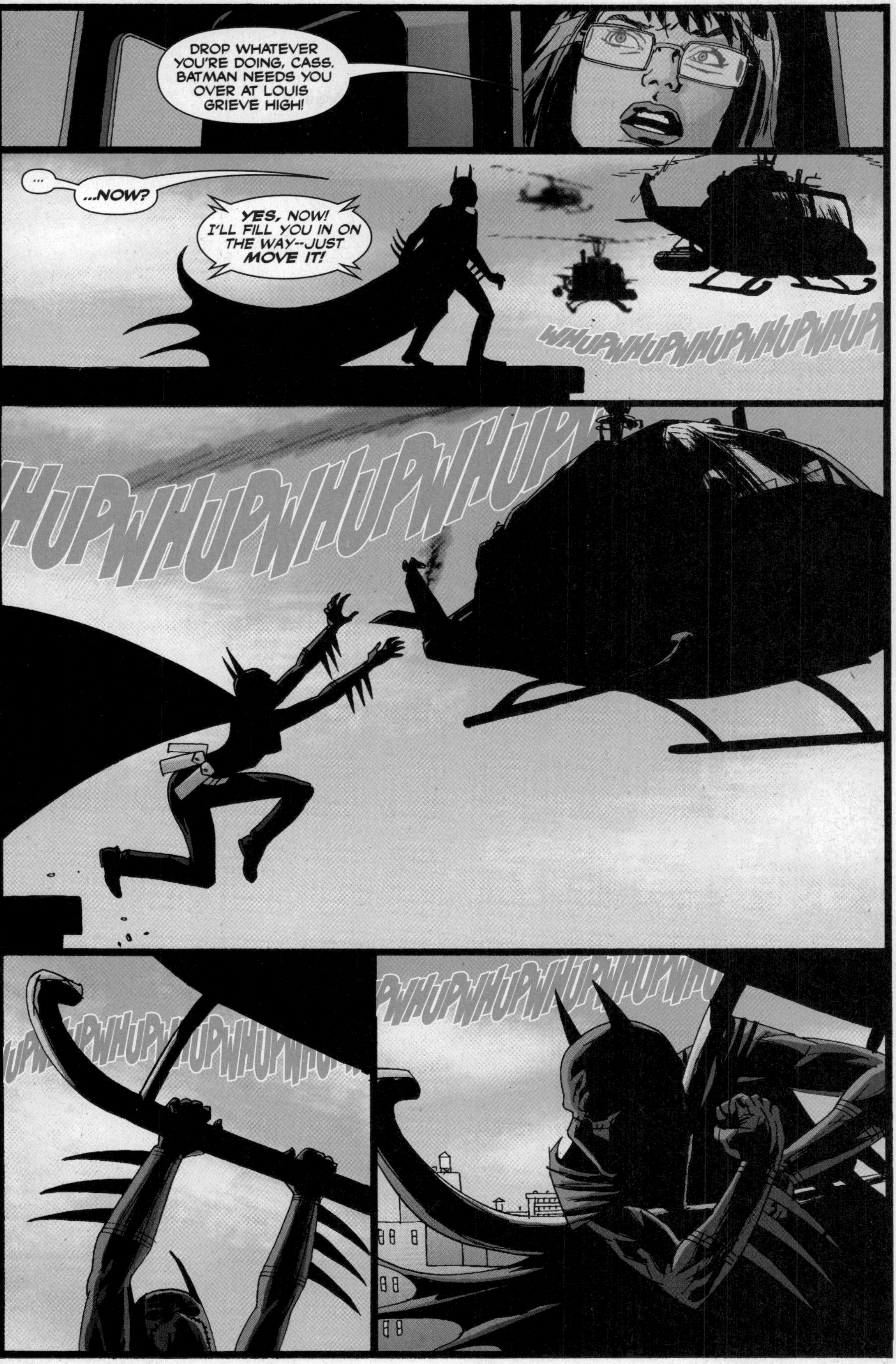

DROP WHATEVER YOU'RE DOING, CASS. BATMAN NEEDS YOU OVER AT LOUIS GRIEVE HIGH!
...
...NOW?
YES, NOW! I'LL FILL YOU IN ON THE WAY--JUST MOVE IT!
WHUPWHUPWHUPWHUPWHUP

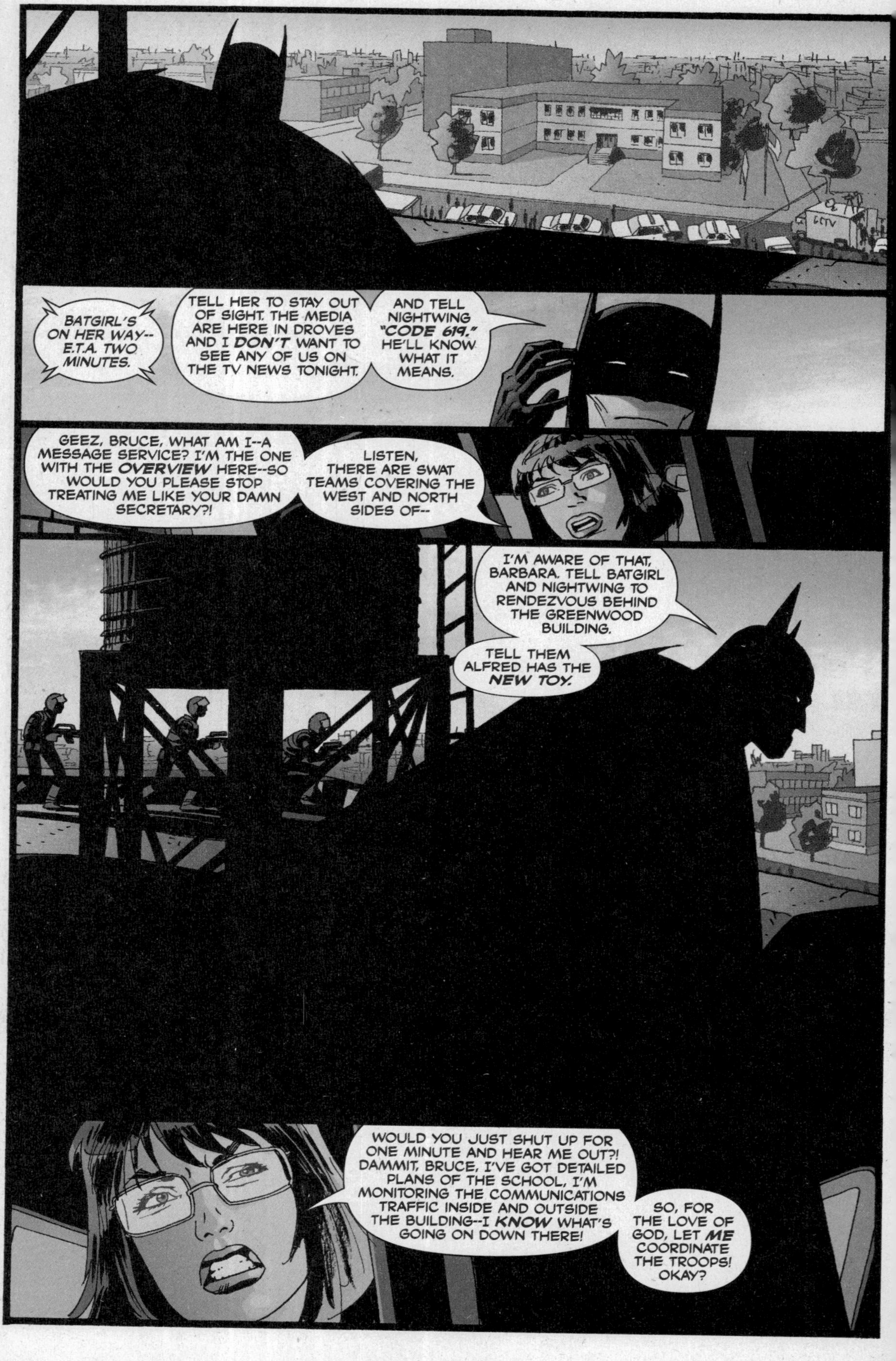
BATGIRL'S ON HER WAY-- E.T.A. TWO MINUTES.
TELL HER TO STAY OUT OF SIGHT. THE MEDIA ARE HERE IN DROVES AND I DON'T WANT TO SEE ANY OF US ON THE TV NEWS TONIGHT.
AND TELL NIGHTWING "CODE 619." HE'LL KNOW WHAT IT MEANS.
GEEZ, BRUCE, WHAT AM I--A MESSAGE SERVICE? I'M THE ONE WITH THE OVERVIEW HERE--SO WOULD YOU PLEASE STOP TREATING ME LIKE YOUR DAMN SECRETARY?!
LISTEN, THERE ARE SWAT TEAMS COVERING THE WEST AND NORTH SIDES OF--
I'M AWARE OF THAT, BARBARA. TELL BATGIRL AND NIGHTWING TO RENDEZVOUS BEHIND THE GREENWOOD BUILDING.
TELL THEM ALFRED HAS THE NEW TOY.
WOULD YOU JUST SHUT UP FOR ONE MINUTE AND HEAR ME OUT?! DAMMIT, BRUCE, I'VE GOT DETAILED PLANS OF THE SCHOOL, I'M MONITORING THE COMMUNICATIONS TRAFFIC INSIDE AND OUTSIDE THE BUILDING--I KNOW WHAT'S GOING ON DOWN THERE!
SO, FOR THE LOVE OF GOD, LET ME COORDINATE THE TROOPS! OKAY?

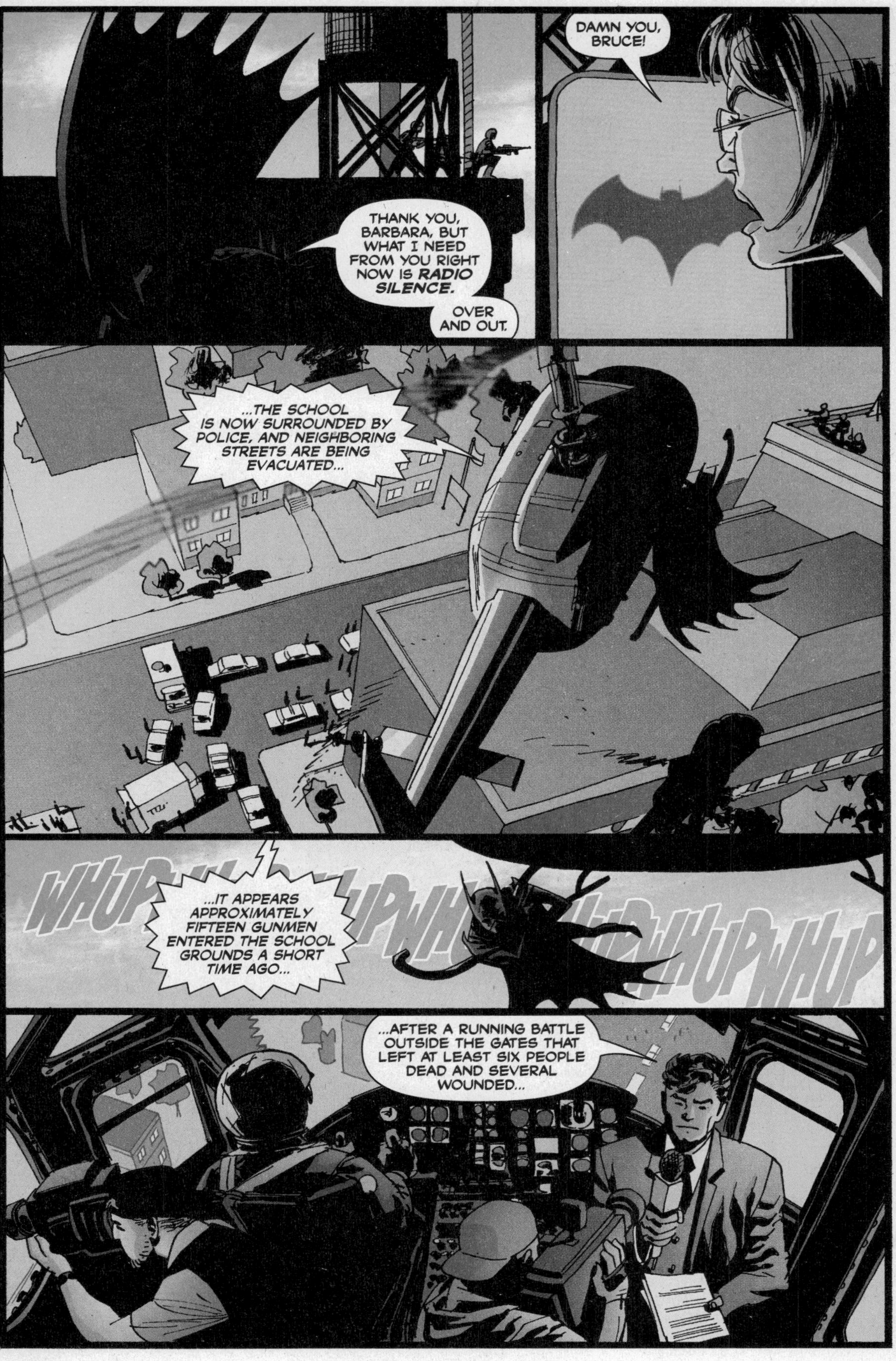
DAMN YOU, BRUCE!
THANK YOU, BARBARA, BUT WHAT I NEED FROM YOU RIGHT NOW IS RADIO SILENCE.
OVER AND OUT.
...THE SCHOOL IS NOW SURROUNDED BY POLICE, AND NEIGHBORING STREETS ARE BEING EVACUATED...
...IT APPEARS APPROXIMATELY FIFTEEN GUNMEN ENTERED THE SCHOOL GROUNDS A SHORT TIME AGO...
WHUPWHUPWHUPWHUPWHUPWHUP
...AFTER A RUNNING BATTLE OUTSIDE THE GATES THAT LEFT AT LEAST SIX PEOPLE DEAD AND SEVERAL WOUNDED...

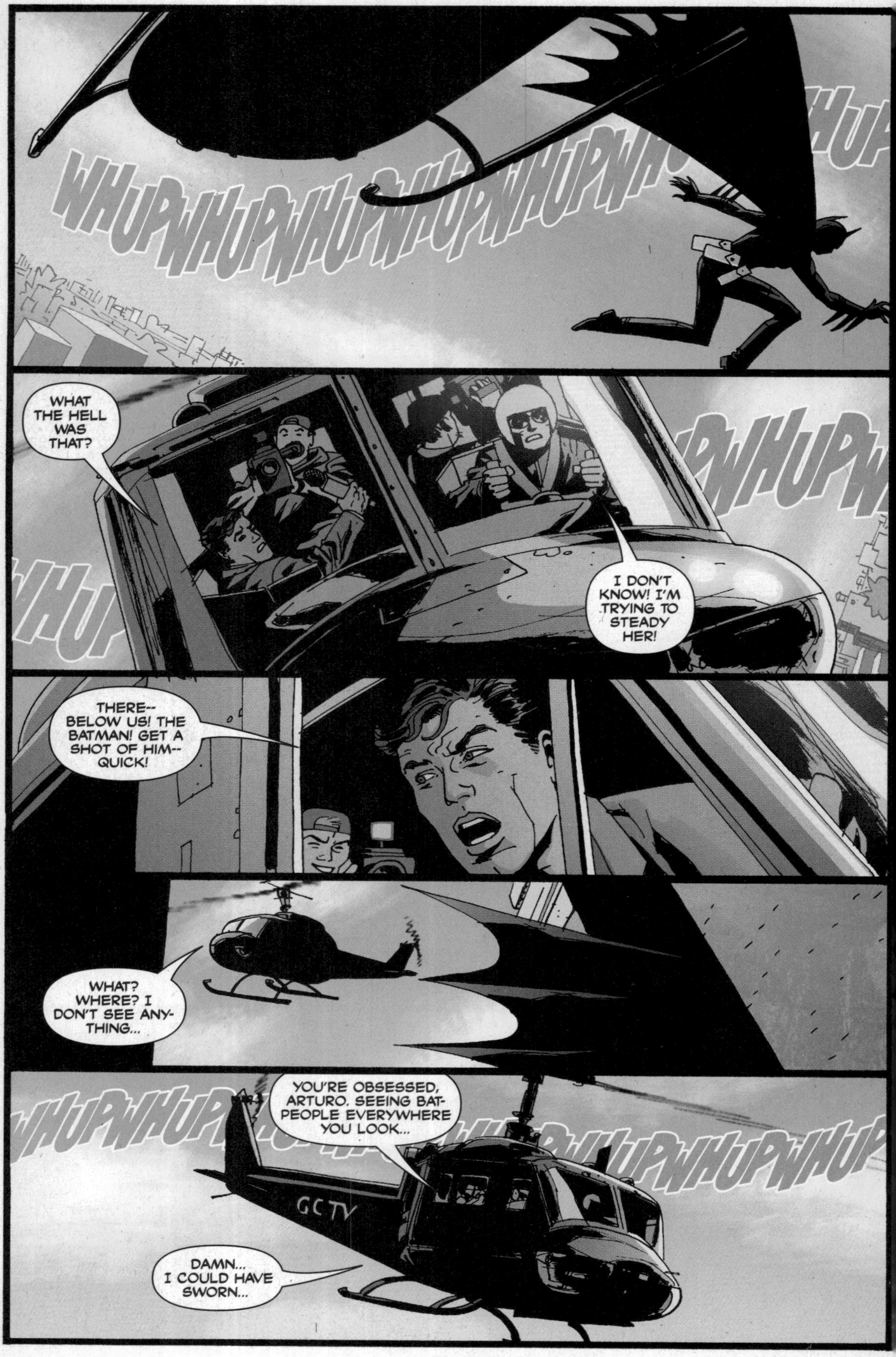
WHUPWHUPWHUPWHUPWHUPWHUPWHUP
WHAT THE HELL WAS THAT?
I DON'T KNOW! I'M TRYING TO STEADY HER!
THERE-- BELOW US! THE BATMAN! GET A SHOT OF HIM-- QUICK!
WHAT? WHERE? I DON'T SEE ANYTHING...
YOU'RE OBSESSED, ARTURO. SEEING BAT-PEOPLE EVERYWHERE YOU LOOK...
GCTV
DAMN... I COULD HAVE SWORN...

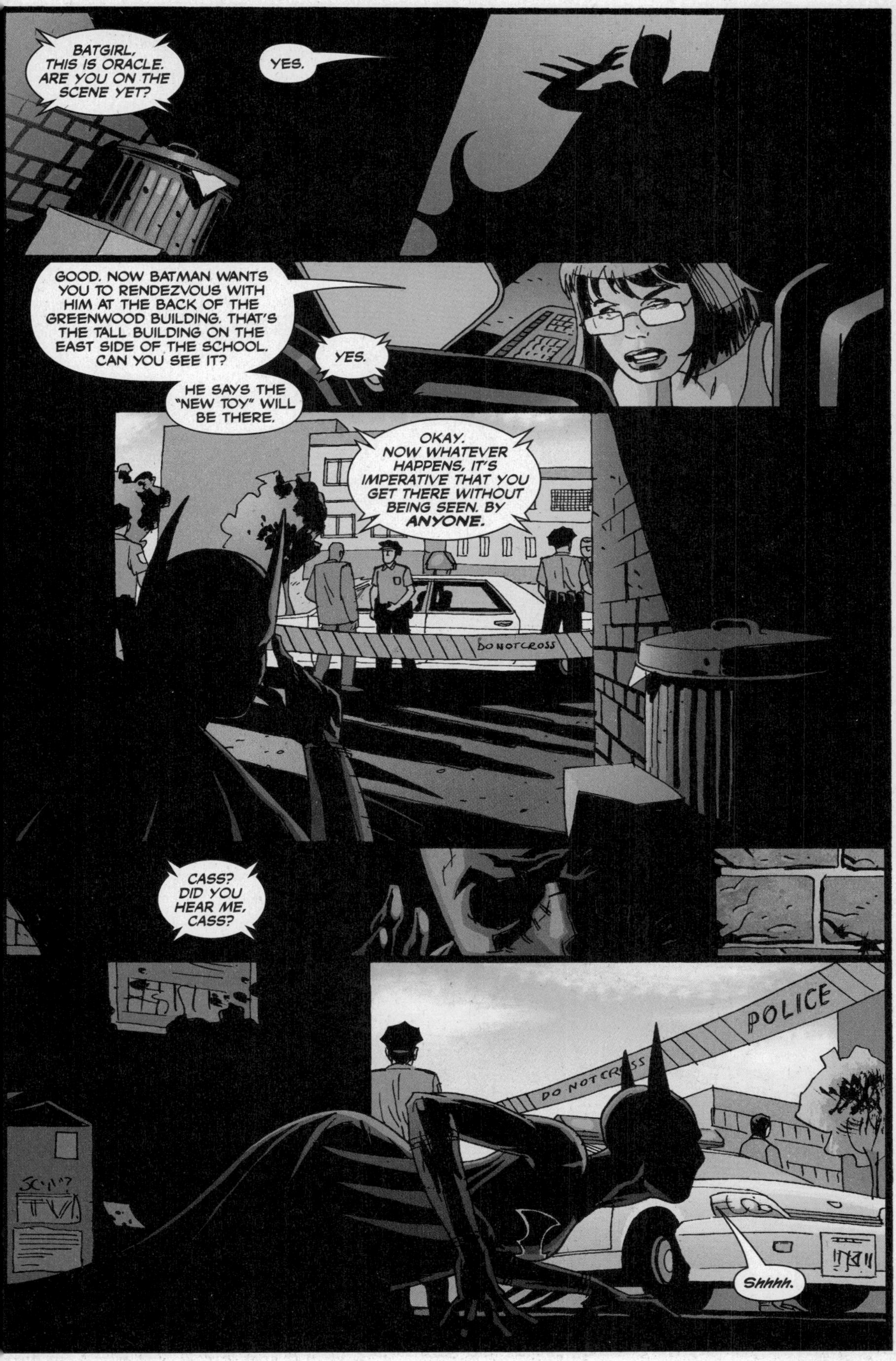
BATGIRL, THIS IS ORACLE. ARE YOU ON THE SCENE YET?
YES.
GOOD. NOW BATMAN WANTS YOU TO RENDEZVOUS WITH HIM AT THE BACK OF THE GREENWOOD BUILDING. THAT'S THE TALL BUILDING ON THE EAST SIDE OF THE SCHOOL. CAN YOU SEE IT?
YES.
HE SAYS THE "NEW TOY" WILL BE THERE.
OKAY. NOW WHATEVER HAPPENS, IT'S IMPERATIVE THAT YOU GET THERE WITHOUT BEING SEEN. BY ANYONE.
DO NOT CROSS
CASS? DID YOU HEAR ME, CASS?
POLICE
DO NOT CROSS
Shhhh.

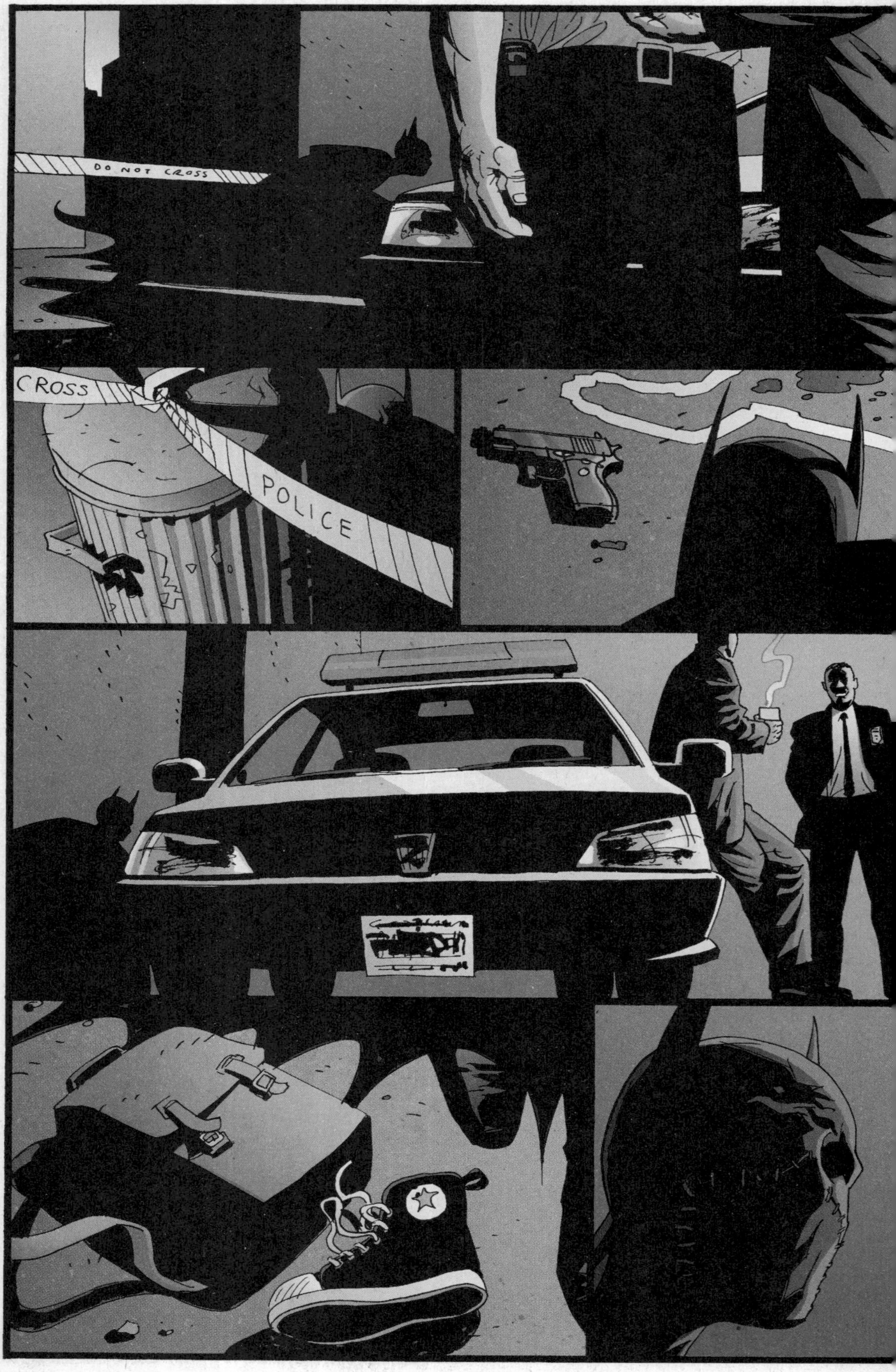
DO NOT CROSS
CROSS
POLICE

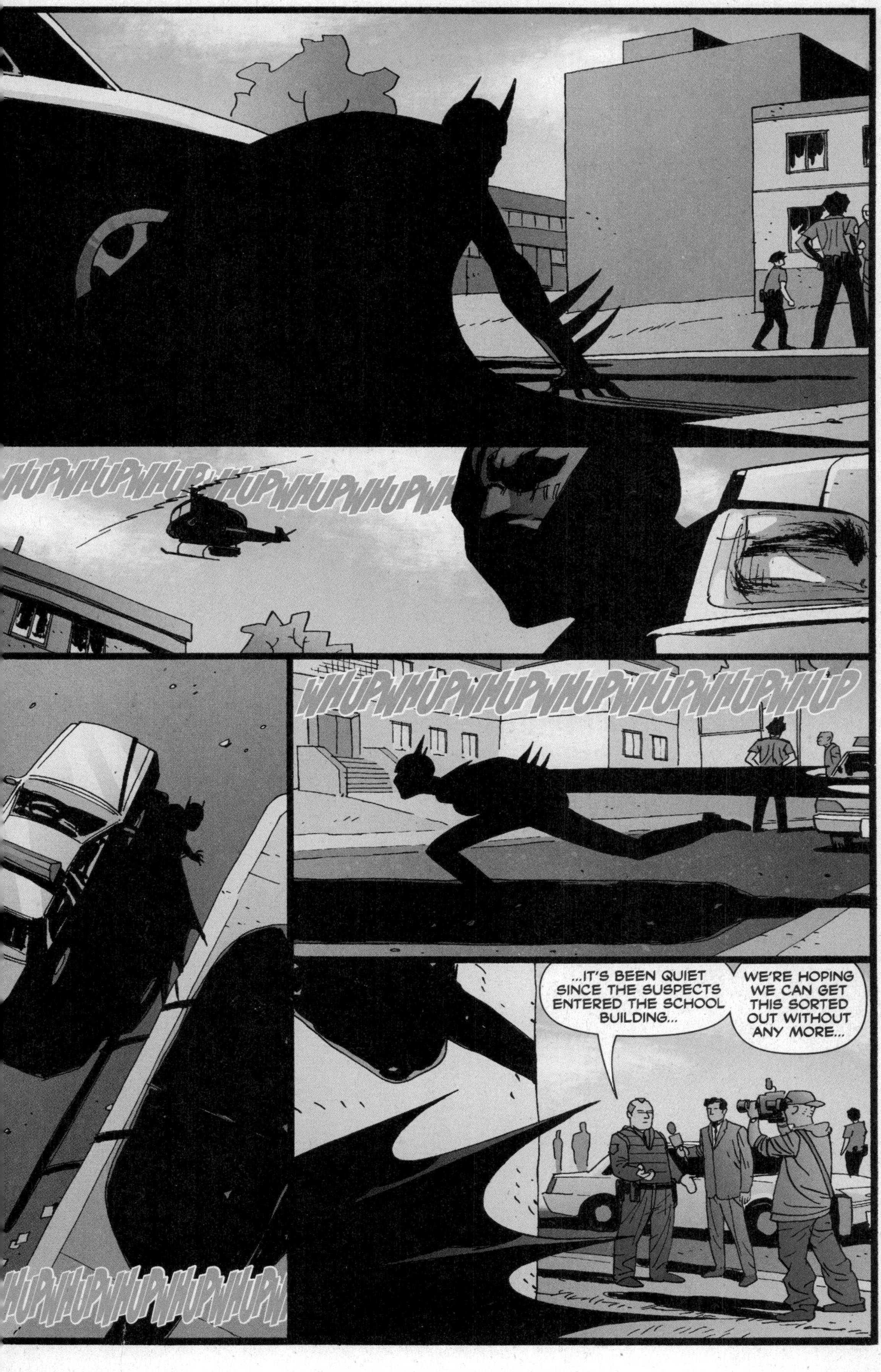
WHUPWHUPWHUPWHUPWHUPWHUPWH
WHUPWHUPWHUPWHUPWHUPWHUPWHUP
WHUPWHUPWHUPWHUPWH
...IT'S BEEN QUIET SINCE THE SUSPECTS ENTERED THE SCHOOL BUILDING...
WE'RE HOPING WE CAN GET THIS SORTED OUT WITHOUT ANY MORE...

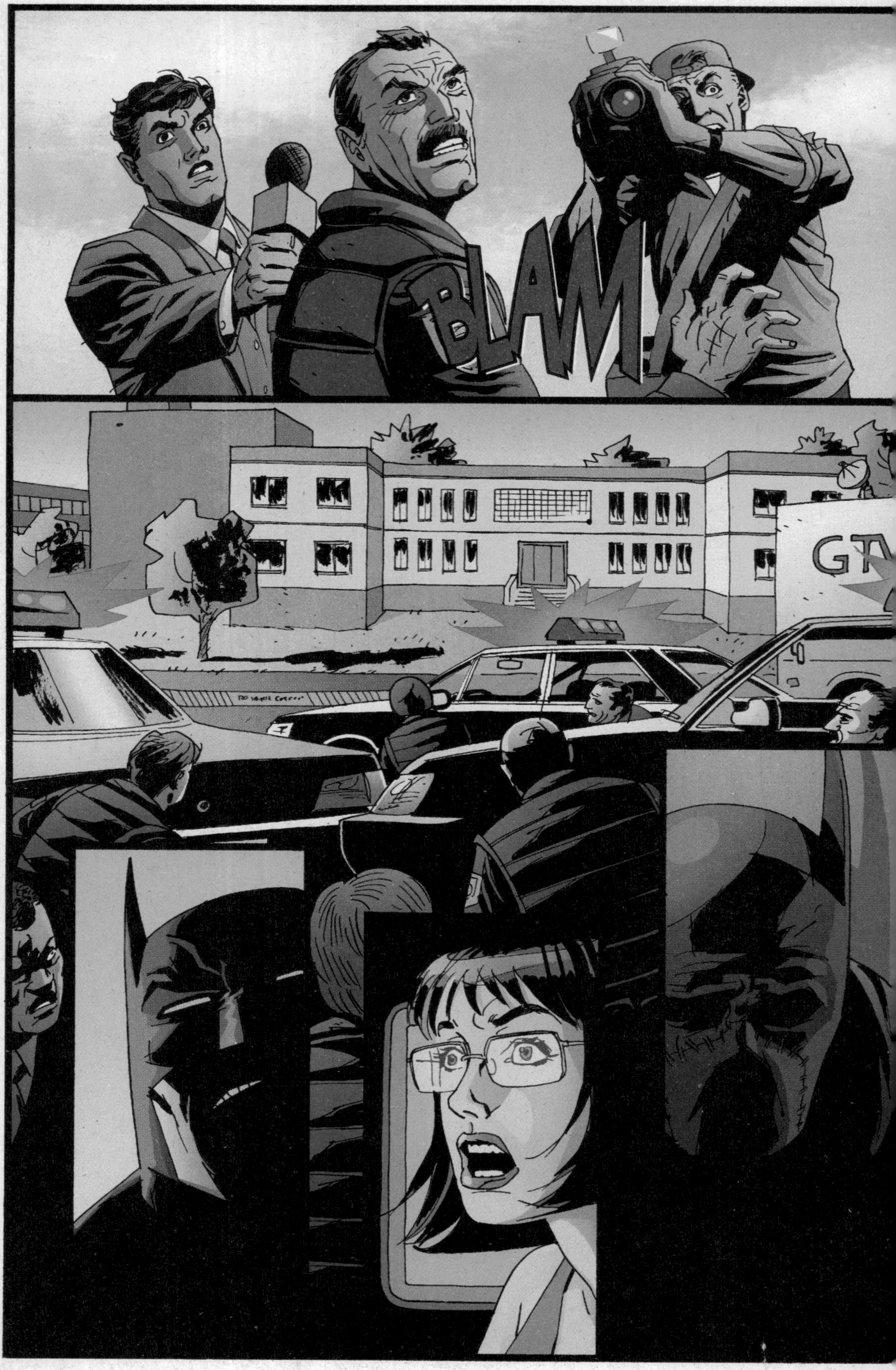
BLAM

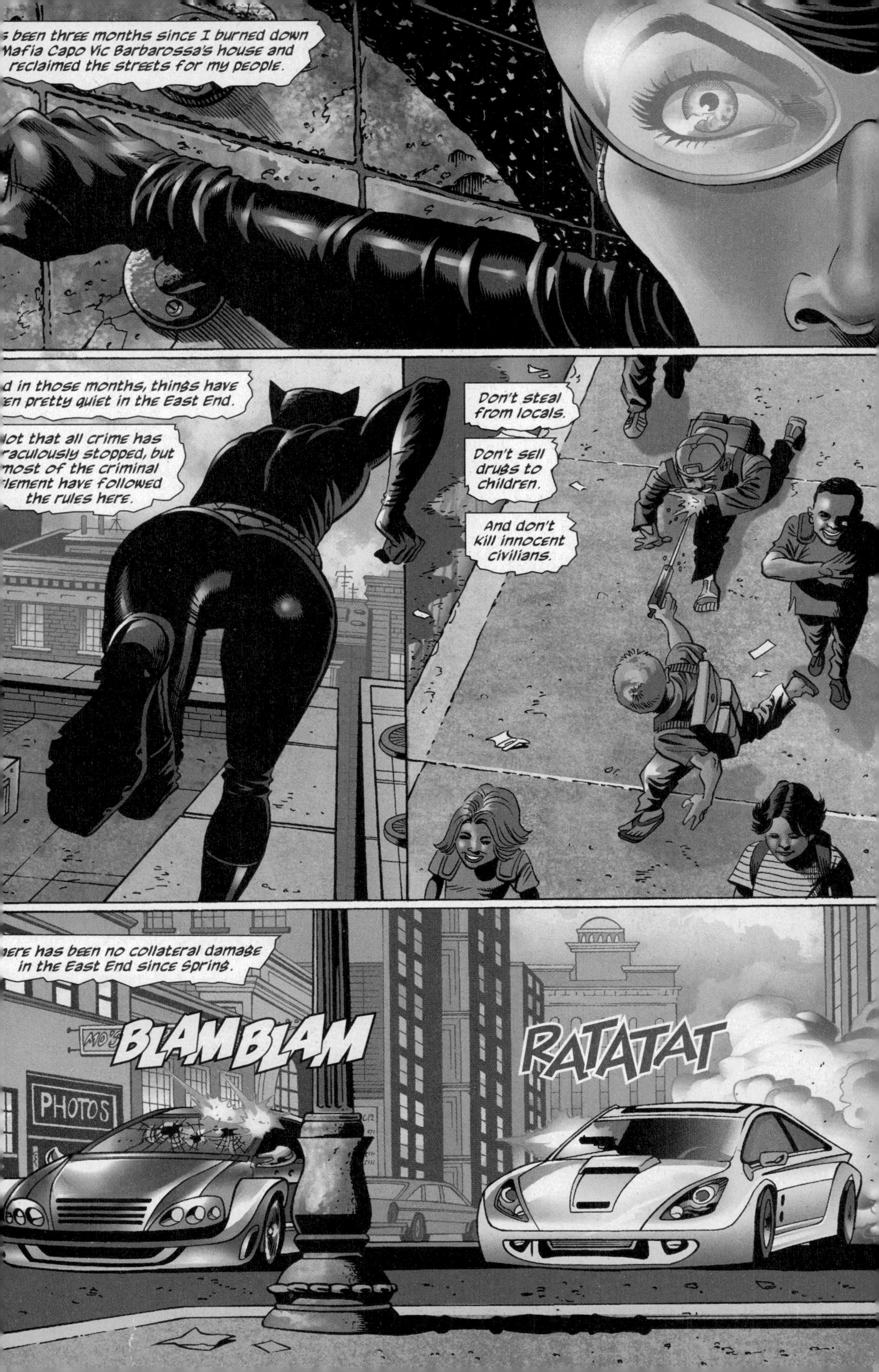

s been three months since I burned down Mafia Capo Vic Barbarossa's house and reclaimed the streets for my people.
d in those months, things have en pretty quiet in the East End.
lot that all crime has raculously stopped, but most of the criminal element have followed the rules here.
Don't steal from locals.
Don't sell drugs to children.
And don't kill innocent civilians.
here has been no collateral damage in the East End since Spring.
MO'S
BLAM BLAM
PHOTOS
RATATAT

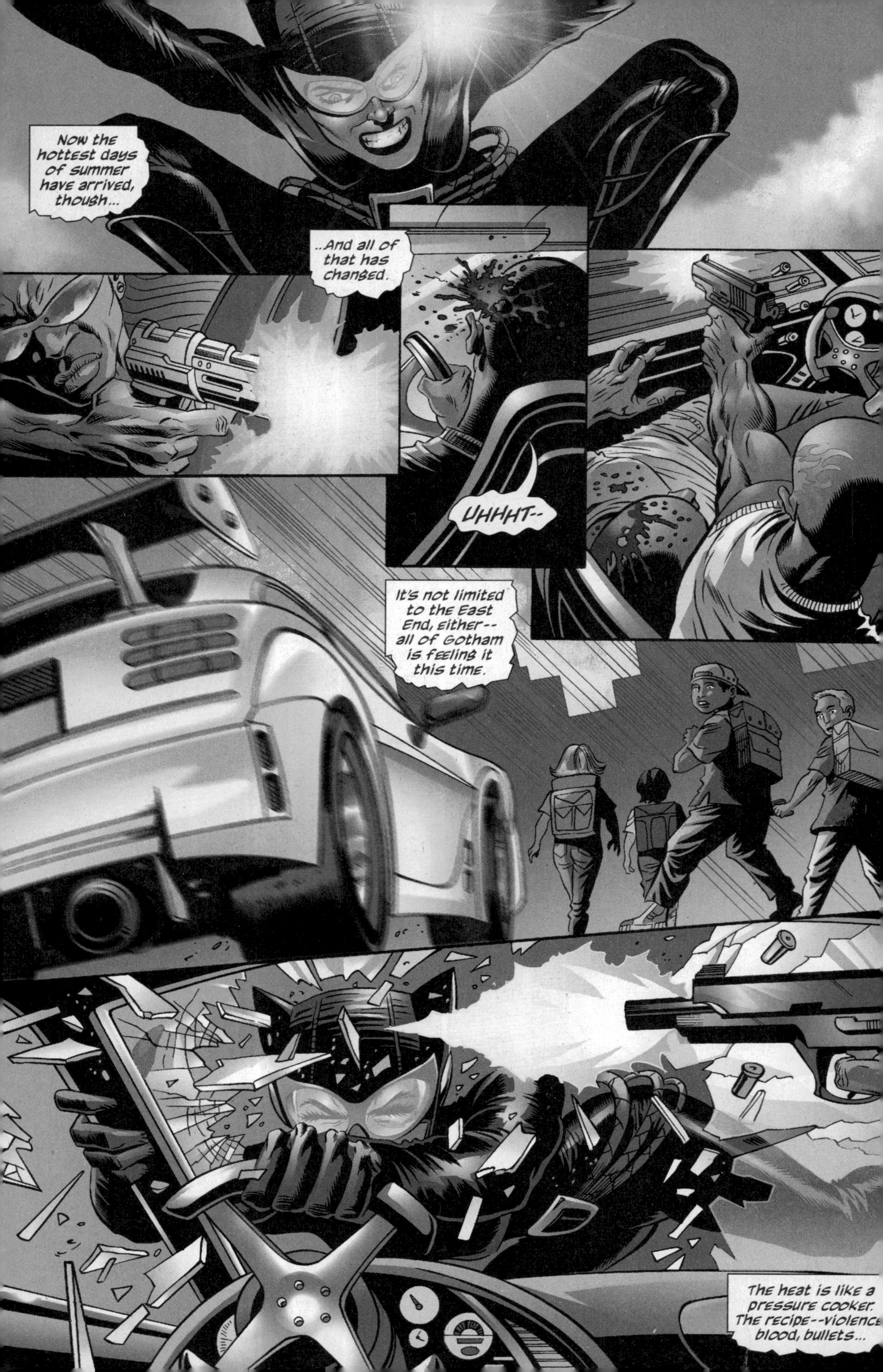
Now the hottest days of summer have arrived, though...
..And all of that has changed.
UHHHT--
It's not limited to the East End, either--all of Gotham is feeling it this time.
The heat is like a pressure cooker. The recipe--violence, blood, bullets...

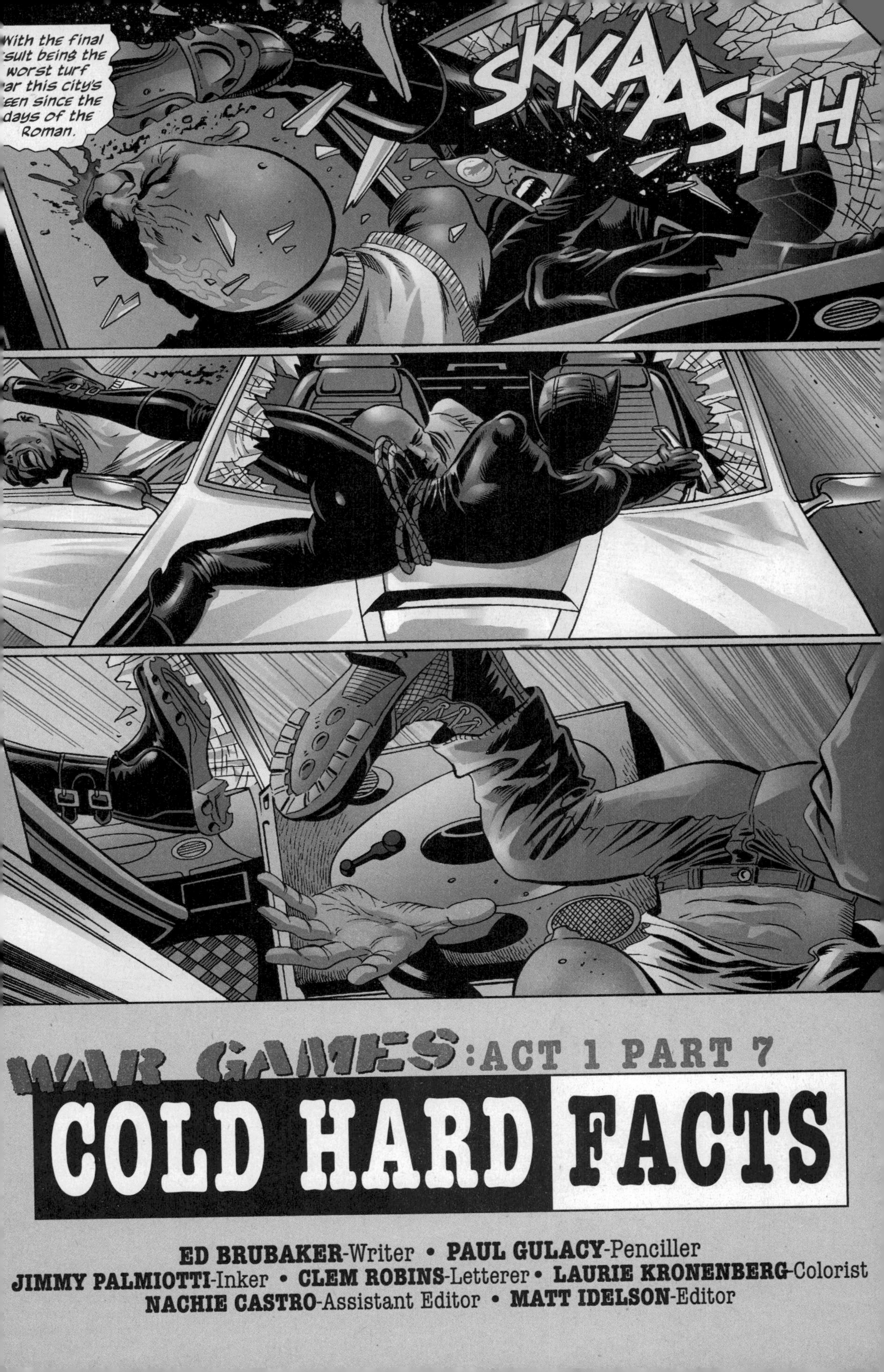
With the final
sult being the
worst turf
ar this city's
een since the
days of the
Roman.
SKKAASHH

# WAR GAMES: ACT 1 PART 7

# COLD HARD FACTS

**ED BRUBAKER**-Writer • **PAUL GULACY**-Penciller
**JIMMY PALMIOTTI**-Inker • **CLEM ROBINS**-Letterer • **LAURIE KRONENBERG**-Colorist
**NACHIE CASTRO**-Assistant Editor • **MATT IDELSON**-Editor

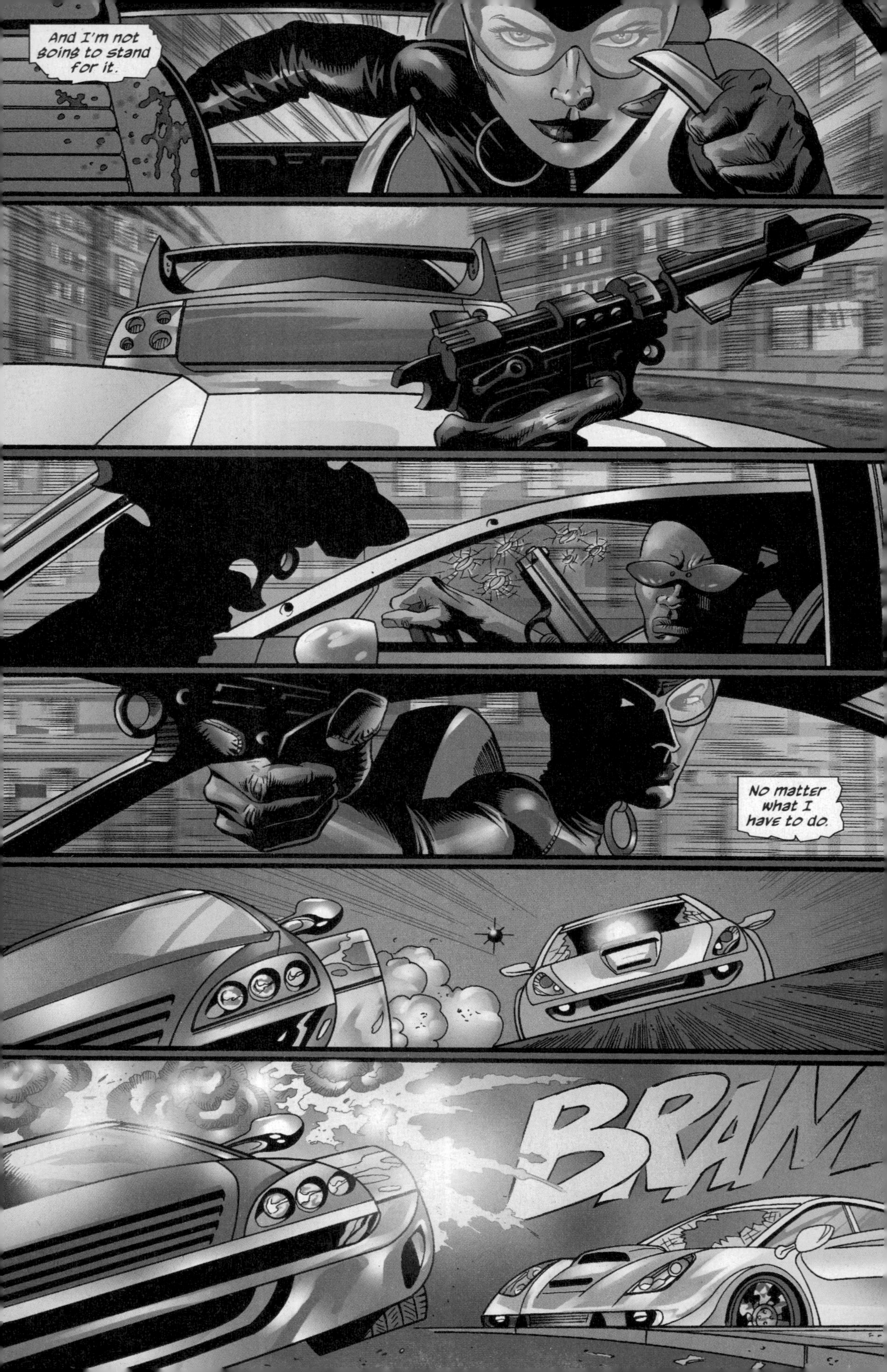
And I'm not going to stand for it.
No matter what I have to do.
BRAM

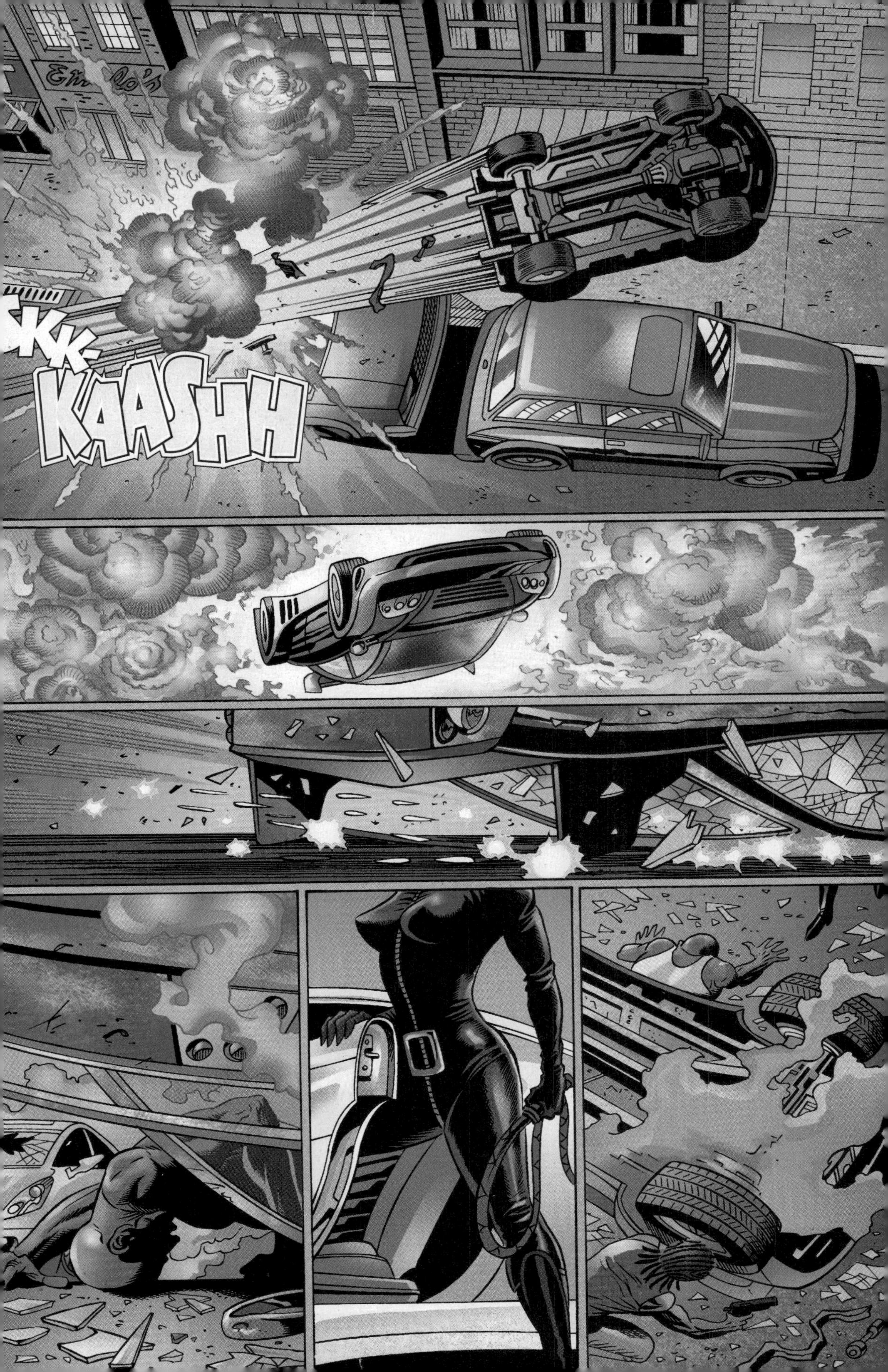
KK-
KAASHH

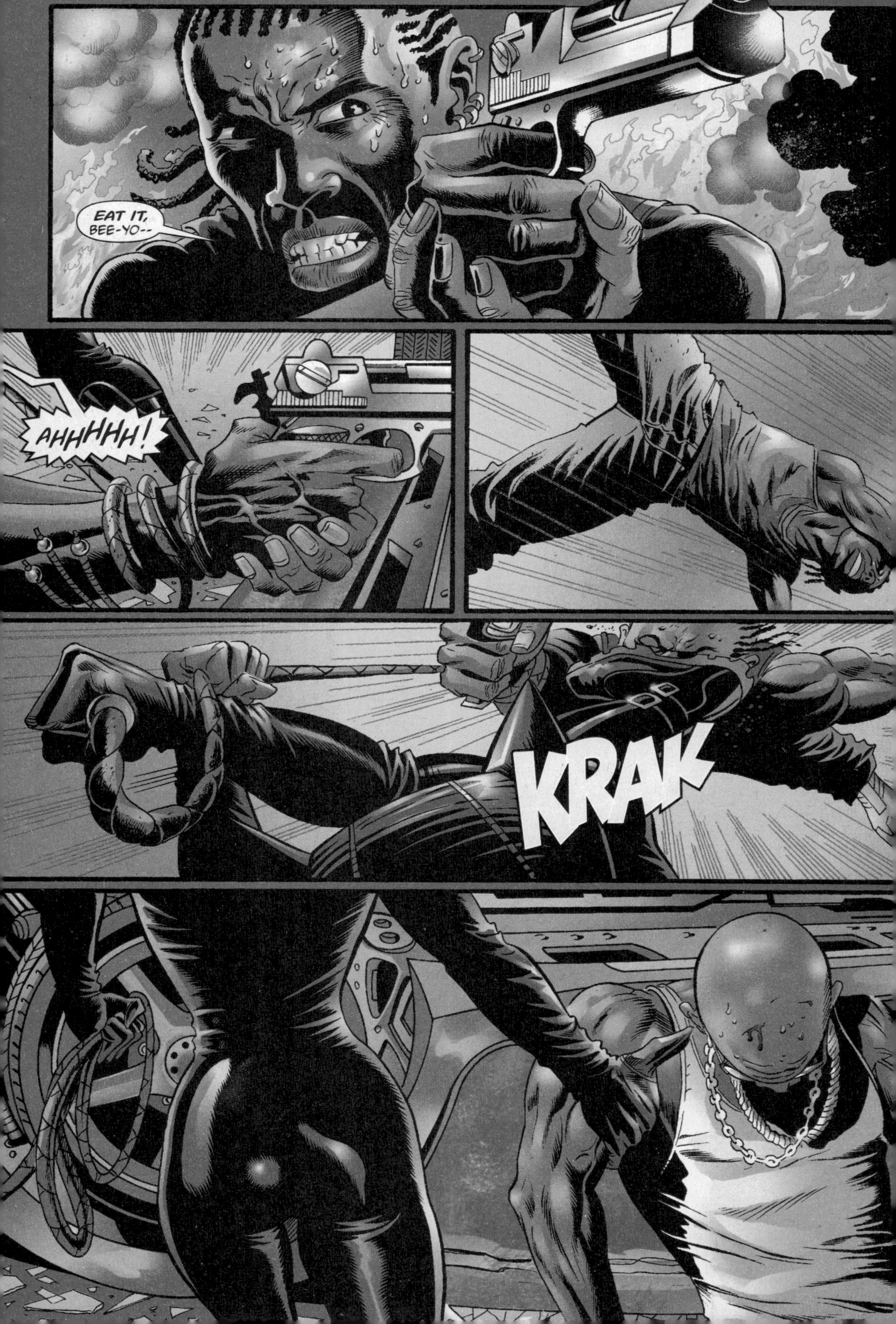
EAT IT, BEE-YO--
AHHHHH!
KRAK

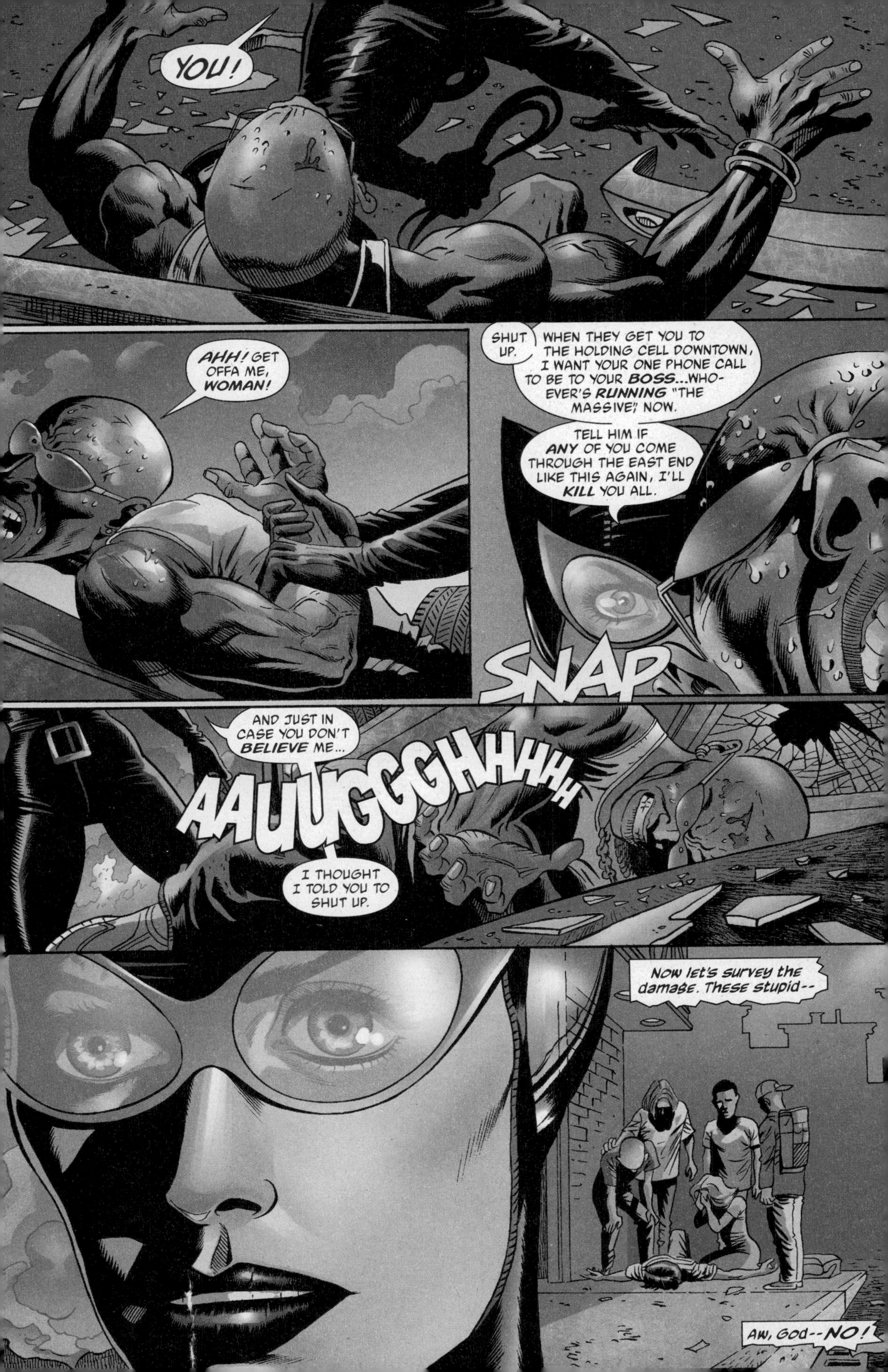
YOU!
AHH! GET OFFA ME, WOMAN!
SHUT UP.
WHEN THEY GET YOU TO THE HOLDING CELL DOWNTOWN, I WANT YOUR ONE PHONE CALL TO BE TO YOUR BOSS...WHO-EVER'S RUNNING "THE MASSIVE," NOW.
TELL HIM IF ANY OF YOU COME THROUGH THE EAST END LIKE THIS AGAIN, I'LL KILL YOU ALL.
SNAP
AND JUST IN CASE YOU DON'T BELIEVE ME...
AAUUGGGHHHHH
I THOUGHT I TOLD YOU TO SHUT UP.
Now let's survey the damage. These stupid--
Aw, God--NO!

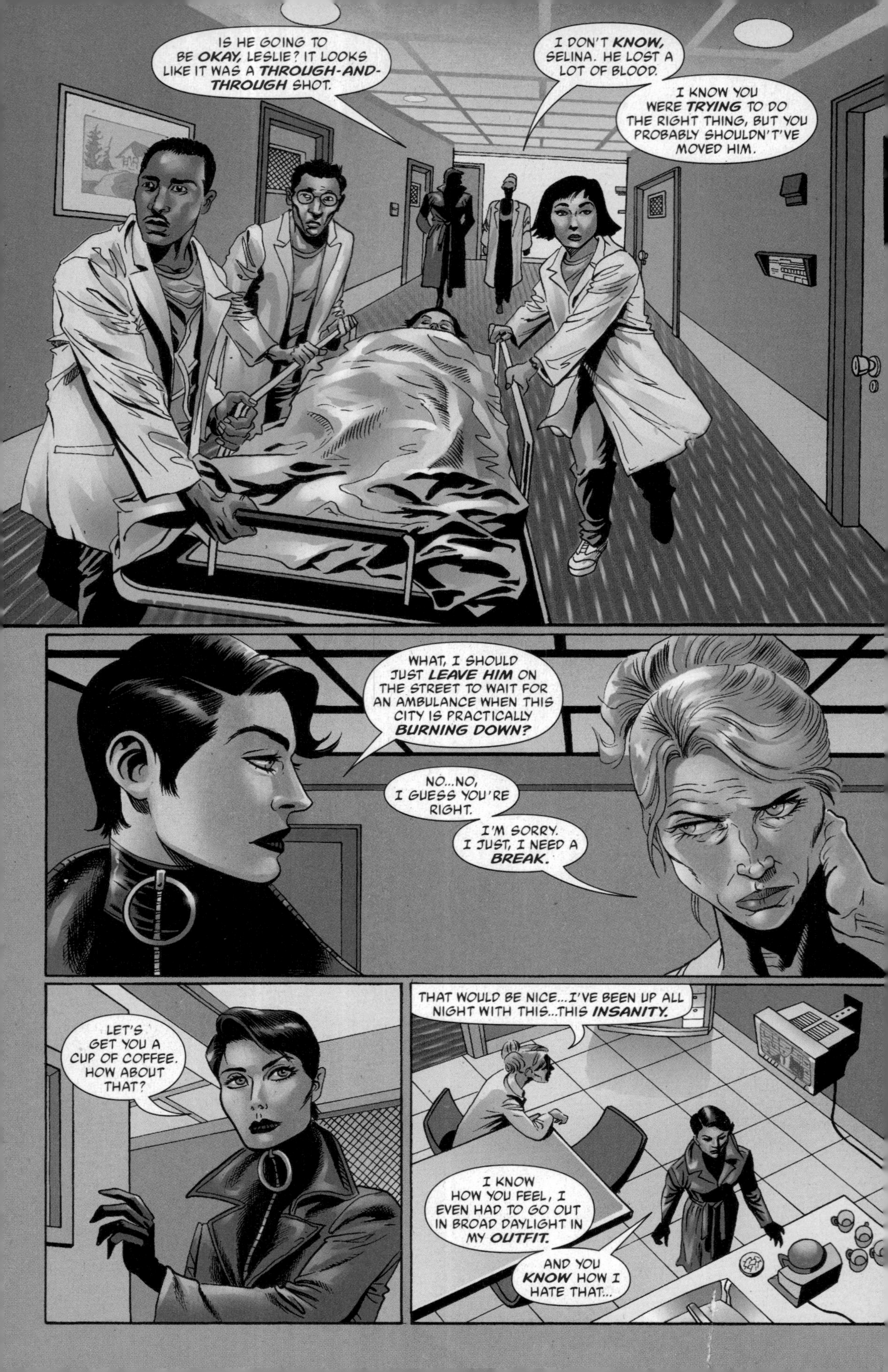
IS HE GOING TO BE OKAY, LESLIE? IT LOOKS LIKE IT WAS A THROUGH-AND-THROUGH SHOT.
I DON'T KNOW, SELINA. HE LOST A LOT OF BLOOD.
I KNOW YOU WERE TRYING TO DO THE RIGHT THING, BUT YOU PROBABLY SHOULDN'T'VE MOVED HIM.
WHAT, I SHOULD JUST LEAVE HIM ON THE STREET TO WAIT FOR AN AMBULANCE WHEN THIS CITY IS PRACTICALLY BURNING DOWN?
NO...NO, I GUESS YOU'RE RIGHT.
I'M SORRY. I JUST, I NEED A BREAK.
LET'S GET YOU A CUP OF COFFEE. HOW ABOUT THAT?
THAT WOULD BE NICE...I'VE BEEN UP ALL NIGHT WITH THIS...THIS INSANITY.
I KNOW HOW YOU FEEL, I EVEN HAD TO GO OUT IN BROAD DAYLIGHT IN MY OUTFIT.
AND YOU KNOW HOW I HATE THAT...

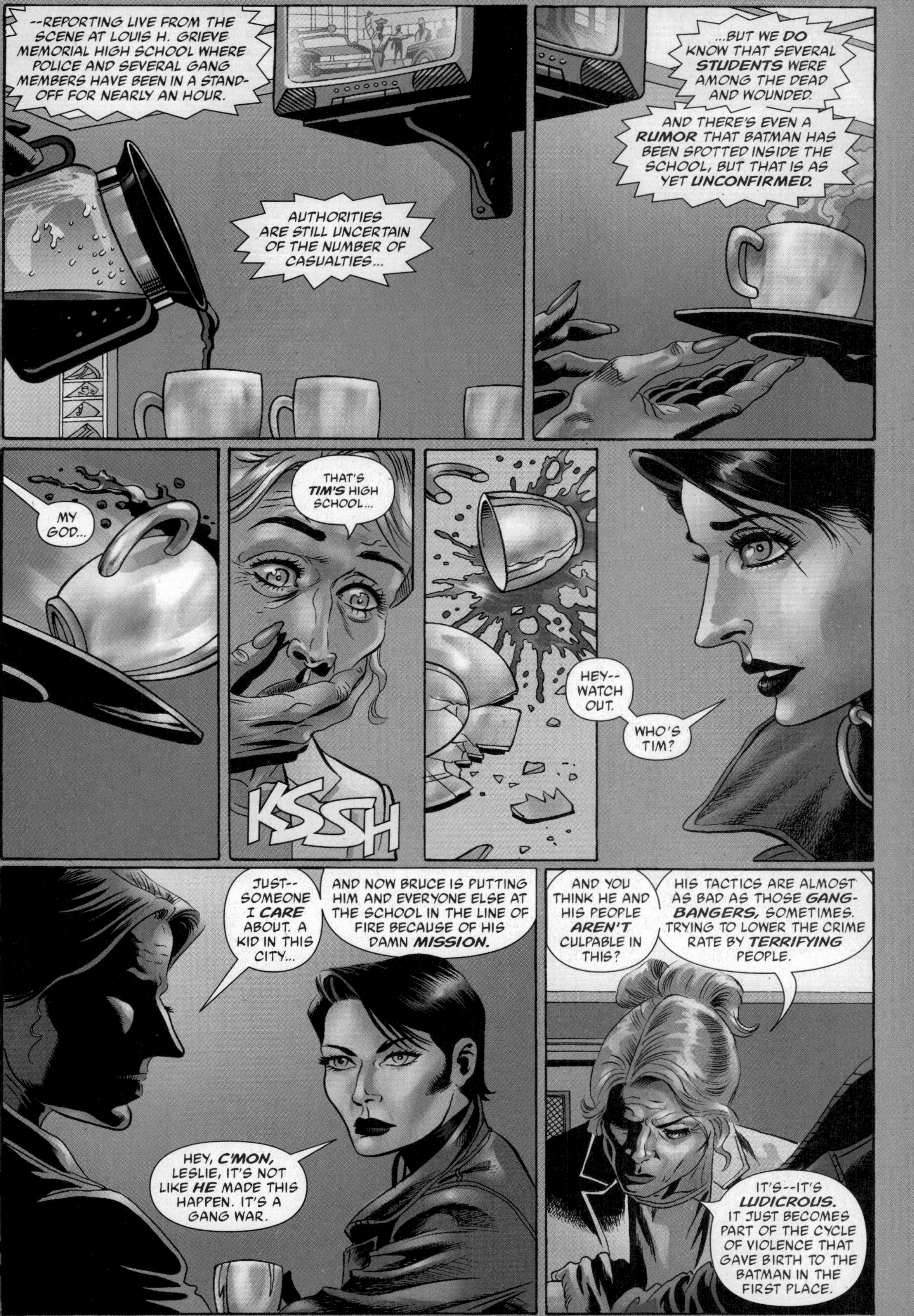
--REPORTING LIVE FROM THE SCENE AT LOUIS H. GRIEVE MEMORIAL HIGH SCHOOL WHERE POLICE AND SEVERAL GANG MEMBERS HAVE BEEN IN A STAND-OFF FOR NEARLY AN HOUR.
AUTHORITIES ARE STILL UNCERTAIN OF THE NUMBER OF CASUALTIES...
...BUT WE **DO** KNOW THAT SEVERAL **STUDENTS** WERE AMONG THE DEAD AND WOUNDED.
AND THERE'S EVEN A **RUMOR** THAT BATMAN HAS BEEN SPOTTED INSIDE THE SCHOOL, BUT THAT IS AS YET **UNCONFIRMED.**
MY GOD...
THAT'S ***TIM'S*** HIGH SCHOOL...
KSSH
HEY-- WATCH OUT.
WHO'S TIM?
JUST-- SOMEONE I ***CARE*** ABOUT. A KID IN THIS CITY...
AND NOW BRUCE IS PUTTING HIM AND EVERYONE ELSE AT THE SCHOOL IN THE LINE OF FIRE BECAUSE OF HIS DAMN ***MISSION.***
HEY, ***C'MON,*** LESLIE, IT'S NOT LIKE ***HE*** MADE THIS HAPPEN. IT'S A GANG WAR.
AND YOU THINK HE AND HIS PEOPLE ***AREN'T*** CULPABLE IN THIS?
HIS TACTICS ARE ALMOST AS BAD AS THOSE ***GANG-BANGERS,*** SOMETIMES. TRYING TO LOWER THE CRIME RATE BY ***TERRIFYING*** PEOPLE.
IT'S--IT'S ***LUDICROUS.*** IT JUST BECOMES PART OF THE CYCLE OF VIOLENCE THAT GAVE BIRTH TO THE BATMAN IN THE FIRST PLACE.

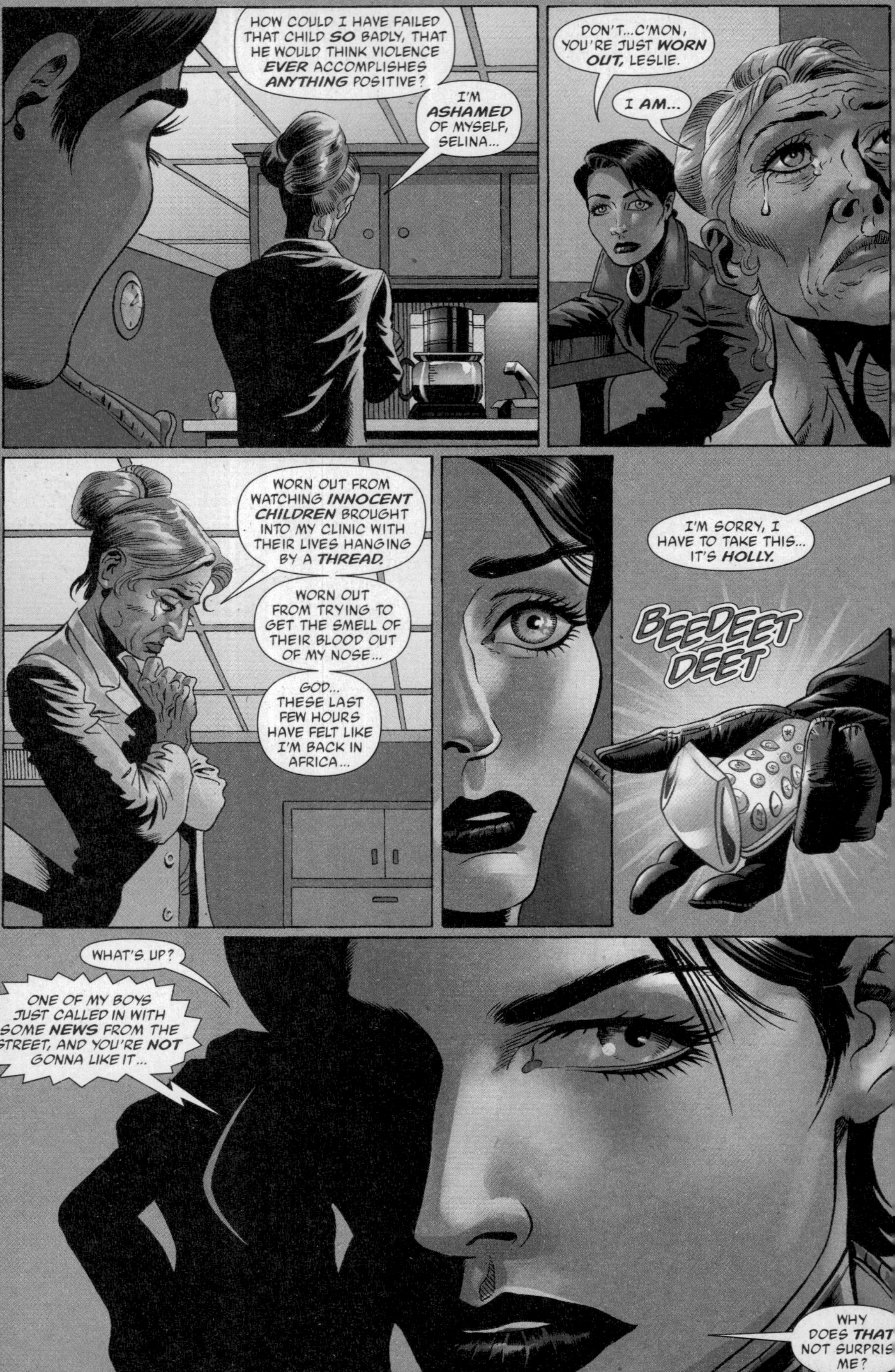
HOW COULD I HAVE FAILED THAT CHILD SO BADLY, THAT HE WOULD THINK VIOLENCE EVER ACCOMPLISHES ANYTHING POSITIVE?
I'M ASHAMED OF MYSELF, SELINA...
DON'T...C'MON, YOU'RE JUST WORN OUT, LESLIE.
I AM...
WORN OUT FROM WATCHING INNOCENT CHILDREN BROUGHT INTO MY CLINIC WITH THEIR LIVES HANGING BY A THREAD.
WORN OUT FROM TRYING TO GET THE SMELL OF THEIR BLOOD OUT OF MY NOSE...
GOD... THESE LAST FEW HOURS HAVE FELT LIKE I'M BACK IN AFRICA...
BEEDEET DEET
I'M SORRY, I HAVE TO TAKE THIS... IT'S HOLLY.
WHAT'S UP?
ONE OF MY BOYS JUST CALLED IN WITH SOME NEWS FROM THE STREET, AND YOU'RE NOT GONNA LIKE IT...
WHY DOES THAT NOT SURPRIS ME?

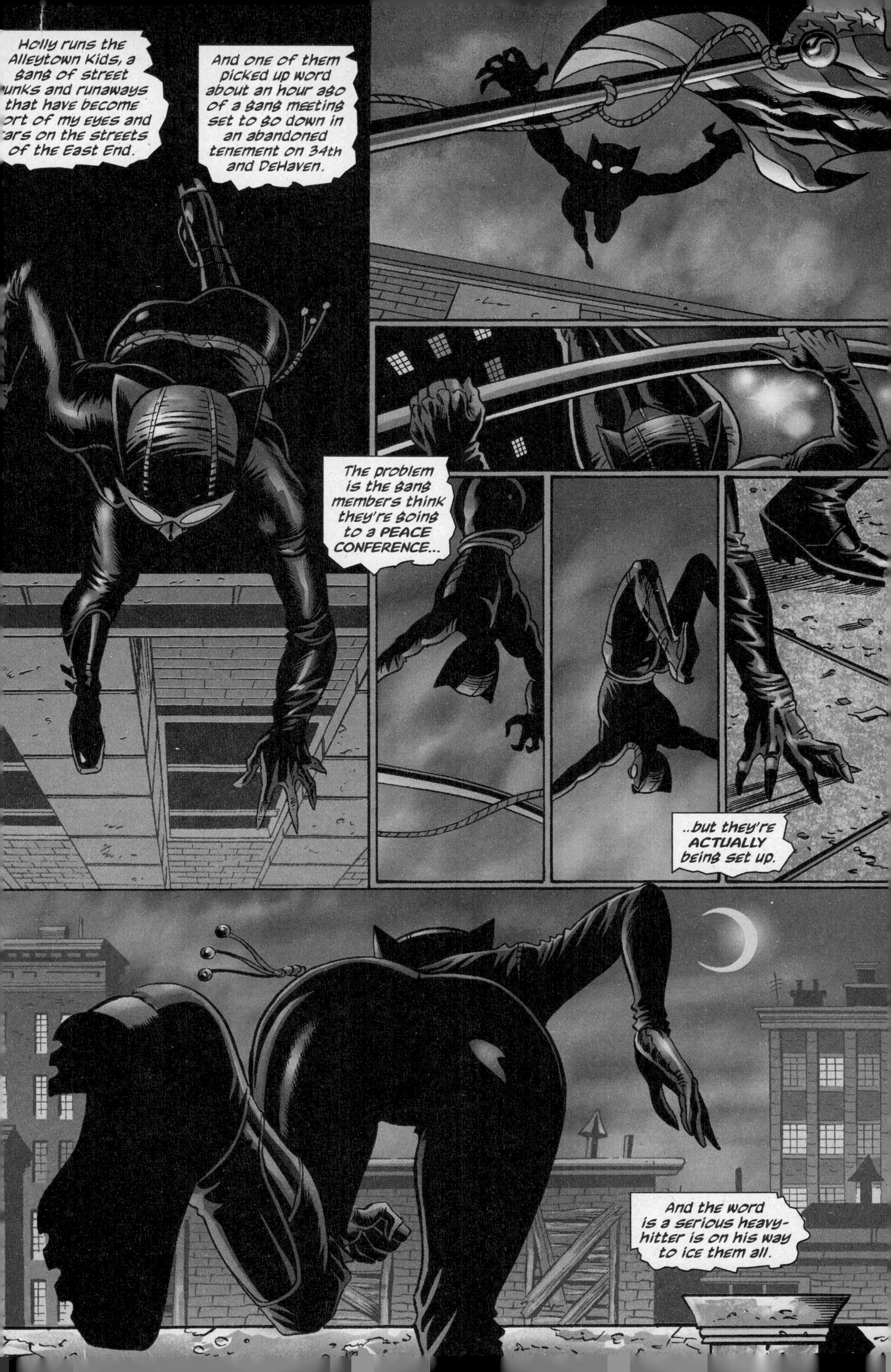
Holly runs the Alleytown Kids, a gang of street unks and runaways that have become ort of my eyes and ars on the streets of the East End.
And one of them picked up word about an hour ago of a gang meeting set to go down in an abandoned tenement on 34th and DeHaven.
The problem is the gang members think they're going to a PEACE CONFERENCE...
...but they're ACTUALLY being set up.
And the word is a serious heavy-hitter is on his way to ice them all.

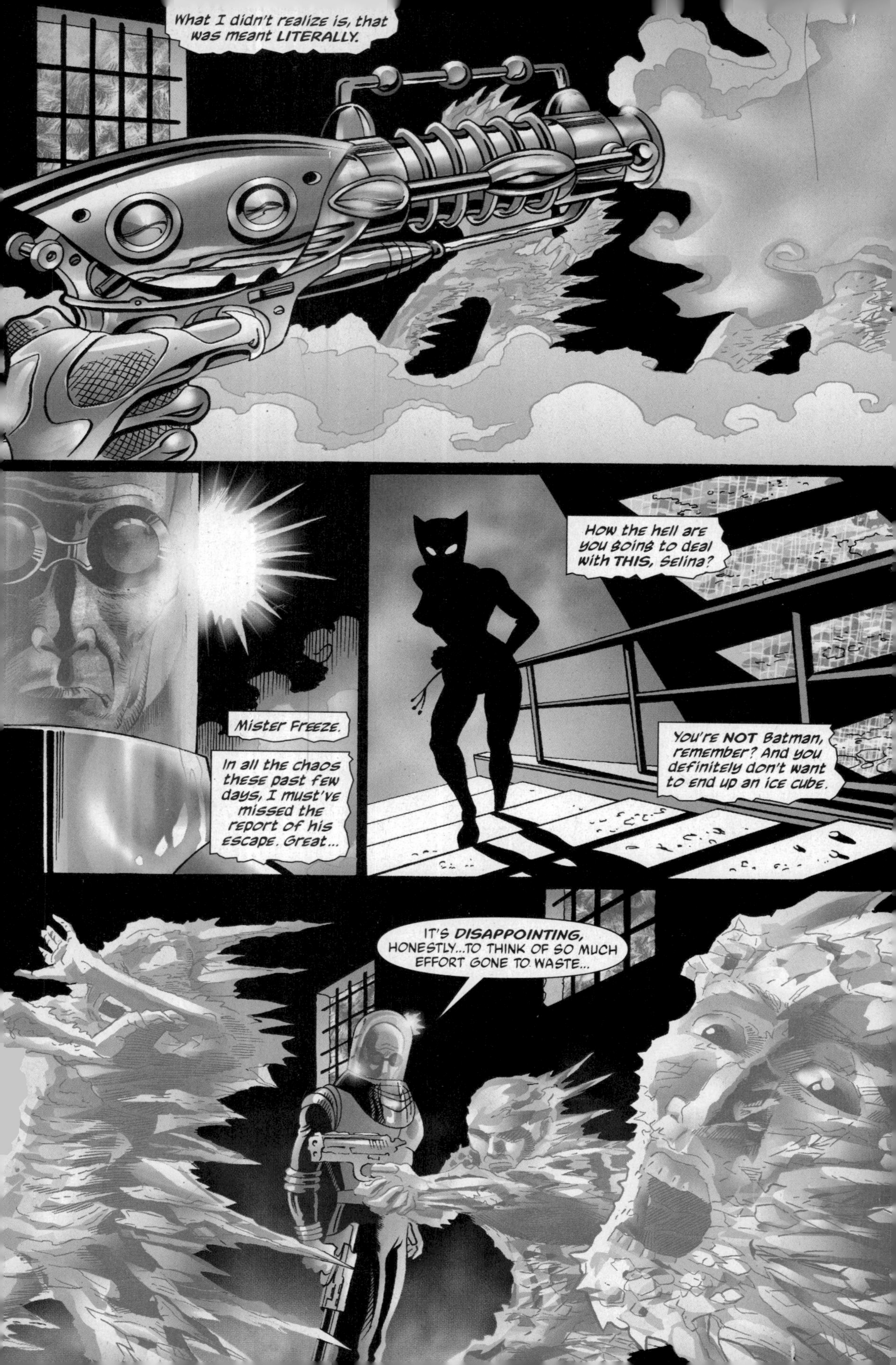

What I didn't realize is, that was meant LITERALLY.
Mister Freeze.
In all the chaos these past few days, I must've missed the report of his escape. Great...
How the hell are you going to deal with THIS, Selina?
You're NOT Batman, remember? And you definitely don't want to end up an ice cube.
IT'S DISAPPOINTING, HONESTLY...TO THINK OF SO MUCH EFFORT GONE TO WASTE...

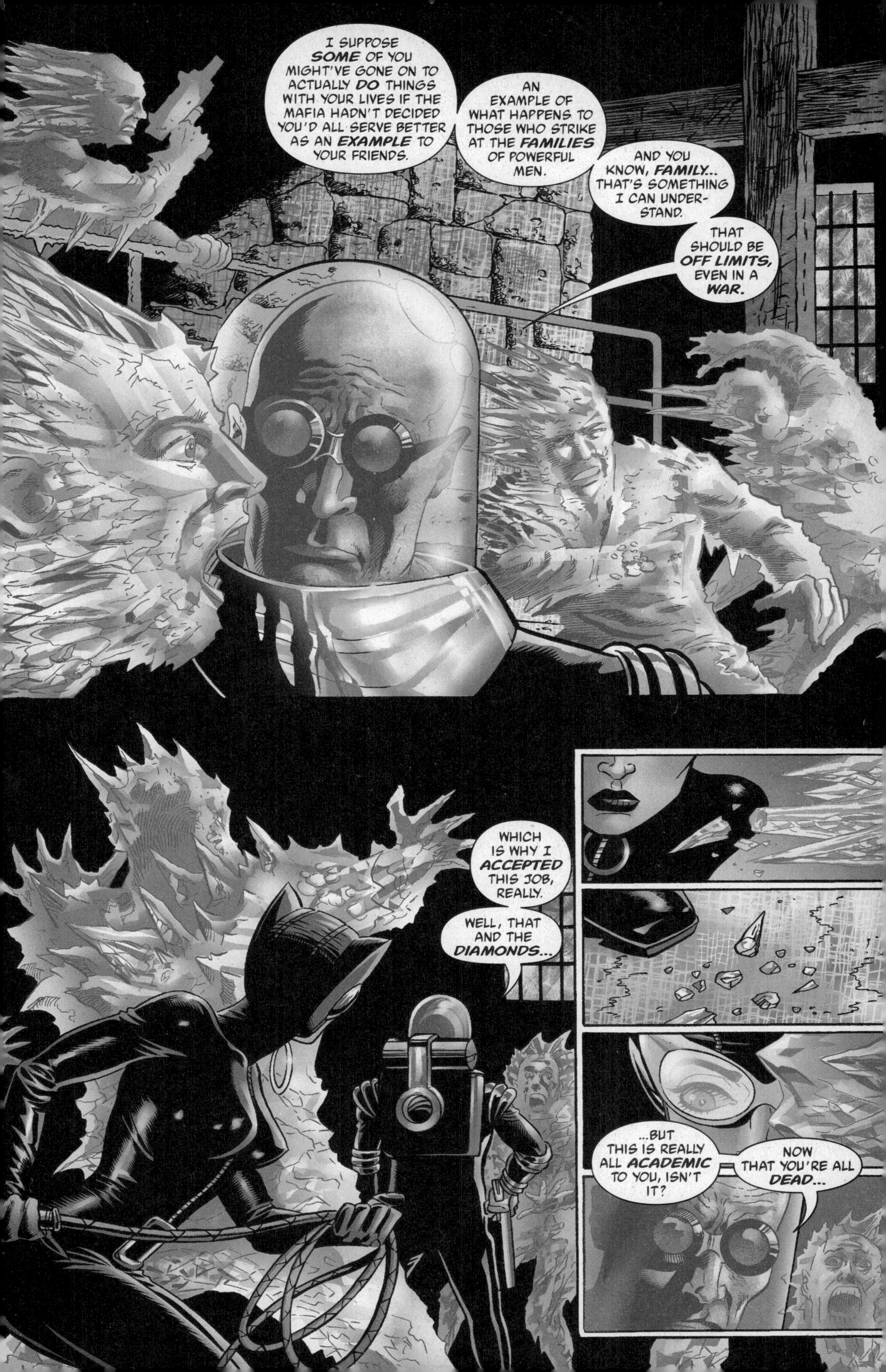
I SUPPOSE SOME OF YOU MIGHT'VE GONE ON TO ACTUALLY DO THINGS WITH YOUR LIVES IF THE MAFIA HADN'T DECIDED YOU'D ALL SERVE BETTER AS AN EXAMPLE TO YOUR FRIENDS.
AN EXAMPLE OF WHAT HAPPENS TO THOSE WHO STRIKE AT THE FAMILIES OF POWERFUL MEN.
AND YOU KNOW, FAMILY... THAT'S SOMETHING I CAN UNDER-STAND.
THAT SHOULD BE OFF LIMITS, EVEN IN A WAR.
WHICH IS WHY I ACCEPTED THIS JOB, REALLY.
WELL, THAT AND THE DIAMONDS...
...BUT THIS IS REALLY ALL ACADEMIC TO YOU, ISN'T IT?
NOW THAT YOU'RE ALL DEAD...

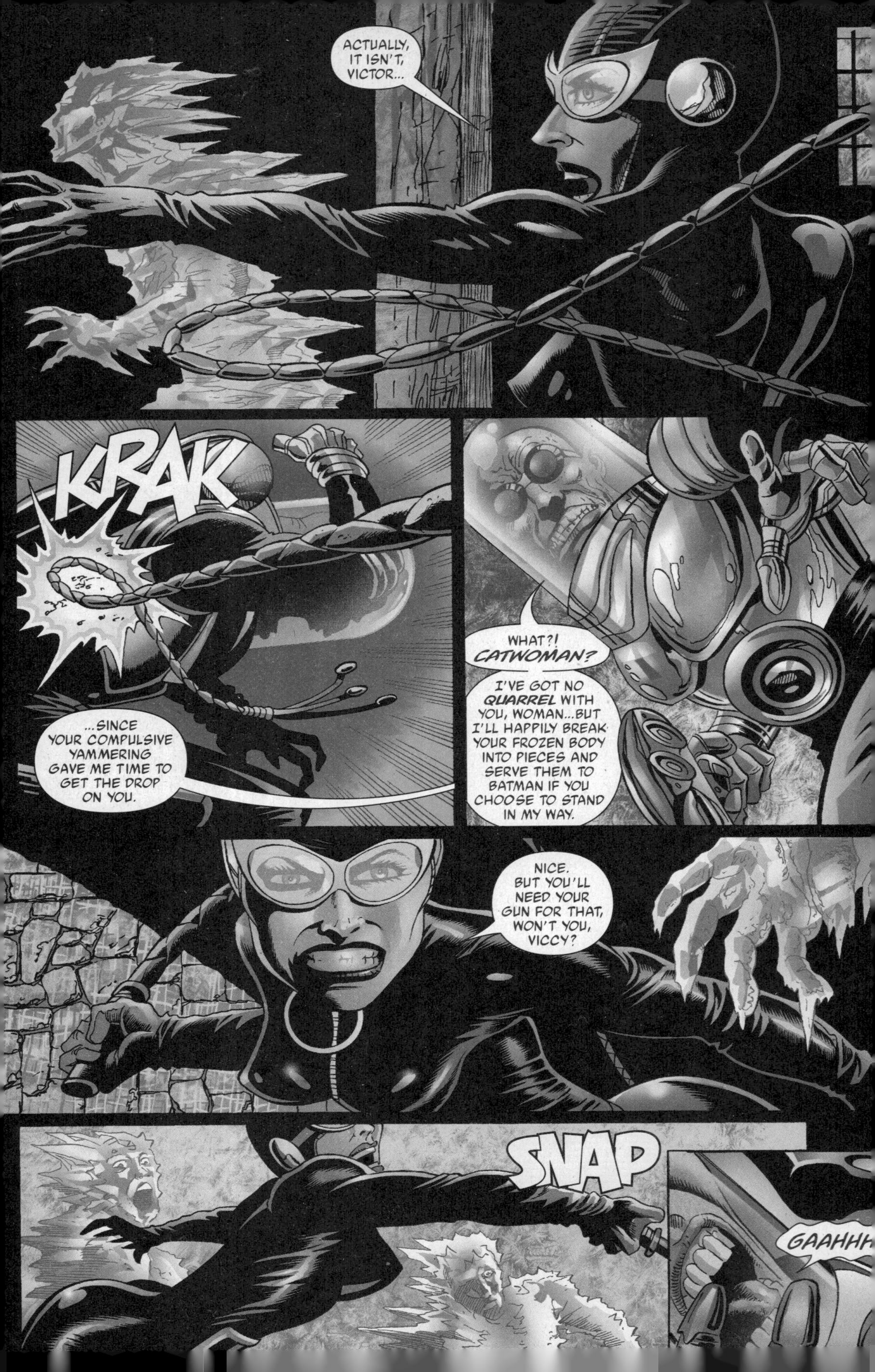
ACTUALLY, IT ISN'T, VICTOR...
KRAK
...SINCE YOUR COMPULSIVE YAMMERING GAVE ME TIME TO GET THE DROP ON YOU.
WHAT?! CATWOMAN?
I'VE GOT NO QUARREL WITH YOU, WOMAN...BUT I'LL HAPPILY BREAK YOUR FROZEN BODY INTO PIECES AND SERVE THEM TO BATMAN IF YOU CHOOSE TO STAND IN MY WAY.
NICE. BUT YOU'LL NEED YOUR GUN FOR THAT, WON'T YOU, VICCY?
SNAP
GAAHHH

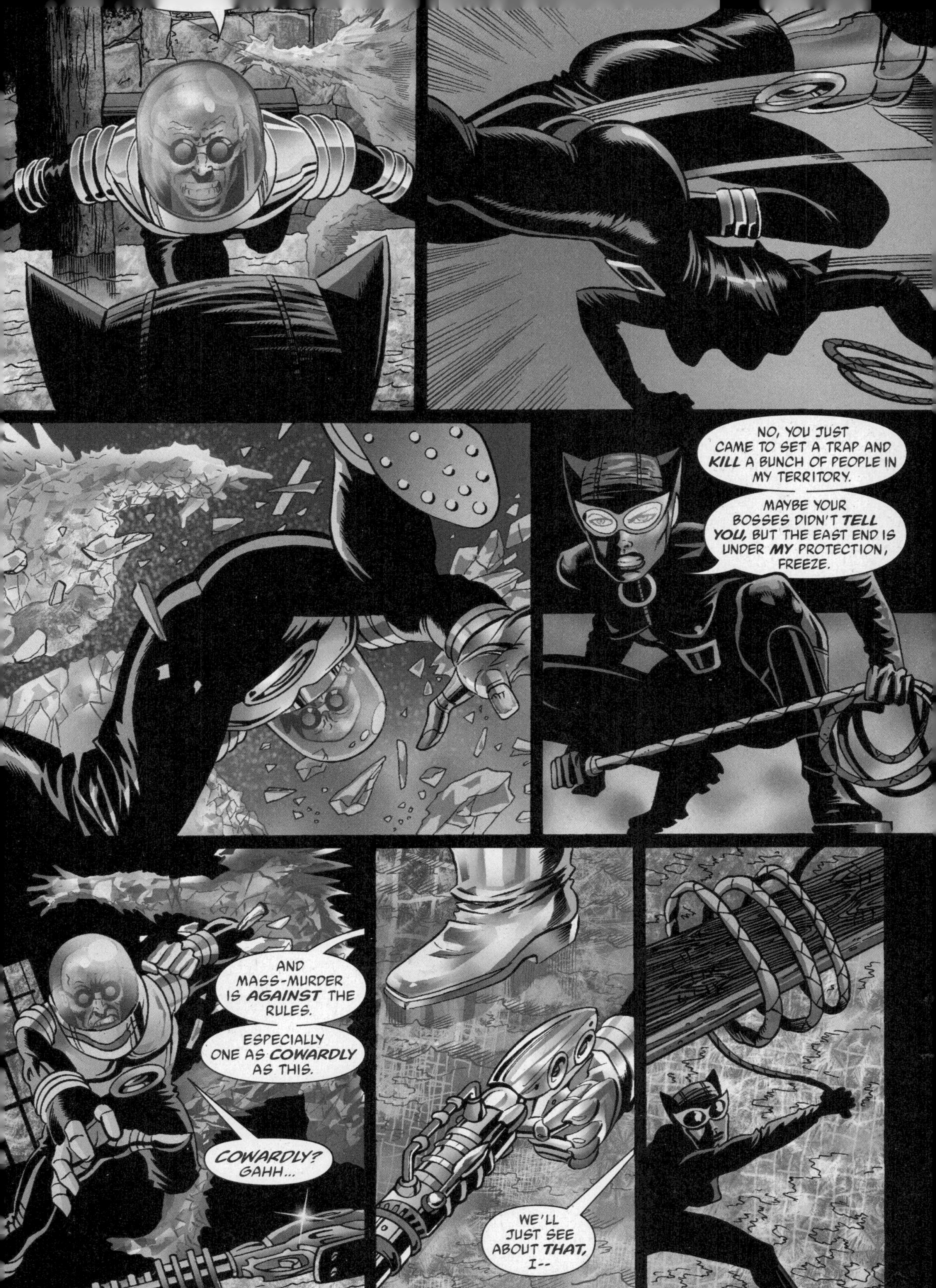
NO, YOU JUST CAME TO SET A TRAP AND KILL A BUNCH OF PEOPLE IN MY TERRITORY.
MAYBE YOUR BOSSES DIDN'T TELL YOU, BUT THE EAST END IS UNDER MY PROTECTION, FREEZE.
AND MASS-MURDER IS AGAINST THE RULES.
ESPECIALLY ONE AS COWARDLY AS THIS.
COWARDLY? GAHH...
WE'LL JUST SEE ABOUT THAT, I--

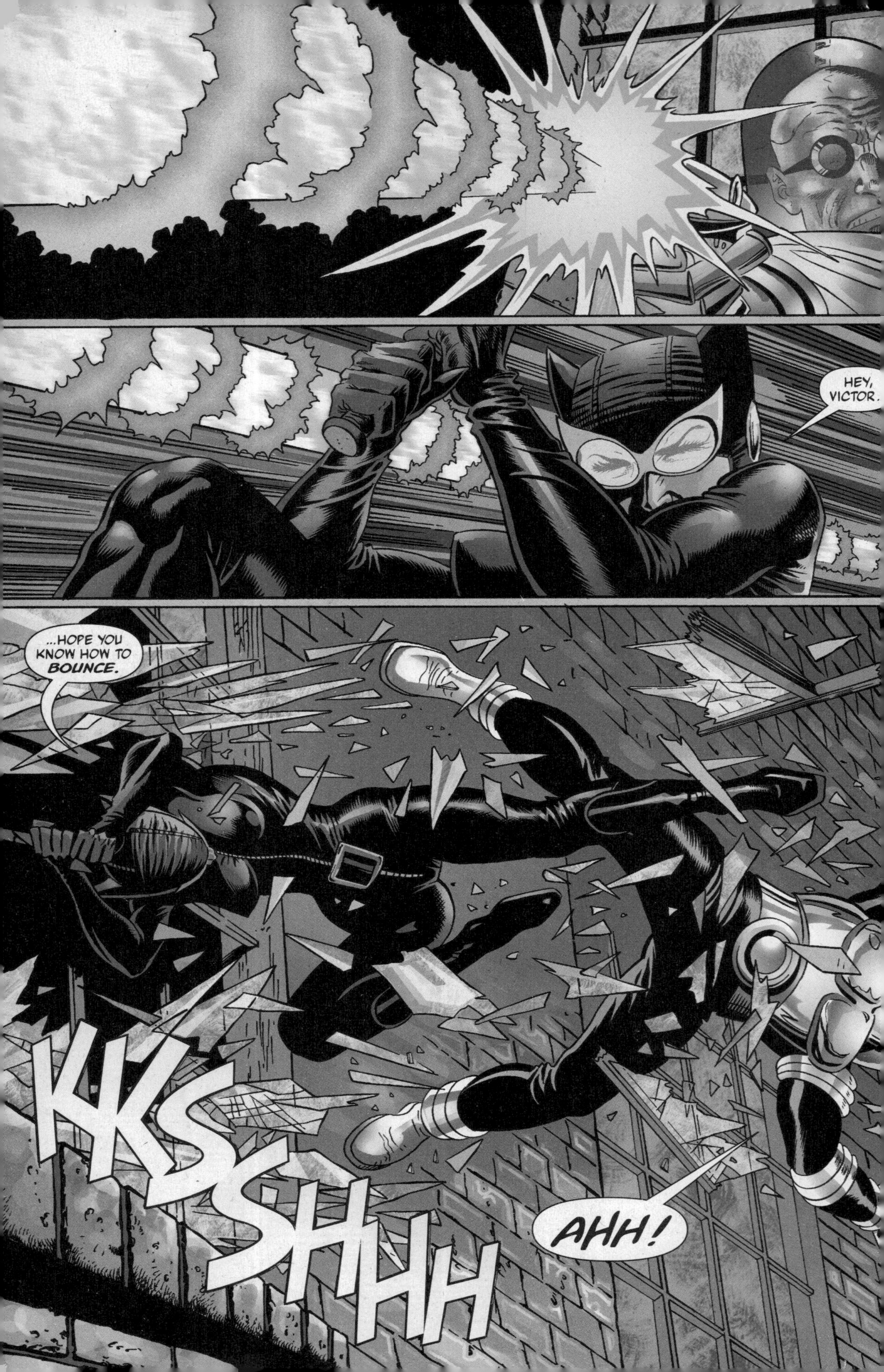
HEY, VICTOR.
...HOPE YOU KNOW HOW TO BOUNCE.
KKSSHHHH
AHH!

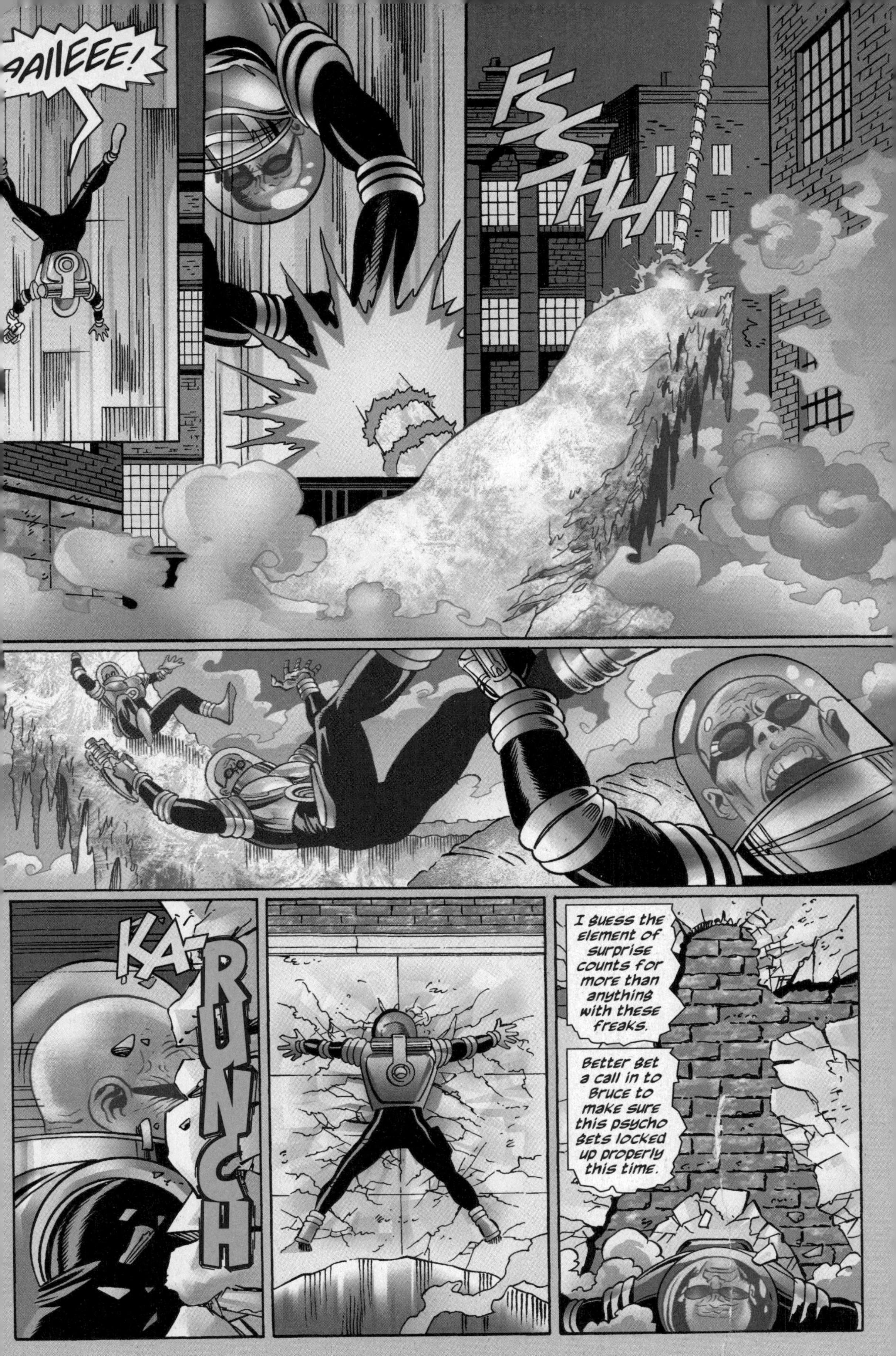
AAIIEEE!
FSSHH
KA-RUNCH
I guess the element of surprise counts for more than anything with these freaks.
Better get a call in to Bruce to make sure this psycho gets locked up properly this time.

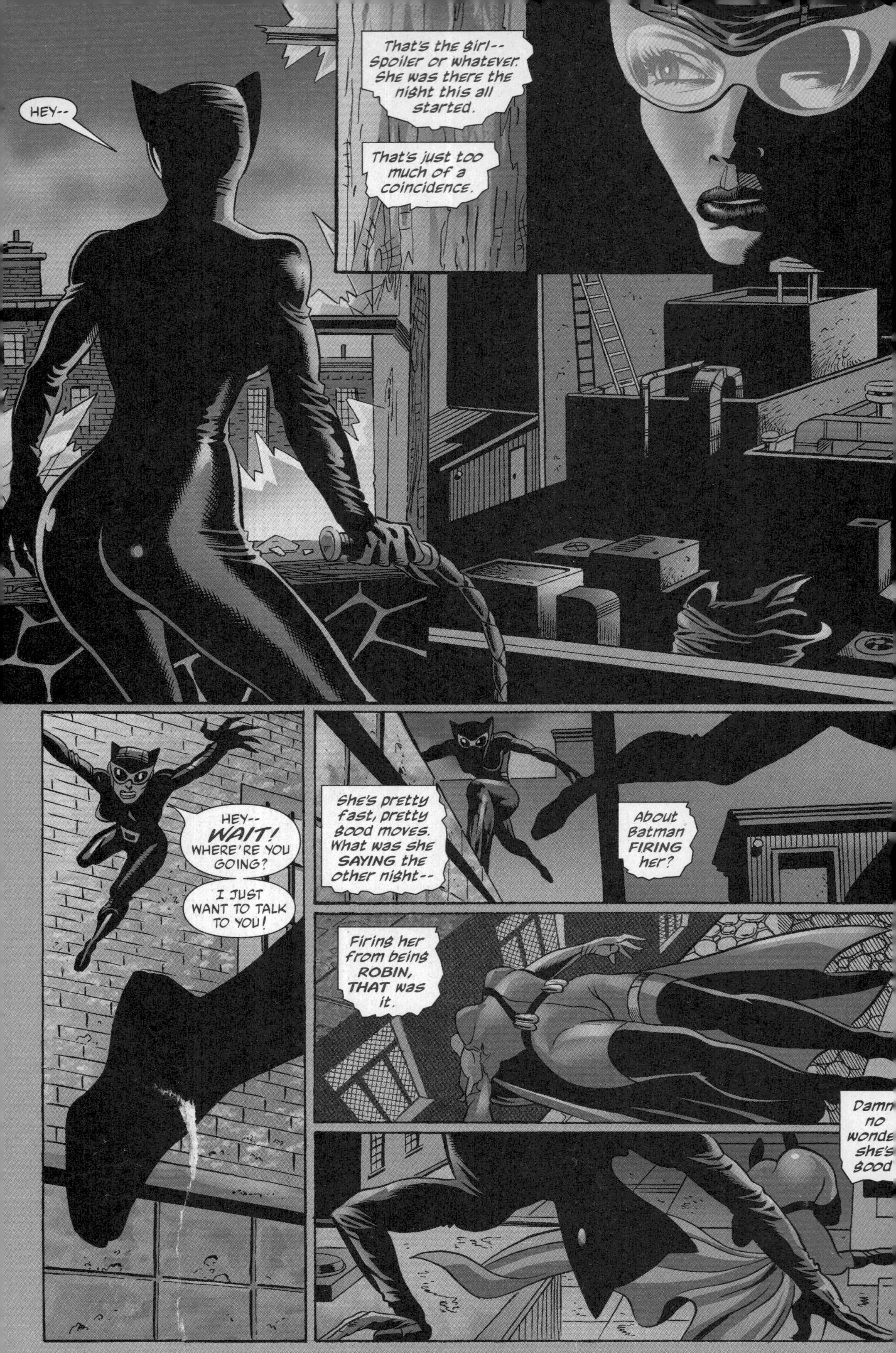
HEY--
That's the girl--Spoiler or whatever. She was there the night this all started.
That's just too much of a coincidence.
HEY-- WAIT! WHERE'RE YOU GOING?
I JUST WANT TO TALK TO YOU!
She's pretty fast, pretty good moves. What was she SAYING the other night--
About Batman FIRING her?
Firing her from being ROBIN, THAT was it.

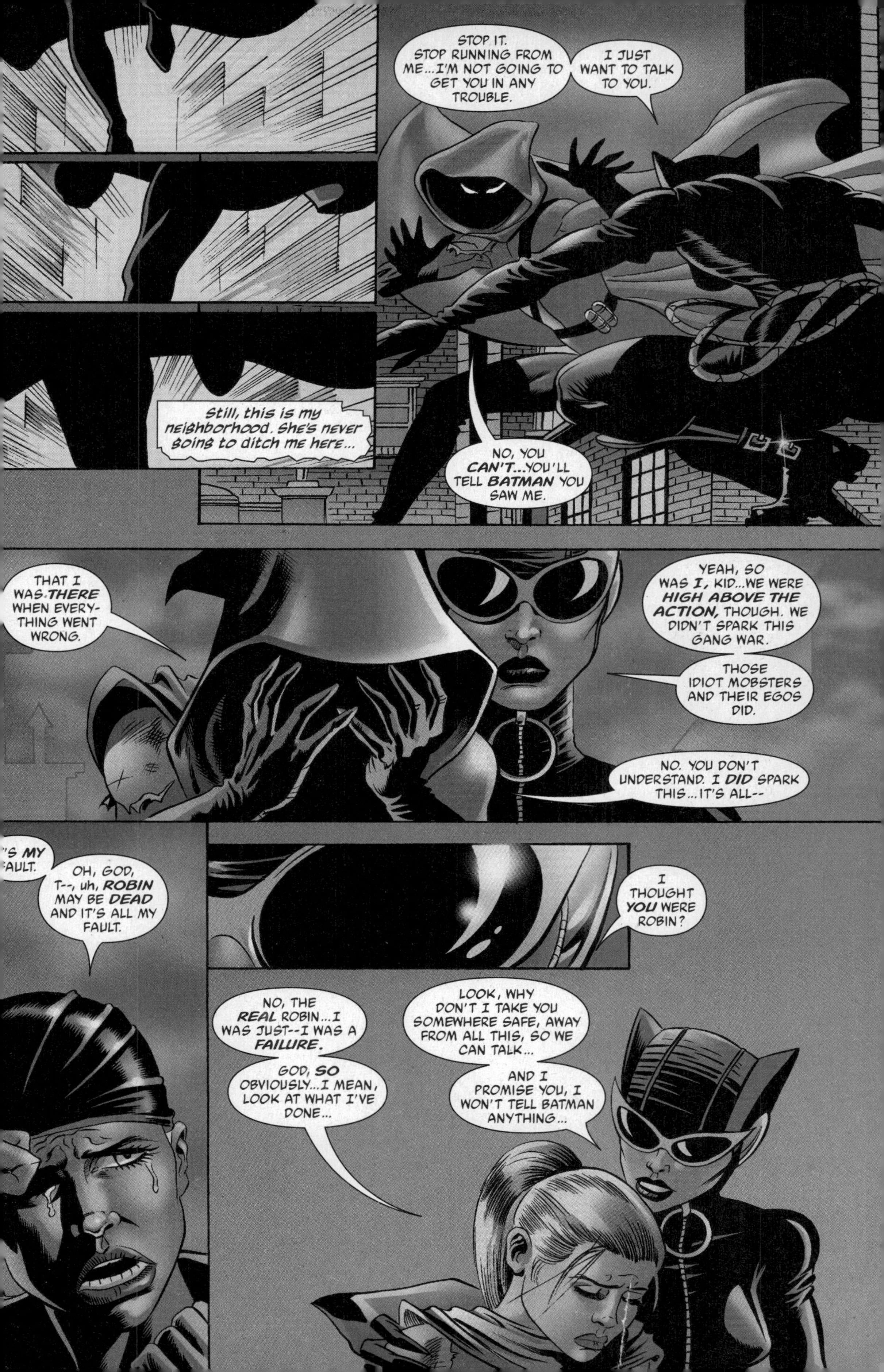
STOP IT. STOP RUNNING FROM ME...I'M NOT GOING TO GET YOU IN ANY TROUBLE.
I JUST WANT TO TALK TO YOU.
Still, this is my neighborhood. She's never going to ditch me here...
NO, YOU CAN'T...YOU'LL TELL BATMAN YOU SAW ME.
THAT I WAS THERE WHEN EVERYTHING WENT WRONG.
YEAH, SO WAS I, KID...WE WERE HIGH ABOVE THE ACTION, THOUGH. WE DIDN'T SPARK THIS GANG WAR.
THOSE IDIOT MOBSTERS AND THEIR EGOS DID.
NO. YOU DON'T UNDERSTAND. I DID SPARK THIS...IT'S ALL--
'S MY FAULT.
OH, GOD, T--, uh, ROBIN MAY BE DEAD AND IT'S ALL MY FAULT.
I THOUGHT YOU WERE ROBIN?
NO, THE REAL ROBIN...I WAS JUST--I WAS A FAILURE.
GOD, SO OBVIOUSLY...I MEAN, LOOK AT WHAT I'VE DONE...
LOOK, WHY DON'T I TAKE YOU SOMEWHERE SAFE, AWAY FROM ALL THIS, SO WE CAN TALK...
AND I PROMISE YOU, I WON'T TELL BATMAN ANYTHING...

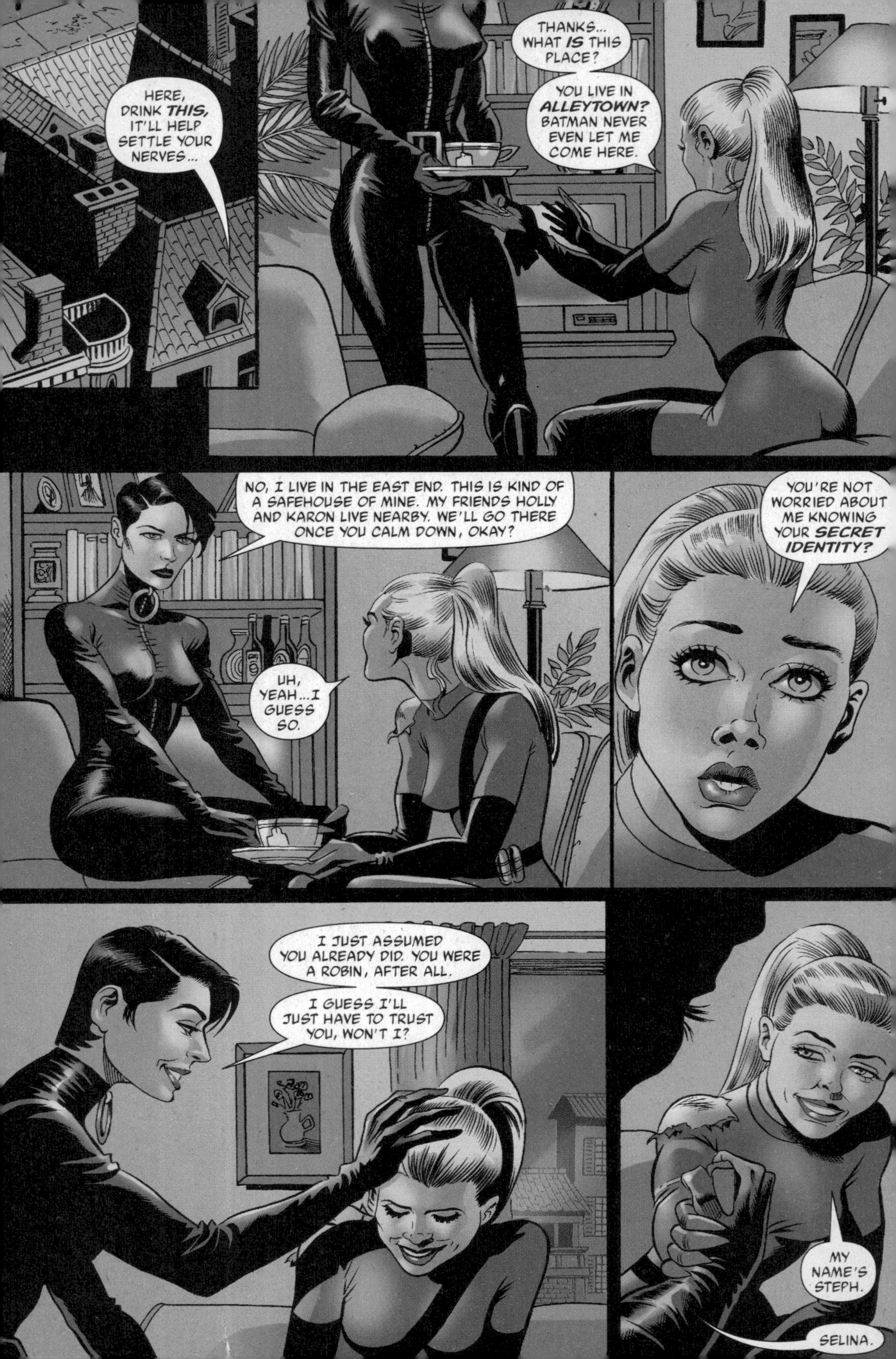
HERE, DRINK THIS, IT'LL HELP SETTLE YOUR NERVES...
THANKS... WHAT IS THIS PLACE?
YOU LIVE IN ALLEYTOWN? BATMAN NEVER EVEN LET ME COME HERE.
NO, I LIVE IN THE EAST END. THIS IS KIND OF A SAFEHOUSE OF MINE. MY FRIENDS HOLLY AND KARON LIVE NEARBY. WE'LL GO THERE ONCE YOU CALM DOWN, OKAY?
UH, YEAH...I GUESS SO.
YOU'RE NOT WORRIED ABOUT ME KNOWING YOUR SECRET IDENTITY?
I JUST ASSUMED YOU ALREADY DID. YOU WERE A ROBIN, AFTER ALL.
I GUESS I'LL JUST HAVE TO TRUST YOU, WON'T I?
MY NAME'S STEPH.
SELINA.

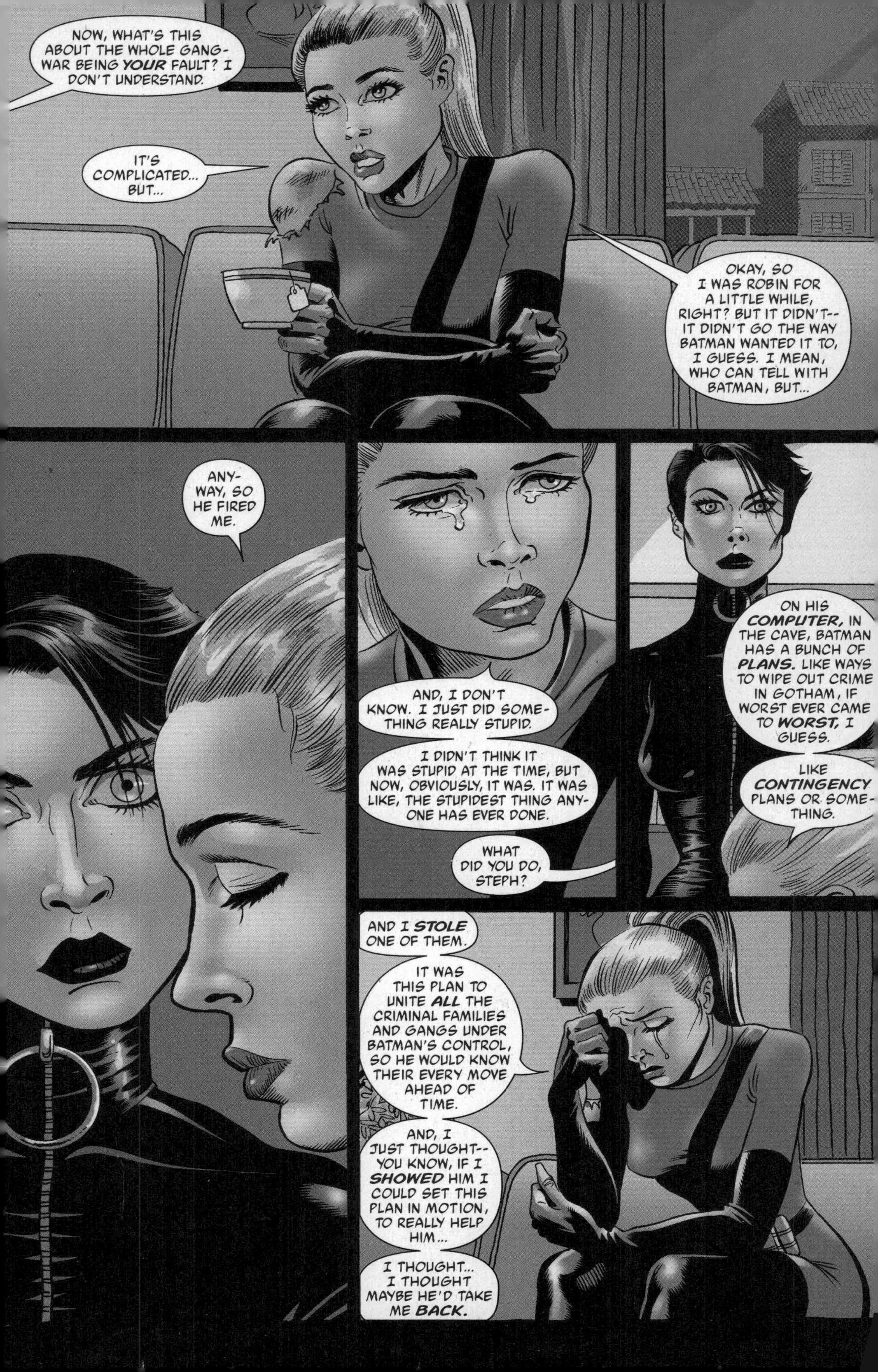
NOW, WHAT'S THIS ABOUT THE WHOLE GANG-WAR BEING YOUR FAULT? I DON'T UNDERSTAND.
IT'S COMPLICATED... BUT...
OKAY, SO I WAS ROBIN FOR A LITTLE WHILE, RIGHT? BUT IT DIDN'T-- IT DIDN'T GO THE WAY BATMAN WANTED IT TO, I GUESS. I MEAN, WHO CAN TELL WITH BATMAN, BUT...
ANY-WAY, SO HE FIRED ME.
AND, I DON'T KNOW. I JUST DID SOME-THING REALLY STUPID.
I DIDN'T THINK IT WAS STUPID AT THE TIME, BUT NOW, OBVIOUSLY, IT WAS. IT WAS LIKE, THE STUPIDEST THING ANY-ONE HAS EVER DONE.
WHAT DID YOU DO, STEPH?
ON HIS COMPUTER, IN THE CAVE, BATMAN HAS A BUNCH OF PLANS. LIKE WAYS TO WIPE OUT CRIME IN GOTHAM, IF WORST EVER CAME TO WORST, I GUESS.
LIKE CONTINGENCY PLANS OR SOME-THING.
AND I STOLE ONE OF THEM.
IT WAS THIS PLAN TO UNITE ALL THE CRIMINAL FAMILIES AND GANGS UNDER BATMAN'S CONTROL, SO HE WOULD KNOW THEIR EVERY MOVE AHEAD OF TIME.
AND, I JUST THOUGHT-- YOU KNOW, IF I SHOWED HIM I COULD SET THIS PLAN IN MOTION, TO REALLY HELP HIM...
I THOUGHT... I THOUGHT MAYBE HE'D TAKE ME BACK.

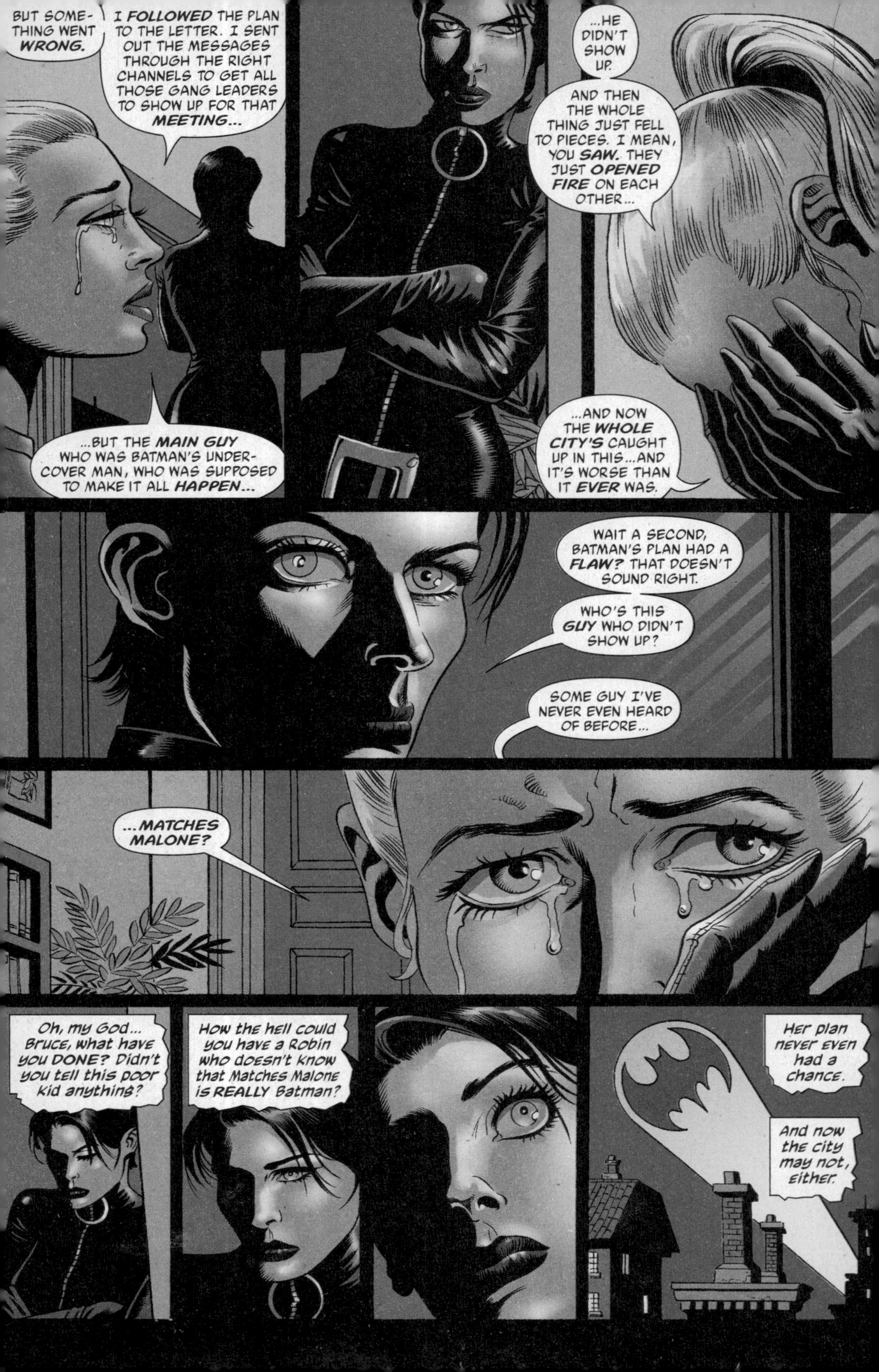

BUT SOMETHING WENT WRONG.
I FOLLOWED THE PLAN TO THE LETTER. I SENT OUT THE MESSAGES THROUGH THE RIGHT CHANNELS TO GET ALL THOSE GANG LEADERS TO SHOW UP FOR THAT MEETING...
...BUT THE MAIN GUY WHO WAS BATMAN'S UNDERCOVER MAN, WHO WAS SUPPOSED TO MAKE IT ALL HAPPEN...
...HE DIDN'T SHOW UP.
AND THEN THE WHOLE THING JUST FELL TO PIECES. I MEAN, YOU SAW. THEY JUST OPENED FIRE ON EACH OTHER...
...AND NOW THE WHOLE CITY'S CAUGHT UP IN THIS...AND IT'S WORSE THAN IT EVER WAS.
WAIT A SECOND, BATMAN'S PLAN HAD A FLAW? THAT DOESN'T SOUND RIGHT.
WHO'S THIS GUY WHO DIDN'T SHOW UP?
SOME GUY I'VE NEVER EVEN HEARD OF BEFORE...
...MATCHES MALONE?
Oh, my God... Bruce, what have you DONE? Didn't you tell this poor kid anything?
How the hell could you have a Robin who doesn't know that Matches Malone is REALLY Batman?
Her plan never even had a chance.
And now the city may not, either.

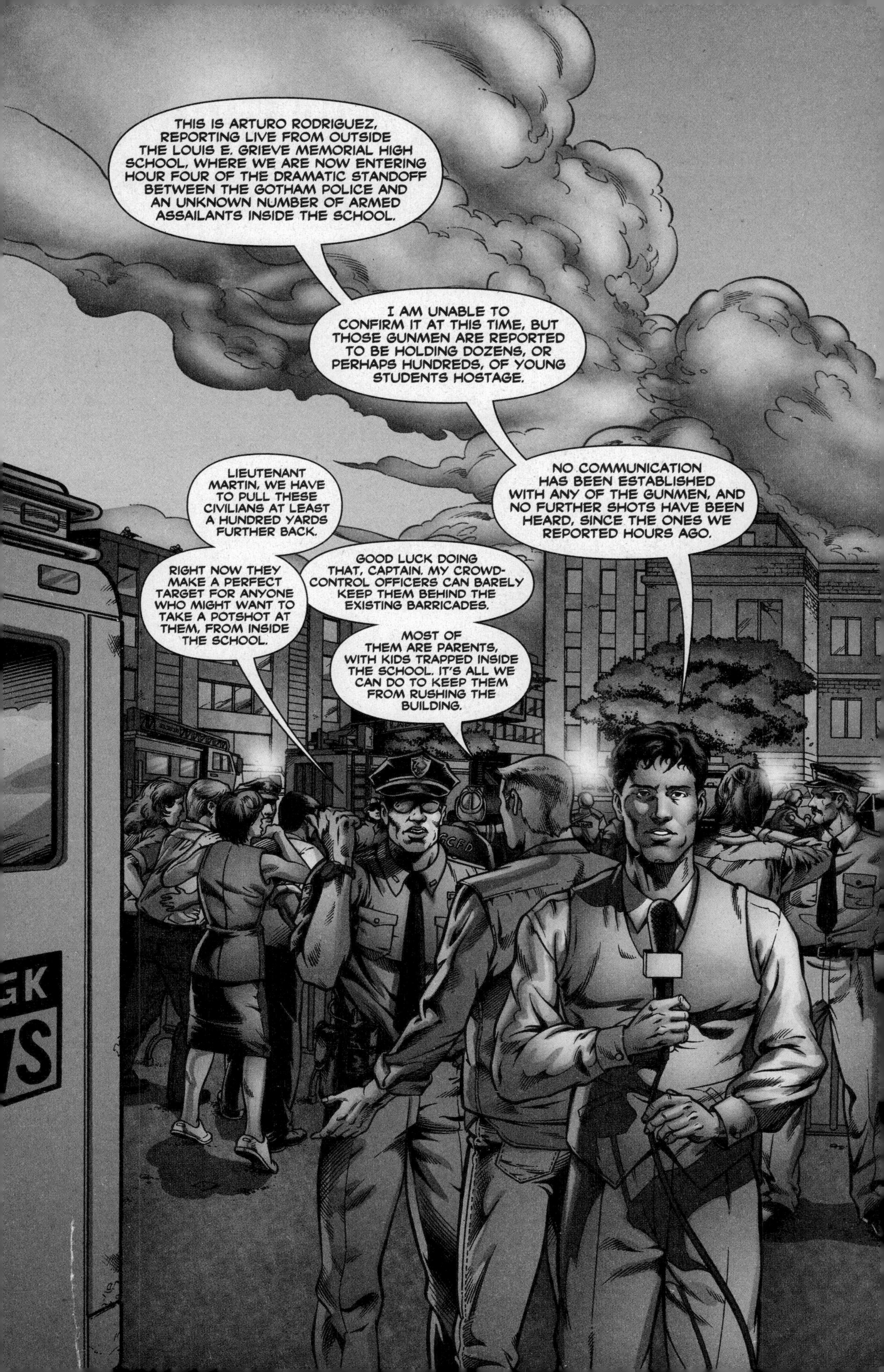
THIS IS ARTURO RODRIGUEZ, REPORTING LIVE FROM OUTSIDE THE LOUIS E. GRIEVE MEMORIAL HIGH SCHOOL, WHERE WE ARE NOW ENTERING HOUR FOUR OF THE DRAMATIC STANDOFF BETWEEN THE GOTHAM POLICE AND AN UNKNOWN NUMBER OF ARMED ASSAILANTS INSIDE THE SCHOOL.
I AM UNABLE TO CONFIRM IT AT THIS TIME, BUT THOSE GUNMEN ARE REPORTED TO BE HOLDING DOZENS, OR PERHAPS HUNDREDS, OF YOUNG STUDENTS HOSTAGE.
NO COMMUNICATION HAS BEEN ESTABLISHED WITH ANY OF THE GUNMEN, AND NO FURTHER SHOTS HAVE BEEN HEARD, SINCE THE ONES WE REPORTED HOURS AGO.
LIEUTENANT MARTIN, WE HAVE TO PULL THESE CIVILIANS AT LEAST A HUNDRED YARDS FURTHER BACK.
RIGHT NOW THEY MAKE A PERFECT TARGET FOR ANYONE WHO MIGHT WANT TO TAKE A POTSHOT AT THEM, FROM INSIDE THE SCHOOL.
GOOD LUCK DOING THAT, CAPTAIN. MY CROWD-CONTROL OFFICERS CAN BARELY KEEP THEM BEHIND THE EXISTING BARRICADES.
MOST OF THEM ARE PARENTS, WITH KIDS TRAPPED INSIDE THE SCHOOL. IT'S ALL WE CAN DO TO KEEP THEM FROM RUSHING THE BUILDING.
GCFD
GK
WS

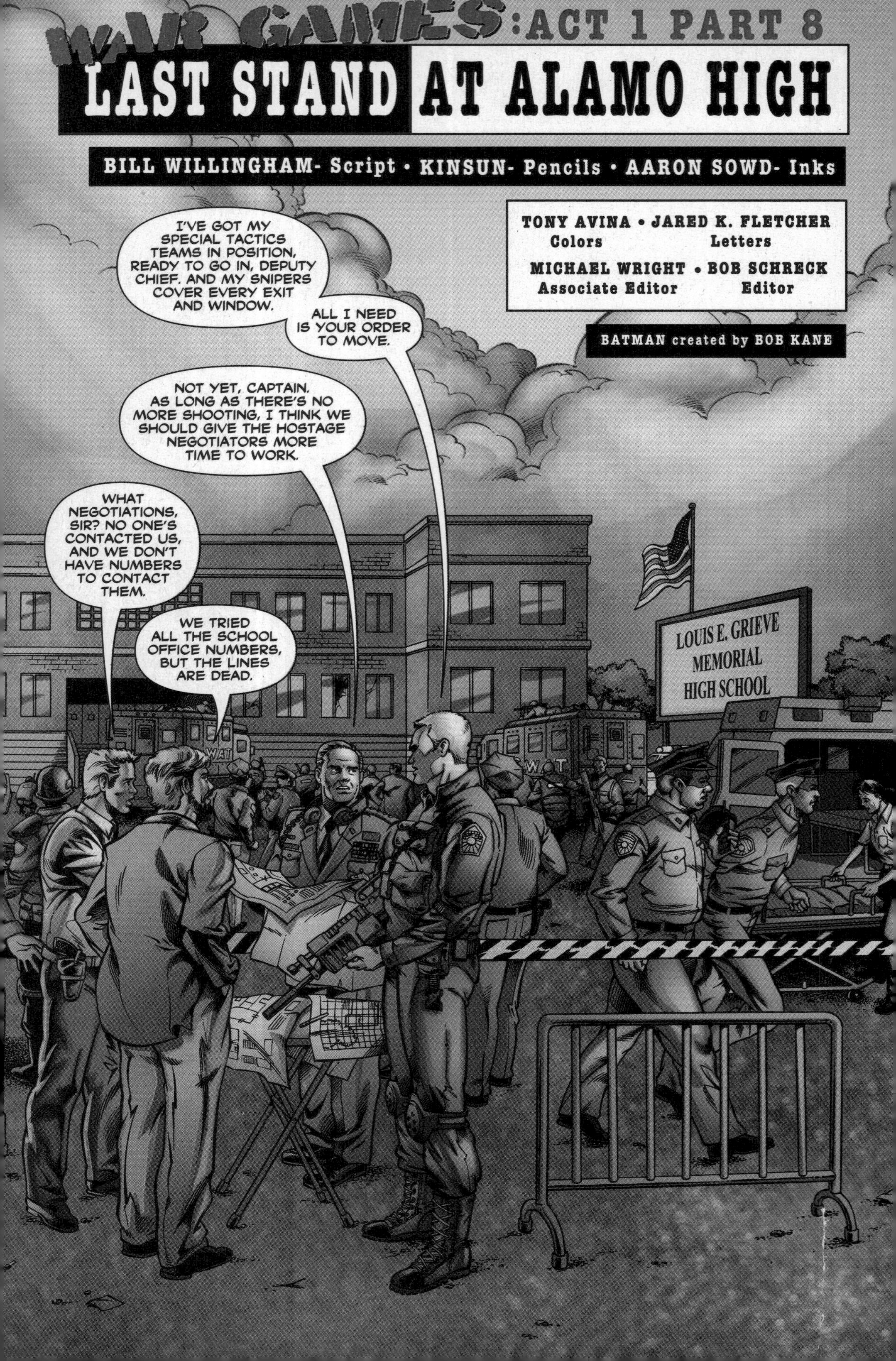
WAR GAMES: ACT 1 PART 8
LAST STAND AT ALAMO HIGH
BILL WILLINGHAM- Script • KINSUN- Pencils • AARON SOWD- Inks
TONY AVINA • JARED K. FLETCHER
Colors Letters
MICHAEL WRIGHT • BOB SCHRECK
Associate Editor Editor
BATMAN created by BOB KANE
I'VE GOT MY SPECIAL TACTICS TEAMS IN POSITION, READY TO GO IN, DEPUTY CHIEF. AND MY SNIPERS COVER EVERY EXIT AND WINDOW.
ALL I NEED IS YOUR ORDER TO MOVE.
NOT YET, CAPTAIN. AS LONG AS THERE'S NO MORE SHOOTING, I THINK WE SHOULD GIVE THE HOSTAGE NEGOTIATORS MORE TIME TO WORK.
WHAT NEGOTIATIONS, SIR? NO ONE'S CONTACTED US, AND WE DON'T HAVE NUMBERS TO CONTACT THEM.
WE TRIED ALL THE SCHOOL OFFICE NUMBERS, BUT THE LINES ARE DEAD.
LOUIS E. GRIEVE MEMORIAL HIGH SCHOOL

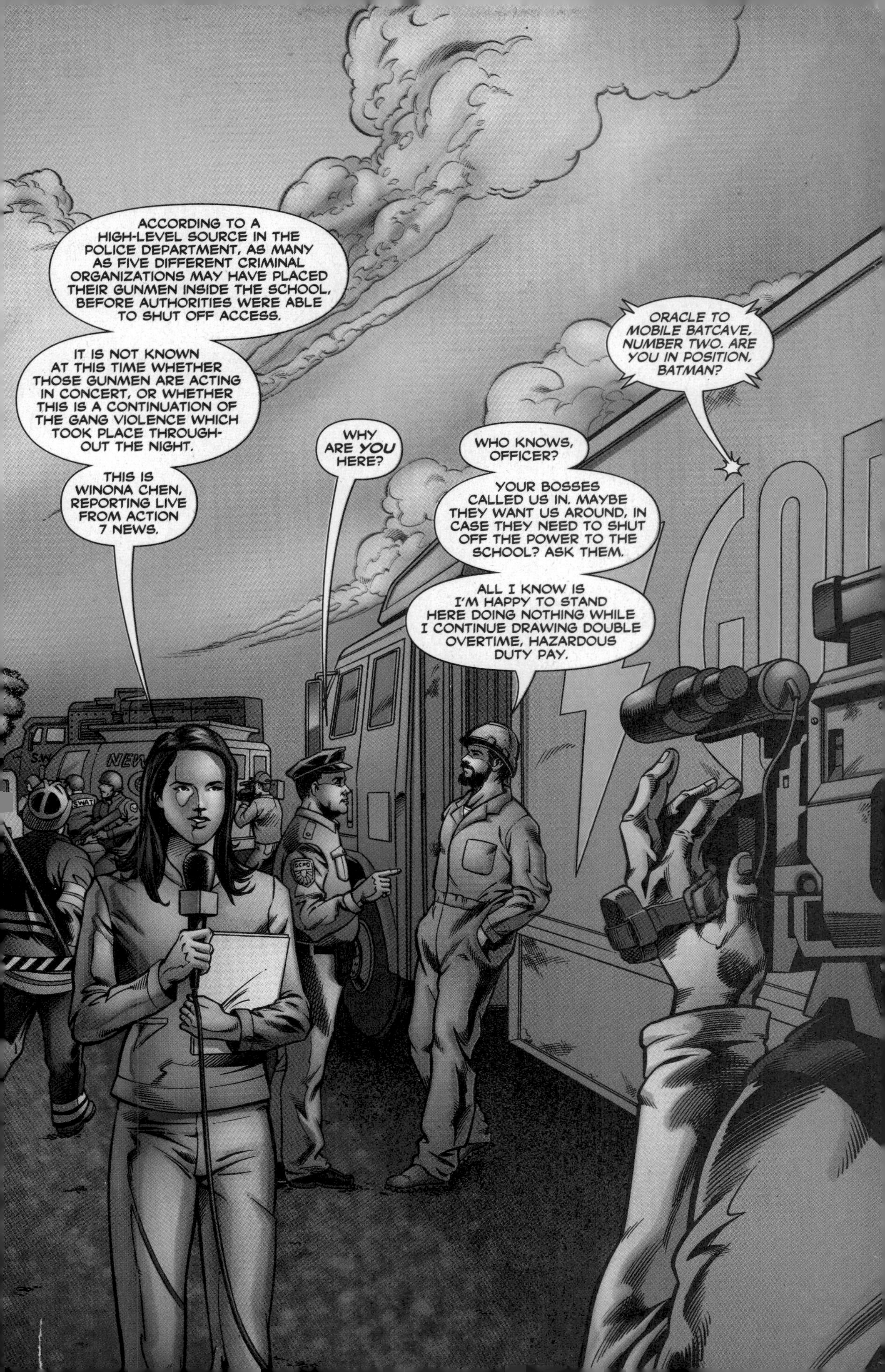
ACCORDING TO A HIGH-LEVEL SOURCE IN THE POLICE DEPARTMENT, AS MANY AS FIVE DIFFERENT CRIMINAL ORGANIZATIONS MAY HAVE PLACED THEIR GUNMEN INSIDE THE SCHOOL, BEFORE AUTHORITIES WERE ABLE TO SHUT OFF ACCESS.
IT IS NOT KNOWN AT THIS TIME WHETHER THOSE GUNMEN ARE ACTING IN CONCERT, OR WHETHER THIS IS A CONTINUATION OF THE GANG VIOLENCE WHICH TOOK PLACE THROUGH-OUT THE NIGHT.
THIS IS WINONA CHEN, REPORTING LIVE FROM ACTION 7 NEWS.
WHY ARE *YOU* HERE?
WHO KNOWS, OFFICER?
YOUR BOSSES CALLED US IN. MAYBE THEY WANT US AROUND, IN CASE THEY NEED TO SHUT OFF THE POWER TO THE SCHOOL? ASK THEM.
ALL I KNOW IS I'M HAPPY TO STAND HERE DOING NOTHING WHILE I CONTINUE DRAWING DOUBLE OVERTIME, HAZARDOUS DUTY PAY.
ORACLE TO MOBILE BATCAVE, NUMBER TWO. ARE YOU IN POSITION, BATMAN?

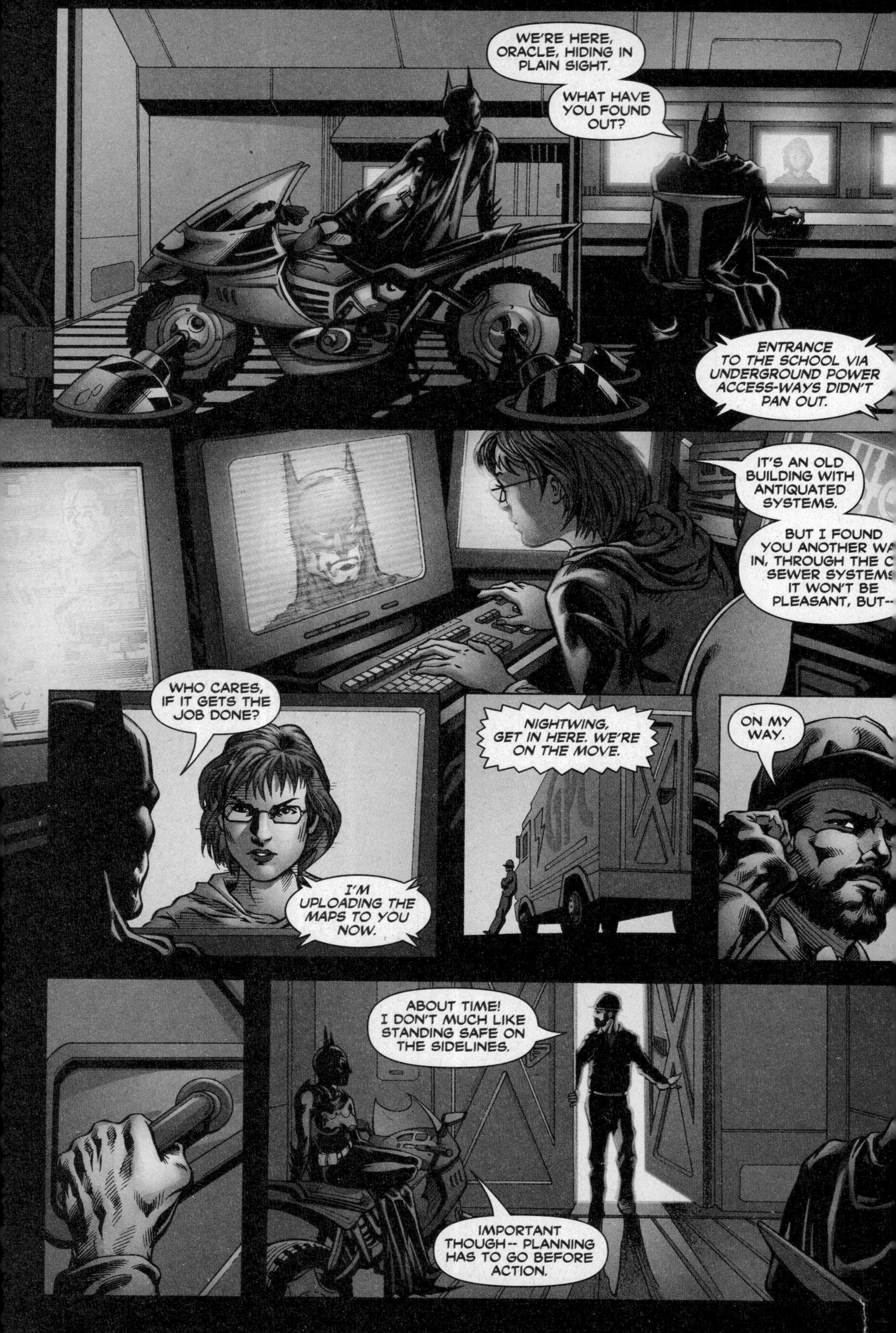
WE'RE HERE, ORACLE, HIDING IN PLAIN SIGHT.
WHAT HAVE YOU FOUND OUT?
ENTRANCE TO THE SCHOOL VIA UNDERGROUND POWER ACCESS-WAYS DIDN'T PAN OUT.
IT'S AN OLD BUILDING WITH ANTIQUATED SYSTEMS.
BUT I FOUND YOU ANOTHER WA IN, THROUGH THE C SEWER SYSTEMS IT WON'T BE PLEASANT, BUT--
WHO CARES, IF IT GETS THE JOB DONE?
I'M UPLOADING THE MAPS TO YOU NOW.
NIGHTWING, GET IN HERE. WE'RE ON THE MOVE.
ON MY WAY.
ABOUT TIME! I DON'T MUCH LIKE STANDING SAFE ON THE SIDELINES.
IMPORTANT THOUGH-- PLANNING HAS TO GO BEFORE ACTION.

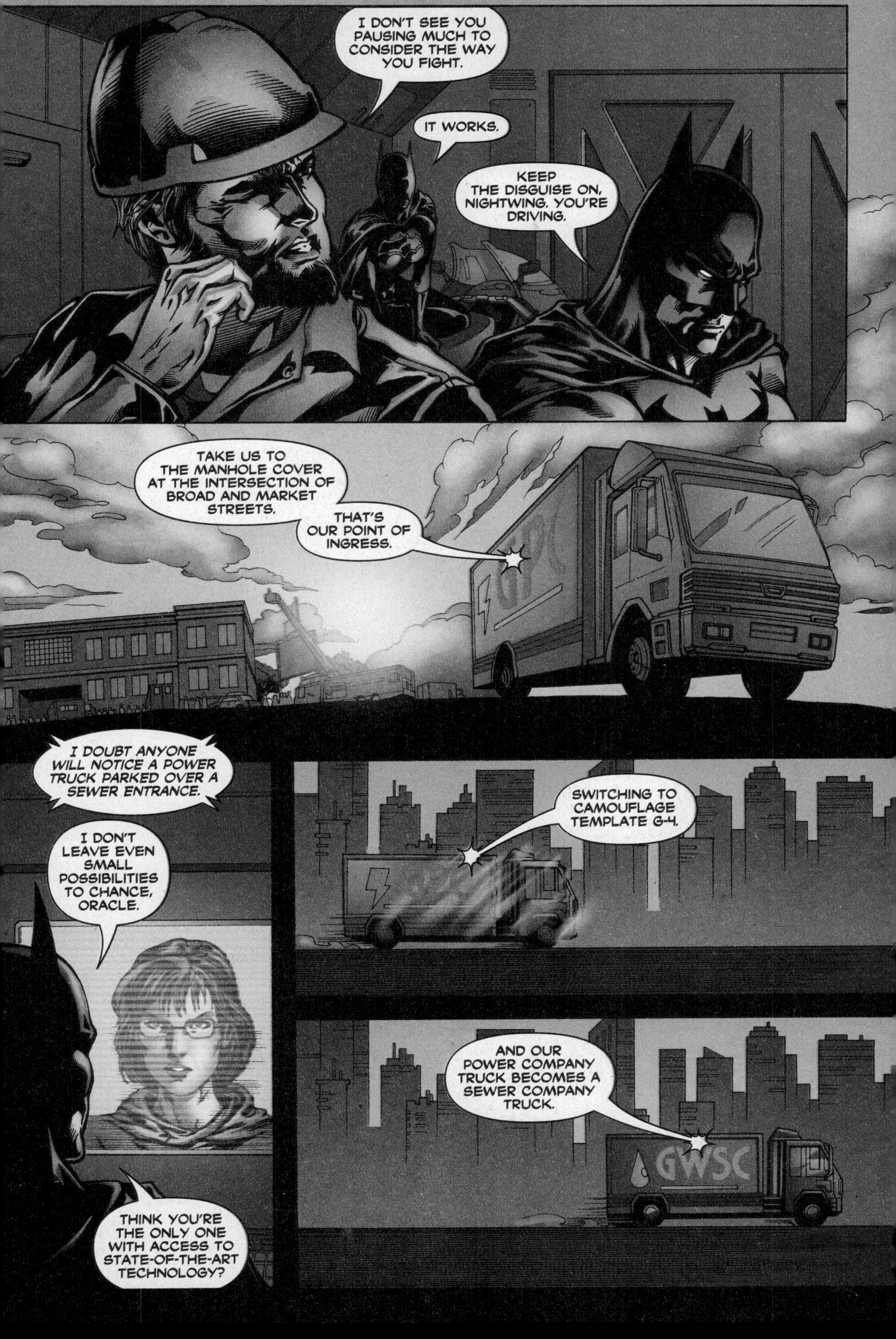
I DON'T SEE YOU PAUSING MUCH TO CONSIDER THE WAY YOU FIGHT.
IT WORKS.
KEEP THE DISGUISE ON, NIGHTWING. YOU'RE DRIVING.
TAKE US TO THE MANHOLE COVER AT THE INTERSECTION OF BROAD AND MARKET STREETS.
THAT'S OUR POINT OF INGRESS.
I DOUBT ANYONE WILL NOTICE A POWER TRUCK PARKED OVER A SEWER ENTRANCE.
I DON'T LEAVE EVEN SMALL POSSIBILITIES TO CHANCE, ORACLE.
THINK YOU'RE THE ONLY ONE WITH ACCESS TO STATE-OF-THE-ART TECHNOLOGY?
SWITCHING TO CAMOUFLAGE TEMPLATE G-4.
AND OUR POWER COMPANY TRUCK BECOMES A SEWER COMPANY TRUCK.
GWSC

DON'T PANIC! IT JUST MAKES A BAD SITUATION WORSE!

WHY ARE YOU RUNNING AWAY FROM--

WHAT HAPPENED, LARRY? I SENT YOU GUYS TO THE CAFETERIA.

MEN CAME IN. GUNS. SOME OF US GOT AWAY, BUT NOT BILLY HORNER, OR MR. SANDWATER, OR--

THERE'S LOTS STILL CAUGHT THERE AND--

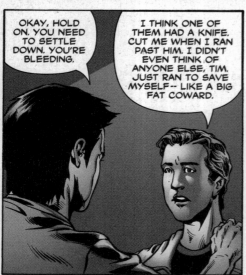

OKAY, HOLD ON. YOU NEED TO SETTLE DOWN. YOU'RE BLEEDING.

I THINK ONE OF THEM HAD A KNIFE. CUT ME WHEN I RAN PAST HIM. I DIDN'T EVEN THINK OF ANYONE ELSE, TIM. JUST RAN TO SAVE MYSELF-- LIKE A BIG FAT COWARD.

NOW THEY'LL PROBABLY KILL MR. SANDWATER, AND LISA JOLIAN, AND--

SHHHHH.

DON'T WORRY ABOUT THAT NOW. LET'S GET YOU DOWN TO THE NURSE'S OFFICE. SOME OF US HAVE BEEN HIDING OUT THERE.

ON THE WAY, WHY DON'T YOU DESCRIBE THOSE MEN WHO TOOK OVER THE CAFETERIA?

IS THAT BLOOD ON YOUR SHIRT?

IT'S NOT MINE.

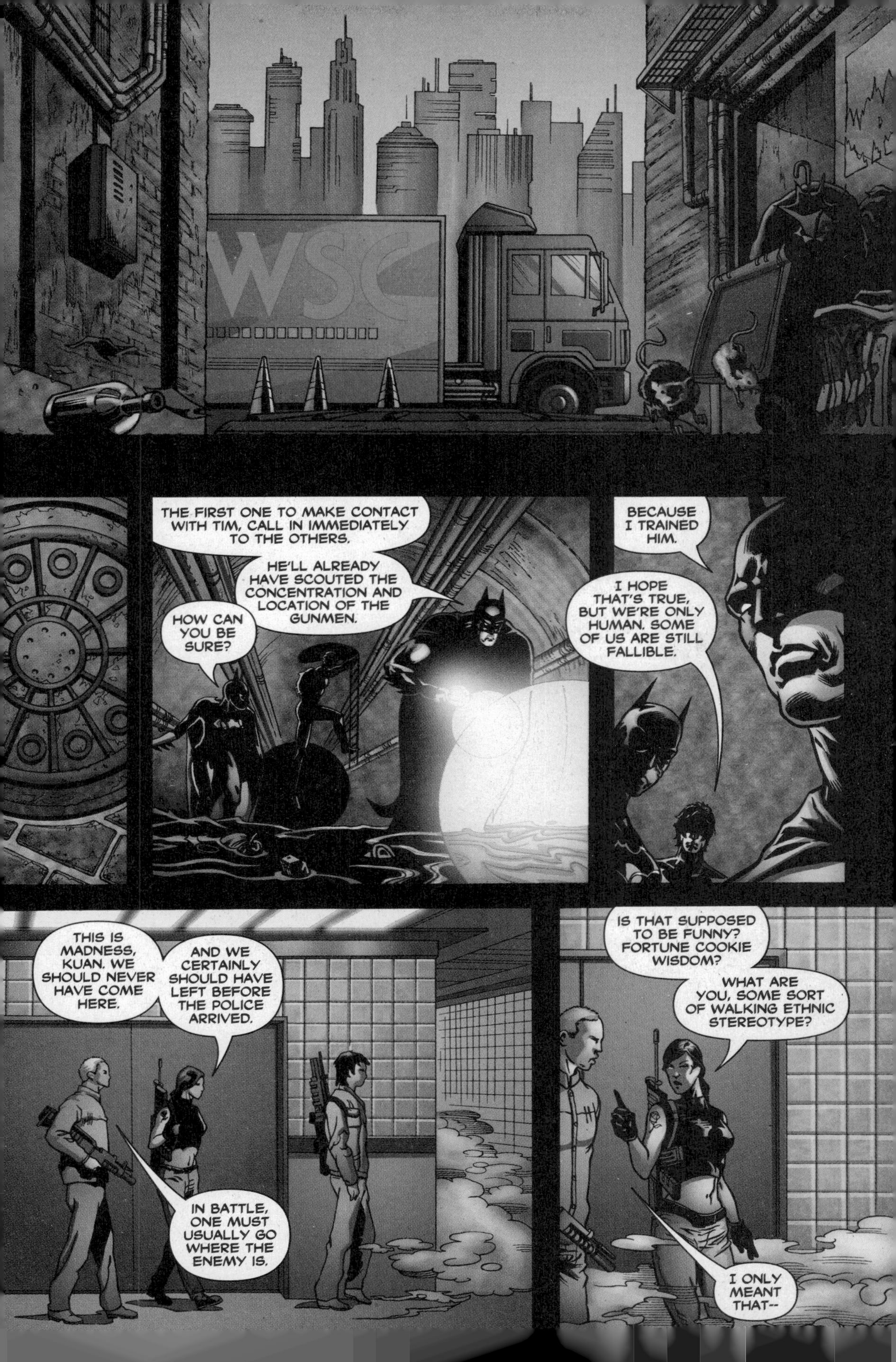
WSC
THE FIRST ONE TO MAKE CONTACT WITH TIM, CALL IN IMMEDIATELY TO THE OTHERS.
HE'LL ALREADY HAVE SCOUTED THE CONCENTRATION AND LOCATION OF THE GUNMEN.
HOW CAN YOU BE SURE?
BECAUSE I TRAINED HIM.
I HOPE THAT'S TRUE, BUT WE'RE ONLY HUMAN. SOME OF US ARE STILL FALLIBLE.
THIS IS MADNESS, KUAN. WE SHOULD NEVER HAVE COME HERE.
AND WE CERTAINLY SHOULD HAVE LEFT BEFORE THE POLICE ARRIVED.
IN BATTLE, ONE MUST USUALLY GO WHERE THE ENEMY IS.
IS THAT SUPPOSED TO BE FUNNY? FORTUNE COOKIE WISDOM?
WHAT ARE YOU, SOME SORT OF WALKING ETHNIC STEREOTYPE?
I ONLY MEANT THAT--

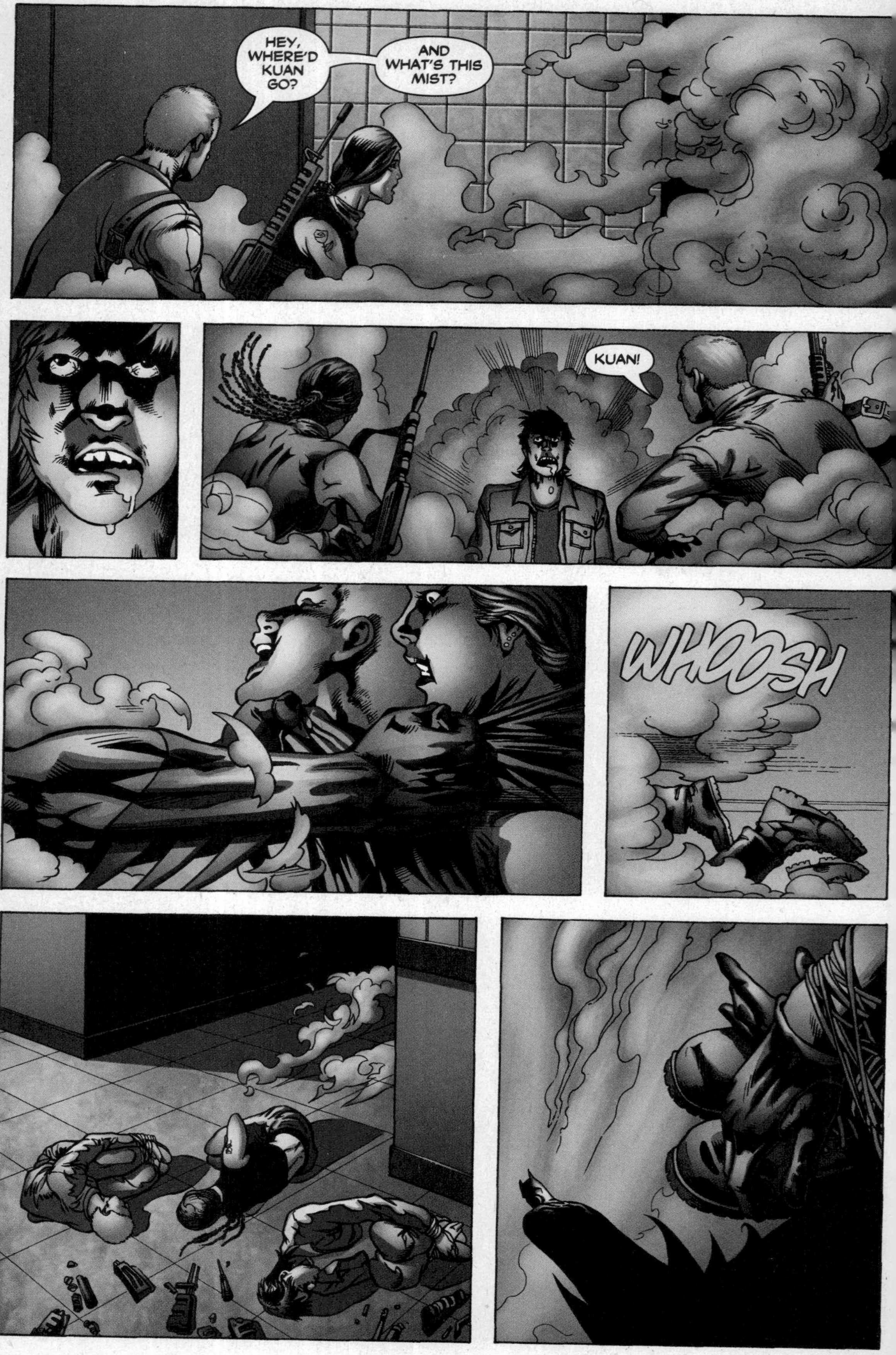
HEY, WHERE'D KUAN GO?
AND WHAT'S THIS MIST?
KUAN!
WHOOSH

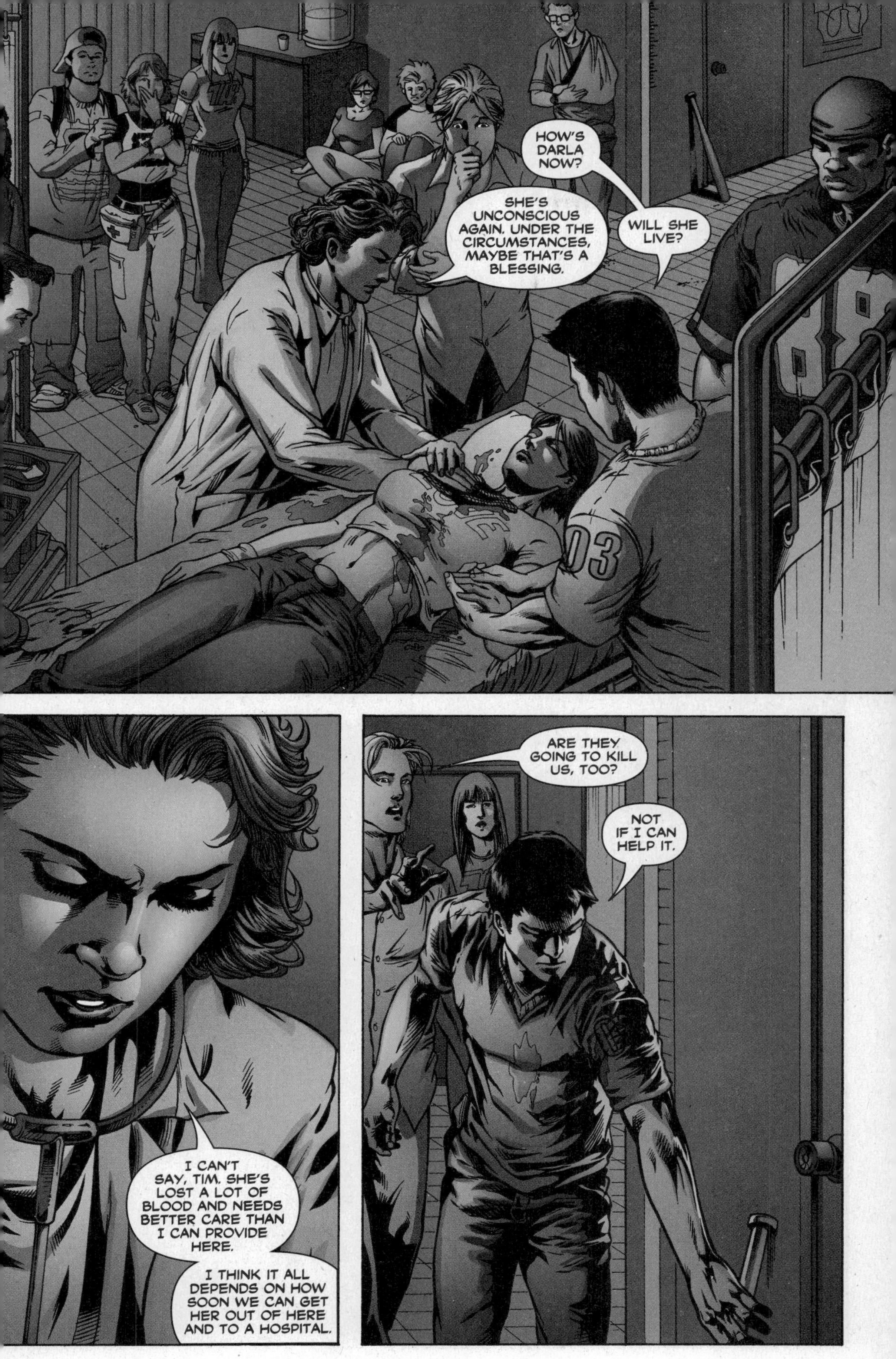
HOW'S DARLA NOW?
SHE'S UNCONSCIOUS AGAIN. UNDER THE CIRCUMSTANCES, MAYBE THAT'S A BLESSING.
WILL SHE LIVE?
I CAN'T SAY, TIM. SHE'S LOST A LOT OF BLOOD AND NEEDS BETTER CARE THAN I CAN PROVIDE HERE.
I THINK IT ALL DEPENDS ON HOW SOON WE CAN GET HER OUT OF HERE AND TO A HOSPITAL.
ARE THEY GOING TO KILL US, TOO?
NOT IF I CAN HELP IT.

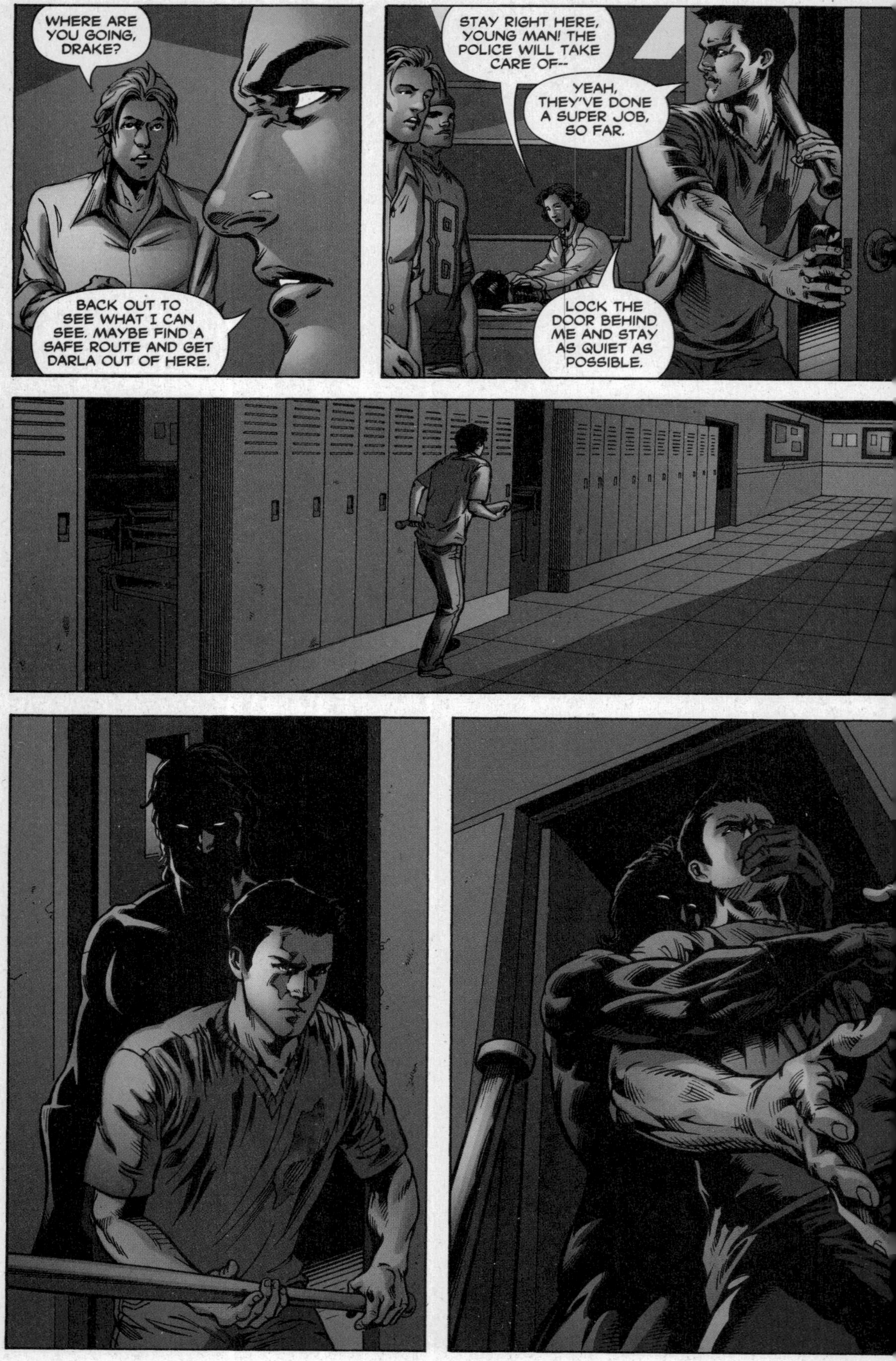
WHERE ARE YOU GOING, DRAKE?
BACK OUT TO SEE WHAT I CAN SEE. MAYBE FIND A SAFE ROUTE AND GET DARLA OUT OF HERE.
STAY RIGHT HERE, YOUNG MAN! THE POLICE WILL TAKE CARE OF--
YEAH, THEY'VE DONE A SUPER JOB, SO FAR.
LOCK THE DOOR BEHIND ME AND STAY AS QUIET AS POSSIBLE.

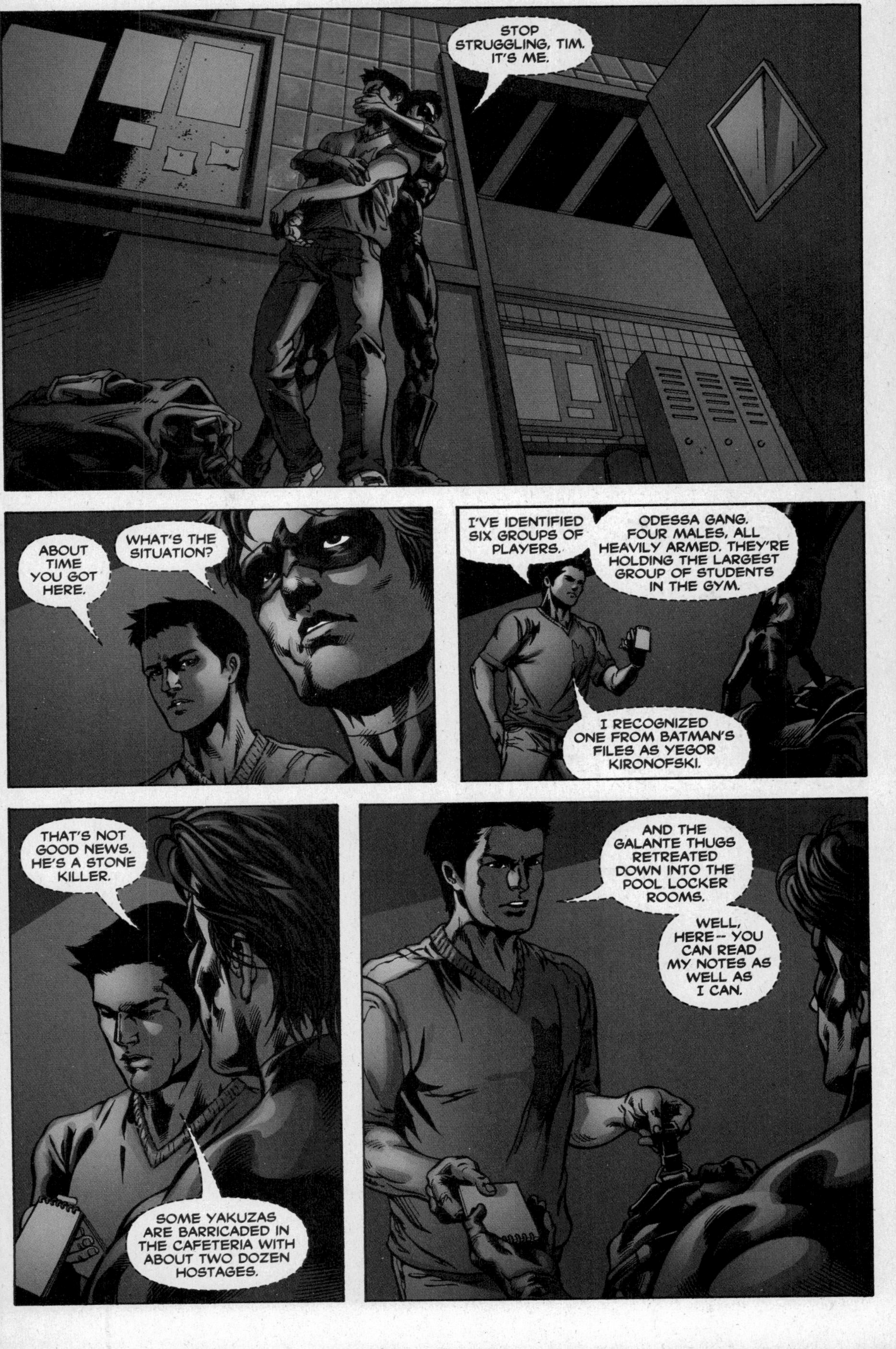
STOP STRUGGLING, TIM. IT'S ME.
ABOUT TIME YOU GOT HERE.
WHAT'S THE SITUATION?
I'VE IDENTIFIED SIX GROUPS OF PLAYERS.
ODESSA GANG. FOUR MALES, ALL HEAVILY ARMED. THEY'RE HOLDING THE LARGEST GROUP OF STUDENTS IN THE GYM.
I RECOGNIZED ONE FROM BATMAN'S FILES AS YEGOR KIRONOFSKI.
THAT'S NOT GOOD NEWS. HE'S A STONE KILLER.
SOME YAKUZAS ARE BARRICADED IN THE CAFETERIA WITH ABOUT TWO DOZEN HOSTAGES.
AND THE GALANTE THUGS RETREATED DOWN INTO THE POOL LOCKER ROOMS.
WELL, HERE-- YOU CAN READ MY NOTES AS WELL AS I CAN.

VICTIM STATUS?

ONLY ONE LIFE-THREATENING INJURY, TO MY KNOWLEDGE-- BUT SHE'S CRITICAL.

TELL BATMAN WE NEED TO WRAP THIS UP IMMEDIATELY-- THEN MEET ME IN THE SCHOOL NURSE'S OFFICE.

HERE'S SOME TREATS FOR YOU. GAS GRENADES, SMOKE AND STUN BOMBS, SOME TANGLERS - A CORNUCOPIA OF NON-LETHAL WEAPONRY.

LOAD UP, WHILE I CALL THIS IN.

WHY'D THEY ALL DECIDE TO COME HERE IN THE FIRST PLACE?

PEP RALLY

CHESS CLUB

VOLUNTEER AID WALK

ORACLE PIECED SOME OF IT TOGETHER FROM CELL-PHONE TRAFFIC.

AS NEAR AS WE CAN TELL, THE FIRST GROUP WAS AFTER SOME MOBSTER'S DAUGHTER WHO GOES TO SCHOOL HERE.

THEN OTHERS CAME HERE LOOKING TO WHACK THE FIRST GROUP, WHICH, OF COURSE, THE TV STATIONS STARTED BROADCASTING.

WHICH INSPIRED EVEN MORE THUGS TO SHOW UP, LOOKING FOR A TARGET-HEAVY ENVIRONMENT, FULL OF THEIR ENEMIES IN THIS GANG WAR.

IT CASCADED, OUT OF CONTROL FROM THERE, WITH ONE EVENT FEEDING ON ANOTHER.

DARLA.

HUH?

VOLUNTEER AID WALK

THE MOB GIRL'S NAME IS DARLA AQUISTA.

OKAY, BUT THAT INFORMATION DOESN'T REALLY HELP US. STAY FOCUSED, LITTLE BROTHER.

TRUE, BUT--

HOLD ON A SEC.

BATMAN, BATGIRL, I'VE MADE CONTACT WITH OUR FRIEND.

PREPARE TO COPY THE CURRENT TACTICAL SITUATION.

GOT A LIGHT, COWBOY?

SURE, WINNY, BUT THOSE THINGS'LL KILL YOU.

IN THE THREE YEARS I'VE BEEN ON THE AIR IN THIS MARKET, I'VE COVERED SIX RIOTS, A DOZEN MURDER SPREES, AN EARTHQUAKE-- I'VE EVEN BEEN BITTEN BY THE TIGER AT THE GOTHAM ZOO.

SOMEHOW I DON'T THINK IT'S SMOKING THAT WILL EVENTUALLY KILL ME.

GOOD POINT.

CONGRATULATIONS ON GETTING THAT ON-AIR QUOTE FROM THE CITY ATTORNEY. MY BOSS WAS LIVID THAT I DIDN'T GET IT.

YEAH, BUT YOU SKUNKED US BY ACTUALLY GETTING VISUALS OF THOSE GUNMEN THROUGH THE CAFETERIA WINDOW BEFORE THEY CLOSED THE BLINDS.

SO HOW ABOUT THIS MESS, HUH? THINK THOSE KIDS WILL SURVIVE THE DAY?

OF COURSE. BATMAN AND HIS CREW WILL COME THROUGH. THEY ALWAYS DO.

I CAN'T BELIEVE YOU STILL SUPPORT THOSE VIGILANTE KOOKS.

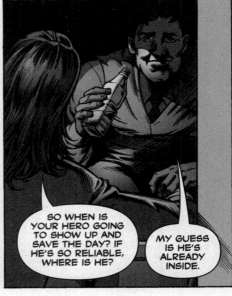

SO WHEN IS YOUR HERO GOING TO SHOW UP AND SAVE THE DAY? IF HE'S SO RELIABLE, WHERE IS HE?

MY GUESS IS HE'S ALREADY INSIDE.

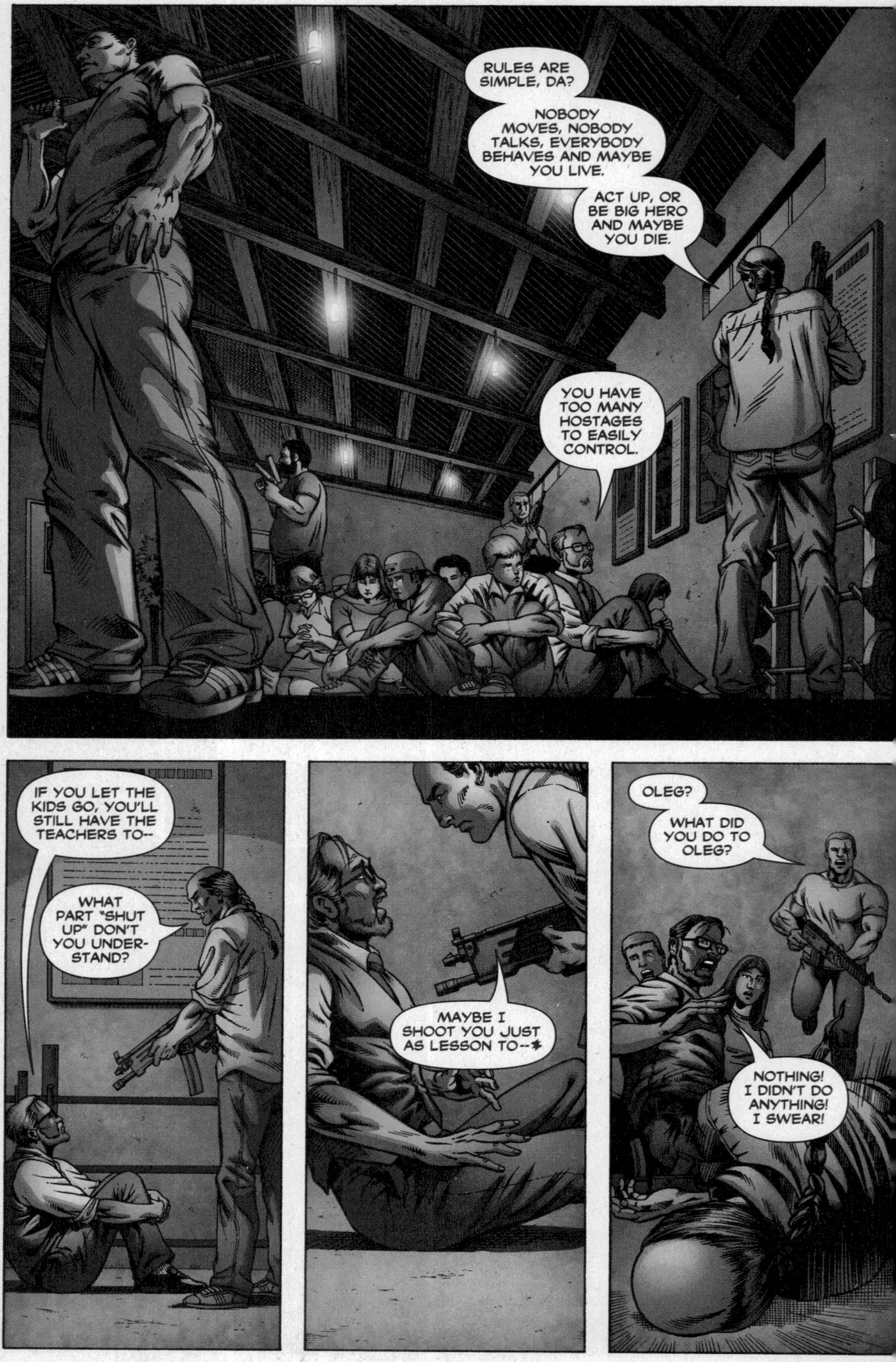
RULES ARE SIMPLE, DA?
NOBODY MOVES, NOBODY TALKS, EVERYBODY BEHAVES AND MAYBE YOU LIVE.
ACT UP, OR BE BIG HERO AND MAYBE YOU DIE.
YOU HAVE TOO MANY HOSTAGES TO EASILY CONTROL.
IF YOU LET THE KIDS GO, YOU'LL STILL HAVE THE TEACHERS TO--
WHAT PART "SHUT UP" DON'T YOU UNDER-STAND?
MAYBE I SHOOT YOU JUST AS LESSON TO--
OLEG?
WHAT DID YOU DO TO OLEG?
NOTHING! I DIDN'T DO ANYTHING! I SWEAR!

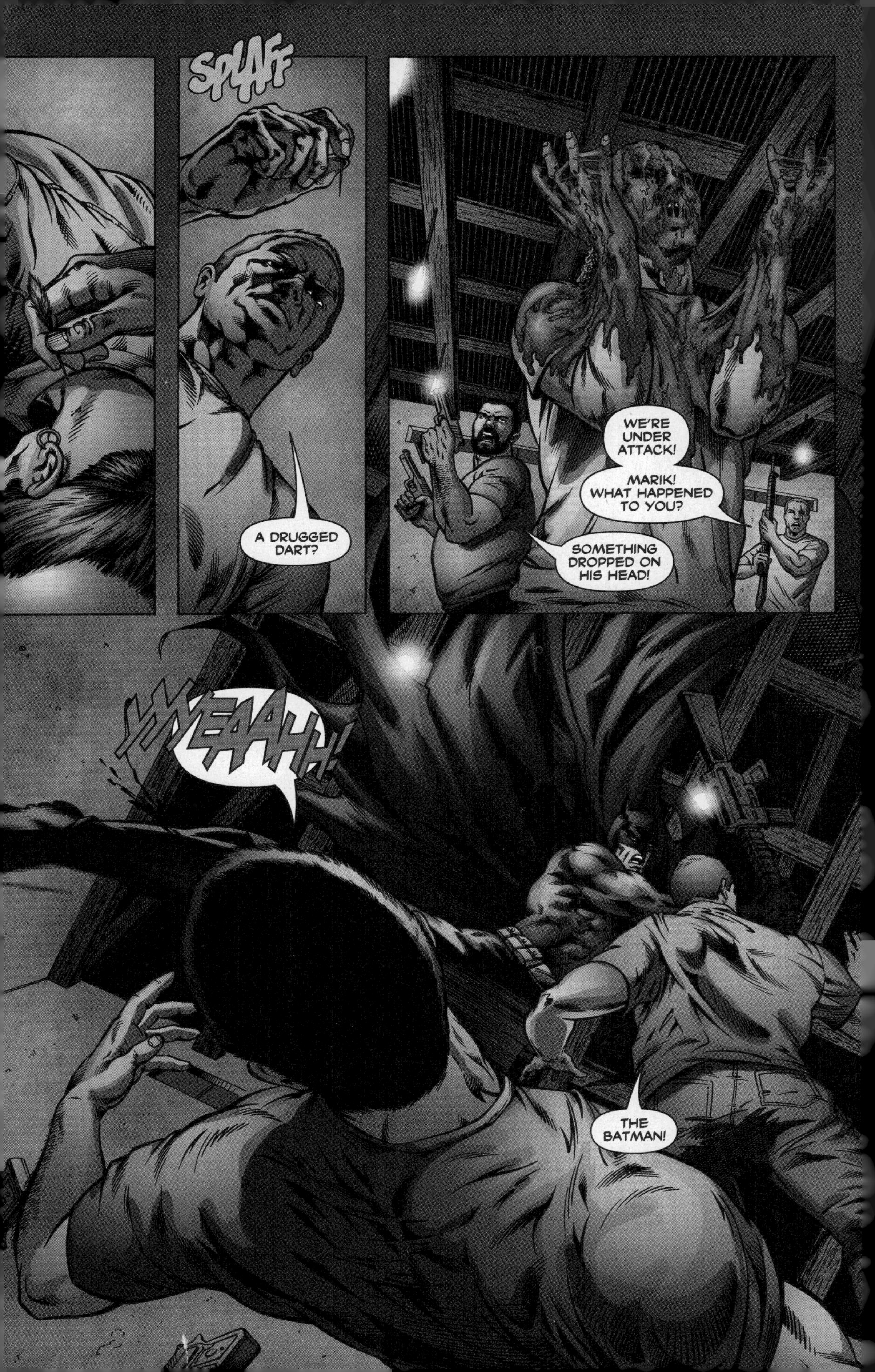
SPLAFF
A DRUGGED DART?
WE'RE UNDER ATTACK!
MARIK! WHAT HAPPENED TO YOU?
SOMETHING DROPPED ON HIS HEAD!
YYYEAAHH!
THE BATMAN!

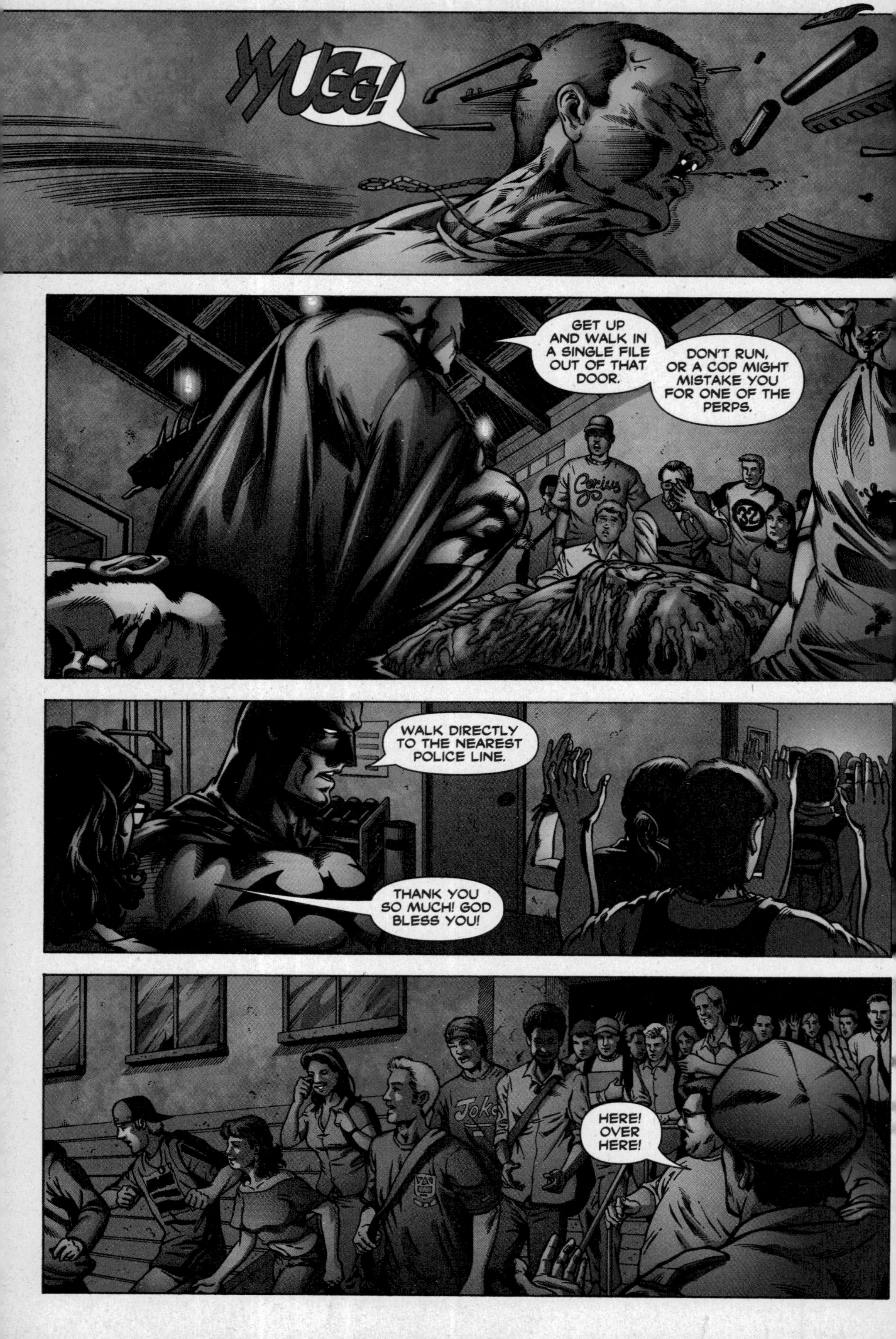
YYUGG!
GET UP AND WALK IN A SINGLE FILE OUT OF THAT DOOR.
DON'T RUN, OR A COP MIGHT MISTAKE YOU FOR ONE OF THE PERPS.
WALK DIRECTLY TO THE NEAREST POLICE LINE.
THANK YOU SO MUCH! GOD BLESS YOU!
HERE! OVER HERE!

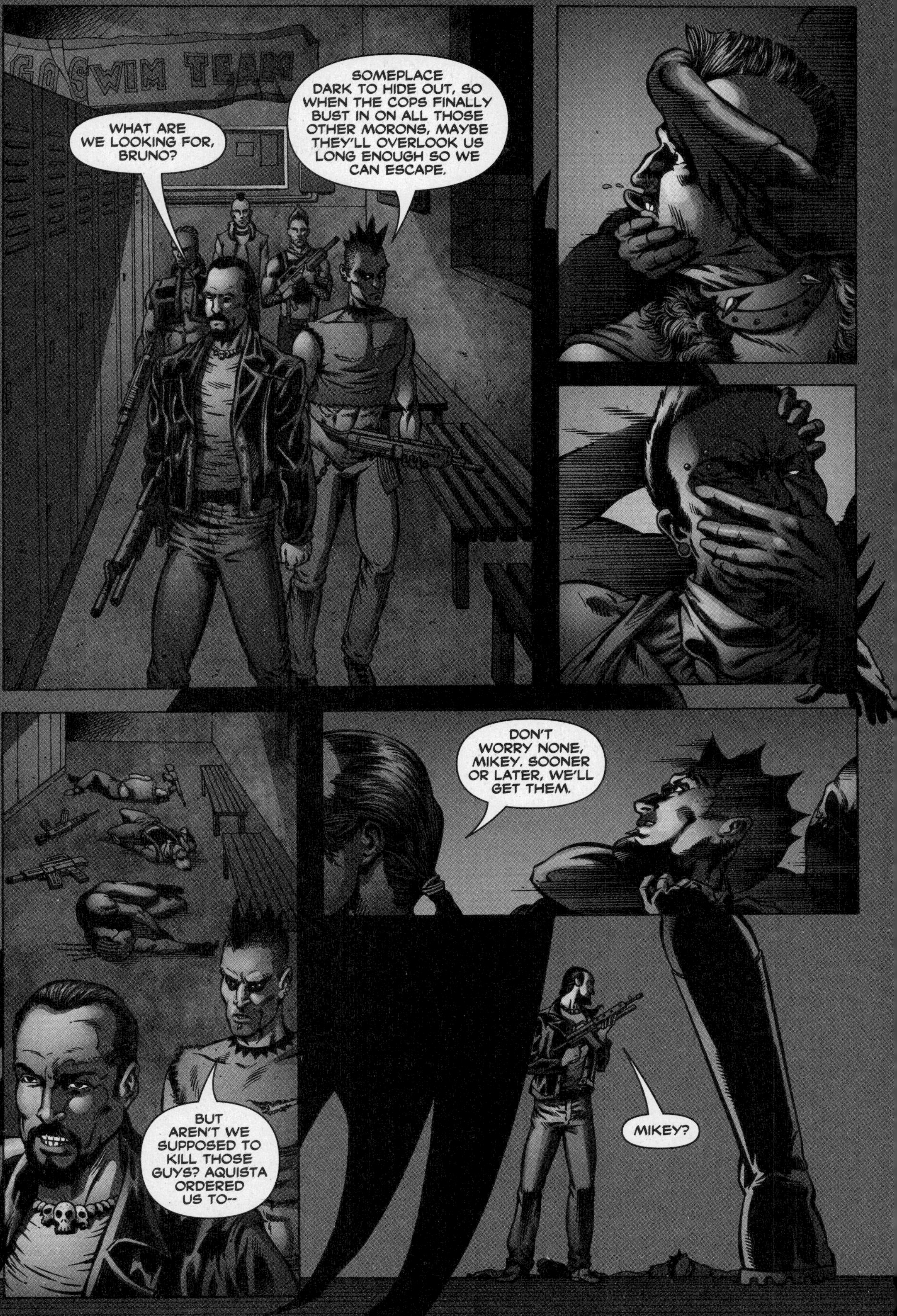
GO SWIM TEAM
WHAT ARE WE LOOKING FOR, BRUNO?
SOMEPLACE DARK TO HIDE OUT, SO WHEN THE COPS FINALLY BUST IN ON ALL THOSE OTHER MORONS, MAYBE THEY'LL OVERLOOK US LONG ENOUGH SO WE CAN ESCAPE.
BUT AREN'T WE SUPPOSED TO KILL THOSE GUYS? AQUISTA ORDERED US TO--
DON'T WORRY NONE, MIKEY. SOONER OR LATER, WE'LL GET THEM.
MIKEY?

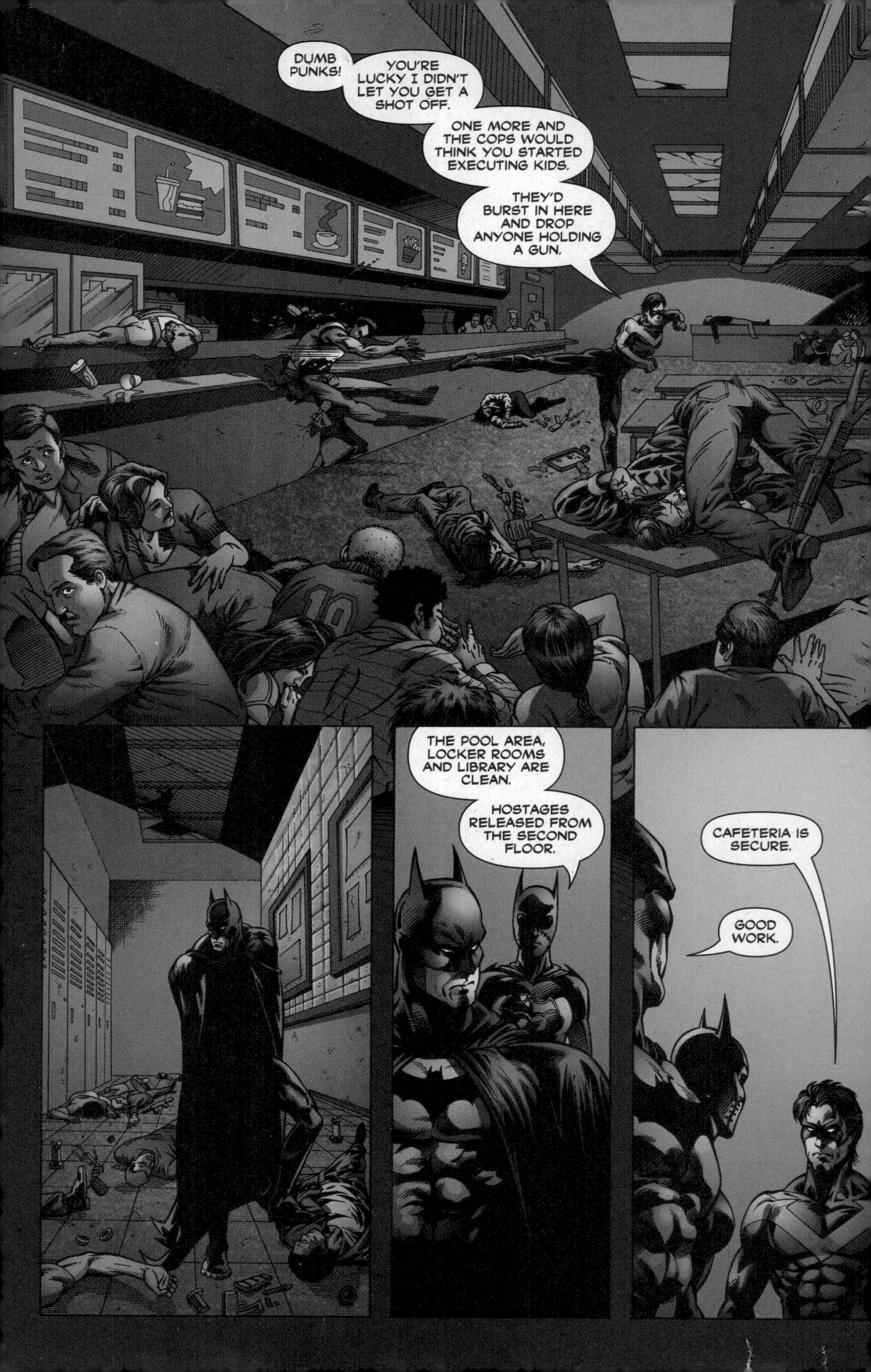
DUMB PUNKS!
YOU'RE LUCKY I DIDN'T LET YOU GET A SHOT OFF.
ONE MORE AND THE COPS WOULD THINK YOU STARTED EXECUTING KIDS.
THEY'D BURST IN HERE AND DROP ANYONE HOLDING A GUN.
THE POOL AREA, LOCKER ROOMS AND LIBRARY ARE CLEAN.
HOSTAGES RELEASED FROM THE SECOND FLOOR.
CAFETERIA IS SECURE.
GOOD WORK.

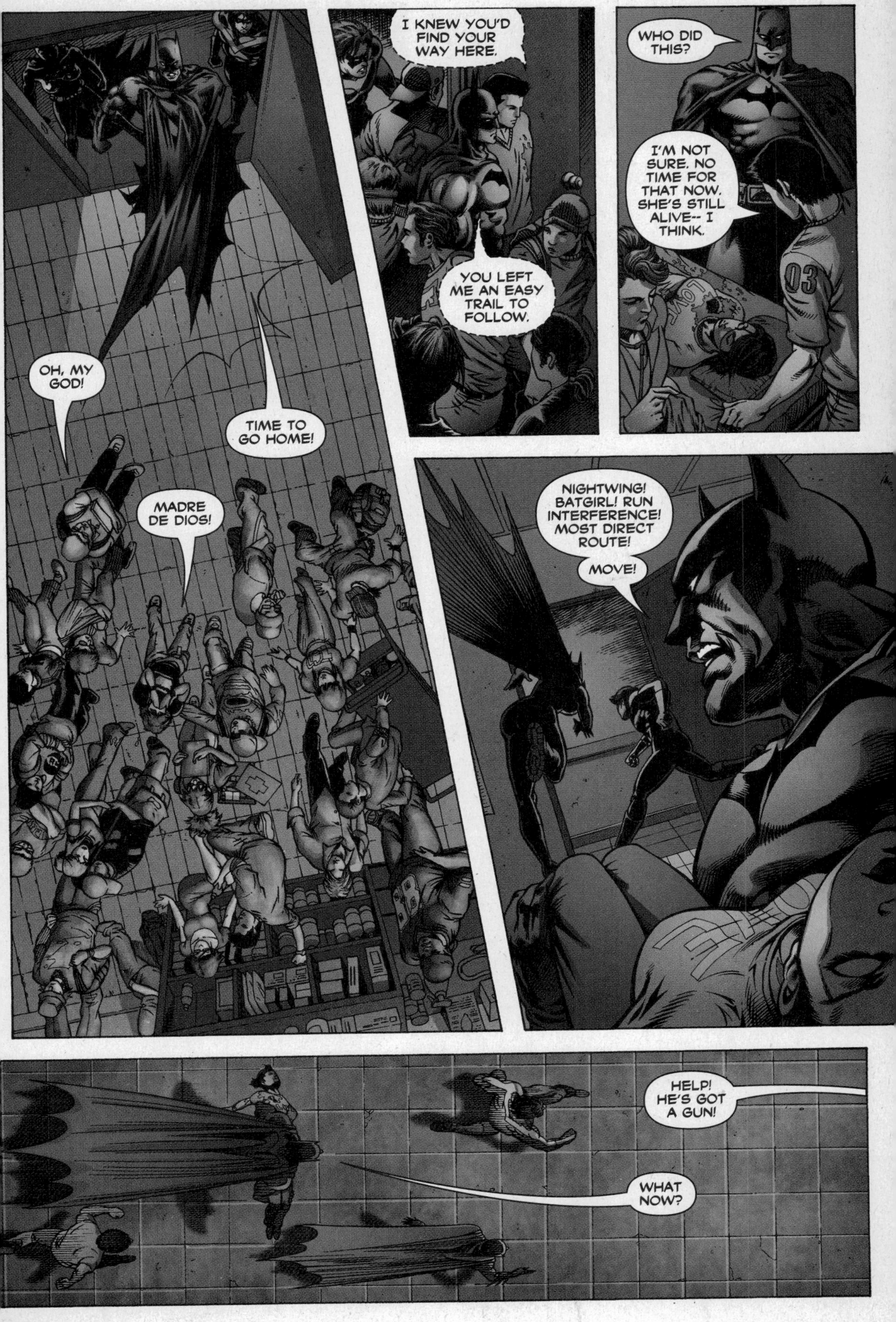
OH, MY GOD!
TIME TO GO HOME!
MADRE DE DIOS!
I KNEW YOU'D FIND YOUR WAY HERE.
YOU LEFT ME AN EASY TRAIL TO FOLLOW.
WHO DID THIS?
I'M NOT SURE. NO TIME FOR THAT NOW. SHE'S STILL ALIVE-- I THINK.
NIGHTWING! BATGIRL! RUN INTERFERENCE! MOST DIRECT ROUTE!
MOVE!
HELP! HE'S GOT A GUN!
WHAT NOW?

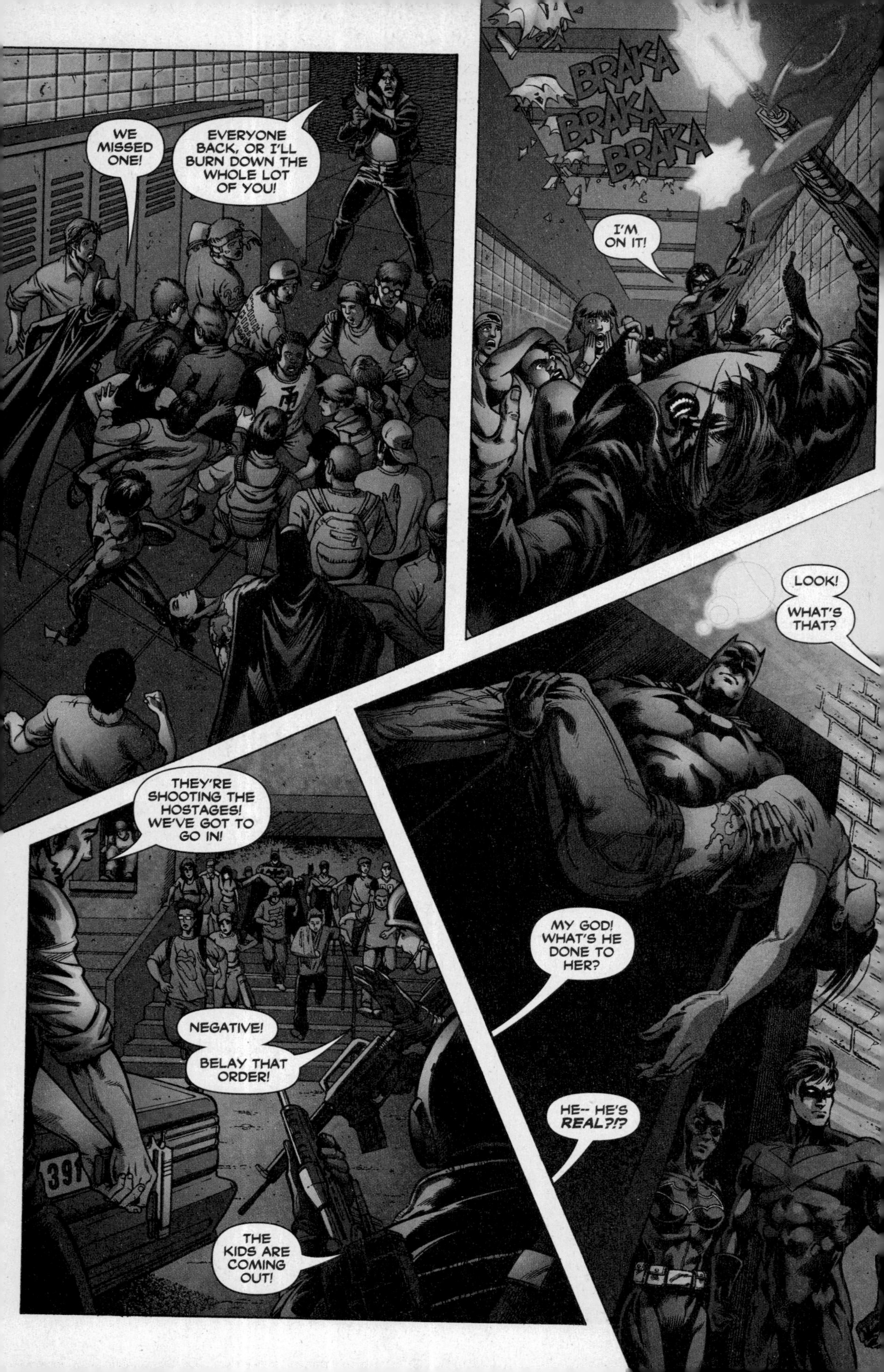
WE MISSED ONE!
EVERYONE BACK, OR I'LL BURN DOWN THE WHOLE LOT OF YOU!
BRAKA BRAKA BRAKA
I'M ON IT!
THEY'RE SHOOTING THE HOSTAGES! WE'VE GOT TO GO IN!
NEGATIVE!
BELAY THAT ORDER!
THE KIDS ARE COMING OUT!
LOOK!
WHAT'S THAT?
MY GOD! WHAT'S HE DONE TO HER?
HE-- HE'S *REAL?!?*

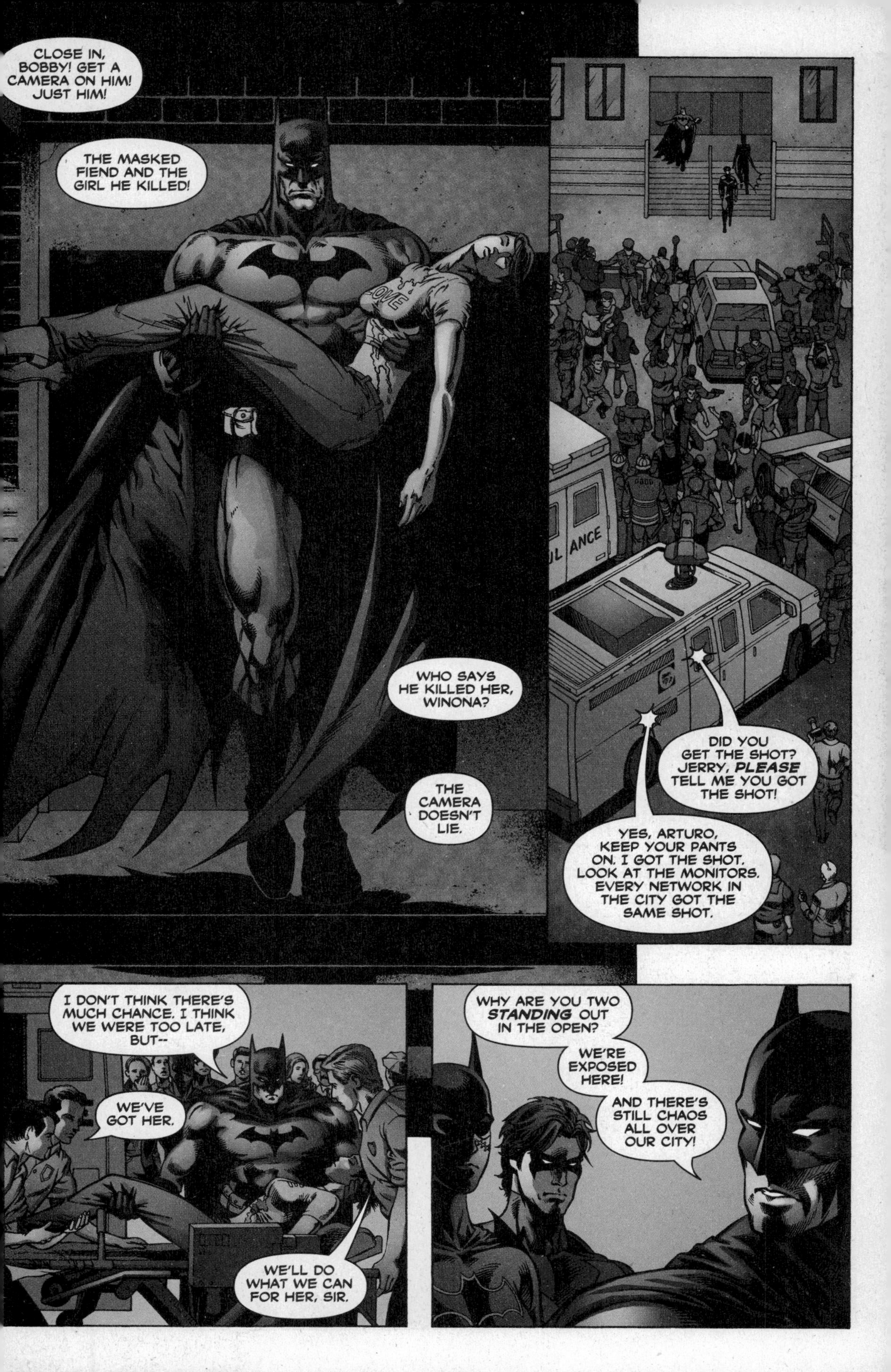
CLOSE IN, BOBBY! GET A CAMERA ON HIM! JUST HIM!
THE MASKED FIEND AND THE GIRL HE KILLED!
WHO SAYS HE KILLED HER, WINONA?
THE CAMERA DOESN'T LIE.
DID YOU GET THE SHOT? JERRY, PLEASE TELL ME YOU GOT THE SHOT!
YES, ARTURO, KEEP YOUR PANTS ON. I GOT THE SHOT. LOOK AT THE MONITORS. EVERY NETWORK IN THE CITY GOT THE SAME SHOT.
I DON'T THINK THERE'S MUCH CHANCE. I THINK WE WERE TOO LATE, BUT--
WE'VE GOT HER.
WE'LL DO WHAT WE CAN FOR HER, SIR.
WHY ARE YOU TWO STANDING OUT IN THE OPEN?
WE'RE EXPOSED HERE!
AND THERE'S STILL CHAOS ALL OVER OUR CITY!

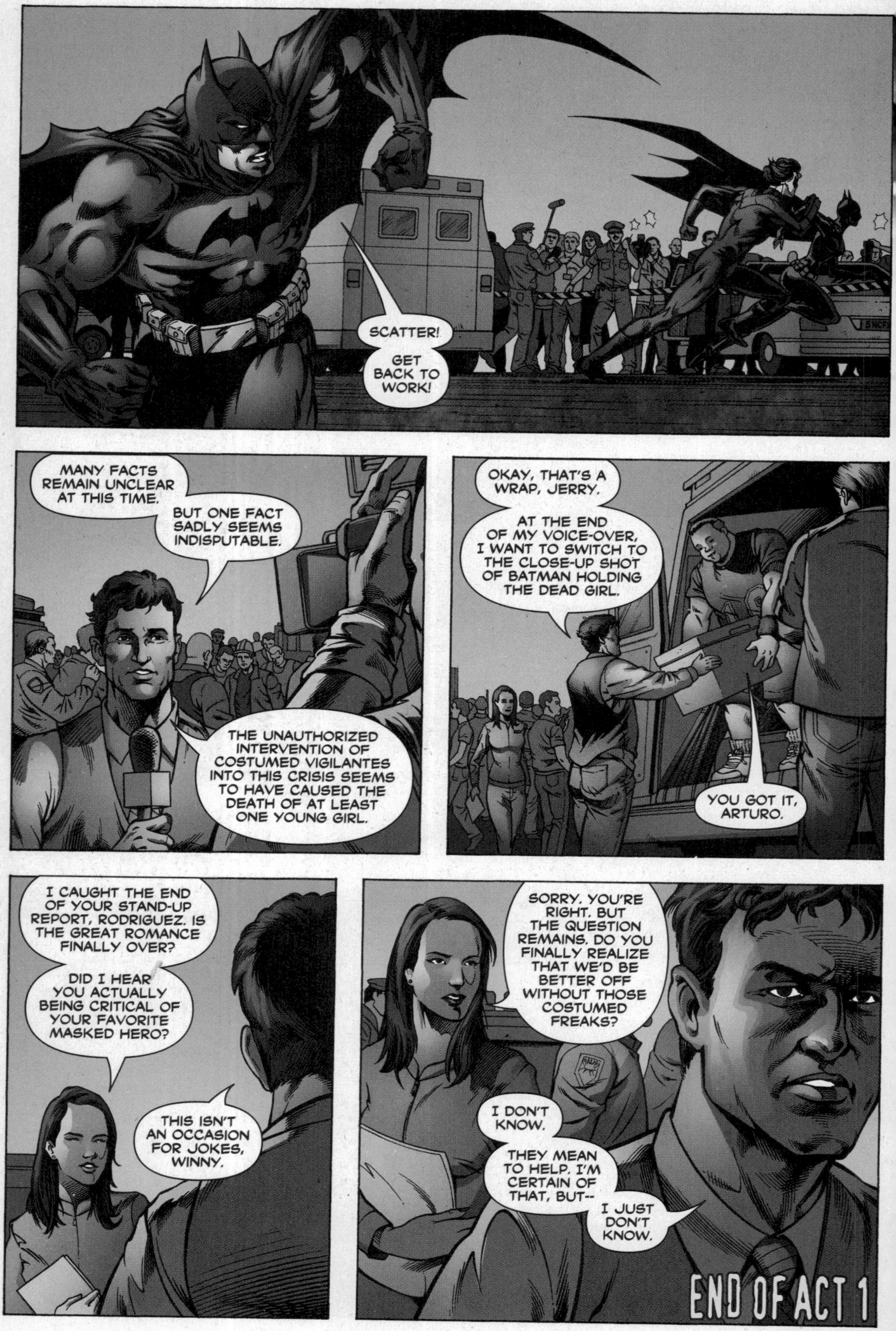
SCATTER!
GET BACK TO WORK!
MANY FACTS REMAIN UNCLEAR AT THIS TIME.
BUT ONE FACT SADLY SEEMS INDISPUTABLE.
THE UNAUTHORIZED INTERVENTION OF COSTUMED VIGILANTES INTO THIS CRISIS SEEMS TO HAVE CAUSED THE DEATH OF AT LEAST ONE YOUNG GIRL.
OKAY, THAT'S A WRAP, JERRY.
AT THE END OF MY VOICE-OVER, I WANT TO SWITCH TO THE CLOSE-UP SHOT OF BATMAN HOLDING THE DEAD GIRL.
YOU GOT IT, ARTURO.
I CAUGHT THE END OF YOUR STAND-UP REPORT, RODRIGUEZ. IS THE GREAT ROMANCE FINALLY OVER?
DID I HEAR YOU ACTUALLY BEING CRITICAL OF YOUR FAVORITE MASKED HERO?
THIS ISN'T AN OCCASION FOR JOKES, WINNY.
SORRY. YOU'RE RIGHT. BUT THE QUESTION REMAINS. DO YOU FINALLY REALIZE THAT WE'D BE BETTER OFF WITHOUT THOSE COSTUMED FREAKS?
I DON'T KNOW.
THEY MEAN TO HELP. I'M CERTAIN OF THAT, BUT--
I JUST DON'T KNOW.
END OF ACT 1

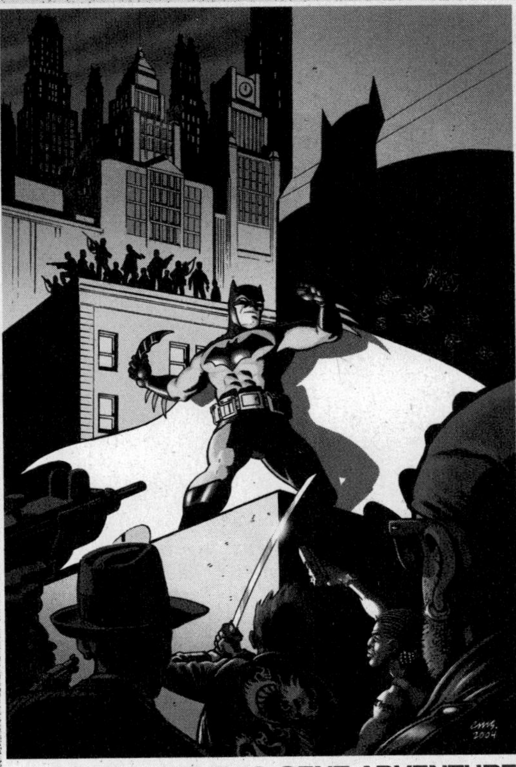

CMS 2004


**BATMAN: THE 12-CENT ADVENTURE**
**Cover by Cameron Stewart**

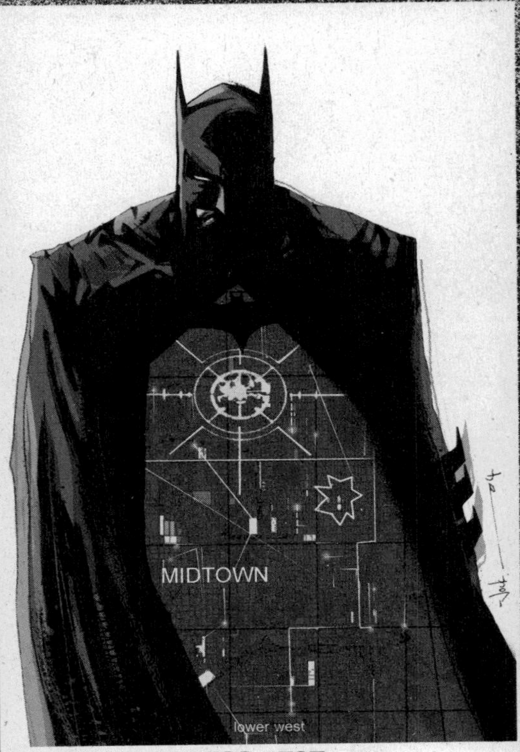

MIDTOWN
lower west


**DETECTIVE COMICS #797**
**Cover by Jock**

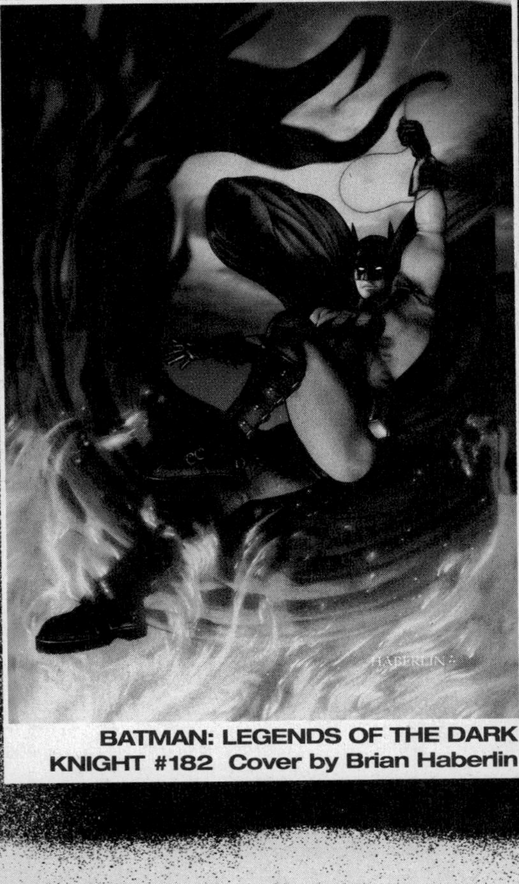

HABERLIN


**BATMAN: LEGENDS OF THE DARK KNIGHT #182 Cover by Brian Haberlin**

# COVER GALLERY

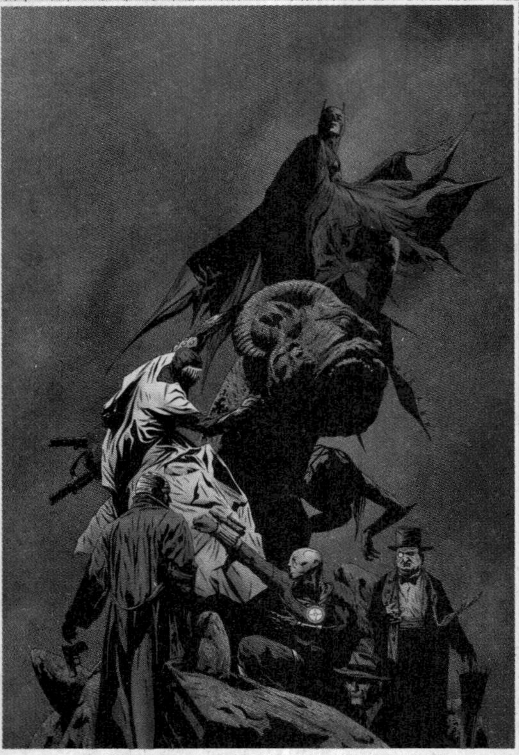

**BATMAN: GOTHAM KNIGHTS #56**
**Cover by Jae Lee**

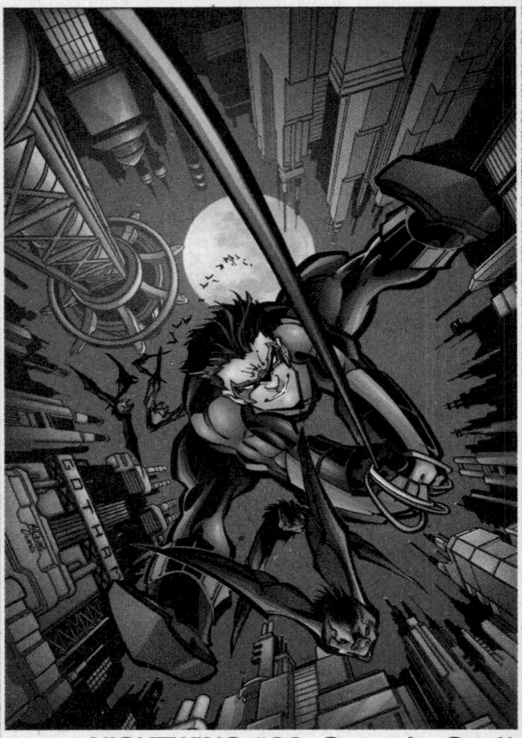

**NIGHTWING #96 Cover by Scott McDaniel & Andy Owens**

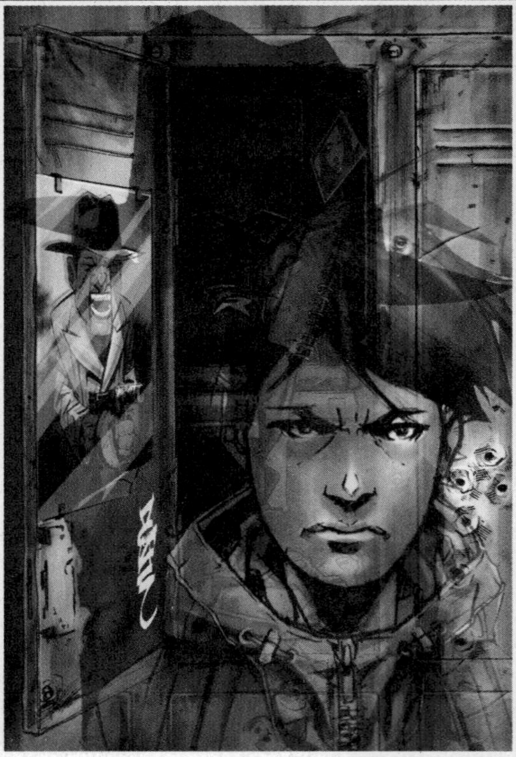

**ROBIN #129**
**Cover by Dustin Nguyen**

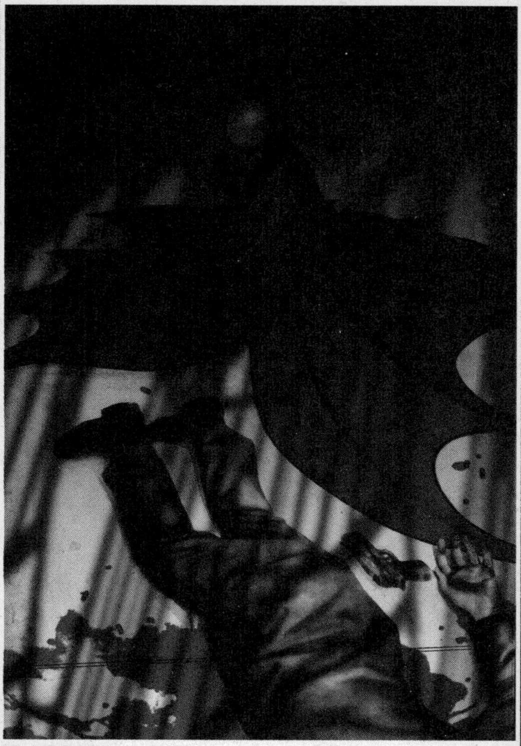

**BATGIRL #55**
**Cover by James Jean**



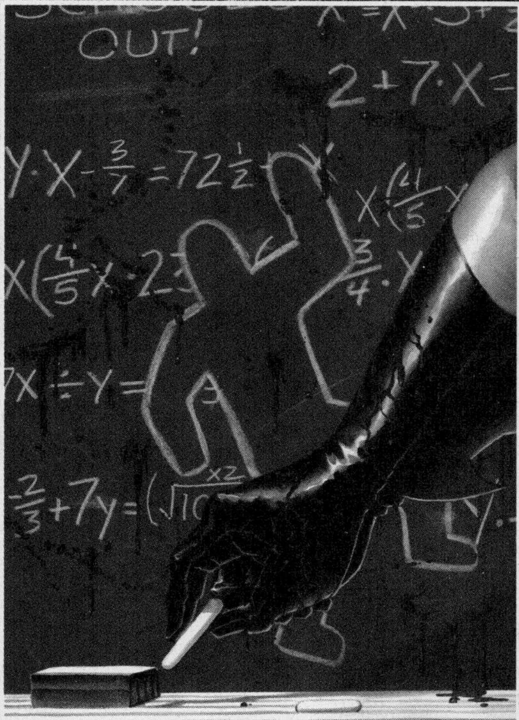
CUT!

**BATMAN #631**
**Cover by Matt Wagner**

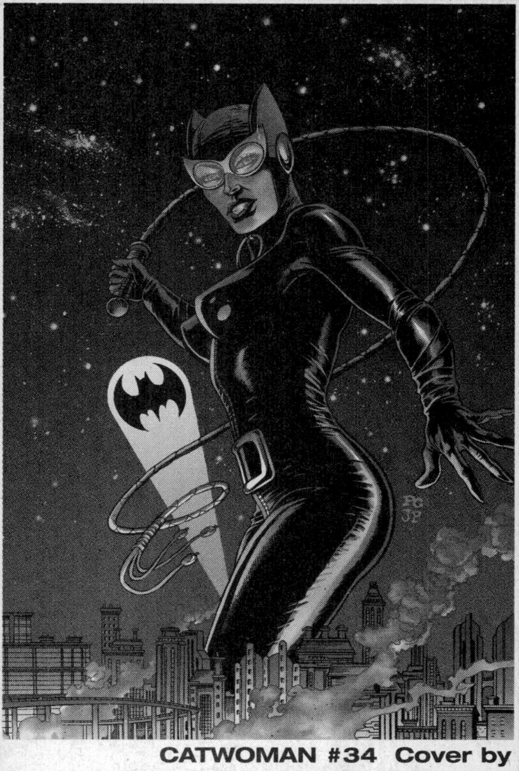

**CATWOMAN #34 Cover by**
**Paul Gulacy & Jimmy Palmiotti**

# COVER GALLERY

# BATMAN
## THE QUEST FOR JUSTICE CONTINUES IN THESE BOOKS FROM DC:

TO FIND MORE COLLECTED EDITIONS AND MONTHLY COMIC BOOKS FROM DC COMICS,
CALL 1-888-COMIC BOOK FOR THE NEAREST COMICS SHOP OR GO TO YOUR LOCAL BOOK STORE.

Visit us at www.dccomics.com

BM0012